Contemporary Social Theory

This book is arguably the definitive undergraduate textbook on contemporary social theory. Written by one of the world's most acclaimed social theorists, Anthony Elliott provides a dazzlingly accessible and comprehensive introduction to modern social theory from the Frankfurt School to globalization theories and beyond.

In distilling the essentials of social theory, Elliott reviews the works of major theorists including Theodor Adorno, Herbert Marcuse, Michel Foucault, Jacques Lacan, Jacques Derrida, Anthony Giddens, Pierre Bourdieu, Julia Kristeva, Jürgen Habermas, Judith Butler, Slavoj Žižek, Manuel Castells, Ulrich Beck, Zygmunt Bauman, Giorgio Agamben and Manuel DeLanda.

Every social theorist discussed is contextualized in a wider political and historical context, and from which their major contributions to social theory are critically assessed. This book is essential reading for students and professionals in the fields of social theory, sociology and cultural studies, as it is both an original enquiry and a consummate introduction to social theory.

Anthony Elliott is Professor of Sociology at Flinders University, Australia and Visiting Research Chair at the Open University, UK. He is presently Head of Department at Flinders University, and has served as Associate Deputy Vice-Chancellor (Research). He was previously Professor of Sociology at the University of Kent at Canterbury, UK, as well as Foundation Director of the Centre for Critical Theory, University of the West of England. His writings have been published in over twenty languages, and he is internationally acclaimed for his research in social theory, the sociology of culture and psychoanalytic studies. His recent books include *Critical Visions* (2003), *Social Theory Since Freud* (2004), *The New Individualism* (with Charles Lemert, 2006), *The Contemporary Bauman* (2007), *Concepts of the Self* (2007, 2nd ed.), *Making The Cut: How Cosmetic Surgery Is Transforming our Lives* (2008) and *Identity In Question* (coedited with Paul du Gay, 2008).

"Here is the latest example of what Anthony Elliott does best: He brings his readers in on the key social, personal and political issues of our time. Always readable and interesting, *Contemporary Social Theory: An Introduction* includes a wide range of modern social thought, from structuralism, to feminism, to globalization, and engagingly demonstrates these theories' relevance in our own lives. As importantly, Elliott provides us a way to think critically, making the reader a more thoughtful reader of social theory as well as a participant in contemporary social debates. A book that is stimulating to both teacher and student alike and that enlivens the classroom experience."

Professor Jeffrey Prager *Sociology, UCLA, USA*

"Anthony Elliott has written a wide ranging and appealing book, setting new standards for introductory texts in social theory. *Contemporary Social Theory* is clear in style and accessible in presentation. It is sure to stimulate students and beginners in the field whilst proving of considerable interest to their teachers. It will also strike sparks with those with a professional research interest in social theory."

Professor Paul du Gay *Organisational Behaviour, Warwick University, UK*

"Extraordinary in scope, *Contemporary Social Theory* takes the reader on a world tour of social theory since the Second World War and offers the student clear and accessible guidance around what are often complex and obscure theoretical edifices. More than this, Anthony Elliott provides not just description but evaluation and critique, and the originality of his mind will make this a pleasure to read for all thoughtful people engaged with the politics of living."

Professor Paul Hoggett *Director of the Centre for Psycho-Social Studies, UWE, UK*

"The renewal of the teaching of social theory can now take place! For in Anthony Elliott's scholarly, thorough and limpid volume, teachers of theory have the perfect support text, one guaranteed to bring students fully into the exciting drama that it lays out: the drama of contemporary social life as social theorists from the Frankfurt School to Giorgio Agamben have mapped it out."

Professor John Lechte *Higher Degree Convenor (SOC) Macquarie University, Australia*

"Social theory gives us the building blocks to make sense of our lives and explore how they link to the processes which shape what we can do and how we live. But it takes a master of the craft to turn the blocks into a building in which it is possible to live and flourish. This book shows that Anthony Elliott is a master of the craft.

The house that is built within the pages of this comprehensive book is one of many rooms, in which all students will find a place in which they can think and, moreover, in which they will be given in an exceptionally accessible and well-informed style the resources which that thinking needs if it is going to succeed.

I have little doubt that thanks to its encyclopaedic spread, authoritative content and keen eye for the excellent illustration, this book will be valued highly by everyone who wants or needs to think – and live – with social theory. And ultimately that means all of us."

Professor Keith Tester *Cultural Sociology, University of Portsmouth, UK*

"Elliott provides a sweeping survey that is both accessible and sophisticated. Organised in thematic chapters that make excellent use of vignettes from the lives of everyday people to draw the reader into the issues, Elliott elegantly summarises the main points of each theorist's work, provides some discussion that stretches the reader's understanding, and rehearses the main criticisms. The book weaves together the disparate strands of social theory, including psychoanalysis, feminism, (post)structuralism, and critical theory alongside the issues of globalization and postmodernity. This book will set the agenda for many university courses in contemporary social theory."

Professor Douglas Ezzy *Head of School, Sociology and Social Work,*
University of Tasmania, Australia

"For the last twenty years Anthony Elliott has been bringing his unique personal and intellectual insights to the major debates of our time, in an impressively wide-ranging series of texts on social theory and psychoanalysis. More recently he has produced a provocative series of works on risk and globalization, the allure of celebrity and plastic surgery, and the trials and terrors of the new individualism. Here, in his new introductory text, Elliott returns with new insights to some of the classics of social theory, and charts a path through the most interesting and important contemporary social theorists. I can think of few writers better equipped to carry off this task, and Elliott has done it here magnificently. Elliott combines his deep knowledge of social theory, his lightly worn erudition, and an engaging style that is a pleasure to read. The personal stories that begin most chapters were a highlight and manage to bring home what is at stake in the theories and ideas that follow. What he has achieved here should win over a generation of new students to social theory."

Anthony Moran *Lecturer in Social Sciences, La Trobe University, Australia*

"Covering an impressive range of theories and theorists, and presenting them in an accessible and elegant fashion, reading Anthony Elliott's text is an ideal way to navigate the often complex terrain of modern social thought."

Professor David Inglis *University of Aberdeen, UK*

"This is the best introduction to social theory we are ever likely to need. The writing is crystal clear, the arguments are complex but accessible and this is likely to become the best friend of every sociology undergraduate. This book has been especially written for those who want to know why social theory is so important to under-standing the world right now. At last we finally have a book we can recommend to our students with confidence."

Nick Stevenson *University of Nottingham UK*

"This is the best contemporary social theory text currently on the market. It is highly accessible, explaining ideas in the clearest possible language without compromising depth and complexity. Accordingly, it is a book that would work well for students at all levels. Undergraduates with no background in social theory will be able to easily engage with this text, and this is something that cannot be said of any other contemporary social theory textbook that considers the range of theorists and complexity of ideas that this book does. More advanced students, including professional social theorists, will find that Elliott provides great clarity on some of the most difficult, yet most influential, ideas in contemporary social thought. "

Ann Branaman *Associate Professor of Sociology,*
Florida Atlantic University, USA

Contemporary Social Theory

An Introduction

Anthony Elliott

Routledge
Taylor & Francis Group

LONDON AND NEW YORK

First published 2009 by Routledge
2 Park Square, Milton Park, Abingdon, Oxon, OX14 4RN

Simultaneously published in the USA and Canada
by Routledge
270 Madison Avenue, New York, NY 10016

Routledge is an imprint of the Taylor & Francis Group, an informa business

Typeset in ScalaSans by Keystroke, 28 High Street, Tettenhall, Wolverhampton
Printed and bound in India by Gopsons Papers Ltd., Noida

British Library Cataloguing in Publication Data
A catalogue record for this book is available from the British Library
Library of Congress Cataloging in Publication Data
Elliott, Anthony.
    Contemporary social theory : an introduction / Anthony Elliott.
        p. cm.
    1. Sociology—Philosophy. 2. Social sciences—Philosophy.
    3. Sociology—Philosophy—History—20th century. 4. Social sciences—
    Philosophy—History—20th century. I. Title.
    HM447.E55 2009
    301.01—dc22   2008026790

ISBN10: 0-415-38633-0 (pbk)
ISBN13: 978-0-415-38633-3 (pbk)

For Niamh

Contents

Preface and Acknowledgements

There are few areas of academic enquiry as diverse, multidisciplinary and politically important as social theory. In writing this book, I have sought to develop a readable, comprehensive and critical introduction to the field of contemporary social theory. This, in itself, might be considered something of a tall order – given that social theory now manages to scoop up everything from self-identity, sexuality and signifiers to gender, globalization and governance. In seeking to provide a reasonably comprehensive account of contemporary social theory, I have tried to cover most of the major traditions of thought – from the Frankfurt School to postmodernism, from structuralism to post-feminism – along with overviews of many recent cutting edge developments. As such, the book includes detailed discussions of globalization and the global electronic economy, postmodernism, the rise of networks and processes of societal liquidization – among other new topics of key importance.

At the outset, this is perhaps the place to comment on and clarify not only the developments in social theory reviewed in the chapters that follow, but also some of the omissions from this book. Social theory emerged in the context of the European Enlightenment, and has for the most part remained a largely continental affair in its traffic with the fundamental questions about the social dynamics of our lives and of our lives in the age of modernity. If contemporary social theory represents, among other things, a kind of academic shorthand for the intellectual contributions of, among others, Michel Foucault, Jacques Lacan, Jacques Derrida, Julia Kristeva, Jean Baudrillard and Luce Irigaray, this says something about not only the richness, diversity and esotericism of social theory itself, but also the ambitious critique it has developed of our current ways of life. Contemporary social theory, as I argue throughout this book, is a kind of doubled enterprise: a resourceful, high-powered and interdisciplinary project of the social sciences and humanities on the one hand, and an urgent critique of ideological thought and the discourses of reason, freedom, truth, subjectivity, culture and politics on the other. At its best – and my argument is that the best is to be found in the writings of Herbert Marcuse, Jürgen Habermas, Pierre Bourdieu, Anthony Giddens, Judith Butler, Zygmunt Bauman, Giorgio Agamben and many others – contemporary social theory provides a sophisticated, scintillating critique of the arrogance of power as well as engaging the future of progressive politics.

All of which brings me to the omissions of this work. The first is of any serious appraisal of the North American traditions of social theory. Readers will no doubt discern various thematic cross-references to some aspects of American social thought – of, say, Daniel Bell, Christopher Lasch or Noam Chomsky – in the mainly European social theory I discuss. It is the case that I discuss some of the most important social theorists working in the United States today: Fredric Jameson, Judith Butler, Manuel Castells, Charles Lemert and Manuel DeLanda. Yet all these figures are substantially indebted to the European tradition of social theory in some form or another. Moreover, it seems to me that the large bulk of current American social thought, at least that which is politically progressive, is also derivative of continental traditions of social theory. The other omission arises as a result of the embarrassment of riches which social theory presents in our own time. Some readers may be surprised to discover that, for example, there is no coverage of the 'systems theory' of Niklas Luhmann. Nor the hermeneutics of Paul Riceour. Nor the actor-network theory of Bruno Latour. The omission of such figures is, of course, partly a consequence of pro-ducing a book that didn't end up the size of a door-stooper. But it also reflects my own rating of not merely the 'stock-market' fortunes of particular theorists, but the political usefulness and value of the work of certain critics. There is, in short, no value-free way of doing social theory; and to that degree my choices reflect my preferences. Then there are those whose work I should have very much liked to include had space permitted: again, among others – Stuart Hall, Jean Laplanche, Richard Rorty, Gianni Vattimo, Umberto Eco, Roberto Unger, Noberto Bobbio, Emanuel Levinas and Manfred Frank. These figures I hope to include in some future edition of the book, or perhaps a companion volume.

I should like to thank various people who have helped in the writing of this book. I am very grateful to Gerhard Boomgaarden, my friend and editor at Routledge, for 'insisting' that I write this book: almost every introduction to social theory I have read seems, somehow, to fall wide of the mark. This is perhaps less a reflection of poor scholarship than an indication of a dynamic interdisciplinary terrain. Against this backdrop I was often doubtful that I could come up with an approach that would be at once theoretically serious and personally engaging. To the extent that I might have succeeded, I remain grateful for the many ways in which Gerhard, along with his assistant Miranda Thirkistle, has assisted with the project.

Since there is no value-free way of engaging with social theory, perhaps this is the place for me to record my own debt of acknowledgement to those with whom I have studied, and learnt from, over the years. The late Alan Davies at Melbourne University was marvellously helpful in gearing me to think in novel ways about the relationship between our social and private worlds. The period of study I undertook with Tony Giddens at Cambridge University in the late 1980s was transformative, and I remain profoundly indebted to him for the various ways in which he has helped to shape my sociological outlook. I owe to the late Cornelius Castoriadis an immense intellectual debt, specifically as regards the analysis of the creativity of action. To Zygmunt Bauman I also own much – particularly for his instruction on the value of persistence, as well as how to both think and act against the grain of academic orthodoxy. And to Charles Lemert, with whom it has been my good fortune to work these recent years, who reviewed the manuscript and made some superb last-minute suggestions for improvement.

I should like to thank the following colleagues and friends: Bryan S. Turner, John Urry, Nick Stevenson, Jeffrey Prager, David Held, Paul du Gay, Jessica Evans, Anthony Moran, John B. Thompson, Mary Holmes, Bob Holton, Sharyn Roach Anleu, Peter Redman, Stephen Frosh, Alison Assiter, Larry Ray, Paul Hoggett, Deborah Maxwell, Elizabeth Williams, John O'Neil, Keith Tester, Kriss McKie, Jean and Keith Elliott, Carmel Meiklejohn, Conrad Meyer, Simon Smith, and Jem Thomas.

Daniel Chaffee and Eric Hsu played an absolutely fundamental role in the whole project, especially towards its final stages. They were really wonderful to work with, and I am especially grateful for their labours in pulling threads of the project together. Eric also undertook bibliographic and reference research, and I owe to him huge thanks for his input to this. Many thanks to Rictor Norton for expert proof-reading and also thanks to Maggie Lindsey-Jones at Keystroke for project managing this title through to printing stage. Tamara Waraschinski undertook valuable research into various social theory websites. I also wish to thank students involved in the Flinders Social Theory Group.

Above all, I should like to thank Nicola Geraghty – along with our children Caoimhe, Oscar and Niamh – for their support, encouragement and help. This book has been a number of years in the making – written variously in Bristol, Dublin, Canterbury and Adelaide – and I most certainly could not have done so without their love. To the extent that our youngest, Niamh, is the budding social theorist of the family – the child's instinctive curiosity (as Freud argued) is disabling to the established adult world, and thus a suggestive model for social theory – I dedicate the book to her.

Anthony Elliott
Adelaide, 2008

chapter 1

The Textures of Society

Contents

Natalie is a 26-year-old fashion designer living and working in London. Her design studio is located at Notting Hill Gate, where she spends part of her working week; for the rest of the week she is regularly in Paris – attending to the business details of her fledgeling fashion company. The routine air travel between London and Paris is something that now seems 'normal' to Natalie after four years of flitting between cities, but the travel she undertakes to see her boyfriend Ross, who relocated to Finland last year, is more difficult for her to schedule. It is not the travel itself she finds difficult; rather it is finding the time to travel. Time is a resource that for Natalie is in short supply.

Natalie, a daughter of Taiwanese immigrants to America, grew up in Brooklyn – where her parents still live. Her father worked as a waiter, and her mother worked long hours in a dry-cleaning store. Natalie's life has been remarkably different from that of her parents – largely the result of her parents' efforts to get a good college education for their only daughter. She keeps in regular touch through phone calls; she has also recently purchased a computer for her parents, to 'keep close' through email. In communication as they are, Natalie misses direct contact with her parents, and often feels worried that she lives so far away from them. These anxieties have been tempered somewhat of late, however, as Natalie is planning a holiday to the USA. In addition to seeing her parents, she has also scheduled to meet Ross in Brooklyn – to introduce him to her family.

What might Natalie's life have to tell us about the world today? What might her professional and private life reflect about the changing direction of society? To begin with, it seems evident that Natalie lives a life – like many throughout the expensive cities of the West – which requires ongoing communication and travel across large distances. Natalie's professional success, as well as her private life, depends upon the routine use of systems of transportation (motorways, rail, air) as well as new communication technologies. Yet if technological innovation lies at the core of how Natalie traverses the large distances she has to cover in terms of travel and communication, these social developments are less evident in the lives of her parents – who rarely ever leave Brooklyn. Still, Natalie's parents travel in a kind of 'virtual' way – making use of email communication. Equally significantly, they traverse the different cultures and social landscapes of which they are part, or to which their lives connect – Taiwanese, American, British.

If we seek to broaden out these points, we might say that Natalie's life reflects the dynamic changes occurring within social, cultural and economic life today, and on a global scale. Think, for example, of how her use of new information technologies reflects the social changes now affecting how people and places interweave. There are today more than one billion users of the Internet worldwide, of which Natalie's parents are merely some of the latest users. Or think about Natalie's carbon footprint across the globe as she routinely travels between the UK and Europe as well as across the Atlantic oceans. There are today more than nine hundred million international air flights undertaken each year, a figure predicted to pass one billion in the near future. If these statistics are suggestive of the increasingly complex 'border crossings' (at once geopolitical, communicational and virtual) lived by young women like Natalie in the expensive cities of the West, there are also other human migrations that predominate in our own era of globalization which receive less media attention, but which most certainly disturb. These are not the kinds of travel either Natalie or her parents undertake, but are certainly of fundamental significance to the textures of world society today. It has been estimated by Robert Neuwirth, for example, that 70 million people each year leave their rural villages for the promises of distant cities. These promises remain, for most, forever out of reach: living without the rights of place or citizenship, there are many tens of millions of refugees and asylum-seekers today roaming the globe, experiencing the social humiliation and bodily degradation that the Italian social theorist Giorgio Agamben calls 'bare life'. The notion of bare life may well be apt to describe the plight of illegal immigrant workers scrambling to earn a few dollars or displaced peoples living on the margins, yet it may equally serve to capture the political mood of a world in which three billion of its inhabitants receive the same total income as the richest three hundred individuals.

To raise the question of the 'textures' of society is thus to consider social trends that are intensely worrying on the one hand, as well as those with the most extraordinary potential on the other. However much Natalie may be aware of the global realities of bare life – of peoples living on the margins; of peoples dispossessed, displaced and humiliated – it seems unlikely that she could end up in any such situation herself. For the society to which she belongs is well insulated from too greater awareness of the shocking trends of enforced human migrations in these early years of the twenty-first century. The society to which she belongs, we might suppose, is that of the West – with its mesmerizing information networks, its dazzling digital technologies and its seductive consumer culture. But if we stop and pause for a moment, the question remains: To which society does Natalie actually belong? She was raised in the USA. Yet her family immigrated to America from Taiwan when she was an infant. She now lives in London, but works regularly in Paris. And her boyfriend is based in Helsinki. To which society does she belong?

What is society?

One answer to the question 'to which society does Natalie belong?' derives from common sense: she belongs where she lives, her homeland, her nation. In social theory as in everyday life, this answer emphasizes that social life must be constructed within the province of the nation and its assured rights of belonging – the entitlements and duties of citizenship. On this view, Natalie is an American citizen, one who now lives and works in the UK, and who holds a permanent British visa. Talk about the connections between nations and societies in the social sciences tends to be fairly general, and yet it remains the case that nations have been regarded as providing societal homes for a remarkably long historical period. Nations of course have many different powers and forms at any given historical time, but one reason why they might no longer provide a good enough societal home in our age of intensive globalization is that people are *on the move* as never before. Just think of Natalie's existence. As already noted, she grew up in Brooklyn and now lives in the UK, but she spends part of every week in France, and many weekends in Finland. In which national homeland that we call 'society' does she *belong*? Still further, we might also wonder, how it is that her multi-dimensional experience of nations and the world actually affects both her experience and conception of society.

Perhaps a better answer to the question then of 'to which society does Natalie belong?' is that of the *globe*. Globalization is an answer to this question when, like Natalie, we universalize the daily operations of our lives, compressing the dimensions of time and space through new technological innovations in such fields as travel and communications. On this view, Natalie emerges as a 'global citizen', one with a cosmopolitan appreciation of the complexities of living in an age of transnationalism, and thus becomes defined as *one at home* wherever she happens to find herself. A citizen, in other words, of global society. But whether it is meaningful to speak of global society in the same manner in which we might speak of national society is a contentious issue – as we will see in the discussion of globalization in Chapter 10. For while there is a very specific sense in which we might say that Natalie is a citizen of America or the UK, in what sense is she actually a citizen of the globe? To define society in purely national terms is to circum-scribe its operations in terms of, say, territories, boundaries and geopolitical spaces. To define society beyond the terrain of the nation seems to open the textures of human belonging and association in ways which appear to have no limit, pushing the boundaries of social and political understanding to the edge. In one sense this may be described as a core and intractable problem of our time – a problem that preoccupies social theorists, but one that also arises at the centre of public political debate today.

These considerations bring us to the heart of a core issue in contem-porary social theory – namely, the nature of society. There is, to date, no single adequate definition of society in social theory – and indeed one objective of this book is to trace the various definitions of society that have emerged in social theory during the course of the twentieth century and into the early 2000s. To indicate the range of meanings attached to the notion of society that we will encounter throughout this book, consider the following random list of definitions currently emanating in social theory:

1 the institutionalization of unequal power relations and domination;
2 the conjuncture of reason and repression;
3 the structuring of social institutions and social interactions;
4 the process whereby linguistic structures are converted to social regulation;
5 the social forms in which signifiers and signifieds are interwoven;
6 forms of thought structured by social differences;

7 ideas and ideologies governed by patriarchy, promoting unequal relations between the sexes;
8 the gendered process of encoding sexual signs and human bodies in
social life;
9 systematically distorted communication;
10 reflexively orientated social practices;
11 liquidity;
12 the networks or flows in which self-reflective social actors organize their
daily activities;
13 the globalization of the social, involving an interweaving of global and
local happenings.

There are a number of points that might be noted about this list of definitions. For one thing, some of these definitions view society positively,
others negatively, and some are clearly ambiguous. The more positive of
these definitions see society as an indispensable medium for the production
of social relations, emphasizing the benefits of interpersonal relationships
and the potential gains from intercultural communication. In this sense
society is viewed in a largely technical way, as a process that facilitates not
only the constitution of identity and elaboration of forms of thought but also
the reproduction across time and across space of social interactions (think,
for example, of family life across generations) and of social institutions
(think, for example, of schools, hospitals or prisons). Some of these definitions, however, view society pejoratively – as the inculcation of false beliefs
or ideology – and thus emphasize the role of economic and political forces
in various forms of human exploitation.

Another point is that this list of definitions carries a range of implications for understanding the world in which we live: not just in academic
terms but for everyday life. Some formulations identify profoundly transformative processes, such that the very existence of a thing known as
'society' appears as either an illusion or an unnecessary hangover from
classical social theory. This is a fertile line of social enquiry which emerges
out of structuralist social theory, in which society is recast as a language or
linguistic process, and runs through our own time to postmodernism and
other forms of critical social thought. A number of conceptual approaches
in this respect, from post-structuralism and postmodernism to globalization
studies, suggest that the social sciences must radically rethink its subject
matter – as a world of 'bounded' societies no longer exists, if indeed it ever
once did. Other traditions of thought are much more cautious. Some argue
that the so-called 'openness' of the social has been exaggerated: society,
according to some critics, is alive and well, and it is only in the writings of
obscure social theorists (particularly the French) that the notion recedes into
the shadows.

Society and social theory

Another way of thinking about Natalie's life and current circumstance is by looking in a little more detail at what social theorists have had to say about the concept of 'society'. Social theory, as we will see, is a very sweeping and diverse attempt to engage with major social problems, and for that reason alone any hard-and-fast generalizations about it should be treated with caution. But it is possible to identify three widely held positions, deriving from classical social theory, on what it actually feels like to live in the modern world.

The first position seeking to make sense of what it feels like to live in society is that of Karl Marx. According to Marx as well as authors influenced by Marxism, social bonds are determined to their roots by structured inequalities, or class conflict. In this portrait, society is fundamentally split, torn and divided. The modern world after Marx is *schizoid* to its roots. This is a world that is continuously dynamic at the level of productive industrial forces, and endlessly restless in its search for profits. Yet if capitalism unleashes human creative powers and fosters material growth for some in society, it condemns the bulk of humanity to a degraded, wretched life. 'More than any other mode of production,' writes Marx (see Cohen 1978: 25), 'capitalism squanders human lives, or living labour, and not only flesh and blood, but also nerve and brain.' Capitalism, simply, generates the brutalization of society through its ongoing revolution of economic life. These internal dynamics of the capitalist system produce, in turn, the most tragic social contradictions – namely, the polarization of rich and poor. It is for this reason, said Marx, that we have to free ourselves from capitalism by restoring to society the realization of human powers through communism. For Marx, the anticipated communist society was one in which the active shaping of history involved a more stable, ordered, free and equal world.

The second position on the texture of modern society is that of Max Weber. According to this portrait, modern society imprisons us in the 'iron cage' of bureaucratic rationality. Writing at the turn of the nineteenth century, Weber was as much preoccupied with the threats to humanity presented by modern industrial society as was Marx, but he addressed these threats differently. His focus was more internal than external, concentrating on how individual attitudes come to be shaped by the drab, passionless world of bureaucratic routine. The portrait of modern society he bequeaths to social theory is that of a *bureaucratic machine* – where people may retain some semblance of authenticity (a kind of pseudo-individualism), but are in fact trapped in the 'steel-hard' cage of a rigid rationality. This portrait of society has been tremendously influential – for example, literary works such as George Orwell's *1984* implicitly reference the Weberian model of society as fixed, static and rationalized.

The third position on the texture of modern society is that of Emile Durkheim, according to which social cohesion falls on hard times as a result of the rise of individualism. Perhaps more clearly than either Marx or Weber, Durkheim saw the significance of morality in modern social development. There must be a moral bond for society to exist at all according to Durkheim, and it is from that angle that the moral framework may be considered to be at the root of both individualism and social relations. In *Elementary Forms of the Religious Life* (1912), Durkheim invoked the term *conscience collective* to show that whenever we think, we think collectively. Less about religion than about the question of morality, Durkheim's *Elementary Forms* sought to demonstrate that social theory cannot explore the terrain of morality if women and men are abstracted from their concrete social surroundings. To study morality after Durkheim means grasping it as intricately interwoven with the fine gradations and subtle nuances of our shared social experiences. In the end, the world is known through the social categories of our shared lives. The dilemma in our own time of intensive individualism, according to Durkheim's standpoint, is how to struggle to retain contact with the common aspects of social life.

There is, however, a problem. History has not exactly been kind to any of these versions of society. The world in which Natalie finds herself today does not really reflect, or simply correspond to, any of the classical portraits of society. Rather than being socially integrated through the impact of shared moral values as described by Durkheim, contemporary societies seem to operate as much through a lack of consensus among social agents as through any implicit shared moral norms. So, too, societies today are not becoming more and more bureaucratic, or predictably ordered, in the fashion Weber anticipated. Finally, as the collapse of the Berlin Wall in 1989 and associated death of Marxism as a political project indicate, class conflict is most certainly not the principal motor of history. It is true that we now live in a global electronic economy, to which the ideas of Marx, Weber and Durkheim still have relevance. But it is a very different world from that anticipated in classical social theory, one that neither reduces to a single overriding dynamic of social explanation nor one subject to rational pre-diction and scientific control.

As it happens, Natalie has a powerful sense of the breadth and speed of social change currently sweeping the globe. She believes, for example, that no single force – neither governments nor corporations – is in control of the global economy. She thinks the idea that the nation-state can manage capitalism has been exposed as fatally flawed. Consequently, she is con-cerned that the welfare state – an institution she has grown to admire while living in the UK, but which was virtually unknown to her while growing up in America – will not be able to meet the demands placed upon it by citizens, especially the growing numbers of elderly people. But there are other anxieties too, perhaps deeper ones, that Natalie has about the future of society. She feels that the entire globe is in a 'state of emergency'. There are tremendous new risks. Terrorism, and particularly the threat of high technology nuclear terror, convinces Natalie that the world in which she grew up is gone, and gone for good. Other high risks of today's world that she mentions include global warming and environmental destruction. And yet she still identifies other social trends more promising for her future, and the future of the next generation. She describes her life today as a constantly shifting terrain of exciting experiences. As she moves between cities and countries, her professional and personal lives bring her into regular contact with people who think differently, and live quite different lives, from her. She embraces this social complexity, and welcomes moves towards increased cultural diversity and cosmopolitan living.

Natalie's instinctive sense that the world in which she lives is changing fast mirrors contemporary intellectual assessments of the human condition in the current age. What the 'deep drivers' of society are, and whether they are in point of fact new, are the focus of intense controversy in social theory. I discuss many of the most significant assessments of society – of the complex ways in which we now live – throughout this book. Some of these social theories, as we will see, seek to develop the structural method proposed by classical thinkers such as Marx, Weber and Durkheim, but apply it to novel areas of social enquiry. That is to say, the classical insight that social structures – such as the economy or bureaucracy – operate in ways invisible to the naked eye has been extended by various contemporary analysts of society to encompass, among others, the linguistic field, the unconscious, sexuality, the body, new technologies and virtual networks. Other social theorists reject classical perspectives on the grounds that they are ill-equipped to comprehend the novel global circumstances in which we now find ourselves. In this viewpoint, industrialism and market capitalism are dying, if not dead, and a new world has been born. Various social theories have been proclaimed to challenge classical orthodoxies in this respect, ranging from post-industrialism and post-structuralism to post-feminism and postmodernity.

New times demand fresh thinking. Tracing the rise of contemporary social theory from the 1920s to the present day, this book explores how path-breaking theoretical and sociological concerns have brought topics such as selfhood, power, domination, sexuality and gender to the fore of intellectual and public political debate over recent years. In reviewing developments in social theory, my aim is to introduce readers to some of the most challenging perspectives, and surprising innovations, on the multidimensional aspects of contemporary social processes. Social theorists from a wide variety of perspectives agree – even if they agree on little else – that we live in new worlds of social and cultural organization. To capture the spirit of these new times, a vast array of terms and terminology has been developed. What must urgently be engaged with according to Theodor Adorno are the institutional transformations associated with 'the totally administered society', whereas for Herbert Marcuse the core of our social pathologies stems from 'surplus repression'. Jürgen Habermas speaks by contrast of 'systematically distorted communication' warping contemporary societies, and Axel Honneth widens this focus on communication to encompass problems of recognition and disrespect. If communication and culture brook large in some recent analyses, then structuralist, post-structuralist and deconstructive theories focus attention on the relation between language and social realties in startling new ways. The French semiologist Ferdinand de Saussure's procla-mation that we must analyse 'the life of signs in society' has served to establish signifiers, sexualities and simulations as legitimate objects of study in contemporary social theory. The pioneering works of Roland Barthes, Jacques Lacan, Michel Foucault, Louis Althusser and Jacques Derrida on the intricate entwinement of signs and society call attention to the fundamental importance of languages, discourses and codes in everyday life.

Some of the new social theories, by contrast, seek to anchor their pre-occupations in less cultural and more institutional concerns. Anthony Giddens speaks of the current age as one of 'reflexive modernization'. Ulrich Beck writes of 'risk society'. Zygmunt Bauman of 'liquid modernity'. Manual Castells of 'the network society'. Fredric Jameson of 'late capitalism'. All of these social theories, in very different ways, attempt to account for changes in social conditions and institutional life associated with modernity. They represent powerful approaches to thinking about the rise of new information technologies and the current world economy, among others, in these early years of the twenty-first century. Then there are other, perhaps more familiar attempts to theorize what is truly new today. The term 'globalization' has been social theory's most famed recent reply to the complexities of people's lives today. The adventures of the concept of globalization range all the way from the emergence of transnational financial economies to global satellite communications. Again, social theorists have invented new terms to cap-ture, and indeed define, our new global times: to mention just a few that we will review in this book, 'global transformations' (David Held), 'border-less world' (Kenichi Ohmae) and 'glocalization' (Roland Robertson).

Social theory as practical life: Charles Lemert

Like Natalie, most people – most of the time – possess a *basic social theory*, which they use to orientate themselves to others and the wider world.

What does it mean to say that the quality of daily life is informed by a person's basic social theory? Perhaps we should start with what this statement does not mean. The notion of a person's basic or implicit sociology does not mean that people are necessarily practised in the scholarly arts of social theory – even though a large number of women and men who have, say, attended university or college, or read widely, may have engaged at some point with the social theories of Marxism, feminism, structuralism or postmodernism. To say that people possess a basic social theory is rather to underscore that a social agent's under-standing of social things plays a facilitative role in the actual production of social life. Consider again Natalie, who holds that the contemporary world is not controlled by any single authority or agency. While not elaborated in any detail, Natalie's thoughts, beliefs and assumptions about the multidimensional, chaotic aspects of current social experience not only reflect themes to be found in current social theory (such as postmodernism) but actually help serve to constitute the world as fractured and fracturing. How others in contemporary society understand and deal with the world at any given time will obviously vary widely. For some people, the world today involves various high risks. For others, it might be about thick credit and consumerism. For still others, it is about growing inequalities between the West and the rest. All such notions about how society works play a role in facilitating social relations. All such notions may be found in more sophisticated and detailed forms in contemporary social theory.

For Charles Lemert, the doyen of contemporary American social theory, our capacity to imagine social things competently is an essential part of our practical sociologies. To see the world sociologically is to see it in the light of its organizing structures and orderings of power. This means seeing it also in the shadow of its own potential transformation – the possibility of society lived otherwise. Lemert (2005b: 5) explains our common social sense for imagining social life competently:

> Whenever you enter a room and 'just know' you don't belong there, when you see a stranger on the subway and understand intuitively that it is safe to return his not-quite-delivered smile, when you are introduced to someone elegantly dressed in a certain way and know she is not to be called by her first name even if she offers it – these are among the evidences for the sociology in each of us. They may seem to be trivial manners by contrast to the urgency of survival through dark nights. And so they are. But, however small,

they are not unimportant. They may seem inconsequential just because they come to us so naturally. But think of what life would be like if we regularly encountered people who were sociologically incompetent.

What Lemert underwrites is the very fact that social theory is implicated in how we live in the present. The present for us is always filtered through certain social-theoretical assumptions, precepts and ideas – however basic or elementary – of the social realities all around us. Thus we cannot choose to live non-theoretically: social life, its regulations, orderings and structurings, is quite as much theoretical as practical.

How useful do you find the idea that all social actors possess 'practical sociologies'? How would you describe your own 'basic social theory' on life?

Key themes in contemporary social theory

Contemporary Social Theory: An Introduction is organized around a number of key themes, to which we will turn at various points throughout the chapters that follow. The first key theme is that of *the relation between the individual and society*, or between human action and social structure. This is perhaps one of the most vexing issues in social theory. Most of the social theorists we examine throughout this book, from Theodor Adorno, Hebert Marcuse, Roland Barthes and Michel Foucault to a variety of contemporary authors including Anthony Giddens, Ulrich Beck, Julia Kristeva and Judith Butler, resolve this issue either by emphasizing the agency of individuals or the power of social structures – or, indeed, through a conceptual combination of these opposing orientations. What side you take in this debate depends on whether or not you favour the idea of individuals-first, or society-first, in understanding how practical social life comes about and is sustained throughout history. For those sympathetic to the idea that it is the agency of individuals that creates patterned social life, the systematic study of the reasons, motives, beliefs, emotions and desires of people is regarded as the most appropriate way in which to develop critical social analysis. Understanding what motivates individual human interests, and particularly the complex ways in which individual actions lead over time to collective social habits, is essential from this standpoint if social theory is to engage adequately with the society in which we live and the fundamental conflicts in values, ethics and morality of our own time. A response that focuses on social structure, by contrast, refuses the emphasis on the agency of individuals and instead concentrates on the institutions or organizations of modern societies as the key ingredient of social explanation. On this approach, it is mistaken to believe that people are the source of the common will. Rather, it is social institutions – from the impact of families, schools and prisons to capitalist organizations and large-scale bureaucracies – which ensure that individual practices conform to collective ones. One reason why society-first explanations of social life hold great appeal is that we live in a society where a great many people have to undertake activities they would prefer not to do – such as holding down a dull job, tidying up one's bedroom when angry parents insist, or looking after a sick relative. Understanding how structures determine our individual actions – in the above cases, as a result of the powerful structures of economics, socialization or morality – is vital for grasping how power operates and unequal social relations are sustained in modern societies.

Whenever one is pondering the dynamics of social relations, it is always useful to raise the question of the relation between agency and structure. Is society reproduced by the impersonal structures of politics, culture and the economy as these forces press down on the activities of individual agents, or is it rather the variety of choices and decisions which individuals make in their daily lives that make up social structures? Throughout this book, we will consider various judgements of social theorists on this issue – from those critical of the individualistic bent of a soft subjectivism to those wary of a steel-hard objectivism. My own view is that both individuals-first and society-first standpoints have their uses, and much simply depends on the social practices under examination as to which is the most appropriate approach to adopt. If one wishes to understand an individual's response to a particular film, absorption in popular music or love of a book, then it no doubt makes sense to consider those theoretical approaches – from psychoanalysis to post-feminism to postmodernism – that adopt strands of the individuals-first case. If one wishes to study, by contrast, political voting systems or the economic trading patterns of multinational companies, then an emphasis on how structures shape activities is understandable enough. As will become evident throughout this book, this contrast as I have drawn it here is overstated – and certainly part of the current debate in social theory is that social theory cannot adequately engage with social life by focusing only on structures (which thereby liquidates individuals) or only on individual agents (which thereby downgrades the impact of social systems upon individuals). One way out of this impasse, as examined in Chapter 5 when we turn to the contributions of Anthony Giddens and Pierre Bourdieu, is to blend the two opposing approaches – examining how action is structured in everyday life, and how the structured features of action are thus reproduced in modern societies.

A second, related theme of the book is that of *the degree of consensus or conflict in modern societies*. This concerns the debate in social theory about the hold of values or norms which are dominant in society. Such values or norms, according to some social theorists, may effectively unify societies – such that individuals come to agree with one another in either open or tacit ways. From the import of early socialization in the family and at school through to the propagation of dominant values or norms in communications media, the idea is that the reproduction and legitimacy of the social order is sustained through such mechanisms for the transmission of unifying beliefs and values. To say that society is a successfully achieved unity is to say that we live in a world where people are effectively drawn into the bigger social forces surrounding them, such that individuals come to imbibe the expectations others have of them and the norms that cultural life lays down for them. There is no need for students of society to assume, however, that such an internalization of the dominant values of society involves the full consciousness or understanding of human agents. After all, many people's experience of the world, especially today, is that of increasing social complexity, cultural diversity and political conflict. Accordingly, sensitivity to the diversity of society and the subtleties of culture is necessary to ensure that social theory does not over-simplify the mixed, ambiguous experience individuals have of their own identities and of the wider social world.

In examining issues surrounding consensus and conflict in modern societies, we will explore various social theories throughout this book in terms of what they have to say about the reproduction of social formations and the transformation of culture. Some analysts of social theory argue that the unity of society is to be sought in the economic contradictions of capitalism; members of the Frankfurt School, for example, discern in the blending of rationalization and repression that operates in modern culture a unity they term the 'totally administered society'. Some analysts, by contrast, contend that the unity of society is to be found elsewhere. For some social theorists, we cannot conceive of social relations apart from how people talk about them, which means focusing on language. In this linguistic turn of social theory, which we will focus on in detail in Chapters 3 and 4, how we see the world around us and ourselves is constituted in and through language. On this view, it is language which unifies society – even if, as we will see, this 'unity' is illusory to its roots. Still other critics question whether social order presupposes some kind of consensus. This questioning of the so-called unity of society takes a number of forms. One approach is to suggest that social reproduction involves less an explicit than a practical consensus: in the work of Pierre Bourdieu, for example, the unity of society arises from a 'cultural unconscious' which gears individual practices to objective social conditions. Another approach underscores the dispersal or fragmentation of social formations. Such a fragmentation of beliefs, values and norms, it is argued, serves not to produce opposition to the current social order but the reproduction of society as a dispersed, postmodern or liquid orchestration.

A third theme is that of *change*, or social transformation. We live today in an era of enormous social change. Globalization, new information technologies, the seemingly unstoppable growth of consumerism, the techno-industrialization of war: such transformations are taking place not only in modern institutions but also within the very textures of everyday life. Contemporary social theory has been concerned to assess the pace of change occurring in our lives today, as well as to critique the large-scale institutional forces driving such social change. Some theorists of modern societies place an emphasis on capitalist transformations in explaining the emergence of a new – post-industrial, post-Fordist or postmodern – economy. The shift away from industrial production (of factories and large-scale assembly plants) in the West during the 1980s and 1990s, and the subsequent outsourcing of manufacture to low-wage economies in developing countries, is considered key by many social theorists to transformations in the whole capitalist system. For other social theorists, the economy has now become effectively cultural – in the sense that industrial manufacture has been traded throughout the West for a wholesale move into the service, communications and finance sectors. Still other critics see more cultural or institutional factors as central to explaining the recent changes. The establishment of commercial satellites above the Earth during the 1970s, facilitating in time the spread of instantaneous communication through, say, the Internet, is at the heart of the communications revolution that has redefined our age. Or, the crisis in scientific or expert knowledge during the final decades of the twentieth century has been viewed by some as heralding new cultural attitudes – loosely called 'postmodern' – towards society, culture, the arts and lifestyle issues. In all of these standpoints, change or social transformation is essential, and this theme will provide a framework for the review of social theories offered within the chapters that follow.

A fourth theme concerns *gender issues*. Social theory has long engaged with feminism, particularly the feminist argument that women's personal troubles should in fact be seen as broader social and political troubles that arise from living in male-dominated societies. Classical social theory by no means sidelined issues of gender and sexuality, although much of the analysis it offered was woefully insufficient. Contemporary social theory, by contrast, has directly engaged with the social, political, psychological and cultural inequalities between men and women – and in many cases has played a direct role in the women's movement and its search for social justice. Chapter 7 specifically explores developments in both feminist and post-feminist social theory, concentrating in particular on the gendering of feelings, desires, behaviours and social roles in modern societies. Nancy Chodorow, Jessica Benjamin, Jane Flax, Julia Kristeva, Luce Irigaray and Judith Butler are arguably the central voices in feminist and post-feminist social theory that have brought to prominence the complex ways in which sexual desire is entangled with broader questions of pleasure and power, with the politics of the body, and the reproduction of individual and collective identities. Issues of gender and sexuality, as feminist and post-feminist analysis highlights, must be urgently engaged with in social theory, and accordingly the chapters that follow return regularly to this most vital matter.

A final theme concerns the relation between the *social* and the *emotional*, between our public and private worlds. Contemporary social theory powerfully questions many of the oppositions in both mainstream social science and broader public life governing the relationship between public and private life. Instead of viewing, say, tumultuous political events or the forces of globalization as outside happenings in society, there are various traditions of social theory which critically examine the complex ways in which social, cultural and political processes come to be anchored, regulated and lived at the levels of identity and emotional life. In fact, the ways in which public life organizes the private domain, while in turn being reshaped by the emotional responses and reactions of individuals, has bulked large in many traditions of recent social theory. Theodor Adorno, Herbert Marcuse, Jacques Lacan, Roland Barthes, Anthony Giddens, Julia Kristeva, Luce Irigaray and Judith Butler have all explored, in very different ways, the meshing of the social and the erotic, the symbolic and the unconscious, cultural conditions and lived experience, the global and the local. As a result, questions of identity, desire and emotion have certainly emerged as fundamental concerns in social theory. Consequently, throughout this book, I emphasize that to critically study a social situation means analysing it at both the cultural and personal levels – looking at how the public and private interlock.

Further questions

1   What do you think your own life reflects about our fast-changing world?

2   What do you understand by the notion of society?

3   If you think of key social institutions – for example, schools, hospitals, prisons and government – what role do they play in society?

4   To what extent is participation in various social institutions consensual or coercive?

5   We live in a world of radical change: do you agree?

Further reading

This chapter covers a broad sweep of introductory concerns in social theory, but the following books should provide useful discussions for further consideration.

Classical social theory is not treated in any detail here, as my core focus is contemporary social theory. For a guide to the main theories and issues in classical social theory, I refer the beginning reader to two of the world's foremost social theorists: Anthony Giddens, *Capitalism and Modern Social Theory: An Analysis of the Writings of Marx, Weber and Durkheim*, Cambridge University Press, 1971; and Charles Lemert, *Thinking The Unthinkable: The Riddles of Classical Social Theories*, Paradigm Publishers, 2007, and *Social Things: An Introduction to the Sociological Life*, Rowman & Littlefield, 2005.

Some of the main arguments and issues in relation to how the self navigates the social world may be found in Anthony Elliott, *Concepts of the Self*, Polity Press, 2007. The more adventurous reader should try Erving Goffman's sociology of everyday life. The best overview of Goffman is Ann Branaman and Charles Lemert (eds), *The Goffman Reader*, Blackwell, 1997. See also Ann Branaman, *Self and Society*, Blackwell, 2000, and Anthony Elliott, *Subject To Ourselves*, Paradigm Publishers, 2004.

Finally, in discussing Natalie's life and experience of the world I have drawn from various works of social theory – either explicitly or implicitly – on current social trends as well as the likely future texture of society. For social theories of current social trends in these early years of the twenty-first century see, among others, Anthony Giddens, *Runaway World*, Profile Books, 1999; Terry Eagleton, *After Theory*, Allen Lane, 2003; and John Urry, *Mobilities*, Polity Press, 2007. For a disturbing portrait of the more tragic textures of the contemporary era see Giorgio Agamben, *Homo Sacer: Sovereign Power and Bare Life*, Stanford University Press, 1998.

Internet Links

www.theory.org.uk
www.thechangingworld.org
www.open2.net/society/socialchange/newsociety_mnv.html
www.socialtheory.info

chapter 2

The Frankfurt School

Contents

Of all the classical sociological traditions, Marxism arguably provides the most scintillating storyline regarding the ongoing, frantic expansion of capitalism. 'The bourgeoisie', wrote Marx, 'has through its exploitation of the world market given a cosmopolitan character to production and consumption in every country.' From San Francisco to Sydney, from New York to New Delhi: anyone shopping in a downtown mall, surveying flashy designer goods and hi-tech products flown in from China, Taiwan or India, would most likely agree with Marx's assessment. What happens to people under capitalism for Marx is an extravagant inflation of sensory life and human desire, creating a sort of permanent revolution across society in which pleasure depends upon the continual accumulation of more and more things. People, simply, want newer and newer experiences. One can argue about whether designer jeans, mobile phones or iPods really constitute an advance in societal well-being, but the essential point from a Marxist perspective is that such consumption has today become perversely self-constituting, self-breeding, self-referential.

Next to watching TV, shopping is now the most popular leisure pursuit the world over. Think about that for a moment. Today, more and more people define their lives in terms of what they buy and what they own, and arguably more so than in terms of what they think or what they do for a living. In the new consumer society of the twenty-first century, individuals consume not only material goods but various seductive products and services targeted to the insatiable wants of mass society. Shopping in today's free-floating consumer landscape – in which shops, services and Internet sites are open around the clock – individuals go about trying to quench their insatiable wants in societies where there just seem to be not enough hours in the day. From online grocery shopping at Tesco to Rolex watches, from figure-hugging Calvin Klein jeans to the ultra-fashion sportswear of Nike, from age-reversing cosmetics and creams to the designer clothes of Armani or Versace: the near-universal pursuit of shopping in the West has established itself as fundamental to experiences of personal liberty and human freedom.

The ascendancy of universal consumerism is a remarkable phenomenon. It has, for one thing, transformed modern societies away from industrial production (that having been 'outsourced' to other developing countries) and towards the post-industrial consumption of products, services and brands. It has also helped fashion a new set of social attitudes in which shopping has become redefined as an end in itself. Unlike Sigmund Freud's psychoanalytic description of society as a trade-off in which people sacrifice happiness for security, today's consumer society is all about instant self-gratification and pleasure. The freedom to consume, or so runs the global *laissez-faire* doctrine, is essential to how contemporary women and men consume freedom.

contemporary social theory

Yet there are powerful reasons to question the supposed liberty that arises from our culture of consumerism. Do so-called lifestyle statements – Apple iPods, Gucci watches, Mont Blanc pens – really satisfy our deeper personal strivings, or are they just a further stimulus to a society that cannot stop desiring to desire? How many online shoppers find that they really have more quality time available in their lives – for family, friends or meaningful pursuits? How many parents avoid spending time with their children as a result of our culture of shopping? And do today's consumer industries – from travel agencies selling pre-packaged holidays to IKEA-inspired firms selling pre-packaged living – promote new freedoms or new insecurities?

One influential contribution to thinking about the societal consequences of advanced capitalism, and especially tracking the contours of the cultural and consumer industries that people must now navigate, is that of the Frankfurt School. Central to the parameters of Frankfurt School social theory is Theodor Adorno's vision of the 'administered society' and Herbert Marcuse's thesis of 'one-dimensional society' in which individuals suffer from 'surplus-repression'. The work of Adorno and Marcuse is incorrigibly interdisciplinary (involving certain traditions of classical social theory, and especially Freudian psychoanalysis), purveying a view of society that may well be unrecognizable to many contemporary men and women who inhabit the fast-paced, consumer-orientated societies of today. Yet as two of the most important German intellectuals of the twentieth century, their writings – and indeed the work of the Frankfurt School as a whole – are of profound importance for engaging not only with recent world history, but with the impacts of large-scale societal processes upon individuals and their private worlds.

The Frankfurt School, as it came to be called, was formed in the decade prior to the Nazi reign of terror in Germany, and not surprisingly many of its leading theorists conducted numerous studies seeking to grasp the wave of political irrationalism and totalitarianism sweeping Western Europe. In a daring theoretical move, the School brought Freudian categories to bear upon the sociological analysis of everyday life, in order to fathom the myriad ways that political power imprints itself upon the internal world of human subjects and, more specifically, to critically examine the obscene, meaningless kind of evil that Hitler had actually unleashed. Of the School's attempts to fathom the psychopathologies of fascism, the writings of Adorno, Marcuse and Fromm particularly stand out; each of these authors, in quite different ways, drew upon Freudian categories to figure out the core dynamics and pathologies of post-liberal rationality, culture and politics, and also to trace the sociological deadlocks of modernity itself. The result was a dramatic underscoring of both the political dimensions of psychoanalysis and the psychodynamic elements of public political life.

Adorno and Horkheimer: *Dialectic of Enlightenment*

While in exile in the United States, Adorno and Horkheimer wrote *Dialectic of Enlightenment* (1944) – a brilliant work of social theory that sought to grasp the dark side of the modern age. Written with remarkable philosophical range and sociological insight, the task Adorno and Horkheimer set for themselves was spelt out thus: 'The discovery of why mankind, instead of entering into a truly human condition, is sinking into a new kind of barbarism.' The hell to which the authors referred was the political nightmare they had left behind in Germany – the fascism of the Third Reich. However, such was the increasingly comprehensive sweep of instrumental reason throughout modern societies that Horkheimer and Adorno also found signs or symptoms of fascist domination in liberal democracies too, especially America. In fact, the American entertainment industry – from jazz to Hollywood – was a fundamental part of this process of commercialized brainwashing, and thus indicative of the rise and domination of fascist ideology. The idea then that enlightenment and domination are intricately interwoven lies at the core of *Dialectic of Enlightenment*, and is fundamental to the comprehensive sociological diagnosis of modernity that Horkheimer and Adrono expounded.

Reason is, of course, essential to human existence. With Horkheimer and Adorno's critical theory, however, the philosophy of the Enlightenment and instrumental reason are revealed as having capsized into a form of sickness. Reason at its extreme limit, transformed into a mirror-image of the very madness it seeks to repress, is explored by Horkheimer and Adorno with reference to various definitions of the term 'enlightenment'. One key definition is associated with a variety of political and intellectual currents which shaped social upheavals in Europe, from the great French Revolution of the eighteenth century to the Russian Revolution in the early decades of the twentieth century. This is the revolutionary idea of enlightenment as rationalist, republican and universal in scope. Another key definition springs from modern science, especially the age of discoveries and transformations occurring in science as a result of technological innovations such as the telescope, microscope, compass and clocks. In examining these versions of enlightenment reason, Horkheimer and Adorno observe a general shift in people's attitudes towards their own lives, the lives of others and in the external world. Whereas traditional societies turned to mythology in governing human affairs, modern societies greeted the force of human reason as decisive. Such an emancipatory notion of enlightenment was essential, for both liberals and conservatives, to the supposed erosion of mythology – facilitative of contemporary developments in science, technology and the economy.

This modern idea – that reason destroys myth – is however nothing but sheer illusion, according to Horkheimer and Adorno. On the contrary, enlightenment and myth are closely allied. This means, however, that there is a secret complicity between what founds enlightenment – reason – and that which it seeks to overcome, namely myth. On this view, the rational becomes more and more entangled in myth, as the social order comes to define itself as enlightened. 'In the most general sense of progressive thought,' write Horkheimer and Adorno, 'the Enlightenment has always aimed at liberating man from fear and establishing their sovereignty. Yet the fully enlightened earth radiates disaster triumphant.' From fascism in Europe to commercialized mass culture in the United States, the Enlightenment's promise of freedom had produced disastrous social consequences on both sides of the Atlantic.

'Enlightenment', write the authors of *Dialectic of Enlightenment*, 'is totalitarian.' From the rise of National Socialism in Germany to the culture industry in America, from Hitler's annihilation of European Jews to the unparalleled destruction of modern technological warfare: enlightenment reason has failed the West and indeed humanity as a whole. At the core of this sceptical, indeed bleak, assessment of the modern age is the concept of domination. While Horkheimer and Adorno do not define domination with any degree of sociological precision, it seems clear that they seek to underscore the power of instrumental, technological and scientific reason in the establishment of domination over the self, over one's inner nature and over external nature and society.

The enslavement to nature of people today cannot be separated from social progress. The increase in economic productivity which creates the conditions for a more just world also affords the technical apparatus and the social groups controlling it a disproportionate advantage over the rest of the population. The individual is entirely nullified in face of the economic powers. These powers are taking society's domination over nature to unimagined heights. While individuals are vanishing before the apparatus they serve, they are provided for by that apparatus and better than ever before. In the unjust state of society the powerlessness and pliability of the masses increase with the quantity of good allocated to them. The materially considerable and socially paltry rise in the standard of living of the lower classes is reflected in the hypocritical propagation of intellect. Intellect's true concern is a negation of reification. It mut perish when it is solidified into a cultural asset and handed out for consumption purposes. The flood of precise information and brand-new amusements make people smarter and more stupid at once.

Theodor Adorno and Max Horkheimer (2002 [1944]) *Dialectic of Enlightenment: Philosophical Fragments*, ed. Gunzelin Schmid Noerr and trans. Edmund Jephcott. Stanford, CA: Stanford University Press, p. xvii.

By dominating nature, argue Horkheimer and Adorno, society and social relations are secured, while individual identity is transformed from blind instinct to reflective consciousness of the self. This is, in effect, a shift from nature to culture. But in a tragic irony, the violence which wrested society out of nature turns back upon itself, mutilating identities and robbing people of possibilities for happiness and freedom. That is to say, the aggression, rage and violence which were initially necessary to protect the social order from the ravages of nature do not magically disappear once culture and political life are constituted. On the contrary, violence is written into the very fabric of social order; aggression strikes at the heart of every attempt by social actors to change the world, no matter how noble or high-minded their intentions might be. This means that the unstoppable urge to 'administer' society through the application of rationalist blueprints is always dangerously in excess of necessity. There is something delusional about the desire for reason: it is delusional because reason conceals a mind-shattering repression which is, in fact, the exact opposite of autonomy. One symptom of this disease of enlightenment is fascism, especially anti-Semitism. Hatred of Jews, contend Adorno and Horkheimer, is a projection of modern society's ferocious inner compulsion on to a marginalized group. Yet anti-Semitism is not the only symptom of the frightful excess of enlightenment reason, which is why domination in our own era runs all the way from the destruction of nature to the colonization of developing nations.

Freudian revolution: the uses of psychoanalysis

One of the most distinctive features of the development of critical theory undertaken by the Frankfurt School was its use of Freudian psychoanalysis for the study of identity, politics, culture and ideology. The fundamental concern of the Frankfurt School with domination – that is, with the process and products of our increasingly administered, manipulated world of advanced capitalism – also involved a particular focus on the individual, self-identity and emotional life. This orientation involved a shift well beyond the confines of classical social theory, and towards the terrain of psychology – principally in the form of psychoanalysis. In Adorno's work from the 1940s, and in Marcuse's writings from the 1950s, psychoanalysis becomes a central intellectual and political resource not only for examining the entanglements of reason and repression, but for rethinking the question of happiness and pleasure at the level of whole societies. The political motivation prompting this turn to psychoanalysis had its roots in Adorno and Marcuse's attempts to explain the rise of fascism, Nazism, and the emotional impacts of bureaucratic capitalism on private life. Significant moves in this direction had already been taken in the 1930s by Erich Fromm, whose work with the Frankfurt School we will consider shortly, and who sought to champion Freudian analysis (against Freud's more pessimistic political judgements) as a tool in the struggle for social liberation and the pacification of violence.

As a result of the Frankfurt School's use of Freud, psychoanalysis has come to exert a major impact on contemporary social theory. This impact will be discussed in detail in Chapter 4, where the post-structuralist rereading of Freud undertaken by Jacques Lacan and his followers is critically examined. For the moment, however, it is necessary to consider what drew members of the Frankfurt School to Freud, and in particular to examine how psychoanalytic concepts were reformulated and extended to fit with the core emphases of critical theory. Almost all of Freud's central discoveries – the unconscious, sexual repression, the Oedipus complex, and the like – were deployed by key Frankfurt School theorists to reconsider the relation between selfhood and society, the family and socialization, ideology and political domination. In an essay 'Sociology and Psychology', for example, Adorno defended the importance of Freud to social theory. He argued that psychoanalysis is valuable because it explored in detail the processes of identity formation in the late nineteenth and early twentieth centuries, and to that extent could be marshalled in the service of critical theory for the development of a critique of identity. Paradoxically, however, psychoanalysis is at its most radical when its concepts are pushed to breaking point – as with some of the wilder 'armchair' conjectures of Freud. 'In psychoanalysis,' Adorno wrote in *Minima Moralia* (1974), 'nothing is true except the exaggerations.' What Adorno meant by this remark, it seems, is that the more outrageous features of Freud's work – the fictions of psychoanalysis, if you will – actually contain key insights into the contemporary social and political world. From this angle, Freud's theory of, say, castration anxiety (a theory which, as a universal condition, has been rejected even within psychoanalytic circles) can be recast as an appropriate *metaphor* for the destructive and brutal nature of social relationships promoted in an age of advanced capitalism. As Martin Jay (1984: 90) observes, what 'drew Adorno to the early Freud was the way in which his theory unflinchingly registered the traumas of contemporary existence. Telling the harsh truth was itself a kind of resistance to the acceptance of those traumas as inevitable.'

Marcuse's use of Freud in critical theory to understand modern society parallels some of the perspectives advanced by Adorno, but his writings were far more influential. Like Adorno, Marcuse focuses on the early 'biological' Freud, or what is termed 'drive theory'. While this reliance on the traditional Freudian vocabulary of repressed drives and sexual energies is unfashionable today, and ultimately accounts for certain limitations in Marcuse's critical theory of society, it also provides the conceptual context for many of his most important insights into how modern societies penetrate the internal landscape of identities in a profoundly repressive fashion. Both Marcuse and Adorno were, for example, deeply suspicious of American ego-psychology, a rewriting of Freudian theory away from its traditional focus on the split and fractured nature of the individual self and towards integration. Such a reading of Freud, argued Marcuse, robbed psychoanalysis of its revolutionary potential. Rather than graft society on to psychoanalysis, Marcuse sought to unfold psychoanalysis from the inside in order to reveal its inherently critical edge. Unlike Adorno, however, Marcuse argues that the undoing of sexual repression opens the possibility for a radical transformation of identity, society and culture.

What has been of incomparable value, however, is the School's analysis of why human subjects, apparently without resistance, submit to the dominant ideologies of late capitalism. The general explanatory model developed by the Frankfurt School to study the socio-psychological dimension of the relation between the individual and culture has received considerable attention in social theory.

Fromm: fear of freedom

Fromm, who had been practising as an analyst since 1926 and was a member of the Frankfurt Psychoanalytic Institute, sought in his early studies to integrate Freud's theory of the unconscious with Marxist sociology. Influenced by Wilhelm Reich's book *Character Analysis* (1972 [1933]), which connected society to the functioning of the unconscious, Fromm became preoccupied with the themes of sexuality and repression, as well as the mediating influence of the family between the economy and the individual. According to Fromm, Freudian psychoanalysis must supplement Marxism in order to grasp how social structures influence, indeed shape, the inner dimensions of personal life. Fromm's analysis of repression, however, differed substantially from that worked out by Reich. In Fromm's view, Reich had been unable to develop an adequate theory of society because he had reduced Freud's theory of sexuality to the level of individual psychology. Yet Freudian psychoanalysis, Fromm maintained, was fundamentally a 'social psychology'. For Fromm, the individual must be understood in his or her relation to others.

The social system, in Fromm's reinterpretation of Freud, shapes people's lives to fit the economic and cultural context of the historical age.

Feudal society produced individuals adapted to the roles of serfs and lords; market capitalism produced individuals as capitalists and workers; and advanced monopoly capitalism churns out people as, first and foremost, consumers. Fromm describes this as the production of 'socially necessary character types'. Society goes to work, in effect, on individuals, ordering the psyche along pre-set social pathways, projecting social values and attitudes into the deepest recesses of the self. The result, says Fromm, is people 'wanting to act as they have to act'.

For Fromm, as for Freud, the family plays a key role in the emergence of repression. The winning of parental love entails the repression or denial of inner selfhood, and the adaptation to socially prescribed patterns of behaviour. As Fromm puts it: 'The family is the medium through which the society or the social class stamps its specific structure on the child, and hence on the adult. 'The family is the psychological agency of society' (Fromm 1985 [1932]: 483, emphasis in original). The family is an institution that implants external, social contradictions at the heart of personal life, sustains economic conditions as ideology, and shapes perceptions of the self as submissive, self-effacing and powerless. The central thread of Fromm's argument is that the destructive effects of late capitalism are not only centred on economic mechanisms and institutions, but involve the anchoring of domination within the inner life and psychodynamic struggles of each individual. If society, in Fromm's eyes, is a matter of sexual repression, libidinal renunciation and pathologies of self, then it is really not all that far from the general tenets of classical Freudianism. In arguing that social and political relations affect self-identity in different and changing ways, Fromm enriches Freud's account of repression. Fromm's later writings, however, change direction quite dramatically. Increasingly sceptical of Freud's dualistic theory of the life and death drives (see subsequent discussion of Freud later in this chapter), he argued that classical Freudianism could not adequately grasp the importance of interpersonal relationships. In particular, Fromm rejected Freud's notion of the death drive, arguing that it only served to legitimate the increasingly destructive and aggressive tendencies of modern societies.

As the 1930s progressed, Fromm became increasingly sceptical of orthodox Freudianism. He strongly criticized Freud's notion of the death drive for its biological reductionism, and argued that it only served to legitimate at a theoretical level the destructive and aggressive tendencies of capitalism. Significantly, Fromm also became influenced by neo-Freudian analysts – such as Harry Stack Sullivan and Karen Homey – who stressed larger social and cultural factors in the constitution of selfhood. This emphasis on cultural contributions to identity formation was underscored in some of Fromm's major books, notably *Escape from Freedom* (1941) and *The Sane Society* (1955). These books put the argument for an essential 'nature of man', a nature repressed and distorted by capitalist patterns of domination.

In *The Sane Society* (1955), Fromm examines modern society in terms of the pathologies it inflicts upon selfhood, considering the extent to which the pressures of social life deform intimate relationships. In particular, he argues that Freud underemphasized social and cultural relations, and also the general impact of culture upon human needs. Selfhood, says Fromm, is best understood in terms of interpersonal processes. From this angle, psychical life is composed of emotional configurations derived from relations between self and others. For Fromm, self-organization, though influenced by unconscious drives and passion, is reflexively organized through 'awareness, reason and imagination'. Fromm's theory of selfhood can be stated in five theses:

1   *Relatedness vs. narcissism.* The human condition is rooted in an essential need for relatedness – a thesis from which Fromm challenges Freud's so-called solitary individual. The need for relatedness is not instinctual, but arises from the separation with nature. The flourishing of intimacy depends upon creative social relations. Without such relations the self is impoverished, as in pathological narcissism.

2   *Transcendence-creativeness vs. destructiveness.* Against the backdrop of our biological needs, personal and social creativity unfold in both positive and negative forms. Creation and destruction, Fromm argues, 'are both answers to the same need for transcendence, and the will to destroy must rise when the will to create cannot be satisfied'.

3   *Rootedness-brotherliness vs. incest.* Mature social life, Fromm argues, depends upon an interplay of masculine and feminine values. Against what he considers the masculinist bent of Freud's work, Fromm contends that the potential of the self depends upon the integration of feminine qualities (such as care and nurturing) into the masculine realm of reason. But for this very reason, feminine qualities are considered dangerous in modern society since they threaten incorporation back into a 'state of nature'.

4   *Sense of identity-individuality vs. herd conformity.* The search for self-identity is intrinsic to the human condition, and modern societies play an essential role in structuring socio-economic possibilities for self-organization. The repressive transformation of this need, he argues, produces authoritarian ideologies such as fascism and anti-Semitism.

5   *The need for a frame of orientation and devotion-reason vs. irrationality.* The need for emotional connection with the world is a precondition for human autonomy. Without emotional connection, the individual is drained of ego-strength.

The central feature of Fromm's work then is that helplessness or isolation are key building blocks in relations between the self and other people. In this respect, intimate relationships can be either progressive or regressive. Progressive relations with other people involve emotional qualities of care, empathy and love. The pain of individual isolation must be confronted and accepted in order for healthy interpersonal relations to develop. By contrast, a regressive involvement with other people is caused by denying individual separateness. In this mode of functioning, inner pain and emptiness are sidestepped by a neurotic immersion in infantile illusions. An endless menu of regressive fantasies is offered by mass consumer culture in this connection, fantasies which produce narcissistic pathology and related disturbances. The key feature in this neurotic, regressive zoning of the self is that other people are used instrumentally in order to bolster self-identity, and thus to avoid inner emptiness and isolation. Here Fromm's standpoint converges on a crucial object relational distinction between self-development and self-distortion – as in Fairbairn's formulation of good and bad object relations, or Winnicott's account of the true self and the false self. However, Fromm proposes a more open psychoanalytic theory of the self by directly linking interpersonal relations and social context. The core of his argument is that problems of self, which link with social relationship pathologies, have their roots in already-existing patterns of cultural domination. Because the spheres of economic, political and cultural life are shot through with the sadistic satisfactions of power and domination, regressive self-solutions are reproduced in the individual domain.

What is so deceptive about the state of mind of the members of a society is the 'consensual validation' of their concepts. It is naively assumed that the fact that the majority of people share certain ideas or feelings proves the validity of these ideas and feelings. Nothing is further from the truth. Consensual validation as such has no bearing whatsoever on reason or mental health. Just as there is a 'folie à deux' [madness with two] there is a 'folie à millions' [madness with millions]. The fact that millions of people share the same vices does not make these vices virtues, the fact that they share so many errors does not make the errors to be truths, and the fact that millions of people share the same forms of mental pathology does not make these people sane.

Erich Fromm (1955) *The Sane Society*. New York; Chicago; San Francisco: Holt, Rinehart & Winston, pp. 14–15.

Given that contemporary social arrangements so violently deform and warp self-constitution, is there anything that can be done to reverse this pathological state of affairs? Can human beings create, and sustain, any kind of meaningful liberation? Fromm believes that they can. Surprisingly, given the pessimistic tone of the preceding analysis, Fromm contends that it is still possible to face the painful realities of life in a mature and rational way. To do this, Fromm argues, it is vital for the self to *disengage* from the corrupting influences of the contemporary epoch. To live authentically means fashioning a creative and responsive selfhood, a self that can productively engage in intimacy and mutuality. Such a capacity, he contends, depends on coming to terms with individual separation and aloneness – realities that are usually experienced as isolation or emptiness in modern culture. A shorthand way of describing this is that Fromm is encouraging a more reflexive involvement with the self. But what then of social conflict? In this context, Fromm attempts to develop a moral dimension as an energizing vision for emancipation. The more that human subjects reclaim the possibility of authentic existence through introspection and self-reflection, the more a social order based on mutual respect and autonomous activity will develop.

Although Fromm's early studies on the integration of individuals into capitalism was broadly accepted by other members of the Frankfurt School, his subsequent, more sociological diagnosis of an essential human nature twisted out of shape by capitalism was strongly rejected. Marcuse, for example, charged Fromm (and other neo-Freudian revisionists) with undoing the critical force of Freud's most important ideas, such as the unconscious, repression and infantile sexuality. According to Marcuse, Fromm's revisionism underwrites the smooth functioning of the ego only by displacing the dislocating nature of the unconscious. Marcuse (1956: 240–1) sums up the central point in the following way:

> Whereas Freud, focusing on the vicissitudes of the primary drives, discovered society in the most concealed layer of the genus and individual man, the revisionists, aiming at the reified, ready-made form rather than at the origin of the societal institutions and relations, fail to comprehend what these institutions and relations have done to the personality that they are supposed to fulfil.

Fromm's attempt to add sociological factors to psychoanalysis, says Marcuse, results in a false political optimism as well as a liquidation of what is truly revolutionary in Freud: the discovery of the repressed unconscious.

Fromm's writings rank among the most important post-Freudian mappings of the relations between self and society. Indeed, his model has had a major influence upon the reception of psychoanalysis into social and cultural theory. There are, however, important problems in Fromm's humanistic psychoanalysis. It has been argued, for example, that his account of self-constitution and the social process leads to a form of sociological reductionism. What is meant by this charge is that Fromm reduces the complex, contradictory relations between self and society to a dull, mechanical reproduction of pre-existing social values. The subject is repressively constituted through certain agencies of socialization, which stamp the prescriptive values of society into the human soul and thereby deform the essential needs of the self. In this critique, Fromm presents an account of self-constitution that eliminates the profound role of unconscious imagination, and leaves unexamined the diverse human possibilities for agency, creativity, critical reflection and transformation. He reduces Freud's notion of the unconscious to a totalistic conception of libidinal malleability. The limitations of such an approach are plain. The ambivalence that Freud locates between self and society – the tension between psychical and social reality – is obliterated. Although wanting to compensate for Freud's focus on unconscious drives, Fromm's cultural analysis proceeds too far in the other direction – sociologizing psychical reality out of existence. Ironically, then, it is the *post*-Freudian Erich Fromm who ultimately speaks up for a *pre*-Freudian conception of the 'total personality'.

A related criticism is that Fromm evaluates society against some 'human essence' of a non-cultural kind. It is as if Fromm, having diagnosed modern selfhood as thoroughly ideological, has to safeguard some resistant kernel of the human condition in order to articulate an emancipatory claim at all. Rationality, individualism, transcendence: these ideals may be absent from modern society, but they underlie all human experience and will potentially transform the social world. But in arguing that there is a transhistorical, universal 'human condition', Fromm seems blind to the fact that ideals such as rationality and self-mastery are often quite explicitly oppressive. Many contemporary world problems – global warming, the risk of massively destructive warfare, the exploitation and pollution of nature – are intimately bound up with the expansion of Western rationality and mastery. As one commentator puts it: 'Fromm revives all the time-honoured values of idealist ethics as if nobody had ever demonstrated their conformist and repressive features' (Marcuse 1956: 258). Significantly, the ideals which Fromm stresses are also those of a male-dominated realm. Little is said about gender or the repression of female sexuality in Fromm's work. His humanistic psychoanalysis, and its underwriting of the 'essential needs of mankind', thus reproduces at a theoretical level masculinist fantasies of omnipotent self-control. Seen in this light, the inadequacy of Fromm's belief that authentic living is possible through social disengagement becomes plain: to turn inward in the hope of discovering authentic existence represents not a 'radical endeavour' but rather an illusory wish to overcome domination and suffering by escaping society.

Adorno: the authoritarian personality, anti-Semitism and the psychodynamics of modernity

Like Fromm, Adorno thought it important to study pathologies of culture – especially fascism – both sociologically and psychologically. For Adorno, investigating the role of irrational authoritarianism in the rise of fascism and anti-Semitism throughout Europe during the Second World War was of the utmost political importance. But so too was studying whether such evil could ever firmly take root in the United States. To that end, Adorno joined with Else Frenkel-Brunswik, Daniel J. Levison and R. Nevitt Sanford in the late 1940s to conduct a large-scale analysis of the 'potentially fascistic individual'. The result was one of Adorno's best known books, *The Authoritarian Personality* (1950).

In contributing to *The Authoritarian Personality*, Adorno was arguably seeking to find empirical confirmation for the social theory of domination he developed with Horkheimer in *Dialectic of Enlightenment*. Again, Freudian psychoanalysis loomed large. Adorno found in fascist leaders, fascist regimes and fascist propaganda the psychodynamic logic of the 'sado-masochistic character' – of identities split between the bloodthirsty desire to denigrate and destroy outgroups on the one hand, and a submissive orientation to social authority on the other. Yet this was far from any simple-minded Freudianism. Like Fromm and Marcuse, Adorno sought to discern how the repressed unconscious shaped, and yet was itself shaped by, social and political conditions. 'The political, economic and social convictions of an individual', wrote the authors of *The Authoritarian Personality*, 'often form a broad and coherent pattern, as if bound together by a "mentality" or "spirit", and that this pattern is an expression of deeplying trends in his personality.'

For our purposes, there are three key elements in Adorno's thesis of irrational authoritarianism spreading throughout modern societies. Succinctly put, these are: (1) the thesis of the 'end of the individual'; (2) the triumph of the unconscious over consciousness of self; and (3) the murderous rage associated with fascist tendencies or authoritarian identities. Let us briefly consider each of these points in turn.

Adorno's account of the rise of irrational authoritarianism proceeds from the insight that there has been a major shift in how society constitutes the individual. He contends that today, throughout the West, we witness the 'end of the individual'. Contemporary society overpowers the individual through a standardized, monotonous mass culture, leaving little room for authentic individualism. Instead, society produces authoritarian social character types. These claims are advanced by Adorno through an interpretation of Freudian psychoanalysis as revealing large-scale historical shifts in identity formation. From this angle, Freud's theory of the Oedipus complex – the psychosexual drama involving the small infant's emotional dealings with its mother's love and father's authority – maps the realization of mature identities in the age of bourgeois capitalism. Throughout the liberal phase of capitalism, according to Adorno, the child's emerging sense of identity was dramatized through resistance to, and internalization of, the authority of the Oedipal father. The new world of administered capitalism, however, changes all that. In late modern society, massive changes in the economy directly serve to undermine the father's authority within the nuclear family. As businesses become corporate, and as jobs shrink or disappear at an unprecedented pace, men as fathers suffer a loss in economic and social standing. A father who becomes unemployed experiences new kinds of insecurity – not just economic, but emotional and social. One significant consequence of these changes from liberal capitalism to the administered society is that the child aspires less and less to be like its father, according to Adorno. In post-liberal societies, therefore, changes in family life mean that the father no longer functions as an agency of social repression. Instead, individuals are increasingly brought under the sway of the logic of techno-rationality itself, as registered in and through the rise of the culture industries. As Adorno summarized these historical developments in identity constitution: 'The prebourgeois world does not yet know psychology, the oversocialised knows it no longer.' Repressive desublimation functions in Frankfurt School sociology as that psychic process which links what Adorno called the 'post-psychological individual' to the historical emergence of fascism and totalitarian societies.

These psychological and historical shifts in identity formation lead to the second aspect of Adorno's account of authoritarian irrationalism, namely the individual's susceptibility to fascist ideologies. In 'Freudian Theory and the Pattern of Fascist Propaganda', written in 1951, Adorno argues that Freud's work on group psychology foresaw the rise of fascist movements, and that psychoanalysis provides a powerful explanation of the relation between leaders and followers. The psychological mechanisms uncovered by Freud's analyses of group processes are vitally significant to critical theory, Adorno argues, since they draw attention to the ways in which individuals yield to political manipulation by external, social agencies. For Adorno, as for Freud, the individual, when in a large group, is likely to identify less with its own 'ego-ideals' and more with impersonal 'group ideals'. This identification with the group involves the undoing of various repressions at the level of the individual, and Adorno argues that fascist propaganda transposes aggression into hatred of the outgroup – in short, racism. With reference to the theme of the 'end of the individual', Adorno contends that fascist leaders become the guarantor of the social bond to the extent that fathers no longer represent a superior social authority. This is a complex psychoanalytic point, but broadly speaking Adorno underscores that fascist leaders rarely present themselves as traditional figures of authority. The fascist leader is more likely to model himself in the style of an elder brother, as one who challenges traditional forms of patriarchal authority. Hitler as Führer was just such a fascist leader, says Adorno: less a patriarchal president than an elder brother, the 'great little man'. 'Hitler', wrote Adorno, 'posed as a composite of King Kong and the suburban barber.' This complex combination of power and personalism spoke to the Nazi movement's followers in a profound way, and ultimately resulted in the masses hell-bent on violence. Adorno interprets such mobilizations of fascist, and especially anti-Semitic, aggression as suggestive of key changes in structures of personal subjectivity in modern societies as a whole. Indeed, he writes of individuals today as 'postpsychological de-individualized social atoms' (1951: 136).

> The individual owes his crystallization to the form of political economy, particularly to those of the urban market. Even as the opponent of the pressure of socialization he remains the latter's most particular product and likeness. . . . Socially, the absolute status granted to the individual marks the transition from the universal mediation of social relation – a mediation which, as exchange, always also requires curtailment of the particular interests realized through it – to direct domination, where power is seized by the strongest. Through this dissolution of all the mediating elements within the individual himself, by virtue of which he was, in spite of everything, also part of a social subject, he regresses, impoverished and coarsened, to the state of a mere social object. . . . If today the trace of humanity seems to persist only in the individual in his decline, it admonishes us to make an end of the fatality which individualizes men, only to break them completely in their isolation.
>
> Theodor Adorno (1974 [1951]) *Minima Moralia: Reflections from Damaged Life*, trans E.F.N. Jephcott. London: NLB, pp. 148–50.

It is obvious from the above that the individual subject, dominated by archaic unconscious impulses, languishes in the grip of an insanely powerful social order. What this period of Adorno's work represents, in fact, is psycho-analytic criticism transfigured by social theory. This is social theory as a more individually focused and less dispassionate enterprise, and which is thus able to harness the unconscious aspects of human activity to social research. Adorno's version of critical theory consists in generalizing beyond an image of the bureaucratized, administered world of advanced capitalism to consider how such alienated forms of consciousness become deeply implanted at the level of personal identity itself. This takes us to his final point concerning irrational authoritarianism – namely that fascist ideology is a core mechanism for the seamless monolith of contemporary social processes. In *The Authoritarian Personality*, Adorno and his co-authors sought to identify how an all-pervasive social authority is internalized by women and men in what they called the F scale – designed as a measurement of fascist potential. Through over two hundred questionnaires and detailed psychoanalytic profiles, Adorno and his colleagues explored such topics as their respondents' early childhoods, family relationships and wider political 'worldviews'. The F scale sought to measure implicit 'pre-fascist tendencies' towards anti-Semitism, ethnocentrism and political and economic conservatism. To clarify the personal dimensions of fascist ideology, *The Authoritarian Personality* identified nine emotional traits of interviewees who were judged to be high as regards possible authoritarian tendencies:

1   *Conventionalism*: A rigid adherence to middle-class values and inflexible attitudes to others.
2   *Authoritarian submission*: An uncritical, submissive orientation to figures of authority.
3   *Authoritarian aggression*: A tendency to actively search out people who transgress conventional values, with the desire to see them punished.
4   *Anti-intraception*: Rejection of imagination, creativity or the emotionally minded.
5   *Stereotype and superstition*: Belief in the mystical determinants of fate, as well as ordering of the world through rigid stereotypes.
6   *Power and toughness*: An exaggerated assertion of strength, coupled with a preoccupation with dichotomies – dominance/submission, strong/weak, leader/follower.
7   *Destructiveness and cynicism*: Generalized hostility and even hatred of the human condition.
8   *Projectivity*: The projection of unwanted emotional aspects of the self on to others.
9   *Sex*: An exaggerated concern with the sexual activities of others.

While Adorno and his colleagues did not discuss in any detail how widespread the authoritarian personality might be in conditions of advanced capitalism, the study did suggest that this syndrome is especially characteristic of the lower middle classes in Europe. The conclusion of the book is that the authoritarian suffers from ego weakness, idealizes social authority, submits in the face of powerful social forces, and demonstrates propensities for racial prejudice and ethnic hatred.

The Authoritarian Personality has been criticized as an attempt to reduce the complex social phenomenon of authoritarianism to the level of individual psychology. If, indeed, Adorno and his colleagues had meant to show that every social formation with authoritarian or fascist potential could be explained away through reference to childhood experiences or stereotypical character traits, then the criticism of 'psycho-babble' could reasonably apply. However, such criticism is surely wide of the mark. For Adorno in particular, transformations in identity formation – and especially pathologies of the self – are inscribed in the very structures of social life; while the analysis of personality traits in relation to authority, and particularly anti-Semitism, can only be adequately undertaken with sociological reference to major changes in the family, culture and the economy. What is pathological about authoritarianism for Adorno is traced not only to disturbances of the psyche, but to general developments in the nature of rationality. Whether Adorno's social theory will do as an explanation of social pathologies is, however, perhaps more questionable. His general theoretical and political conclusions, for one thing, would appear to render individuals mere ciphers of the wider society. This is problematic because, if an unconscious authoritarian submission exerts its hold everywhere, this must presumably extend to the realm of critical social theory itself; what is striking about the more pessimistic elements of Adorno's cultural diagnosis, in other words, is that logically it would appear impossible for the Frankfurt School to have unearthed the thesis of the 'end of the individual' in the first place. Adorno does indeed speak of personal autonomy as essential to the flowering of democracy, but the global tone of his pessimistic social theory overrides such occasional contrasts to the dominance of authoritarian identities. And even within the sociological terms of the 'dialectic of enlightenment', it seems likely that Adorno overestimated the degree of cultural cohesion operating within modern societies. To that extent, as Terry Eagleton (1990: 47) comments, Adorno judged the contemporary social order 'as it would *wish* to appear'.

Written in the stars: Adorno on astrology

The weekend magazine of one current newspaper contains a section entitled 'Diversions' – made up of various 'Brain Trainers' and a 'Mystic Medusa'. Leafing through the astrological forecast, the following advice for Pisces is dispensed:

Make Monday to Wednesday your hardest-working and most audacious days of the week for brilliant results. Keep your ideas contemporary as you ditch ye olde approaches. Thursday is exciting in love as long as you detach from drama and are super-frugal.

And for Taurus:

Book your week up for meetings and meaningful dialogue; just schedule around Thursday and its volatile Venusian aspects. Your best stance? Straight-arrow communication and actions.

What's in a star forecast? For many people, reading a magazine astrology column is merely a source of amusement. As the above newspaper labels it, a 'diversion'. But not so, says Theodor Adorno, who sees in such commodified mass culture something far more sinister and disabling. For Adorno, the newspaper or magazine astrology column follows the social logics of the American entertainment industry – from TV soaps to Hollywood movies. Instead of the differentiated elements of selfhood on the one hand and culture on the other, astrology collapses the former into the latter, promoting conventional and contented attitudes in the process. Unable to accommodate social contradictions without commodifying them, newspaper and magazine astrology columns offer stereotypical scenes to remind us of the dependency of our social existence in the administered world of late capitalism.

In the early 1950s, during a return visit to the United States from Germany, Adorno undertook a study of an astrology column in the *Los Angeles Times*. The result was *The Stars Down to Earth*. According to Adorno, Caroll Righter's 'Astrological Forecasts' column in the *Los Angeles Times* promoted attitudes of fatalism. This is the attitude that, while we live in a threatening world where things are out of control, it is none the less a world where things are likely to turn out for the best in the long run. As Adorno (1994: 56–57) develops this point:

The semi-rationality of 'everything will be fine' is based on the fact that modern American society in spite of all its conflicts and diffi-culties succeeds in reproducing the life of those whom it embraces. There is some dim awareness that the concept of the forgotten man is outdated. The column feeds on this awareness by teaching the readers not to be afraid of being weak. They are reassured that all their problems will solve themselves even if they feel that they themselves are unable to solve them. They are made to understand – and in a way rightly – that the very same powers by which they are threatened, the anonymous totality of the social process, are also those which will somehow take care of them.

The situation is arguably made more stressful by the fact that middle-class society tends to try to reconcile social contradictions not in, say, Freudian terms of promoting pleasurable self-development, but in terms of hard work, thrift and industry. By disavowing the complexity of social experience – principally by dividing life into 'sectors' for work, romance, friendships and so on – the daily astrology column promotes social conformism.

What, in your view, does the regular newspaper or magazine astrology column tell us about the nature of modern societies? Is Adorno's thesis of psychological dependency and social conformism still relevant to today's global realities?

Marcuse: Eros, or one-dimensional futures?

For Marxist social theorist Herbert Marcuse, one-time member of the Frankfurt School and close colleague of Horkheimer and Adorno, this deranged logic of capitalism is, among other things, imposed through the culture industries of advertising, marketing and entertainment. Capitalism for Marcuse operates on a deeply unconscious level, a realm of chimerical fantasy in which sexuality is paradoxically stripped of erotic aura and transferred to the selling of things – both products and people. Marcuse calls this insidious process 'repressive desublimation'. The power of capitalism is that we are all embroiled in a social landscape of commodities and wages, prices and profits. Gradually but unstoppably, people in such a world come to feel personally content only when their appetites and desires are dictated by the emotional system in advance, by socially controlled desublimation.

Marcuse was in broad agreement with Horkheimer and Adorno as regards the thesis of a 'decline of the individual'. Having departed Germany when Hitler came to power, Marcuse joined with his Frankfurt School colleagues in the United States and, throughout the late 1930s and 1940s, worked on a series of research projects investigating transformations of state and monopoly capitalism, the dynamics of mass communication and popular culture, social dislocation, racism, anti-Semitism and other forms of authoritarianism. According to Marcuse, modern culture is repressive, often tyrannically so. However, the transformation of society remains the key to utopian thinking, critical theory and progressive politics. In an early book, *Reason and Revolution* (1941), Marcuse speaks up for the progressive side of utopian thinking. Yet he takes to task those Marxists who argued either that socialism was an inevitable outcome of history, or that workers were the revolutionary agent of social change. Such standpoints for Marcuse were far too simple. The collapse of the Russian Revolution into Soviet Marxism, the failure of various working-class movements and the decline of political dissidence as a result of the rise of mass communications and popular culture were all for Marcuse signs that there could be no privileged agents in the transformation of social life. That this is the case is not necessarily bad news for progressive politics, however. Just because political developments had not unfolded in the manner predicted by orthodox Marxism did not mean that social change was either unjustified or unlikely. A non-repressive society for Marcuse always remained a theoretical and political possibility, and in attempting to address these problems he opened new perspectives in critical social theory by turning to Freud and psychoanalysis.

It is against this political and intellectual backdrop that Marcuse's seminal *Eros and Civilization* (1955) should be contextualized, as a work that was at once resolutely critical of existing capitalist societies and profoundly utopian in its defence of the possibilities for radical social change. Repression is Marcuse's theme from beginning to end in *Eros and Civilization*, and in particular the Freudian insight that the renunciation of emotional energy and sensuality is always filtered through both historical and transhistorical forces. People suffer from too much repression in contemporary society, says Marcuse. The contradictions of capitalism, he argues, pass all the way down into the deepest textures of lived experience and personal subjectivity. Capitalist processes of technological mechanization and standardization have become inscribed within the inner fabric of identity, particularly as a result of the oppressive, dull labour to which people are subjected. Here Marcuse's ideological target was the cultural conformity of middle America, of faceless bureaucrats coping with the crushing repetitions demanded by the workplace and of middle-class housewives bored with their lives at home in the suburbs. Something was deeply amiss. America in the 1950s was easily the wealthiest and most industrially advanced society on Earth, and yet such economic prosperity seemed to run directly counter to the constrained and constraining lives that people experienced, most especially in terms of emotional literacy and inter-personal relationships. Repression, for Marcuse as for Freud, was vital in converting nature into culture, and he interpreted the classical psychoana-lytic account of the Oedipus complex as a kind of social parable regarding sexual and social reproduction. According to Marcuse, however, the torments and repressions of contemporary women and men are not quite the same as those of Freud's era. In his view, repression has become heightened, with particularly excessive restrictions placed on sensuality and eroticism in a world organized around prices and profits, money and monopolistic corporations.

Freud's cultural message: sufferings, submissions and discontents

How can we understand the heightening of repression throughout modern societies using Freudian concepts? Why did Marcuse think that Freud was especially relevant for grasping contemporary social conditions? Freud's provocative challenge to social theory consists in his radical claim that the malaise of repression, anxiety and unhappiness is the emotional cost we pay for social order. At the cornerstone of Freud's theory of modern discontents lies the notion of the 'death drive'. In 'Civilization and its Discontents' (1930), Freud outlines a conception of the 'death drive' as forever organizing disabling repressions at the centre of social and cultural life. By the death drive Freud understands a will to negation, of self-destructiveness or primary aggression. Human misery and oppression are not only the outcome of sexual repression – an idea put forward by Freud in some of his earliest writings on society and culture. In his writings of the 1930s, Freud comes to equate culture with the urge for, and repressive constraints upon, self-destructiveness. Civilization protects against the aggressive demands of the death drive. 'The main renunciation culture demands of the individual', writes Paul Ricoeur (1970: 307) of Freud's interpretation of culture, 'is the renunciation not of desire as such but of aggressiveness'.

By incorporating this new dualism into his analysis of modern culture, Freud is able to rewrite the problem of self and society as a contest between love and hate, or between love and death. Love involves the flowering of civilized co-belonging. Hatred, aggression and the death drive are forces that threaten to tear culture apart. The Freud of 'Civilization and Its Discontents' (1930: 122) unfolds love and hate, Eros and Thanatos (Greek words for 'love' and death', respectively), in the following way:

> [C]ivilization is a process in the service of Eros, whose purpose is to combine single human individuals, and after that families, then races, peoples and nations, into one great unity. . . . These collections of

men are libidinally bound to one another. Necessity alone, the advantages of work in common, will not hold them together. But man's natural aggressive instinct, the hostility of each against all and of all against each, opposes this programme of civilization. The aggressive instinct is the derivative and main representative of the death drive which we have found alongside of Eros and which shares world-dominion with it.

The pathological compulsions of everyday life are rooted in a repressive structuring of love and hatred. Freud remains faithful to his earlier view that the reproduction of society depends upon sexual repression; but in his late sociological vision, sexual repression becomes integrated into a deathly self-preservation, organized as a destructive assault on the human body, on others, and on nature. Freud particularly had in mind the highly authoritarian European societies before the First World War that sent thousands of young men to their deaths in 1914. But he also became acutely aware of the psychopathologies of fascism, racism and anti-Semitism in the 1920s and 1930s – which, for him, represented a kind of breakdown of civilization. This breakdown resulted from a degeneration of sexual repression into a will to exterminate the alien and disorderly. In today's world, it arguably finds expression in the phenomenon of 'ethnic cleansing', as well as homophobia and 'moral panics' about people perceived as deviant.

Freud's writings on the fate of the self in contemporary culture have strongly influenced debates in critical theory – from the Frankfurt School approaches of Marcuse and Adorno to the contemporary approaches of Jürgen Habermas and Axel Honneth. Too much repression, Freud says, leads to intense unconscious anguish, hostility and rage. At such a point, the intensification of unconscious desire can release the 'mental dams' of sexual repression in a far-reaching way. The issue of the subjective seeds of social and political transformation is thus at the heart of Freud's contribution to social theory.

How to explain this? Marcuse presented much of his historical analysis in the language of Freud, but throughout *Eros and Civilization* he sought to contextualize psychoanalytic insights within the broader Marxist tradition of critical theory. In contemporary societies, the unconscious is denied true expression as a result of the reproduction of capitalist profit and exploitation. In Marcuse's view, however, Freud's interpretation of the conflict between repressed desire and social order was ahistorical, which in turn renders a picture of social repression the same in all possible worlds. To recapture this potential historical dimension of psychoanalysis, Marcuse distinguished between two kinds of repression: 'basic repression' and 'surplus repression'. Basic repression refers to the minimum level of sexual renunciation for facing social life and the tasks of culture. Marcuse contends that a certain amount of repression is always necessary for effective socialization and social order. Surplus repression, by contrast, refers to the intensification of self-restraint generated by capitalist exploitation and asymmetrical relations of power. Marcuse gives as an example of this repressive surplus the conjugal family, in which the conventional sexual norms of patriarchy are strictly enforced in the interests of maintaining existing values and society. The repression this surplus generates is not necessarily understood very well by individuals in terms of its emotional damage. According to Marcuse, repression becomes surplus to requirements as a result of the 'performance principle', a culturally specific form of sexual and social demands instituted by the economic order of capitalism. According to Marcuse, the capitalist performance principle recasts repression as surplus in several key ways. The performance principle causes human beings to face one another as 'things' or 'objects', replaces general eroticism with genital sexuality, and fashions a disciplining of the human body (what Marcuse calls 'repressive desub-limation') so as to prevent repressed desire from interfering with capitalist exchange values.

In a subsequent book, *One-Dimensional Man* (1964), Marcuse takes the analysis of the forces of domination to extreme lengths. In the course of the twentieth century, says Marcuse, our personal and social lives are constantly being pulled in two directions at the same time. Arguably, with the advent of advanced industrial society, people's encounter with culture becomes more individuated, complex and subtle. Yet on another level, this potential cultural and aesthetic liberation within advanced capitalism has been thoroughly stunted. Advanced capitalism has brought little more than domestic appliances, Hollywood movies and packaged holidays within reach of many people in the West. In this age of mass consumerism and popular culture, according to Marcuse, a new social order has emerged that sharply curtails individuality, dissent and opposition. Advanced capitalism generates a one-dimensional society based on 'false' consumer needs, and increasingly integrates individuals into the smooth running of a mass system of domination and social inequality. In Marcuse's view, the most striking feature of the modern world is conformity. Contemporary forms of repression and domination are suffocating, and it is against this backdrop that Marcuse raises the issue of how society might confront the systematic erosion of critical thinking, dissent and opposition to capitalism and indus-trial management. 'How', writes Marcuse, 'can the administered individuals – who have made their mutilation into their own liberties and satisfactions

. . . liberate themselves from themselves as well as from their masters? How is it even thinking that the vicious circle be broken.'

The desublimation rampant in advanced industrial society reveals its truly conformist function. This liberation of sexuality (and of aggressiveness) frees the instinctual drives from much of the unhappiness and discontent that elucidate the repressive power of the established universe of satisfaction. To be sure, there is pervasive unhappiness, and the happy consciousness is shaky enough – a thin surface over fear, frustration and disgust. This unhappiness lends itself easily to political mobilization; without room for conscious development, it may become the instinctual reservoir for a new fascist way of life and death. But there are many ways in which the unhappiness beneath the happy consciousness may be turned into a source of strength and cohesion for the social order. The conflicts of the unhappy now seem far more amenable to cure than those which made for Freud's 'discontent in civilization,' and they seem more adequately defined in terms of the 'neurotic personality of our time' than in terms of the eternal struggle between Eros and Thanatos.

Herbert Marcuse (1964) *One-Dimensional Man*. Boston, MA: Beacon, pp. 76–7.

What, then, of the possibilities for change? Marcuse differs sharply from Freud as regards the nature of emancipation. Marcuse contends that the performance principle, ironically, generates the cultural conditions necessary for a radical transformation of society. What promise an end to surplus repression are the industrial-technological advancements of late capitalism itself. For Marcuse, the material affluence generated by Western capitalist industrialization and techno-science opens the way for an unravelling of sexual repression. The overcoming of cultural domination will release repressed unconscious forces, permitting the reconnection of sexual drives and fantasy to the social network. Such a reconciliation between culture and the unconscious will usher in a new, sensuous reality – a reality Marcuse calls 'libidinal rationality'. Libidinal rationality, though abstract as a concept, involves a radical reversal of surplus repression. Liberation from this surplus will facilitate a general eroticism, not only of the body, but of nature and cultural organization. Yet Marcuse's grounding of social theory in psychoanalysis stresses that emancipation requires more than just sexual freedom. It demands an integration of sexuality and love into transformed social, institutional life.

How are we to understand this notion of libidinal rationality? Is it just some emancipatory dream of the Frankfurt School theorist Herbert Marcuse, or does it unearth certain psychical tendencies that point towards an alternative social condition? As a resexualizing of social life, libidinal rationality may be interpreted as an encouragement of emotional communication and intimacy. Fantasy occupies a special place in this context, Marcuse says, since desire contains a repressed truth value. As he puts it:

> Imagination envisions the reconciliation of the individual with the whole, of desire with realization, of happiness with reason. While this harmony has been removed into utopia by the established reality principle, fantasy insists that it must and can become real, that behind the illusion lies knowledge.

Fantasy is itself a longing for reconciliation – between pleasure and rationality, desire and reality. For Marcuse, this recovery of unconscious desire will facilitate the resexualization of the human body, thus creating harmonious social relations. Against the repressive structuring of 'sex' under the performance principle, the release of fantasy will eroticize all aspects of society, allowing for a spontaneous and playful relation to life.

Utopia and social transformation: Marcuse on libidinal rationality

The dark side of the modern age which Marcuse mourns – the totalitarianism of the administered society, the decline of the individual, the manipulation of the unconscious – are to be redeemed by a utopian transformation he terms 'libidinal rationality'. This possible world, says Marcuse (1956: 224), involves 'a new *rationality of gratification* in which reason and happiness converge'. In contrast to today's surplus repression, libidinal rationality promises a world of individual gratification and fulfilment. According to Marcuse (1972: 17):

> [Liberation] involves a radical transformation of the needs and aspirations themselves, cultural as well as material. . . . Moral and aesthetic needs become basic, vital needs, and drive toward new relationships between the sexes, between the generations, between men and women and nature. Freedom is understood as rooted in these needs, which are sensuous, ethical, and rational in one.

Such a world, according to Marcuse, is not merely 'pie in the sky'. The key drivers pushing such change arise, paradoxically, from the industrial and technological advancements of late capitalist society itself. Technological progress, he contends, has now reached a stage that makes the goal of overcoming economic scarcity and surplus repression possible. In fact, Marcuse is adamant that the very technological reason which created surplus repression and stunted human capacities in the first place has now developed to the point where such afflictions can be fully eliminated. Thus, while Marcuse clearly laments the mechanistic and destructive quality of advanced capitalism, he also claims that technological reason bears the stamp of its own collapse, in ways which help to transform the social order.

From this angle, Marcuse says Freud's equation of civilization with repression should be rejected. The task of a critical social theory, he claims, is to advance beyond the hold of surplus repression, seeking to recover certain longings for freedom lodged deeply in the social unconscious. The radical imagination inspired by social theory is especially significant, and Marcuse focuses especially on the import of memory, desire and fantasy – not as escape from the social world, but as prefiguring new possibilities for society. The importance of unconscious memory is spelt out by Marcuse (1956: 19) thus:

> According to Freud's conception the equation of freedom and happiness tabooed by the conscious is upheld by the unconscious. Its truth, although repelled by consciousness, continues to haunt the mind; it preserves the memory of past stages of individual development at which integral gratification is obtained. And the past continues to claim the future: it generates the wish that the paradise be re-created on the basis of the achievements of civilization.

Marcuse's valorization of phantasy is connected with the assumption that the individual body needs to be resexualized for the creation of harmonious social relations. In contrast to the repressive insistence on procreational genitality under the 'performance principle', Marcuse claims that the release of phantasy will lead to the development of a sensual Eros. This liberation, in brief, will involve the activation of pregenital impulses which will extend to all parts of the body. Drawing upon the work of Friedrich Schiller, Marcuse claims that this transfiguration of the human body will directly help to produce a 'senuous order' in which spontaneous cooperation, play and intimacy can be forged. The new reality principle arising from the transformative power of phantasy, however, does not involve some kind of 'release' of sexuality – as in Wilhelm Reich's programme of 'sexual revolution'. Enthusiastic though he is for the transformation of desire, the new sensuous order for Marcuse (1956: 202) signifies a transfiguration of Eros and the very notion of sexuality:

> In contrast, the free development of transformed libido within transformed institutions, while eroticizing previously tabooed zones, time and relations, would *minimize* the manifestations of mere sexuality by integrating them into a far larger order, including the order of work. In this context, sexuality tends to its own sublimation.

Once desire is for the first time allowed full expression, it can become transformative of the conflict between the life and death drives, Eros and Thanatos. Eros would redeem aggressive and destructive drives into the service of life itself. In this sense, Marcuse (1956: 235) looks to Freud's death drive as a source of hope: as that which aims at peace, quiescence, and the absence of pain.

> Death would cease to be an instinctual goal. It remains a fact, perhaps even an ultimate necessity – but a necessity against which the unrepressed energy of mankind will protest, against which it will wage its greatest struggle. In this struggle, reason and instinct could unite.

Freed from the destructive forces of surplus repression, the preconditions of libidinal rationality will allow people to die with dignity.

If this sounds somewhat fantastic, which in a certain sense it is *meant* to be, it is important to stress again that the philosophical basis of Marcuse's doctrine cannot be regarded as social escapism. In connecting the subjective desires of individuals to institutionally immanent possibilities, Marcuse defends this political project by asserting that these ideals have become increasingly realistic in modern times. The relation between human wants and current material resources has reached the point where we can imagine a fundamental social transformation to the good society. As Marcuse remarks, in such conditions 'the pertinent question is whether a state of civilization can be reasonably envisaged in which human needs are fulfilled in such a manner and to such an extent that surplus-repression can be eliminated' (1956: 151). And while it may be difficult to know exactly how such a state as 'libidinal rationality' may ever come about, Marcuse argues that social critique must seek to further these possibilities of a fulfilling and satisfying life for everyone.

Appraisal of Marcuse

The road Marcuse travelled in his career from working in Germany with the Frankfurt School to his celebrity in the United States as a prophet of the student and sexual liberation movements was remarkable. His fame by the 1960s was truly international in scope, with students the world over painting on walls 'Marx, Mao and Marcuse' in protest against the oppressions of capitalist society. Given that Marcuse identified his own work as part of a broader search for liberation, sexual freedom and a new cultural sensibility, it is hardly surprising that he became directly embroiled in the social movements of the 1960s. In everything from 'flower power' to sexual liberation movements, Marcuse's name was tirelessly invoked. Moreover, there can be little doubt that his critique of advanced industrial societies chimed with the political dissent of a generation of people in the 1960s enraged by growing economic inequalities in the age of consumer society, the oppression of Afro-Americans and other minority cultures as well as the Vietnam War. Notwithstanding this, it is mistaken, as Douglas Kellner has argued, to simply equate Marcuse's social theory with the politics of the 1960s. For one thing, Marcuse himself did not equate sexual liberation with a non-repressive society. The transformation of culture, he argued, 'involves not simply a release but a *transformation* of libido'. Against this backcloth, the conflict between life and death will diminish as Eros reinfuses personal life and social relations. This is a very different standpoint from that advocated by the 'free love' movements of the 1960s, and on various occasions Marcuse indicated that he did not wish his work to be associated with such simplistic views. But there are also other reasons why Marcuse's renown as guru of the 1960s Left is inadequate as the sole measure of his revised critical theory. His distinctive arguments across a span of topics, from memory to mass culture, do not easily reduce to the political doxa of the 1960s. We thus need to attend more closely to the contributions of Marcuse's social theory.

There are various aspects of Marcuse's work that remain of incomparable value, in particular the centrality he accords to the individual subject as an agent of social change and human freedom. In an age which has witnessed the 'death of the subject', Marcuse's preoccupation with the relations between societal structures of surplus repression and the nature of personal experience and the passions is daringly unfashionable. In conjoining critical theory with psychoanalysis, Marcuse expanded the conceptual reach of Marxism to take account of individual needs, desires and potentialities. In doing so, he demonstrated Marxism to be a changing and flexible tradition of thought – one capable of addressing social suffering and political oppression in the widest possible human terms, rather than a set of dogmatic doctrines. But if Marcuse looked to Freudian psychoanalysis in order to reconsider the problem of individual subjectivity in social analysis, he also appropriated other intellectual traditions such as German Idealism, Romanticism and avant-garde modernism in order to develop a more adequate sociology of culture. His belief that critical theory must specifically address, for example, the denial, or distortion, of human needs and potentials in existing culture has served as a major resource for many working in the social sciences. Indeed, this thread of his work has been fruitfully refined and extended in contemporary critical theory – especially by Habermas. In the critique of modern society, then, it is not enough to attend to institutional processes of capitalist commodification or bureaucratic techniques. What must also be addressed is the whole area of subjectivity, defined in its broadest emotional sense to encompass both conscious and unconscious forms of repression.

There remain, however, many unresolved difficulties in Marcuse's work. Among these it is important to mention deficiencies in his approach to human agency, particularly his long-standing emphasis upon the concept of the repressed unconscious as the key to social transformation; the limitations of his analysis of contemporary societies, especially as regards the critique of domination and exploitation; and a series of problems to do with human needs, meanings, ethics and justice. Let me briefly address these three criticisms in turn.

First, in an age of media sound-bites, spin and seduction, Marcuse's ironic concept of 'repressive desublimation' serves as a powerful tool with which to grasp how apparent forms of sexual liberalization actually serve to promote heightened repression. Marcuse's argument is that the glossy commercialization of sexuality we see everywhere in the West today confines human desire, eroticism and intimacy to only a partial and restrictive understanding of sexuality. In this view, the sex industry in all its guises, from porno movies to lap-dancing clubs, serves to dull human sexuality and instead promotes conventional behaviour and values. Yet if such a viewpoint offers a powerful critique of the repressive contradictions of capitalism and mass culture, it none the less remains certainly vulnerable to charges of oversimplifying both the psychoanalytic understanding of emotional life as well as the complex, contradictory relations between self and society. Many would now agree, for example, that Marcuse's conceptualization of surplus repression is wanting. His recasting of repression as surplus in order to capture aspects of the dismantling of emotional contradictions fostered by one-dimensional mass culture, while provocative, ultimately gives rise to a top-heavy version of cultural domination, where society stands over and above the individual agent. The problem with this is that it overlooks the fact that the psyche is shot through with unconscious conflict, which in Freudian terms is one important reason why selfhood can never be serenely inserted into social relations without tensions and contradictions. A related difficulty

contemporary social theory

stemming from Marcuse's wall-to-wall image of surplus repression is that he is subsequently forced to round the individual subject back upon itself in order to find an escape route from the contemporary performance principle. The way forward is through the unconscious – which, somehow, is beyond the scope of social domination, and thus prefigurative of an alternative society. Despite this stress on alternative political visions, however, Marcuse has remarkably little to say about new forms of intimacy, interpersonal relationships or cultural association. His utopianism rather focuses on the overcoming of sexual repression. Yet such a vision of liber-ation is highly questionable. A mechanistic conception of the repressed unconscious, and not people, is key to Marcuse's view of social trans-formation. Human agency is reduced to domination, while the repressed unconscious is linked to emancipation. But this gives rise to a thorny polit-ical issue: if the individual subject is obsolescent and repression complete, who would be in a position to transform, or even to know, the truth of the unconscious? Who, exactly, would be capable of sustaining a liberation known as 'libidinal rationality'? Marcuse's focus upon unconscious poten-tialities, although valuable in some respects, actually mirrors an individualist culture which forecloses issues about social bonds and cultural association. Significantly, Marcuse's argument in favour of the liberation of repressed drives also smacks of essentialism. This argument recalls a pre-Freudian view of human passion as somehow natural and timeless, outside and beyond the reach of the social structure. The view that the repressed unconscious, or fantasy itself, will only gain expression in the non-repressive society falls to see that fantasy structures are already bound up with institutional life. Such a view fails to recognize that the 'truth of the unconscious' is already interconnected with embattled human relation-ships, violent gender tensions and ideological conflict.

Second, there have been a number of sharp criticisms made of Marcuse's analysis of the nature of modern societies, particularly his account of advanced capitalism. It is important to be quite specific about the limitations of Marcuse's social theory in this respect, as there are contra-dictory elements in his analysis of modern societies and it is my view that he did not manage to reconcile these elements successfully. Now the bleak critique of advanced capitalism that Marcuse outlined in *One-Dimensional Man* stands in blunt opposition to his optimistic analysis of the potentialities for radical social transformation in *Eros and Civilization*. Some critics have put this discrepancy down to Marcuse's heavy concentration upon the American post-war boom in the former book, while other critics have noted his implicit indebtedness to German Romanticism in the latter book. Whatever the exact division between these optimistic and pessimistic threads in his thinking, however, it is clear that the idea of an emergent stabilization of capitalism played an important role throughout the bulk of his writings. But there are good reasons to object to Marcuse's outline of such trends of social development. For one thing, in focusing too exclusively on the containment of the contradictions and crisis-tendencies of advanced capitalism, Marcuse seemed to assume that cultural conformity plays a central role in the reproduction of modern societies. But such consequences are not borne out by recent sociological research, which rather indicates that social reproduction can be an unintended consequence of the rejection of the values and norms promoted by popular culture and the mass media. For another, in overemphasizing the intensification of technological rationality in our own time and its capacity to integrate culture, society and personhood into a closed, harmonious system, Marcuse's social theory remains unable to account for what prompted the widespread social revolt of the 1960s – notwithstanding his close association with various aspects of these revolts. Furthermore, his social theory is equally lacking in critical edge if forced to confront, say, the recent war on terrorism or the global economic crisis of the early twenty-first century. Nowhere did Marcuse adequately confront the potential explosive disequilibrium of global capitalist markets nor the massive development of militarization on the part of the world's superpowers.

Finally, some critics have lampooned Marcuse's radical politics and vision of utopia. Marcuse's social theory addresses what the transformation of libido would mean at the level of the whole society, as the notion of 'libidinal rationality' tries to clarify what counts as creative, sensuous reason between individuals, groups and nations. For some of its critics, however, the very idea of an eroticized reason is a contradiction in terms, since rationality and the passions remain stubbornly particular and are separate domains. Reason is universal, emotion is particular. This contradiction, however, is only apparent – and for reasons which Marcuse's writings actually make clear. When social rationalization is pressed beyond all reason, it flips over into surplus repression; and one name for such pathology is 'repressive desublimation'. The problem is not that reason and emotion are separated, but that a deformed, perverse version of the latter has come to exert the upper hand over the former. Historically speaking, however, social conditions now offer the slim possibility of eliminating surplus repression. What social theory needs to engage, in Marcuse's own terms, is a 'new rationality of gratification'. This position, however, still gives rise to the dilemma of how people could ever determine that a form of rationality was sufficiently aesthetic, concerned with creativity, fulfilment, pleasure. As David Held writes of this problem, 'one cannot simply appeal, as Marcuse does, to instincts to settle questions about real wants; for wants cannot be articulated independently of the circumstances of their development and of the way in which they are conceived'. Marcuse may indeed be correct, following Freud, in locating reason or rationality in unconscious desire. But even if this reason is an outcrop of desire, social theory still demands a language for grappling with how individual needs and potentials are constituted, conceived and recognized between social actors. This is not to take issue with Marcuse's vision of freedom in terms of the 'rationality of gratification', but it is to raise questions about how concrete history bears upon the deliberation of the actual needs and desires of individual human beings. Such questions necessarily involve a shift away from the rather solitary Freudian language of individual drives, desires and repressions, and towards a more interpersonal language of communication, discourse and symbolic exchange.

Summary points

1   The Frankfurt School – or first generation of critical theorists – refers to the work of leading German neo-Marxist intellectuals who transcended orthodox Marxism through an interdisciplinary integration of sociology, economics, politics and psychoanalysis. The contribution to social theory of the Frankfurt School remains one of the most important of the twentieth century, and critical theory in particular caught the imagination of intellectuals and new social movements in the 1960s and 1970s.

2   The Frankfurt School, in numerous theoretical projects, was concerned above all with the 'dark side' of the modern age, and traced various social pathologies back to general developments in the nature of reason, rationality and the Enlightenment.

3   Reason, according to the Frankfurt School, has become inherently pathological. In Adorno and Horkheimer's *Dialectic of Enlightenment*, society – in securing its own survival through the domination of nature – secretly mutilates itself and destroys the opportunity for freedom. Reason today is automatically transformed into instrumental rationality, and simply to act as an individual subject is to denigrate and destroy.

4   Utilizing Freudian psychoanalysis, the Frankfurt School undertook various investigations of the psychodynamics of identity, politics, culture and ideology. In Fromm's work, psychoanalysis is used to focus on the family as mediator between self and society. In Adorno, Freud is utilized to analyse fascism, anti-Semitism and authoritarian irrationalism. In Marcuse, Freudian psychoanalysis is read 'against the grain' to develop a general social theory of modern societies.

5   The arrival of the administered world of advanced capitalism, according to Adorno and Marcuse, means that the role of the patriarchal family is undermined in identity formation.

6   The totally administered society eliminates the requirement for adaptive citizens with a measure of autonomy, one result of which is heightened levels of repression. As a result, society extends its domination over the personal domain through increasing levels of control over the individual's unconscious. This societal manipulation produces what Adorno terms the 'boundlessly elastic, subjectless subject'.

7   In Marcuse's work, modern societies are portrayed as increasingly 'one-dimensional' in scope. This gives rise to an oppressive existence for many, in which people suffer from crippling levels of 'surplus repression' and are traumatized by the harsh economic imperatives of the capitalist 'performance principle'.

8   For Marcuse, all sociality contains a utopian possibility. Even the most repressive social regimes cannot shut off the radical imagination. A revitalized society for Marcuse is one in which 'libidinal rationality' will flower, permitting reconcilitations between reason and desire, intimacy and sexuality.

9   One key criticism is that critical theory betrays an overreaction to fascism. The sociological and political claims of Adorno and Marcuse especially tend to elide some of core institutional differences between liberal capitalism and fascist regimes.

Further questions

1   Contemporary Western cultures are obsessed with consumption. Do you agree?

2   The bureaucratic administration of society turns reason into its opposite. Evaluate this claim.

3   Why is the Freudian psyche important for social critique?

4   In our age of global terroism, do people fear freedom?

5   The Frankfurt School sees repression as central to political domination. In our supposed age of liberal, anything-goes society, how does an analysis of repression contribute to cultural critique?

Further reading

Frankfurt School

(edited by Andrew Arato and Eike Gebhardt) *Essential Frankfurt School Reader* (Continuum, 1982).

Theodor Adorno

(with Max Horkheimer) *Dialectic of Enlightenment: Philosophical Fragments*, trans. Edmunt Jephcott (Stanford University Press, 2002).
(with co authors) *The Authoritarian Personality* (Harper & Row, 1950).
Minima Moralia (NLB, 1974).
Negative Dialectics, trans. E.B. Ashton (Routledge, 1973).
The Culture Industry (Routledge, 2001).

Erich Fromm

Escape From Freedom (Farrar & Rinehart, 1941).
The Sane Society (Rinehart, 1955).
The Anatomy of Human Destructiveness (Holt Paperbacks, 1992).
The Art of Loving (Harper & Brothers, 1957).

Herbert Marcuse

Eros and Civilization (Vintage Books, 1955).
One-Dimensional Man (Beacon Press, 1964).
The Aesthetic Dimension (Beacon Press, 1978).

There are many secondary works on the Frankfurt school including Douglas Kellner's *Critical Theory, Marxism and Modernity* (Polity Press, 1989), Rolf Wiggerhaus' *The Frankfurt School: Its History, Theories, and Political Significance* (MIT Press, 1994), Tom Bottomore's *The Frankfurt School* (Tavistock, 1984), and Martin Jay's *The Dialectical Imagination: A History of the Frankfurt School 1923–1950* (University of California Press, 1996).

Two good introductions to the work of Theodor Adorno are Simon Jarvis' *Adorno: A Critical Introduction* (Polity Press, 1998) and Detlev Claussen's *Theodor W. Adorno: One Last Genius* (Belknap Press, 2008). For a more in-depth view see Tom Huhn's *The Cambridge Companion to Adorno* (Cambridge University Press, 2004).

For further sources on Marcuse see Douglas Kellner's *Herbert Marcuse and the Crisis of Marxism* (Macmillan, 1984), Robert Pittin, A. Seenderg and C. Webel's *Marcuse: Critical Theory and the Promise of Utopia* (Macmillan,

1988), and John Bokina and Timothy J. Lukes' *Marcuse* (University of Kansas Press, 1994). See also C. Fred Alford's *Science and the Revenge of Nature: Marcuse and Habermas* (University of Florida Press, 1985).

For an introduction to Fromm see Rainer Funk, Ian Portman and Manuela Kunel's *Erich Fromm: His Life and Ideas* (Continuum, 2000) and Daniel Burston's *The Legacy of Erich Fromm* (Harvard University Press, 1991). Also of note are Rainer Funk's *Erich Fromm: The Courage to be Human* (Continuum, 1982), Richard Evans' *Dialogue with Erich Fromm* (Praeger, 1981) and Gerhard Knapp's *The Art of Living: Erich Fromm's Life and Works* (P. Lang, 1989). A more detailed critique may be found in Bernard Landis and Edward Tauber's *In the Name of Life: Essays in Honor of Erich Fromm* (Holt, Reinhart, & Winston, 1971) and Laurence Wilde's *Erich Fromm and the Quest for Solidarity* (Palgrave Macmillian, 1994).

Internet links

The Frankfurt School

http://carbon.cudenver.edu/~mryder/itc_data/postmodern.html#frankfurt
http://www.ifs.uni-frankfurt.de/english/history.htm
http://www.uta.edu/huma/illuminations/
http://www.marxists.org/subject/frankfurt-school/

Theodor Adorno

http://www.iep.utm.edu/a/adorno.htm

Max Horkheimer

http://www.ub.uni-frankfurt.de/archive/ehork.html

Erich Fromm

http://www.erich-fromm.de/e/index.htm

Herbert Marcuse

http://www.marxists.org/reference/archive/marcuse/works/eros-civilisation/
http://www.marcuse.org/herbert/
http://carbon.cudenver.edu/~mryder/itc_data/postmodern.html#frankfurt

chapter 3

Structuralism

Contents

Chris is a commissioning editor at a major New York publishing house, where he has worked for many years. Over this time, he has developed considerable skills in anticipating the kinds of non-fiction books people hunger to read. He has become quite adept, one might say, at reading the signs of what the general reading public want. Indeed, picking up on the signs of the book market is how he has got to where he is today. He made his reputation commissioning popular works of history, and in recent years has moved more in the direction of popular culture, celebrity and media. In recent months, he has commissioned books on the rise of reality television, the politics of 'size o' fashions, and several celebrity biographies.

It is almost impossible for Chris to travel around New York, or anywhere else for that matter, without thinking about the reading interests of people. Acutely aware that publishing has come under increasing challenges as a result of the Internet and new digital technologies, Chris none the less strives to find the best contemporary writers for his publishing list. He acknowledges that publishing confronts new difficulties in these early years of the twenty-first century, but insists that the *signs* are that people still want to read good books.

While Chris may be gifted in reading the signs of what the general public want to read, like anyone else in our society he also needs certain skills for interpreting messages and information all around him in the general culture. Today, for example, Chris woke to morning television and watched the breakfast news. On the way to work on the subway, he read the morning newspaper, and along the way was confronted by countless advertising promotions and billboards. Walking the streets to his office, he found himself surrounded by branded signs: Starbucks, Gap, McDonald's, Apple, Victoria's Secret. Then there were the various signs of daily interpersonal interaction, as colleagues at the office go through the morning ritual of greeting each other and enquiring how people are and what they have planned for the day.

Like most people going about their morning routine, Chris does not pay much attention to the signs that envelop him. Nor does he pay any particular attention to his own use of signs, from nodding to the man at the subway newspaper stand to greeting his secretary in the customary fashion at work. Yet all of these signs – both those encountered and those used by Chris – are fundamental to the business of social life. Signs not only point us in particular directions, and inform us of what is going on around us; they are essential to the very tissue of human communication and everyday life. Perhaps the best way to think about Chris's 'unthinking attitude' to the world of communication in which he dwells, therefore, is that – like everyone else – he experiences signs as existing independently of himself. Signs are just everywhere. This is not to say that there isn't a factor of choice in our use of signs, or language, and the communicative forms we use to express ourselves. But it is to say, and to recognize people's tacit understanding of the fact, that signs exist independently of us. For when people recognize that language and communication are not fully the product of their own intentional activity, they recognize – even to some minimal degree – the extent to which they are the passive prisoners of signs.

To say that we might be the 'passive prisoners of signs' is to move into territory that social theorists term 'structuralism'. Structuralism flourished in the 1960s as an attempt to apply the insights of linguistics to the study of the impersonal effects of social structures and political systems. As its name suggests, structuralism proceeds from the notion that people live their lives within the context of larger structures – social, cultural, political and historical – and that such structures shape and even determine individual decisions, choices, beliefs and values. Structuralism in general is an attempt to shift away from the humanistic viewpoint that people are self-directing, autonomous agents and to focus instead on the structures which give coherence, regularity and meaning to social interactions. Language is taken as the central model of analysis in structuralism, on the grounds that individual speech – as a universal element of all societies and cultures – would not be possible without an enabling structure to give words meaning. The words that I am writing now, for instance, are able to convey meaning only to the extent to which they accord with the structural rules of language – and structuralism is thus an attempt to interrogate such linguistic rules governing objects, events and interactions in fields beyond language itself. In this chapter, we will look in detail at structuralist social theory, starting with the methods developed in structural linguistics. We will then turn to consider how these methods came to be applied to social analysis in the writings of influential public intellectuals associated with structuralism, principally Roland Barthes and Michel Foucault. Throughout, the aim is to scrutinize the structuralist method for undertanding the production of a social world teeming with *signs*.

Saussure and structural linguistics

Not all of us are necessarily as gifted as Chris in reading the signs of professional or business life, but this does not mean that we are not endowed with a capacity to pick up on and read the signs of the endless forms of daily social life. The practical knowledge of how to read the signs of social life are many and varied, ranging from how to read a road map to how to 'handle oneself' at a party or similar social gathering. In any event, how we pick up on the signs around us – using language along the way to communicate with others – has become a core preoccupation of contemporary social theory. One influential viewpoint is that the signs in which we dwell, and the languages we use daily, are given to us – indeed, assigned to us – by this world and its general social structures. This is a viewpoint derived from modern structural linguistics.

Although he was not a social theorist, the founder of structural linguistics Ferdinand de Saussure (1858–1913) has come to exert a remarkable influence over contemporary social theory – primarily through the traditions of structuralism and post-structuralism. A linguist who worked in both Geneva and Paris on highly technical issues to do with Indo-European languages, Saussure set himself against nineteenth-century linguistics by questioning the view that language functions as a naturalistic representation of things or events in the world. In his work, he attempted to study the systems and structures revealed by language and which are essential to speech and communication. His epoch-making *Course in General Linguistics* (1916), one of the most widely read books in social theory, was published posthumously after a group of his students transcribed and edited Saussure's lecture notes to introductory linguistics. In his *Course*, Saussure advanced five central arguments. These are:

1 The distinction between language (*langue*) and speech (*parole*);
2 The arbitrary character of the sign;
3 The key role of difference in the constitution of meaning;
4 The making of the sign through the bonding of signifier and signified;
5 The division between synchrony and diachrony.

These doctrines, as we will later examine, have come to define the core of structuralist social theory – from the works of Claude Lévi-Strauss to Michel Foucault. In the next chapter, we will consider how a subsequent generation of Parisian intellectuals came to adopt, and then substantially modify, Saussurian linguistics in the development of what was to become post-structuralist social theory. At this point, however, it is worth enquiring into the logic of Saussure's key doctrines in order to better grasp how they came to shape the direction of social theory during the twentieth century.

In Saussure's view, the domain of signs and the realm of language must be approached from the standpoint of society, or the collective, and not the individual. The individual does not just spontaneously create meaning through the free-play of imagination; our language pre-exists us as individuals, and we must assimilate ourselves to its pre-existing forms and rules. This is another way of saying that language is a *social institution*. But if language cannot be divorced from society, then neither should the speech of individuals be isolated from concrete structures of linguistic interaction. Saussure, in point of fact, did not use the term 'structure'. But he did speak of 'system': it is from the systemic character of language (*langue*) that speech (*parole*) is ordered, regularized and reproduced. Our speech does not so much *reflect* our inner world as *instantiate* and *reproduce* discrete spheres of language as system. To put the point differently, language is less something 'within' our minds or selves than something around us in the societal structure – even though, somewhat like God or Santa Claus, language as system is unobservable. No one has ever actually seen, say, the English language: you can read the *Oxford English Dictionary* from cover to cover, but that only involves you in looking at specific words, and not the totality of language. Thus Saussure's purpose, roughly speaking, was to focus analysis on language as a structure – a structure that constitutes us to our very roots.

The individual's receptive and co-ordinating facilities build up a stock of imprints which turn out to be for all practical purposes the same as the next person's. How must we envisage this social product, so that the language itself can be seen to be clearly distinct from the rest? If we could collect the totality of word patterns stored in all those individuals, we should have the social bond which constitutes their language. It is a fund accumulated by the members of the community through the practice of speech, a grammatical system existing potentially in every brain, or more exactly in the brains of a group of individuals; for the language is never complete in any single individual, but exists perfectly only in the collectivity.

Excerpt from Ferdinand de Saussure (1916) *Course in General Linguistics*. London: Fontana, p. 13.

In making this core distinction between *langue* (the abstract structure of language) and *parole* (particular utterances of individual speech), Saussure advanced the thesis of the 'arbitrary character of the sign'. It is sometimes difficult, with Saussure, to know how far to press this anti-rationalist case that our languages do not reflect the real things we see around us in the world. For Saussure expressed various equivocations on this point in the *Course*. What his general argument comes down to, however, is that the relation between language and the object world is conventional – by which he meant structured by society and thus *radically arbitrary*. For Saussure, language does not just magically reflect an unchanging world. There is no such thing as a 'fixed language', one fully locked down and unchangeable. Rather, the world is internally structured along the lines of its languages, by which individuals come to know the social things around them and operate within society. One way that Saussure demonstrated this to be the case was by comparing words across languages. Although the meaning is similar, the sounds conveyed in the pronunciation of 'ox' in English have nothing in common with 'boeuf' in French or 'ochs' in German. Likewise, the word 'sister' is not linked in any way to the sounds expressed in 'soeur' in French. Different societies carve up the world through language in different ways. Another equally, if not more compelling argument he made hinged on discrediting the common-sense view that there is some intrinsic connection between words and the physical objects to which they refer. Consider, for example, the word 'tree'. According to Saussurian linguistics, there is nothing about the linguistic marks – t-r-e-e – which 'fits' or 'captures' the intrinsic properties of actual trees as vegetative things. Again, comparison is useful here: the term in French is 'arbre'. But, and this is fundamental, there is no intrinsic reason why either term is more or less appropriate to a tree as an object. But if there is no necessary relation between these words and objects, then that leaves the relation as *arbitrary* – which is precisely Saussure's argument. The relations between language and the object world are ones which we as a society fashion within given social and historical contexts; these relations are not in any sense independent from the systemic character of language, or the ways in which we deploy speech in daily life.

According to Saussure, the key to understanding language is to be found not in any connection between words and the physical objects designated, but in the *arbitrary nature of linguistic signs* that, in turn, depend upon *differential marks*. It may seem, at first, difficult to make sense of this terminology and particular way of thinking about language and its relation to the world. But let us stay a little longer with some of Saussure's terminological innovations, as it is certainly arguable that the world looks remarkably different once one grasps Saussure's principle of the arbitrary nature of linguistic signs. Meaning for Saussure is composed of combinations of 'signifiers', by which he means sounds and images as well as 'marks' of written text on the one hand, and 'signifieds', the mental image to which signifiers refer, on the other. Taken together, the signifier and signified make up the linguistic sign as realized in speaking and hearing, or reading and writing. But how, exactly, are such 'signifiers' and 'signfieds' brought into mutual connection? Connections are established, according to Saussure, through the power of difference: 'day' is constituted as a sign in terms of its difference from 'night', 'black' from 'white', 'man' from 'woman' and so on. This is a fundamental point in Saussurian linguistics, and he insists in the *Course* that every linguistic sign is inscribed in a structure of difference. 'In language', says Saussure (1974: 120), 'there are only differences. Even more important: a difference generally implies positive terms between which the difference is set up; but in language there are only differences without positive terms.' This is an insight that has major ramifications for grasping the connections between language and the world: the use of a signifier is part of a linguistic process that involves the negating, denying or 'forgetting' of other signifiers. 'Hot' only takes on the force of signifying to others by means of its difference to 'cold'. The semiotic power of signs, so to speak, is always differential.

All of this, from the standpoint of Saussurian linguistics, is to do with the internal structure of language. It is *difference* that creates meaning: terms only acquire meaning, continuity and durability insofar as they are differentiated from one another as oppositions within the structure of language as a whole. This, clearly, goes to the heart of questions concerning the systematic character of language on the one side, and the realization and reproduction of speech in daily life on the other. But it is not just the 'internal' dimensions of language that are addressed here, as this is also a theory rich in implications for society and its processes of linguistic and ideological production. Saussure helps make this point clear in his famous discussion of the 'Geneva-to-Paris train'. In conventional language, says Saussure, we would say that the 'same' train leaves Geneva for Paris every day at 8.25 p.m. – even though it is, in fact, the case that the 8.25 p.m. may actually change daily in terms of its carriages, engine and personnel. It is then the difference of the Geneva-to-Paris 8.25 p.m. from the 10.05 p.m., say, that singles out the identity of the train. Difference fosters the illusion that this is, always, the 'same' train – separating it out from other trains. And it is such linguistic difference that facilitates purposive social life, providing the fundamental distinctions and oppositions that are indispensable to daily social existence.

But in examining the arbitrary nature of linguistic signs, it is not just the object world that is carved up through difference. For language is a structure that goes all the way down, penetrating to the roots of identity and everyday life. The principle of difference, as Saussure develops it at any rate, also refers back to the individual speaker or self. If this is so, a signifier is a sound, image or linguistic mark that has the power to pull individuals this way and that, inscribing them within 'majorities' or 'minorities', 'inclusions' or 'exclusions', the 'centre' or 'periphery'. Saussure himself did not theorize the political forces of language and signs in such a direct fashion, and to that extent we are now pushing ahead of ourselves. But to the degree that Saussure made the point that meaning is an upshot of the differential, decentred forces of language, including the inner workings of lived experience, it becomes possible to see how this brand of linguistics transformed itself in time as a properly social structuralist theory. Saussure's work has given rise, as I have mentioned, to a fertile strain of social theory, and as we will subsequently examine, structuralism as a social theory is powerfully concerned with how the inscription of power and domination may be mapped within language and structures of linguistic relation.

The final thread in Saussure's argument concerns *the distinction between synchrony and diachrony*. Saussure looked at the development of language primarily in terms of its synchronic, or static, structures: it was the systematic character of language, rather than any particular modifications of speech by individuals, to which he addressed the project of structural linguistics. To study the structures of language, according to Saussure, means we must abstract fully from the individual articulations of speech. The privilege accorded to synchrony over diachrony, tied as it is to the placing of *langue* over *parole*, has been interpreted by some critics as an erasure of *time* – or, historical change – in structural linguistics. As Terry Eagleton (2008: 96) argues, for example, 'behind this linguistic model lies a definite view of human society: change is disturbance and disequilibrium in an essentially conflict-free system, which will stagger for a moment, regain its balance and take the change in its stride. Linguistic change for Saussure seems a matter of accident: it happens "blindly".' Stated thus, however, this is not quite accurate. Saussure did not so much eliminate 'change' – especially the unfolding of historical change through *time* – as recast the idea of how structural transformations occur. It is because a linguistic structure (or 'social system' for that matter) is only observable in its particular articulations or practices that the notion of time must be related to connections between the whole of a system and its particular elements. Time is thus much more complex than any strict separation between continuity and change. That said, Saussure did emphasize the independence of the synchronic from the diachronic – an emphasis which, among others of Saussure, gives rise to various problems in social theory that we will now turn to consider.

Critical comments on Saussure

The work of Saussure was limited to the field of linguistics, but as we will see, his influence has been immense. His *Course in General Linguistics* is widely viewed as inspiring structuralism in contemporary social theory, and indeed Saussurian themes have been extensively (and sometimes laboriously) used to analyse all possible aspects of social life – from eating habits to fashion, from myths to literature and the arts. What perhaps remains most suggestive in Saussure, although as we will see also much debated, is the theorem of the arbitrary character of the sign. After Saussure, the view that language just somehow magically 'fits' or 'hooks on' to the object world – in a kind of perfect correspondence – is thoroughly discredited. Saussurian linguistics is given to denying that there is any necessary relation between words and objects. Speech is not, on this view, just some 'reflex' to objects or events in the world; meaning is not the result of intentional acts of thought in the minds of language speakers. The relation between words and world is instead an arbitrary one (and thus conventional) to the extent that signifiers are always active in what they signify. Language is not, as with conventional wisdom, the intentional act of a speaker; and 'meaning' is not just the spontaneous expression of 'things' given in the world. For the fact is that meaning is always produced out of difference, the bonding of signifier and signified – which occurs differently in different places and in specific ways. Sociologically speaking, this provides for a fertile understanding of the social dynamics of language since *transformation* is now written into the relation between language and the material world.

However, critics have raised a number of criticisms of Saussure's theory, of which I want to raise some of the more pressing difficulties here. To begin with, if the production of meaning is radically arbitrary, how does the individual human subject come to navigate its way around the social world at all? Through difference, a bond between signifier and signified is said to be fashioned and meaning produced. But how, exactly, is meaning produced in such an unstable, free-floating linguistic system? Aware of these difficulties, Saussure made it clear that arbitrariness did not mean that speakers were unconstrained in their daily linguistic interactions with others; on the contrary, the speaker has no choice but to follow the rules already established in language. But if this is so it remains difficult to isolate what is actually arbitrary about signs. The idea that objects are wholly internal to the bonding of signifiers and signifieds that constitute them leaves obscure the issue of *reference* – of how ideas or concepts refer to objects or events in the social world. According to some critics, part of the difficulty here stems from Saussure's excessive concentration on the signifier/ signified relation at the expense of how objects are actually referenced. As Benveniste (1971: 44) argues:

> Even though Saussure said that the idea of 'sister' is not connected to the signifier s-o-r, he was not thinking any the less of the *reality* of the notion. When he spoke of the difference between b-o-f and o-k-s, he was referring in spite of himself to the fact that these two terms applied to the same *reality*. Here, then, is the *thing*, expressly excluded at first from the definition of sign, now creeping in by a detour.

What is thus missing in Saussurian linguistics is consideration of a third, higher term – what Benveniste calls 'the thing'. By focusing exclusively on the relation between signifier and signified, Saussure was able to unearth the productivity of language in defining and shaping the world, but at the expense of attending to how language actually refers to objects or events in the world.

That social relations do not exist independently of language, and that speech does not so much reflect the world as signify it, are undoubtedly vital insights of Saussurian linguistics. But there are surely limits as to how far we might press the argument that language is pure form, defined wholly internally through difference. For where difference derives from, arguably, is the social context in which language operates. Consider again Saussure's example of the Geneva-to-Paris train. Saussure, as we have seen, seeks to identify the internal composition of signifiers inscribed around the train in terms of defining a distinct identity. To say that the 8.25 p.m. occupies a distinct identity within a timetable of train scheduling by virtue of its difference from other times is one way of understanding how meaning is produced. But this is not the only way of understanding the matter, and arguably Saussure's position is one that at any rate grants privilege to the position of tourist or traveller. As one commentator (Giddens 1979: 16) argues:

> The identity of the 'Geneva-to-Paris train' cannot be specified independently of the context in which the phrase is used; and this context is not the system of differences themselves, as Saussure mentions, but factors relating to their use in practice. Saussure implicitly assumes the practical standpoint of the traveller, or the time-tabling offical, in giving the identity of the train; hence the 'same' train may consist of quite distinct engines and carriages on two separate occasions. But these do not count as instances of the 'same' train for a railway repair engineer, or a train-spotter.

Difference, in short, is *context dependent*: meaning is fashioned in relation to distinctions and oppositions grounded in social practice.

We have seen that Saussure distinguishes between *synchronic* and *diachronic* ways of analysing language; and we have seen that his version of structural linguistics concentrates on the synchronic – that is, the structural conditions of language – while bracketing off the diachronic, or historical, study of language. However, some critics have rightly objected that we should be dubious of a too hard-and-fast distinction between synchrony and diachrony, or statics and dynamics, in studying processes of change. For the problem that arises (which will become increasingly evident when we turn to consider structuralist social theory) is that to view language as all form and no substance results, ultimately, in the neglect of the social and historical conditions in and through which systems and structures are both produced and modified. That is to say, structuralism has immense difficulties explaining social change or historical transformation. Some critics, such as E.P. Thompson (1978), have gone so far as to argue that structuralism betrays a radically impoverished conception of historical processes, such is its elevation of system statics over and above the creative dynamics of human agency. We need to be careful in assessing this criticism, however, since Saussure himself was at pains to stress that the synchrony/diachrony division was only a methodological one. Thus, the claim that 'structuralism fails to recognize that language is constantly undergoing change' is not strictly accurate. It is arguably the case, though, that such a division – even for methodological purposes – means that the production and reproduction of systems and structures cannot be adequately grasped.

The Raw and The Cooked: Lévi-Strauss and structural anthropology

At first sight, no idea might be more removed from the realm of culture and the social than that of nature. Nature, after all, smacks of physical processes unaffected by human activity, and calls to mind the eternal, the timeless and universal. Nothing, it might be thought, could be more natural than nature. And yet, if we think about it for a moment, it is evident that what we experience as natural is rooted ultimately in culture. From biology and physics to the environment and Mother Nature, what we know about the natural is based in turn upon our culturally specific ways of understanding the world. For Claude Lévi-Strauss, the link between the natural and the human is dazzlingly complex. Rejecting as too simplistic the idea that there are natural aspects of culture, or alternatively that culture incorporates nature in all its variations, Lévi-Strauss instead proposes a *structural link* between the natural and cultural which constitutes social relations from end to end.

Lévi-Strauss became one of the most celebrated and fashionable structuralists throughout Europe during the post-war years, applying with beautiful prose the methods of structural linguistics to the anthropological analysis of kinship, primitive classification systems, myth, music, totemism and art. In particular, Lévi-Strauss drew upon Saussure's structural linguistics to examine cultural production as a *system of oppositional relations of difference* that compose social meanings. From this angle, one of his major contributions to social theory was the insight that the products of culture are organized and ordered in much the same way as we imagine the products of nature to be segmented.

In his book *The Raw and The Cooked* (1964), Lévi-Strauss comments that, in the same manner that all historical societies have spoken languages, so also human societies have processed food, in some fashion or other, through cooking. Cooking may take the form of boiling, roasting, grilling, steaming or frying, but whatever the method, the act of cooking itself is a transformational one involving shifts from nature to culture. According to Lévi-Strauss, the cooking of food is, in effect, a form of mediation between nature and society, between Heaven and Earth, and between life and death. The cooking of food involves the transformation of raw fresh food geared to culture, whereas raw fresh food left to nature is transformed as rotten. To claim, as Lévi-Strauss does, that there is a 'culinary triangle' of foods in human culture everywhere is to claim that various binary oppositions – for example, transformed/normal and cooked/rotten – become internalized in the human mind. As one of Lévi-Strauss's foremost interpreters, Edmund Leach (1970: 32), sums up *The Raw and The Cooked*:

> What Lévi-Strauss is getting at is this. *Animals* just eat food; and food is anything available which their instincts place in the category 'edible'. But *human beings*, once they have been weaned from the mother's breast, have no such instincts. It is the conventions of society which decree what is food and what is not food, and what kinds of food shall be eaten on what occasions. And since the occasions are social occasions there must be some kind of patterned homology between relationships between kinds of food on the one hand and relationships between social occasions on the other.

It is important to be clear here as to what Lévi-Strauss is not saying. He is not saying that nature as such does not exist. For example, fresh raw food is essential to life and without it we would die very quickly. Because culture is natural to us, however, it is what we do with foodstuffs (milk, cheese, meat and so on) that constitutes food as a sign system geared to meaning, symbolism and interpretation. Whether we speak of a Londoner or an Amazonian Indian, according to Lévi-Strauss, food is divided into subcategories – food-type 1, food-type 2, food-type 3 – which are, in turn, accorded differences through social relations. For example, according to Western conventions, the presentation of oysters at a dinner party usually signals an entrée, just roast beef is accorded the status of main course and chocolate mousse is suitable for dessert. Why this should be the case, says Lévi-Strauss, arises from forms of symbolism planted deep in the human mind, and structured by powerful binary oppositions – savoury/sweet, raw/cooked, nature/culture.

Do you agree with Lévi-Strauss that, if we dig deep through culture, we can find universal laws (structured by binary oppositions) governing the human mind? How relevant do you find Lévi-Strauss' *The Raw and The Cooked* to today's world of fast-food outlets and multicultural cuisines?

Roland Barthes: structuralist semiology and popular culture

Though Saussure had coined the term 'semiology', defining his project as the systematic study of signs at the heart of social life, the importance of structuralist semiology to social critique was not to develop until the post-war years in Europe. One way of charting that development is to look briefly at the work of the French critic and semiotician Roland Barthes. In a series of path-breaking books such as *Mythologies* (1957), *Elements of Semiology* (1964) and *The Fashion System* (1967), Barthes staged a decisive encounter between structural linguistics (particularly with semiotics) and popular culture. Analysing the signifying systems of everyday myths, fashion and culture in the era of mass communications, Barthes effortlessly decoded the signs that society generates. The genius of his particular blend of semiology and cultural sociology was that Barthes saw clearly, perhaps more so than any critic associated with structuralism, the extent to which we live in a world teeming with signs that demand critical interpretation.

The early structuralist Barthes appears most decisively in *Elements of Semiology*, a book that illustrates the method of structuralism for the critique of culture in our era of mass communications. Quite beyond the austerely technical details that Barthes rehearses in considering Saussurean linguistics and structuralist semiology, his underwriting of the power of deadly structures upon human lives is what led to widespread critical acclaim of *Elements of Semiology*. The first major exercise in what was to become Barthes' structuralist methodology for a new style of cultural research in decoding signs, *Elements* insisted upon the Saussurian insight that meaning is an upshot of oppositions between signs within a linguistic and cultural system. Barthes took Saussure a step further however, and in at least two key respects. First, while arguing that Saussurian linguistics uncovers the absent structures of meaning – by stressing the unremitting play of differences in society, the power of unconscious convention, and systematic function – he also considered limitations to the structural critique of meaning. For Barthes, oppositions leave out of account the various social elements that do not fit into either of the opposed linguistic categories of Saussurian analysis. To that extent, Saussurian linguistics – if not supplemented with a properly semiological appreciation of the complexity of human experience – runs the risk of downgrading individuality and issues pertaining to individual style. These were matters of considerable importance to Barthes, whose structuralism was always tempered by an appreciation of other theoretical approaches – from sociology to psychoanalysis. But he also extended Saussure in still another respect. *Elements* sets out the method of structuralism for the critique of culture and society, and not simply the functional analysis of language. In Barthes' view, semiology – the study of the signs produced by society – is vital to the critique of capitalist consumerism, of the deep structures that orientate desire for flashy cars, designer clothes and technological gadgets, and which purges the political realm of creativity and alternative possibility.

> Like the linguist who deals only with the phonic substance; in the same way, ideally, a good corpus of documents on the food system should comprise only one and the same type of document (restaurant menus, for instance). Reality, however, most commonly presents mixed substances; for instance, garments and written language in fashion; images, music and speech in films, etc.; it will therefore be necessary to accept heterogeneous corpuses, but to see to it, in that case, that one makes a careful study of the systematic articulation of the substances concerned (and chiefly, that one pays due attention to separating the real from the language which takes it over), that is, that one gives their very heterogeneity a structural interpretation.
>
> Roland Barthes (1967) *Elements of Semiology.* London: Cape, pp. 98–9.

If *Elements of Semiology* details the structuralist method and conceptual tool-box for the critique of culture, it is *Mythologies* that uncovers the ideological consequences of popular culture itself. His most famous work as a 'high' structuralist, *Mythologies* finds Barthes analysing a panorama of 1950s French culture – from wrestling to striptease, from advertising to the Tour de France. Derived from journalistic essays he had penned during the early 1950s, *Mythologies* took French intellectual culture by storm, perhaps partly because these little essays seemed an easier way for readers to engage with structuralism, and partly because Barthes' short, witty reflections revealed a structuralist with a radical political agenda. For his aim throughout the book, wrote Barthes, was to decode the function of myths as rendering social reality 'natural'; alarmed at seeing 'Nature and History confused at every turn', Barthes found in everyday mythologies the making of what is thoroughly cultural seem natural, what he referred to as the ceaseless 'what-goes-without-saying'. In order to uncover how myth converts culture into nature, Barthes brought to bear a lightly worn-on-the-sleeve structuralism upon popular culture. Taking current affairs and various news items as his point of departure, he traced the ideological distortions of myths, the social lies concealed in adverts, films or books, beauty products and other symbolic forms which bound French culture together. He found at work within the mythological façade of culture a dramatic series of displacements, substitutions and repetitions of meaning, all of which served to pass off the signs of culture as natural. The structuralist argument which Barthes weaves throughout *Mythologies* is that culture promotes particular meanings only through a concealment of other ideological ones. Wine, steak and fries, for example, are the apparently natural diet of the French – 'an alimentary sign of Frenchness'.

Perhaps the best way to illustrate Barthes' arrestingly original semiological structuralism is by looking in a little more detail at one of his essays in *Mythologies*. In 'The Brain of Einstein', Barthes reviews the famous scientist's 'body in the library' of popular culture. That is to say, he carefully appraises the complex cultural meanings attributed to Einstein and to natural science. 'Einstein's brain', writes Barthes (1972: 68), 'is a mythical object: paradoxically, the greatest intelligence of all provides an image of the most up-to-date machine, the man who is too powerful is removed from psychology, and introduced into a world of robots.' What Barthes finds notable about Einstein is how the creativity and innovation of natural science is bracketed off from popular consciousness of his scientific genius; instead, Einstein is reduced to a machine, his scientific labours to 'the mechanical making of sausages'. Still further, the complexity of scientific analysis is reduced in our general culture to the utter simplicity of a singular formula, $E = mc^2$. 'There is a single secret to the world', writes Barthes (1972: 69),

> and this secret is held in one word; the universe is a safe of which humanity seeks the combination: Einstein almost found it, this is the myth of Einstein. . . . The historic equation $E = mc^2$, by its unexpected simplicity, almost embodies the pure idea of the key, bare, liner, made of one metal, opening with a wholly magical ease a door which had resisted the desperate efforts of centuries.

The stylish, playful prose of Barthes' writing on Einstein works to occlude the rigours of his structuralist enquiry. For stripped of its elegant writing, Barthes' semiological analysis reveals a series of oppositions which structure the internal relations of meanings attributed to myths that Einstein embodies. Traversing the themes discussed above – from Einstein as the world's 'greatest intelligence' to his insertion into a 'world of robots', from the 'magic' (as Barthes puts it) of his theory of relativity to his 'mechanical making of sausages', and from the complexity of his science to the simplicity of the world's secret unlocked in one equation – we could condense this structuralist analysis to a series of binary oppositions. These would presumably include: human/machine; psychology/anti-psychology; magical/mechnical; and complexity/simplicity. Written in this way, this is obviously not as gripping or eloquent as Barthes' decoding of the myth of Einstein. But my point is to indicate that, notwithstanding Barthes' aesthetic and brilliant style, the core of his structuralist analysis shifts the content of the issue under review to the sidelines in order to concentrate entirely on form. As with Saussure, then, it is the structure of internal relations of the signs under consideration that matters.

Structuralism has sometimes been criticized as apolitical. The criticism is that, with its relentless focus on linguistic units of discourse, structuralism turns away from the historical conditions and actual political struggles of people, substituting an empty formalism. In the light of reading Barthes' *Mythologies*, however, it seems difficult to give much weight to such criticism, such is the penetrating political analysis and ideological engagement of his writing. Famously, Barthes attacked French involvements in Indo-China and Algeria. A key example was his analysis of the cover of an issue of *Paris-Match*, with a photo of a black soldier in uniform saluting the French flag. For Barthes, the magazine cover traded in the mythology of French imperialism. At the time, France was engaged in a prolonged war with Algeria; against the backdrop of the breakup of the French colonial empire, there was considerable debate in France over whether Algeria should be given its independence. The *Paris-Match* cover, said Barthes, tacitly underwrote imperialism. The mythological message of the cover, he wrote, was

> that France is a great Empire, that all her sons, without distinction of colour, serve faithfully beneath her flag, and that there is no better answer to the detractors of a supposed colonialism, than the zeal of this Negro to serve his supposed oppressors.

In Barthes' view, myth is around to make us feel socially 'ordinary' or 'natural'; criticism remains the difficult theoretical labour of demonstrating why myth is a kind of 'social lie'. To see the world through the prism of myth, for Barthes, is akin to having one's head buried in the sand – as culture palms itself off as nature. In 'Myth Today', a theoretical overview of the Saussurean model at the conclusion of *Mythologies*, Barthes details the complex ways in which mythological language is at once intimate and alien to us. Deep in the Saussurean mode, Barthes theorizes a 'pyrimadal' sign divided between the signifier (the voice or graphic mark) and signified (the representation or concept attached to it). The relation between signifier and signified, for Barthes as for Saussure, is arbitrary – that is to say, socially conventional. Barthes calls this a 'first-order' signifying system in which the proliferation of discourse is contingent – signs are always a matter of historical and cultural convention. Language in this sense, for Barthes, is creative, rich in its multiple associations, and capable of turning back upon its own conventional 'arbitrariness' – for example, when people use irony. By contrast, there is a kind of language which is ideological because it blocks its own relative, artificial status and attempts to pass itself off as transcendent, natural and universal. Barthes calls this a 'second-order semiological system' and the ideological language which corresponds to this system is myth. Mythic speech, according to Barthes, draws upon the first-order system of language in the fashioning of a second-order system which offers up a version of reality 'as it is', the 'natural' attitude. Agreeing that appreciation of wine is a mark of sophistication, or that wealth creation is intrinsically beneficial, seems the most obvious thing in the world. Nothing could more mythic than the 'most obvious', according to Barthes – as layers of free-floating 'first-order' signs are gathered up, glued together through repetition, and displaced to the fixed 'second-order' of mythic speech.

Myth hides nothing and flaunts nothing: it distorts; myth is neither a lie nor a confession: it is an inflexion. Placed before the dilemma which I mentioned a moment ago, myth finds a third way out. Threatened with disappearance if it yields to either of the first two types of focusing, it gets out of this tight spot thanks to a compromise – it *is* this compromise. Entrusted with 'glossing over' an intentional concept, myth encounters nothing by betrayal in language, for language can only obliterate the concept if it hides it, or unmask it if it formulates it. The elaboration of a second-order semiological system will enable myth to escape this dilemma: driven to having either to unveil or liquidize the concept, it will *naturalize* it.

Roland Barthes (1972) *Mythologies*. New York: Hill & Wang, p. 129.

Barthes thus presents what might be called the two faces of language. One is associative, free-flowing, relative, artificial, poetic. This is the 'first-order' realm of language, as captured in Saussurean linguistics. The other is fixed, repetitious, closed. This is the 'second-order' realm of language, and for Barthes the preserve of ideology and mythological speech. It is here – in the structural transformations from 'first' to 'second' order signifying systems – that social theorists can most usefully deploy structuralist methods for the analysis of ideology, myth and popular culture. Consider, for example, recent advertisements for Apple iPods – which are relentlessly associated with advanced technology, sophisticated style and innovative design. Such adverts might be critically interpreted, following in the footsteps of Barthes, as involving layers of first-order associations to do with new technologies to the point where a repetitive and substitutive second-order bond is made between the signifier 'Apple' and the signified 'stylish, sophisticated, affluent and cool'. This kind of advertising is rampant throughout consumer culture today, and Barthes' semiological structuralism provides a critical perspective on the sociological and ideological elements of such mediated mythic discourses.

Barthes' structuralist-inspired writings have powerfully challenged traditional forms of sociological analysis, and even today works such as *Mythologies* continue to inspire significant work in critical cultural studies. Barthes' semiological method for the decoding of signs has found many supporters – from Susan Sontag to Julia Kristeva – and subsequent authors working in the structuralist tradition have refined and elaborated Barthes' cultural critique. The ongoing relevance of Barthes' structuralist semiology surely lies in its radical account of the conventional 'arbitrariness' of the sign's relationship to society, its painstaking structural lucidity, and its account of social and ideological forms. On the other hand, it is now widely agreed that there are major limitations to Barthes' early structuralism, and indeed Barthes himself was to express serious reservations about the 'scientific pretensions' of his earlier structuralist writings. One limitation, according to some critics, is that the individual appears diminished – determined exclusively by the powers of structure – in Barthes' work. This may be so in one sense, but it would appear to neglect the broader political thrust of Barthes' work. For the structuralist tradition, social analysis cannot adequately proceed from the individual's 'experience' – for that very 'experience' is, in fact, the effect of an impersonal structure. Thus, Barthes' social theory, at its best, steers a middle course between individual subject and social process by examining instead the *system of differences* in which discourse is embedded. It is here that we find the ongoing political edge in Barthes' work: society reveals itself through the system of differences it produces, while ideology reveals itself through the closure of those differences. In myths, in the obviousness of the 'natural', in pseudo 'common sense', culture seeks to naturalize social reality. But still Barthes' commitment to structures at the expense of identity produces tensions and contradictions – and, at its worst, casts the individual as the passive victim of impersonal processes. 'The excitement of innovative methods and new materials,' writes Rick Rylance (1994: 54) of Barthes, 'contradicts the gloomy scenarios of determinism and limitation.'

Foucault: knowledge, social order and power

Michel Foucault (1926–1984) is perhaps the most influential French intellectual associated with the theoretical current of structuralism. Although he rejected any direct linkage with this tradition of thought, Foucault's early works – such as *The Birth of the Clinic* (1963), *The Order of Things* (1966) and *The Archaeology of Knowledge* (1969) – demonstrate the method of a 'high' structuralist, analysing the origins of modern medicine, psychiatry and systems of classification in terms of the systemic features of language and discourse. Foucault's own typical habit of energetically attacking the present, as well as all things 'familiar' or 'normal', is to dig into the past – examining the archives of previous historical epochs. This historical approach informing Foucault's structuralist criticism produced, in time, powerful insights into the systems of power that people make to entrap themselves – as well as pushing the structuralist method to its limit. In other words, Foucault's work is concerned in the broadest sense with the gentle wiles of modern reason and knowledge; and his structuralist-inspired social theory reveals the subtle and complex ways in which the rules of social formation shape the lives of individuals.

The early structuralist Foucault details the possibility of a scientific method, labelled either 'archaeology' or 'genealogy', which can discern unconscious processes of social change. Such an archaeological or genealogical method in the hands of Foucault sought to trace the unthought processes governing the structure of social things; the aim was to reveal 'a positive unconscious of knowledge: a level that eludes the consciousness of the scientist and yet is part of what is scientific'. Foucault sought to do this by applying structuralism to the rules of social formation whereby certain discourses became deeply layered in social life. In *The Order of Things* (1966) and *The Archaeology of Knowledge* (1969), Foucault set about analysing the production of modern reason and knowledge by 'digging' into the past. At one level, this meant attacking certain taken-for-granted concepts, ideas and structures that have served to legitimize Western knowledge and philosophy – such as the widespread belief in scientific advancement and faith in humanly engineered progress. This he did by working the archives, critically interrogating the ways in which the production of knowledge has been shaped and organized over the centuries by bodies of texts, doctrines and discourses. He sought, in effect, to reread the commentaries, authors and disciplines of the human sciences in terms of the rules of language whereby knowledge becomes the ultimate ground of all power. At a deeper level, Foucault's archaeological or genealogical method sought to rise above certain familiar themes dominant in Western thought – such as the privilege accorded to consciousness – to a point where the production of knowledge through the linguistic systems that structure social, political and technological life could be comprehended. As Foucault represents this, archaeological analysis addresses 'the general space of knowledge' and 'the mode of being of things that appear in it'.

> In a society such as ours, but basically in any society, there are manifold relations of power which permeate, characterize and constitute the social body, and these relations of power cannot themselves be established, consolidated nor implemented without the production, accumulation, circulation and functioning of a discourse. There can be no possible exercise of power without a certain economy of discourses of truth which operates through and on the basis of this association. We are subjected to the production of truth through power and we cannot exercise power except through the production of truth.
>
> Michel Foucault (1980) 'Two lectures', in C. Gordin (ed.) *Power/Knowledge: Selected Interviews and Other Writings, 1972–1977.* New York: Pantheon Books.

According to Foucault, the power of knowledge moves on several levels. First, it is the power of classifying languages – of determining that certain languages will come to have an overarching hold over the organization of discrete aspects of daily life. In *The Order of Things*, Foucault maps the force-fields of the human sciences, from their emergence in the Renaissance to the nineteenth century in the domains of biology, economics and linguistics. Second, it is the power of classifying discourse itself, classifying the rules which underpin formations of discourse and their domains of application. Economic discourses, so to speak, construct 'productive individuals' subject to the laws of economics; biology constructs individuals as 'living organisms' subject to laws of nature; and linguistics locates speaking subjects as governed by structures of signification. Finally, such systems of thought and their classifications govern not only how discourse is produced but the power relations operating throughout society in general – of which we will consider Foucault's treatment of the relation between power and knowledge in more detail shortly.

In order to better understand how knowledge becomes inscribed in techniques of individuation and objectification, let us now turn to consider Foucault's famous work on prisons. In his best-selling *Discipline and Punish* (1977), Foucault develops a genealogical history of punishment and prisons and introduces his celebrated concept 'power–knowledge'. The historical problem to which Foucault turns, in effect, concerns the relations of power and knowledge as imprinted on the human body through disciplinary codes and related forms of punishment. Foucault's aim, he writes, is to 'study the metamorphosis of punitive methods on the basis of a political technology of the body in which might be read a common history of power relations'. To see modern judicial punishment and disciplinary codes through the frame of a genealogical history, for Foucault, is a valuable advance on seeing it simply as an ongoing 'humane improvement' over earlier historical forms of punishment. For it allows us to see that the discipline of the body as performed by prisons scoops up various disciplinary codes that originated at different points in history, and which have come to shape the functioning of wider relations of power in schools, military life and organizations. In modern society, says Foucault, individuals are increasingly subject to what he terms 'disciplinary power', a power that is hidden, monotonous and invisible.

Discipline and Punish asserts that the institutional framework of prisons has its origins in the Panopticon, an organizational proposal for the treatment of offenders put forward by the social philosopher Jeremy Bentham in the nineteenth century. 'Panopticon' was the term Bentham used for a set of proposals he tried to sell to the British government for the retraining of a criminal's mind from irrational law-breaking to rational law-following. The design of Bentham's Panoptical prison was circular in shape, with a guard in a central tower looking out on to prisoners' cells. The purpose of the design was to make it impossible for the prisoner to tell if the guard was watching or not, since the tower windows were fitted with a Venetian blind, thus establishing a kind of one-way, total surveillance of prisoners by the prison staff. It was this element of surveillance of central control that Foucault isolated as fundamental to the exercise of power.

Panoptical surveillance takes several forms. One is the direct monitoring of the prisoner's actions at any time. Whether mixing with other inmates or alone in one's cell, there was to be no place of escape from the Panoptical gaze. For Foucault this principle was a structure of domination at the heart of the penitentiary, but also in other organizations too. 'Is it surprising', asks Foucault (1979), 'that prisons resemble factories, schools, barracks, hospitals, which all resemble prisons?' The panoptical prison, it transpired, was everywhere – organizing the practical knowledge of daily life.

A second form of surveillance consists of record-keeping, the updating of files, and the development of case histories for the reform of criminals. Such administrative paperwork is for Foucault not only essential for the operation of prisons, but crucial to the regulation and disciplining of human bodies. As Mark Poster (1990: 91) observes:

> The principle of one-way, total surveillance of the subject was extended to the keeping of files. Without a systematic record of the subject's behaviour surveillance is incomplete. For the Panoptical machine to have its effect the individual must become a case with a meticulously kept dossier that reflects the history of his deviation from the norm.

Foucault thus sees the organizing influence of Panoptical surveillance at work in more and more modern organizations, such as mental asylums, schools, hospitals, and the military and secret services. In contemporary culture, says Foucault, power is imposed upon people through the bureaucratic surveillance of populations, the routine gathering of information and the continual monitoring of daily life; in effect, the modern age is one of 'panopticism', a society in which individuals are increasingly caught up in systems of power in and through which visibility is a key means of social control. Society for Foucault may be understood as a struggle of discourses in which power relations are shaped, with specific forms of discipline and resistance defining the nature of what it feels like to be alive. Those in positions of power, in order to further their material and symbolic interests, seek to gain control over the policing of discourse – of defining what is acceptable and unacceptable within specific forms of life in society at large. But power, warns Foucault, is never fixed. Power is instead best conceived of as a relationship, a mysterious force between individuals, groups and institutions. It is for this reason that Foucault often speaks of a micro-politics of power, by which he means the multifarious submissions and resistances of individuals in their engagement with social and institutional life.

Society and disciplined bodies

An early use of Foucault's ideas for thinking about the relations between self, society and power is that offered by the British sociologist Bryan S. Turner. In a series of books, from *The Body and Society* (1984) to *Regulating Bodies* (1992), Turner (b. 1945) has sought to develop a sophisticated sociological reading of Foucault. Now Foucault was a philosopher and historian, not a sociologist. Yet Turner argues that there is much in Foucault's work that can be drawn upon with profit for developing a sociology of the 'embodied self'. The self has been passed off for too long, says Turner, as peculiarly disembodied; the body is conceptualized in mainstream sociological approaches as a biological constraint upon human agency and social action. However, Turner sees the embodied self as fundamental to social interaction. The body is something we are, we have and we do in daily life; the body is crucial to an individual subject's sense of self, as well as the manner in which the self relates to and interacts with others. The relationship between self, body and knowledge, says Turner, is central to Foucault's work and, when sociologically interpreted, provides a valuable model for understanding the changing relations between self and society. The body for Turner connects self-identity, physical self-regulation and sexuality in the context of postmodern city culture. The increasing emphases on fitness, hygiene, thinness and youthfulness are central planks in the maintenance of self-regulation in relation to consumer capitalism. This political struggle around the body, particularly the commodification of body images, occurs not only in relation to the regulation of self and sexuality, but also through legislative and administrative structures. *In vitro* fertilization programmes, abortion, child care, the medicalization of AIDS as a modern epidemic: it is here that we witness the progressive institutional management, regulation and surveillance of the embodied self in contemporary culture.

In an essay 'The Government of the Body' (1982), Turner extends Foucault's ideas by analysing the regularization of self, the rationalization of diet and the discipline of the body. Diet, says Turner, is linked to a micro-politics of the human body, since it transfers responsibility for the discipline of the self into the hands of human subjects. The growth of dietetics and social science consolidate the administrative management of food consumption as part of the biopolitics of population, insofar as this involves the regulation of individuals, of health and of mortality. Analysing the rise of expert technical knowledge (medicine, dietetics, social science) as interwoven with the political management of populations, Turner argues:

> Dietary tables were typically aimed at forms of consumption which were regarded as 'irrational' threats to health, especially where overconsumption was associated with obesity and alcoholism. These dietary programmes were originally addressed to those social groups which were exposed to abundance – the aristocracy, merchants and the professional groups of the London taverns and clubs. . . . It was not until the latter part of the nineteenth century that the science of diet became important in the economic management of prisons and the political management of society. The principles for the efficient government of prisons and asylums were quickly applied to the question of an effective, healthy working class supported on a minimum but adequate calorie intake.
>
> (Turner, 1992, pp. 192–3)

Dietetics, with its focus on consumption and the body, led people increasingly to care for themselves according to pre-given administrative rules and regulations; it led people to follow expert information in the management and control of the self.

Turner is refreshingly ambivalent about the wider social and political consequences of the complex interrelationship between self, embodiment and gender. He does not see a single source of social power guiding the government of the body/self. Rather, our growing awareness that the body is socially produced and regulated occurs on many different symbolic levels, from medicine to the fashion industry. Like sexuality and the self, the body is today located within consumer culture as a mark of distinction; bodily appearance and control link to the symbolic representation of identity – as a metaphor of society, as a field for gender differentiation, as a site for racial and ethnic cultures and conflicts. However, the embodied self for Turner is not the passive product of institutional and ideological forces, but rather is integral to the very nature of being and of agency in the routine presenting, interpreting and monitoring of daily life. In contemporary culture there is for Turner a kind of lifting of the care of the self to the second power, with regimens of calorie measurement, jogging, and health clubs the means through which people discipline their bodies. From this perspective the politics of identity is increasingly wrapped around configurations of the body – the fit body, the disciplined body, the body beautiful, body piercing, the body in cyberspace. There is also, of course, the troubled and troubling anorexic body; eating disorders, says Turner, are central self-pathologies of our age. In all of this, however, the body is itself the site of intensified self-management, self-regulation and self-mastery.

The limits of structuralism: Foucault's *History of Sexuality*

During the late 1970s and early 1980s, Foucault moved away from structuralism. Like Barthes, he became increasingly concerned with the limits of structuralist analysis to comprehend the complexities of social transformation and the intricacies of human action and matters pertaining to individual style. But this theoretical move involved less a wholesale break with the core tenets of structuralism than a pushing of structuralist analysis to its limits. This he did in the final part of his academic career through the development of a sweeping, brilliant history of sexuality.

In *The History of Sexuality* Foucault's contends that knowledge about sexuality compels individuals to situate themselves in relation to regimes of the erotic, particularly to what is regulated, forbidden, prohibited. 'Each person', writes Foucault (1988: 40), 'has the duty to know who he is, that is, to try to know what is happening inside him, to acknowledge faults, to recognize temptations, to locate desires.' In the first volume of *The History of Sexuality*, Foucault sets out to debunk what he calls 'the repressive hypothesis'. According to this hypothesis the healthy expression of sexuality has been censured, smothered and forbidden; at any rate, this is held to be the case in the West. However, Foucault takes issue with this hypothesis, and in fact seeks to undermine the conventional wisdom that sex is repressed. Sex, says Foucault, has not been driven underground in contemporary culture. On the contrary, there has been an ever-widening discussion of sex and sexuality. Sexuality for Foucault is the result of a process of endless monitoring, discussion, classification, ordering, recording and regulation. The medicalization of sexuality, particularly notions of sexual perversion and deviance, has brought into focus the complex interrelationship between desire, sex and power. Questioning the conventional view that power constrains sexual desire, Foucault advances the view that power serves not only to regulate 'sexual taboos' but to produce sexuality and its pleasures. That is to say, power and sexual pleasure are intricately intertwined.

To demonstrate this Foucault examines Victorian attitudes towards sexuality in the late nineteenth century. Victorianism, writes Foucault, is usually associated with the emergence of prudishness, the silencing of sexuality, and the rationalization of sex within the domestic sphere, the home, the family. Foucault disagrees. He argues that one sees in the advent of the Victorian era the development of sexuality as a secret, as something forbidden or taboo, which then required administion, regulation and policing. For example, doctors, psychiatrists and others catalogued and classified numerous perversions, from which issues about sex became endlessly tracked and monitored with the growth of social medicine, education, criminology and sexology. These discourses about sex and sexuality form part of a broader realm of techniques for the care of the self in society, techniques which Foucault sees as shaping the mind externally.

To understand the rise of techniques for the care of the self, Foucault argues that it is necessary to connect the West's prohibition against sex to discourses of sexuality in nineteenth-century scientific disciplines and culture. Foucault's approach to the analysis of the intertwining of sex and power is brought out nicely in the opening chapter of *The History of Sexuality*, where he discusses a medical report about a farmworker, apparently simple-minded, who was arrested and then incarcerated in a clinic for sexual transgressions:

> One day in 1867, a farm hand from the village of Lapcourt . . . obtained a few caresses from a little girl, just as he had done before and seen done by the village urchins around him. . . . So he was pointed out by the girl's family to the mayor of the village, reported by the mayor to the gendarmes, led by the gendarmes to the judge, who indicted him and

turned him over first to a doctor, then to two other experts who not only wrote their report but also had it published. What is the significant thing about this story? The pettiness of it all; the fact that this everyday occurrence in the life of village sexuality, these inconsequential bucolic pleasures, could become, from a certain time, the object not only of a collective intolerance but of a judicial action, a medical intervention, a careful clinical examination, and an entire theoretical elaboration. The thing to note is that they went so far as to measure the brainpan, study facial bone structure, and inspect for possible signs of degenerescence the anatomy of this personage who up to that moment had been an integral part of village life; that they made him talk; that they questioned him concerning his thoughts, inclinations, habits, sensations, and opinions. And then, acquitting him of any crime, they decided finally to make him into a pure object of medicine and knowledge – an object to be shut away till the end of his life in the hospital at Maréville, but also one to be made known to the world of learning through a detailed analysis.

(Foucault 1978: 31–2)

For Foucault, the point of this story is that inconsequential pleasures are subjected to the workings of power; he detects in this investigation the emergence of diagnosis, analysis, measurement, classification, and specification of bodies and pleasures; through this investigation state officials and medical specialists attempt to regulate and control pleasures which are, in Foucault's opinion, relatively harmless and innocent.

Foucault sees sex as the focal point of our contemporary cultural fascination with personal identity and the self. By concentrating its gaze more and more on sex, society is able to channel into various discourses a 'regime of truth' in which pathologies and deviations may be read, interpreted, uncovered, disclosed, regulated and restricted. All of this is related to science, as the central discourse which influences many variant actions. Scientists – in the form of medical experts, psychologists, sexologists and assorted specialists – deploy knowledge in order to distinguish between norm and pathology; moreover, Foucault argues that in analysing and interpreting human behaviour science creates sex at the same time as it excavates secrets of the self. The case history, the medical report, the scientific treatise, the questionnaire: these are the means by which science establishes a position from which it discloses, and legislates upon, sex and its regimes of truth. Knowledge and power, once again, tangle and interpenetrate.

Foucault's approach to sexuality, power and the self has sometimes been caricatured by his critics – thus it is important to be clear about his argument. To begin with, it should be stressed that Foucault is not suggesting that the production of sexuality as a process of regulation and normalization is simply the result of external or societal constraint. Rather, his argument is that, while power may prohibit sex in various forms, it also serves to implicate individuals in multiple self-organizations. by inciting desires, dispositions, needs, practices, activities and transgressions. When an adult watches a talk show about marriage infidelities, for instance, he or she participates in mediated talk about sex – talk which is imbued with highly structured rules and conventions, as well as hierarchies of gender power and social prestige. Similarly, people who read self-help manuals about intimate relationships, and how to handle such relationships, are enveloped in a world of instruction as to the protocols of sexual behaviour. Individuals everywhere for Foucault are involved at a personal and emotional level with talk about sex, preoccupied with the cultivation of the self in and through sexuality.

What this amounts to saying, in short, is that individuals today willingly monitor and track down, with a view towards controlling, their sexual feelings, fantasies, inclinations, dispositions and activities. Modern culture in the West has become obsessed with sex as the truth of identity; deviations from accepted adult sexual norms must be guarded against vigilantly. Our lives are lived against a preconscious backdrop of self-policing. Foucault discerns this shift to the self-policing of sexuality in relation to the role of confession, particularly the need for self-punishment, in the psychological sciences, but also within intimate relationships and the family. In fact, Foucault tells us we have become a 'confessing society'; a society which, through confession, continually monitors, and checks against, the dangers of sex. He outlines a number of more general historical developments in this respect, but the broad thrust of his argument is as follows. The Roman Catholic confessional, Foucault contends, was a means of regulating the sexuality of its believers; the Church was the site in which subjects came to tell the truth about themselves, especially in relation to sexuality, to their priests. When seen from this angle, the confessional may be regarded as the source of the West's preoccupation with sex, particularly in terms of the sanctioned inducement to talk of it. Confession became unhooked from its broad religious framework, however, somewhere in the late eighteenth century and was transformed into a type of investigation or interrogation through the scientific study of sex and the creation of medical discourses about it. Sex became increasingly bound up with networks of knowledge and power, and in time a matter for increasing self-policing, self-regulation and self-interrogation. In other words, instead of sex being regulated by external forces, it is much more a matter of attitudinal discipline, which is in turn connected to issues of, say, knowledge and education. Psychotherapy and psychoanalysis, says Foucault, are key instances of such self-policing in the contemporary era. In therapy the individual does not so much feel coerced into confessing about sexual practices and erotic fantasies; rather the information divulged by the patient is treated as the means to freedom, the realization of a liberation from repression.

The publication of Foucault's subsequent volumes on the history of sexuality, *The Use of Pleasure* (1985) and *The Care of the Self* (1986), saw a shift in emphasis away from the modern, Christian world to the classical world, specifically ancient Greek culture. Foucault became interested in the study of Roman morality as a means of undermining the claims to universality of our contemporary system of sexuality in the West. The fundamental difference between classical and Christian sexual moralities, contends Foucault, is that while the latter seeks to regulate sexual behaviour through coercion and compulsion, the former promoted sexuality as something to be self-managed and self-mastered: sexual conduct was something to be indulged in or abstained from at appropriate times. The classical world, says Foucault, initiated a concern with 'care of the self', in which the individual attended to problems of techniques of the self, self-examination and self-stylization. Nowhere was this better demonstrated, according to Foucault, than in the exercise of restrained sexual behaviour both within marriage and in extramarital liaisons. With regard to marital relations, what distinguished the ethical husband was not the demonstration of affection towards his wife but rather the self-control with which he conducted himself in relation to sex and pleasure. 'For the husband,' wrote Foucault, 'having sexual relations only with his wife was the most elegant way of exercising control' (Foucault 1985: 151). For Foucault, the ancient Greek and classical Roman arts of existence demonstrate the intimate connection between self-control and the elegant stylization of sexual conduct: the individual self, in exercising self-restraint and moderation in relation to all sexual conduct, established ethical worthiness and moral authority.

This notion of sexual moderation also pertained to extramarital relations, and Foucault devotes considerable discussion to dissecting the aesthetic values and stylistic criteria governing homosexual conduct in classical Greek society. The Greeks, he argues, did not stigmatize the love felt for a boy by an older man. On the contrary, men were permitted to have love affairs with younger boys; nonmarital sex was not considered dangerous or unnatural in the manner in which it is viewed by Western culture, and homosexual bonds did not prevent a man from maintaining heterosexual intimacy and commitment to his wife; the love between boys and adult males was one use of pleasure among others, with different moral rules of conduct and self-stylization. Note that Foucault is not suggesting that the classical age was some golden period in the history of sexuality; for the Greeks, sexuality was at once a source of pleasure and a source of anxiety. Moreover, there were many regulations governing the nature of Greek homosexuality. Older men could engage in homosexual bonds with boys, but not with other, adult men; the relation between adult men and boys was required to be moderate in its display of sexual desire. Indeed, self-restraint and sexual abstinence, suggests Foucault, were central to the ethical regime in which the individual carried out sexual acts. Self-control, self-awareness and self-mastery in the realm of sexuality defined the ethical regime of the classical age; appropriate forms of sexual moderation shaped a way of being, of living, of a whole technology of the self.

In discussing an ethics of the self in the classical age, in which the language of pleasures and the eroticization of the body figures prominently, Foucault came very close to revealing aspects about his own private life and sexuality. In his later years, Foucault was openly homosexual. Profoundly troubled by his own sexuality as a young man, Foucault long considered French sexual culture restrictive and intolerant. It was not until the 1970s, when he travelled to lecture at universities in the United States, that Foucault encountered the affirmative sexual politics of the gay and lesbian communities. The assertion of gay identity and culture fascinated him, and he described the emergence of American gay urban areas – such as Christopher Street in New York and the Castro Street area in San Francisco – as 'laboratories of sexual experimentation'. Yet he was also ambivalent about the gay sexual liberation movement, particularly the assumption that gayness formed a common sexual identity. Time and again Foucault debunked the idea of a true self; he was scathing of what he called the 'Californian cult of the self', in which the deciphering of sexual desire is treated as revealing the essence of a true self. In contrast to those who spoke of liberating a sexual essence, Foucault argued that gayness meant the *invention* of new identities, the extension of pleasure beyond narrow sexual relations to multifarious parts of the body. Such an ethics of the self, Foucault said of gayness, could herald 'a culture which invents ways of relating, types of existence, types of exchanges between individuals that are really new and are neither the same as, nor superimposed on, existing cultural forms' (1982: 39).

Governmentality

During the final years of his life, Foucault conceptualized technologies of the self and their associated practices of coercion, constraint and domination in terms of the idea of 'governmentality'. In a lecture given at the College de France in 1978, he explained that governmentality referred to all endeavours involving 'how to govern oneself, how to be governed, how to govern others, by whom the people will accept being governed, how to become the best possible governor' (Foucault 1991: 87). Like the theme of 'care of the self', governmentality focused largely on the productive transformation of proposals, strategies and technologies for self-conduct. What subsequently emerged in social theory during the

1980s and 1990s, with the so-called school of governmentalities, was a style of critique which revolved around the socio-historical shaping, guiding and directing of the conduct of individuals. Indeed, one of Foucault's key acolytes summarizes governmentality as capturing 'the ways in which one might be urged and educated to bridle one's own passions, to control one's own instincts, to govern oneself' (Rose 1999a: 3). Like many postmodern forms of thought, the Foucaultian-inspired school of governmentalities turned out to offer a dark, oftentimes sinister, account of social processes.

Nikolas Rose, a card-carrying Foucaultian, sought to advance investigations of governmentality through a series of influential works, all of which are mostly politically pessimistic in temper. In *Governing the Soul* (1999b) and *Inventing Our Selves* (1996), Rose set out to show how the 'psy' professions (from counseling to psychotherapy), as well as medicine, education, welfare, and the social sciences and humanities, lead individuals into devoting attention to their own self-conduct, thereby implicating the self within oppressive structures that underpin society. For Rose, governmentality is the power of shaping language – seducing people to conform to what is acceptably sayable in day-to-day life. It is the power of authenticating ways of doing things, certificating modes of conduct, and thus inscribing the self in multiple modes of power. As Rose writes of the relation between the self, truth and power:

> [Expert knowledge] enables us to appreciate the role that psychology, psychiatry, and other 'psy' sciences have played within the systems of power within which human subjects have become caught up. The conceptual systems devised within the 'human' sciences, the languages of analysis and explanations that they have invented, the ways of speaking about human conduct that they constituted, have provided the means whereby human subjectivity and intersubjectivity could enter the calculations of the authorities.
>
> (Rose 1999b: 7)

For Rose, the growth of 'psy knowledges' connects directly with the government of the self and its increasing regulation. During the course of the twentieth century, in particular, the self became more and more subject to 'psychotherapies of normality' – by which he means to say that psychological knowledge became central in how people related to themselves and to others, to ways of understanding personal problems as well as in planning for the future.

Rose's work is a suggestive conjuncture of Foucaultian theory, sociology and psychology – interestingly, Rose trained as a psychologist before he moved under the influence of Foucault. His work is not, however, without its problems. Politically speaking, this is a covertly libertarian account of the self, which distrusts virtually all arenas of social activity and uncritically celebrates the 'minority politics' of resistance to the organized and systematized power of governmentality. Rose inherits Foucault's wariness of all forms of social routine, and in the process fails to consider the cognitive anchors people require to realize and maintain forms of emotional security in all cultures. At the individual level, Rose's Foucaultianism theorizes processes of personal transformation as the result of discursive forms of governmentality involving scrutiny of self and others. From this angle, the individual is not only free to construct new cultures of the self, but indeed is obliged under the force of governmentalities to do so. The difficulty with this standpoint, however, is that it provides no adequate account of human agency, since the self simply appears as the decentred effect of an analytics of governmentality. At the social level, this kind of analysis is generally too eager to overlook long-term historical trends in its excessive concentration on the 'technological' aspects of governmentality. In short, inadequate attention is given to the active, creative struggles of individuals as they engage with their own social and historical conditions. One key reply to this neglect of social and historical structures in the school of governmentalities has been the rather different doctrine of reflexivity, which – as examined in the previous chapter – displays greater attention to the sociological forms of the relation between self and the individual agent than that offered in its French-inspired counterpart.

Criticisms of Foucault

Notwithstanding its theoretical brilliance, rich historical insight and literary style, Foucault's work has been criticized from many angles. Some have argued, for example, that his early structuralist-inspired writings are too deterministic. In making this charge, critics argue that Foucault's work renders discourse and language as a one-way intrusion of power into the lives of people – such that the workings of society operate 'behind the backs' of actors. Others have claimed that the key notion of 'power–knowledge' is too general, since it fails to illuminate the complex historical factors by which social change comes about. Still others have questioned his later works on sexuality and their debunking of the myth of repression. Yet there are various aspects of Foucault's account of society that are accepted by many; in particular, there are three core insights in Foucault's writings which have profoundly influenced contemporary social theory – though each of these insights also contains various limitations of understanding. These concern (1) power; (2) discourse, and (3) sexuality.

First, 'disciplinary power' as described by Foucault is a valuable advance on traditional conceptualizations of punishment and social control. His work has made clear the degree to which disciplinary power depends not simply upon the direct supervision of individuals, but crucially upon *indirect forms of surveillance* – from information-keeping to the use of new technologies in observing individuals and groups. Indeed, Foucault's thesis of 'disciplinary power' has strongly influenced contemporary studies of crime, surveillance and punishment. Yet his approach to surveillance, and in particular to power/ knowledge or 'bio-power' as he defines it, makes for severe difficulties. It seems mistaken, for example, to treat disciplinary power as representative of power in general within modern societies. Taking Bentham's Panopticon as the epitome of disciplinary power, Foucault focuses on the structural forms through which organizations like prisons and asylums fashioned the daily routines of their inmates through the use of administrative mechanisms such as strict timetabling, continued observation and the keeping of personal records. He argued that such surveillance, and especially the technological devices that are used in ongoing observation, is fundamental not only to prisons and asylums but to the general characteristics of modern organi- zations – from schools to workplace settings. Now certainly prisons and asylums are institutions in which individuals are incarcerated against their will. Such institutions, however, have very clear differences from other mod- ern organizations, such as the school or the workplace, in which individuals spend only part of their day. While it is arguable that workplace and school settings are partly fashioned through the routine bureaucratic monitoring of individuals, it remains the case that disciplinary power is far more fractured and diffuse in such institutions than Foucault recognizes.

Part of the problem in this respect is that power moves in mysterious ways in Foucault's writings. Power in the hands of the early Foucault, as we have seen, is regarded as coextensive with the mushrooming of disciplinary discourses and codes. In this sense, Foucault as high-structuralist focuses on the language of punishment and the codes of discourse. The struc- turalism is evident in Foucault's claim that there has been a shift away from one discourse of punishment (spectacular, violent, open) to another dis- course (disciplinary, covert, monotonous). Following Saussure's structural linguistics, Foucault was interested not in what participants in such orga- nizational settings actually said or did but in the structure that both facilitated and constrained their possible discursive moves – and, even then, with the focus principally on carceral institutions. The neglect of other, less 'total' institutions – such as schools or the workplace – is striking in Foucault, and it is one from which he fails to appreciate the extent to which disciplinary power is routinely contested. Rather than the complexities of social bargaining arising as a central feature of modern organizations, Foucault's focus was, in point of fact, in how the language of discipline shapes the speech and actions of individuals. But this approach to language, as we have seen in reviewing Saussure, is one that privileges structure at the expense of individual action, placing a monolithic system over and above the ordinary activities of people. Foucault's disciplinary society denies the agency and knowledgeability of individuals; the emphasis he places on the social organization of power results in an account of human agents as passive bodies.

Arguably, this top-heavy approach to understanding the reach of power is still evident in Foucault's later writings on sexuality – undertaken long after his earlier structuralist studies of prisons and punishment. Yet the assumption that discourse determines the shape of speech and behaviour of individuals in matters pertaining to sexuality, intimacy and love is questionable. For one thing, it is surely mistaken to suppose – as Foucault does – that the historical development of public discussion about sex was uniformly or generally self-deceptive. The phenomenon of the medicalization of sexuality – the process by which physicians, sexologists, psychiatrists and scientists make sex a site of objective knowledge – is significant, and primarily (as Foucault suggests) for its regulation of human bodies, desires, pleasures, actions and social relations. These proliferating Victorian discourses concerning sexuality, however, were not as widely available to people, nor were they as commonly discussed and analysed, as Foucault contends. Medical, scientific and psychiatric journals on sex were primarily consumed by experts in the field; low levels of literacy during the late nineteenth century blocked the wider dissemination and analysis of such texts, and some have argued that even more educated groups were often denied access to this literature. The medicalization of sexuality certainly helped create a new world of knowledge and discourse, but it also functioned to *restrict* sex to expert fields of discussion – which was in turn linked to gender power, of which more shortly. Another way of putting this point is to say that Foucault assumes too readily that individuals were the passive victims of specific technologies (medical, psychotherapeutical, legal and so on) which unleashed their deadly weight through a fixed intrusion of power/knowledge into the lives of individuals.

This brings us, second, to the limitations of the notion of 'discourse'. Foucault's concentration upon discourse leads, arguably, to a neglect of the creativity of human action. In Foucault's approach to sexuality it is discourse which produces human experience rather than experience (individual dispositions, emotional desires, personal biographies) producing discourse.

The strength of Foucault's position is that he underlines the extent to which individuals, in defining themselves as sexual subjects, become fixed in relation to symbolic discourses and social prohibitions. The making of sexual identities, says Foucault, is always interwoven with a mode of social control. However, the weakness of this standpoint is that it bypasses the complexity of individual agency. Thus Foucault's work often implies a one-way movement of power over and above the individual. This is certainly true, for example, of Foucault's discussion of psychotherapy and psychoanalysis, where he develops a forced account of the links between therapy and confession. His account is forced because, unlike the religious confessional, self-knowledge is seen as inhibited by unconscious blockages in psycho-analysis. This is important for conceptualizing the self because emotional blockages are deeply intertwined with memory, desire and childhood. Frames of experience are at once structured internally, organized in terms of the psycho-sexual development of the individual and, externally, organized by the symbolic textures of society. In analysing sexuality and the self, Foucault ignores this permeability of internal and external worlds, and down-grades the individual to a mere cipher in the reproduction of the larger social world.

Finally, Foucault says little about gender, nor the intimacies of love. Sexuality is usually described by Foucault as a realm of androgynous pleasures and sensations; his views concerning sexual self-practices and self-control informed his broader political strategy of desexualization – that is, pressing beyond the repressive confines of gender polarity (male/female, masculinity/femininity, subject/object). However, while Foucault's plea for a redefinition of the body and its pleasures is important, his failure to link the embodied structure of the self to issues of gender polarity and oppres-sion is a significant problem. Certainly many feminists have argued that Foucault's failure to develop a systematic theory of gender leads in turn to significant political difficulties in relation to a feminist appropriation of his work on the self. Certainly, the world of sexuality that he writes about is, for the most part, one in which virile men undertake the exercise of defining themselves as subjects of sexuality. The troubles of sexuality are mastered by men restraining the self, performing desires, maintaining moderation and stylizing pleasures. Foucault's history of sexuality is thus very much in the masculinist tradition of *history*: it is a world *without women*. It is a world in which gender and love have few long-term social influences. The omission is startling.

The foregoing critical comments concerning the notions of power, dis-course and sexuality in Foucault's work raise, in turn, issues about the status of autonomy and freedom in social theory. The ethical techniques of the self with which Foucault was concerned in *The History of Sexuality* were those of bodily surfaces, pleasures, sensations. Yet Foucault has relatively little to say about how a new order of bodies and pleasures might produce a transformation in intimate relationships and cultural association. Because Foucault saw individualization as a form of self-imprisonment, and because he viewed the self as shot through with modern technologies of power, he steadfastly refused to consider how individuals might reflect on social practices and, in turn, transform aspects of their lives in the process. The issue of what a better society might look like thus remains unaddressed. Foucault's own answer to this gap in his work was to insist that theory cannot legislate in advance the concrete conditions of social life; to do so, as the history of Marxism shows, is only to court the dangers of political totalitarianism. Rather than prescribing what relationships should be like, Foucault regarded his work as opening a potential space for the individual to experiment with self-definition and self-regulation. Again, however, it is Foucault's failure to discuss the interpersonal, moral and ethical implications of his own studies of sexuality that limits the appeal of his call for a new order of bodies and pleasures.

Summary points

1   Structuralism, derived from the structural linguistics of Saussure, examines the linguistic rules governing objects, events and inter-actions in fields beyond language itself.
2   According to Saussure, the analysis of meaning involves the distinction between language and speech; the arbitrary character of the sign; difference; the bonding of signifier and signified in the making of signs; the division between synchrony and diachrony.
3   Saussure contends that the key to language is not in any connection between words and objects, but in the arbitrary nature of linguistic signs. It is through difference that meaning is fashioned.
4   There are many criticisms of Saussure's structural linguistics, including that this approach isolates language as a structure from the social environments of language use. This results in a defective account of the creativity of action, and is a limitation carried through in various versions of structuralist social theory.
5   In the work of Barthes, there is an application of structural linguistics to other areas of cultural analysis – from fashion and film to consumption and myths.
6   The preoccupation with the deadly weight of structures in the lives of individuals appears in various guises in structuralist social theory. In Barthes, it is a series of claims concerning the promotion by culture

of particular ideological meanings at the expense of other meanings. In Foucault's discussion of prisons and punishment, it is largely a set of historical observations about the objectification of individuals through the impacts of power/knowledge.

Further questions

1   What role do you as a member of society play in creating signs?

2   Explain the relationship between sign, signifier and signified.

3   How are speech and language different?

4   From intimacy to nationalism, how does culture work to promote particular meanings?

5   How does discourse determine identities and individual actions?

Further reading

Ferdinand de Saussure

Course in General Linguistics, edited by Wade Baskin (Peter Owen, 1960).

Claude Lévi-Strauss

The Elementary Structures of Kinship (Beacon Press, 1969).
The Raw and The Cooked: Introduction to a Science of Mythology (Jonathan Cape, 1970).

Roland Barthes

Elements of Semiology, trans. Annette Lavers and Colin Smith (Beacon Press, 1970).
Mythologies, selected and trans. Annette Lavers (Granasa, 1973).

Michel Foucault

The Order of Things: An Archaeology of the Human Sciences (Pantheon Books, 1971).

The Archaeology of Knowledge (Pantheon Books, 1972).
Discipline and Punish (Allen Lane, 1977).
The History of Sexuality, Volume 1: An Introduction (Allen Lane, 1978).

Some useful introductions to structuralism in general are John Sturrock's *Structuralism* (Fontana, 1993), Terrence Hawke's *Structuralism and Semiotics* (Routledge & Kegan Paul, 1978), and Jonathan Culler's *Structuralist Poetics* (Routledge & Kegan Paul, 1975). For an introduction to Saussure see Jonathan Culler's *Saussure* (Fontana, 1976).

On Lévi-Strauss, the best introduction remains Edmund Leach, *Claude Lévi-Strauss* (Fontana, 1970).

The standard introduction to Barthes is Jonathan Culler, *Barthes* (Fontana, 1983). See also the erudite overview provided in Rick Rylance, *Roland Barthes* (Harvester Wheatsheaf, 1994).

Some useful introductions to Foucault are Barry Smart's *Michel Foucault* (Tavistock, 1985) and Lois McNay's *Foucault: A Critical Introduction* (Polity Press, 1994). For more detailed treatments see Charles Lemert and Garth Gillan's *Michel Foucault: Social Theory and Transgression* (Columbia University Press, 1982), and Hubert Dreyfus and Paul Rabinow's *Michel Foucault: Beyond Structuralism and Hermeneutics* (University of Chicago Press, 1982).

Internet links

Structuralism

http://www.cus.cam.ac.uk/~blf10/structuralism.html

Ferdinand de Saussure

http://www.sou.edu/English/IDTC/Projects/Saussure/saussrex.htm
http://www.sou.edu/English/IDTC/People/saussure.HTM

Claude Lévi-Strauss

http://www.marxists.org/reference/subject/philosophy/works/fr/levistra.htm

Michel Foucault

http://www.lib.berkeley.edu/MRC/audiofiles.html#foucault
http://www.michel-foucault.com/

chapter 4

Post-structuralism

Contents

We left social theory at the end of the last chapter in the grip of the 'linguistic turn', refashioning concepts taken from the study of language and extending these ideas to other aspects of social activity. In the perspective of structuralism, language is form not substance. The meaning of a word such as 'tree' is not due to some intrinsic property of actual trees as vegetative things. The meaning of 'tree' arises rather because a community of speakers use agreed-upon semantic rules. Meaning is thus always a matter of difference. Words, as the reader will remember, cannot mean their objects. A 'tree' is a 'tree' because it is not 'flee' or a 'bee'. So far, one might suppose, so good. But if the utterance 'tree' is no more or less appropriate to a tree as a real thing than these other terms might be, then this would seem to suggest that the *spacing* internal to language comprises a potentially infinite mass of differences. A 'tree' is what it is because it is not 'flee' or a 'bee', and likewise 'bee' is what it is because it is not 'she' or 'he', and on and on in an endless chain of signification. Suddenly, things look more complex. If a signifier only refers us to another signifier, and if we can never arrive at an ultimate signified, what are we to make of the structuralist insistence that language forms a stable system? How are we to understand the structuralist account of meaning in terms of systemic structures? Is there not a tension between the structuralist emphasis on the differential nature of meaning on the one hand, and the presumption that as speakers or writers we have no choice but to follow patterns of meaning already established in language as a closed system?

To ask these questions is to raise doubts about structuralism as a social theory. Such questions go to the heart of the adequacy of the structuralist conceptualization of the sign as a tidy symmetrical unity of signifier and signified. In dividing the sign from the referent, Saussure and his followers accentuated strongly the arbitrary nature of the sign. To say that meaning in language is formed through the differences which exist between letters, words or sounds, it was argued in the previous chapter, was to advance a novel understanding of how signifiers transform into signifieds. But Saussure, to the extent that his analysis concentrated on the level of the signified, conceptualized this realm of signification as made up only of concepts, ideas or mental images. What remains missing in structuralist linguistics is any detailed treatment of how concepts become firmly tied to signifiers, or indeed of what it is that prevents a signified (that is, a concept or idea) from transforming back into another signifier. Think about it for a moment, as the problem is less abstract than it might first appear. If you look up the meaning of a word in a dictionary, all you find are more words, more signifiers. These words too can, in turn, be looked up. But the same issue arises. For, again, the reader is referred to yet more words, more signifiers.

All of this would seem to suggest that there is no neat or fixed distinction between signifiers and signifieds. If this is correct, however, it is necessary to question the structuralist account of language as a neat, structured system. This is to question, in effect, the prioritization accorded to signifieds over signifiers in structuralist thought. And it is precisely this conceptual move that took off in certain political circles and debates within social theory, particularly continental social thought and philosophy, during the late 1960s and which in general defined the shift from structuralism to post-structuralism.

Jacques Lacan, the French psychoanalyst who has had a major impact upon the development of social theory and whose work I shall examine in this chapter, put the argument that meaning is always somehow suspended, divided and dispersed, a displaced outcrop of the endless productivity and play of signifiers. Lacan developed his exciting method of reading psycho-analysis through the lens of structuralist doctrines, his infamous 'return to Freud', in the most philosophical and avant-garde of world cities, Paris. Although by training a psychiatrist, Lacan appropriated the ideas of various European thinkers – from Hegel and Husserl to Saussure and Lévi-Strauss – to develop a rigorous form of thought – often very abstract, sometimes seemingly unintelligible – on the psychoanalytical constitution of the human subject, specifically in terms of speech and language. In so doing, and long before his work came to the attention of a wider public, his project was to open knowledge to a world of social differences, to explore and affirm Otherness – particularly its effects upon all identities. In 1957, in a now-famous essay titled 'The Agency of the Letter in the Unconscious or Reason since Freud', Lacan reflected on the unstable terrain of language and pushed structuralist doctrines to their limit by advancing the view that meaning is never immediately present in the interlocking of signifier and signified. Lacan tells a most simple, yet powerful, story involving a girl and boy and their encounter with the established world of signs, particularly sexual meanings:

> A train arrives at a station. A little boy and a little girl, brother and sister, are seated in a compartment face to face next to the window through which the buildings along the station platform can be seen passing as the train pulls to a stop. 'Look', says the brother, 'we're at Ladies!'; 'Idiot' replies his sister, 'Can't you see we're at Gentlemen'.

Reading a sign, according to Lacan, cannot be reduced to an imagined unity between one signifier and one signified. For the doors are identical. What, then, distinguishes one toilet door from another? Nothing, says Lacan, but the signifier itself, which enters into, intrudes upon, displaces and derails the signified. The meaning of a sign is a matter of what the sign is not, and so in this instance 'Ladies' is somehow located in a chain of meaning which is traced through with terms that are absent from it, namely 'Gentlemen'. At the same time this play of signifiers enters fully into our sexual and personal lives, locking gender identity into a kind of constant flickering of presence and absence. The 'constant flickering' of signifiers is what most interests Lacan, and is what gives rise to the dispersal and division that marks our identities (sexual, private, public) for the rest of our lives.

Lacan's quite abstract psychoanalytical and philosophical doctrines struck a chord, at first, with Parisian avant-garde intellectuals and artists, and later with a wider public. In underscoring the instabilities of language and the open-ended play of signification, his structuralist-influenced reinterpretation of psychoanalysis struck a chord because, in part, it reflected the growing experiences of dislocation and fracture of many people the world over. As the structuralist 1960s gave way to the post-structuralist 1970s in France, Lacan was to emerge as a celebrity of the cultural Left. Indeed, he became widely hailed as one of the most important European intellectuals of the post-war years, in large part because of his radical insistence on identity and sexuality as decentring, which he in turn linked to a culture that was decentring. In this connection, his intellectual influence was only to be matched by the French philosopher Jacques Derrida, whose powerful blending of linguistics and post-structuralism in the form of deconstructionism will form the major thread of discussion in the second half of this chapter.

Derrida, like Lacan, is much indebted to Saussure and structuralist linguistics, but he gives a new impetus to social theory in his most exciting and brilliant method of understanding the multivocal and shifting textures of speech and language. The pure productivity of language is Derrida's theme from beginning to end. He puts the argument, which I reproduce here from a 1966 lecture delivered in the United States, that the 'absence of the transcendental signified extends the domain and the play of signification infinitely'. Not, perhaps, the easiest of philosophical statements to grasp for the beginning student. But certainly Derrida makes clear the consequences for social theory of the recognition that there is no harmonious one-to-one set of correspondences between words and objects, or as he puts it the 'absence of the transcendental signified'. The consequence Derrida specifies is, precisely, nothing less than the recognition that meaning is an outcrop of a potentially endless 'play of signification'. This tissue of social differences extends, says Derrida, 'infinitely', not only beyond the boundaries of the closed, structuralist system but infinitely. Elsewhere in the lecture, Derrida implicitly links his argument that the process of difference in language can be traced along a chain of broader cultural and political differences. 'In the absence of a center or origin,' argues Derrida, 'everything becomes discourse.'

What, exactly, is this 'absence of a center'? And how is this 'absence of a center' transformative of social relations into discourse or language? To understand the connections between Derrida's early philosophical thinking and the changed social world to which it paid close attention, it is necessary to recall that the late 1960s was a period of mass political unrest throughout many Western capitals. In 1968, student protests in the United States against the Vietnam War generated considerable public support. These student protests subsequently swept across Europe, and in Paris the student movement forged various alliances with the trade unions and working class. Major social upheaval occurred in Paris in May 1968, when millions of workers went on strike and protesters took to the streets. For a brief period, the French Fifth Republic looked gravely threatened, although in time the police and army gained the upper hand and the French political establishment, under the leadership of General Charles de Gaulle, reasserted social control.

Derrida's post-structuralist recasting of social theory – widely referred to as 'deconstruction' – was at once prefigurative of and a reaction to the widespread public discontent which was 1968. Social theory, he argued, should break from the search to identify a centre or origin of meanings. For the centre – the West, its belief systems and its philosophy – was under severe political strain, seeking to respond to, cope with and shore up widespread social protest. His method of deconstruction, as we shall see, was a means of decentring the oppressive search for a political centre, and opened up social theory to the ambiguous, conflicting meanings of social differences. Derrida's deconstruction was both a philosophical and political method for continuing the disruptive revolts of 1968 to the cultural and institutional powers of the West. In devoting his philosophical energies to deconstruction, Derrida's social theory proceeded from an unspoken alliance with those individuals and groups – students, workers, women, blacks, marginalized outsiders, former colonial subjects – questioning the political structures of Western power and the ongoing relevance of a principle of the centre. This was politics carried on under a different name, that of deconstruction or post-structuralism. Let us to consider in more detail the detailed theoretical arguments which produced this shift from structuralist to post-structuralist social theory.

Lacan: The mirror stage and imaginary

Like Saussure, Lacan was no social theorist, yet his influence over contemporary social theory has been profound. That this should be so is, at first sight, hard to figure – not only because of the dense and very difficult conceptual terminology of his work, but because Lacan's central reference point was the founder of psychoanalysis, Sigmund Freud. This was not the first time that Freud was to loom large over social theory. In Chapter 2, I described how for the Frankfurt School the insights of Freud and psychoanalysis are of fundamental relevance for social theory, particularly for grasping how individuals come to submit to unequal social relations based upon political power and domination. It is the writings of Freud himself, rather than those of his followers, which Frankfurt School theorists such as Adorno and Marcuse turned to in refashioning social theory. A similar orientation is to be found in Lacan, who returns to some of Freud's earliest theoretical speculations – particularly his work 'The Intepretation of Dreams' (1900) – in formulating a post-structuralist account of how the individual becomes 'other' to itself. By this reference to 'Othering', Lacan was to draw attention to the split and fractured nature of identity as operationalized through the repressed unconscious.

Like Adorno and Marcuse, Lacan held a negative view of post-Freudian psychoanalysis, particularly the American model of ego-psychology. He argued that ego-psychology represented a flattening of the Freudian revolution. By contrast, Lacan sought to develop a radical language for psychoanalysis, a language adequate to the strange workings of the unconscious. One might better appreciate the metaphors, puns and elliptical nature of his writings if this is borne in mind: Lacan believed that theoretical discourse must reflect the distortions of the unconscious in order to engage with both the practical and poetic textures of who we are as human beings.

When Lacan, early on in his career, formulated the outlines of his new social theory based upon a rigorous 'return to Freud', he focused on the precariousness of the ego and its imaginary lines of engagement with the world. Why? Why *imagination* as the basis upon which to question how individuals come to see themselves, and how individuals understand how other people look at them as actors in the world? Lacan's line of analysis was, in essence, premised on one basic idea: that identity involves a *fundamental division*, one which secures and sets the unconscious life of the subject in the direction of imaginary lures, snares, misrecognitions and misadventures. In perhaps his most influential paper, 'The Mirror Stage as Formative of the Function of the I' (1949), he describes a small infant contemplating its image in a mirror. Noting that from the beginnings of life the infant is physically uncoordinated, psychologically fragmented and without any defined sense of centre, he asks how it is that the small child becomes centred on the world and on itself. Elaborating upon Freud's argument that the ego is built upon self-love or narcissism, Lacan speaks of an 'imaginary' state in which a degree of unity, wholeness and centredness occurs. The infant's drafting of a distinction between itself and the outside between the ages of 6 and 18 months, says Lacan, takes place within the paradoxes and illusions of the visual field, or what he calls the 'mirror stage'. As a metaphorical and structural concept, the mirror provides the subject with relief from the experience of fragmentation by granting an illusory sense of bodily unity through its reflecting surface. Note that Lacan stresses that the image is cast within the field of optics: it is in and through a reflecting surface that the subject narcissistically invests its self-image. This contrasts radically with other conceptions of mirroring, such as the work of Cooley (1902) who speaks of a 'looking glass self' that exists in relation to the gaze of others and also the work of D.W. Winnicott (1960) who views the early interchange between self and others as crucial to the founding of a 'true' self.

> We only have to understand the mirror stage as an identification, in the full sense that analysis gives to the term: namely, the transformation that takes place in the subject when he assumes an image – whose predestination to this phase-effect is sufficiently indicated by the use, in analytic theory, of the ancient term imago.
>
> This jubilant assumption of his specular image by the child at the infant stage, still sunk in his motor incapacity and nursling dependence, would seem to exhibit in an exemplary situation the symbolic matrix in which the I is precipitated in a primordial form, before it is objectified in the dialectic of identification with the other, and before language restores to it, in the universal, its function as subject.
>
> This form would have to be called the Ideal-I, if we wished to incorporate it into our usual register, in the sense that it will also be the source of secondary identifications, which term I would place the functions of libidinal normalization. But the important point is that this form situates the agency of the ego, before its social determination, in a fictional direction, which will always remain irreducible for the individual alone, or rather, which will only rejoin the coming-into-being (le devenir) of the subject asymptotically, whatever the success of the dialectical synthesis by which he must resolve as I his discordance with his own reality.
>
> Jacques Lacan (1949) 'The mirror stage as formative of the function of the I', in *Ecrits: A Selection'* trans. A. Sheridan. New York: W. W. Norton, 1977, p. 2.

The mirror, for Lacan, is therefore not what it seems; it appears to provide a sense of psychological unity and cohesion, but what it in fact does is distort and deform the self. As Lacan proclaims, the mirror situates the self in a line of *fiction*. The self or ego is created as defensive armour to support the psyche against its otherwise terrifying experience of fragmentation and dread. The capture of the self, or what Lacan terms the 'I', by the subject's reflection in the mirror is inseparable from a fundamental

contemporary social theory

misrecognition of its own truth. In a word, the mirror *lies*. The reflecting image, because it is outside and other, leads the infant to misrecognize itself: the image yielded up by the mirror looks pleasingly unified and gratifyingly alluring, but the reality is that the mirror is just *image*. The image is not in reality the subject. Still more, Lacan believes that the 'mirror stage' is not something we ever fully pass through or get over in our personal and social lives; it is rather a 'drama' that defines a core aspect of our ongoing experience of ourselves and others in the social world. Television soaps, media advertising, pop music, Hollywood blockbusters: all the signs that circulate in contemporary society are shot through with imaginary investments and distortions. This is not a point that Lacan himself developed in any detail, but it is a line of argument taken up by some of his followers in media studies and social theory. We will consider these developments in Lacanian-inspired post-structuralist theory later in the chapter.

Lacan's reformulation of structuralism: language, symbolic order and the unconscious

Having argued that the ego is a paranoid structure, an agent of misconstruction and misrecognition, Lacan's subsequent work aimed to demonstrate that the subject is also divided through insertion into a symbolic order of speech and language. Through extensive engagement with Saussure's *Course in General Linguistics* (1916) and Lévi-Strauss' *The Elementary Structures of Kinship* (1969), Lacan derived a structuralist-influenced account of the subject in which the concepts of signifier, system, otherness and difference figure prominently. The central essays in which he elaborates this anti-humanist or structural-scientific conception of psychoanalysis are 'The Field and Function of Speech and Language in Psychoanalysis' (1953) and 'The Agency of the Letter in the Unconscious or Reason since Freud' (1957), to which we will now briefly turn.

In setting out his idea that life, both private and public, is dominated by the primacy of language, Lacan drew from and refashioned Saussure's theory of the arbitrary nature of the linguistic sign. The importance that Saussure placed upon the status of oppositions – upon not things themselves but on the relationship between words – appealed to Lacan's psychoanalytic and structuralist sensibilities. Saussure provided Lacan with the means to bridge his theoretical concerns with both symbolic production and the formal organization of desire. He argued in his seminar, following Saussure, that the linguistic sign comprises two parts: the signifier (the acoustic component or linguistic mark) and the signified (the conceptual element). In line with structuralist thought, Lacan argued that the relationship between signifiers and signifieds is arbitrary. The designation of a signifier – 'man', for example – is defined by difference, in this case by the signifier 'woman'. However, where Saussure placed the signified over the signifier, Lacan inverts the formula, putting the signified under the signifier, to which he ascribed primacy in the life of the psyche, subject and society. For Lacan, all is determined by the movement of signifiers. In fact, the position of each of us as individual subjects is determined by our place in a system of signifiers.

This brings us to the relation between language and the unconscious, a central preoccupation of Lacan. The idea that language might be a product of the unconscious was widespread among many psychoanalysts, and indeed Lacan continually affirmed in his writings and seminars that the importance he placed upon language was in keeping with the spirit of Freud's corpus. However, Lacan's structuralist elaboration of Saussure is, in fact, a radical conceptual departure from the Freudian conception of the unconscious. Whereas Freud sees connections between the psychic systems of unconscious representation (fantasy) and conscious thought (language), Lacan views subjectivity itself as constituted to its roots in language. This linguistification of the unconscious has important ramifications, making of this psychic strata not something which is internal to the subject (as with, say, a bodily heart or kidney), but rather an intersubjective space of communication, with language constantly sinking or fading into the gaps which separate signifier from signified. The unconscious, writes Lacan, represents 'the sum of the effects of the parole on a subject, at the level where the subject constitutes itself from the effects of the signifier' (Lacan quoted in Ragland-Sullivan 1986: 106). Or, in Lacan's infamous slogan: 'The unconscious is structured like a language' (1998b: 48).

If the unconscious is structured like a language, as a chain of signifiers, the apparent stability of the individual's 'mirror image' is alienated twice over. First, the individual is alienated through the mirrored deceptions of the imaginary order, in which the ego is organized into a paranoid structure; second, the person is constituted as an I in the symbolic order, an order or law indifferent to the desires and emotions of individual subjects. Language is thus the vehicle of speech for the person, but this is an *order* in which the individual is *subjected* to received social meanings, logic and differentiation. It is this conception of the function of the symbol which paves the way for Lacan's incorporation of Lévi-Strauss' structural anthropology. Drawing upon Lévi-Strauss' conception of the unconscious as a symbolic system of underlying relations which order social life, Lacan argues that the rules of matrimonial exchange are founded by a preferential order of kinship which is constitutive of the social system:

The marriage tie is governed by an order of preference whose law concerning the kinship names is, like language, imperative for the group in its forms, but unconscious in its structure. . . . The primordial Law is therefore that which in regulating marriage ties superimposes the kingdom of culture on that of a nature abandoned to the law of mating. . . . This law, then, is revealed clearly enough as identical with an order of language. For without kinship nominations, no power is capable of instituting the order of preferences and taboos that bind and weave the yarn of lineage through succeeding generations.

(Lacan 1953: 66)

This 'primordial Law' to which Lacan refers is the Freudian Oedipus complex, now rewritten in linguistic terms. What Lacan terms *nom-du-pére* (name-of-the-father) is the cornerstone of his structural revision of the Oedipus complex. For Lacan, as for Freud, the father intrudes into the imaginary, blissful union of the child/mother dyad in a symbolic capacity, as the representative of the wider cultural network and the social taboo on incest. It is, above all, the *exteriority* of this process which Lacan underlines. Broadly speaking, Lacan is not arguing that each individual father forbids the mother–infant unity. Rather he suggests the 'paternal metaphor' intrudes into the child's narcissistically structured ego to refer her or him to what is outside, to what has the force of the law – namely language.

After Lacan: Althusser and society as interpellation

Throughout his career Lacan was primarily concerned with clinical issues arising from psychoanalysis, though he did often speculate on broader philosophical and aesthetic matters. He was not much concerned, however, with the social and political applications of psychoanalysis. In order to consider the import of Lacanian psychoanalysis for social theory, we need therefore to look briefly at the writings of one of Lacan's followers, the French Marxist philosopher Louis Althusser. In several essays published during the 1960s, Althusser argued for the importance of Lacanian psychoanalytic theory for understanding how social relations are sustained through ideology. Ideology for Althusser was a concept of major importance for grasping how societal arrangements are sustained and reproduced in the daily lives of people, and especially for addressing the many forms of political domination. In order for production to be possible in any society, according to Althusser, it is necessary to reproduce the conditions of production. That is to say, reproduction depends not only on the forces of production, such as raw materials, buildings and machines, but crucially also on labour power, which in turn requires individuals with the requisite know-how and training to carry out particular roles and tasks. The central issue in social theory which Althusser seeks to illuminate thus concerns how it is that individuals come to *submit* to the rules of established society.

There are two major theses on ideology put forward in Althusser's writings. The first thesis asserts that ideology both confers a sense of coherent identity and subjects individuals to a particular social position in class society. Althusser's exploration of the ways in which ideology leads individuals to feel 'centred' in relation to society is perhaps best captured by his oft-quoted slogan, 'ideology interpellates individuals as subjects'. This notion of 'interpellation', while the topic of considerable debate in social theory throughout the 1970s, provides a theoretical underpinning for understanding the social processes through which an individual comes to experience a sense of unitary identity. As a structuralist Marxist, Althusser was particularly insistent that individuals have no essential unity, and derive whatever sense of meaning and value they have in their lives from the signs and social practices which go on around them. Ideology in this sense is less a set of well-articulated political ideas or doctrines than deeply resonant unconscious images and associations generated in everyday interaction which leads individuals to feel centred on others and the wider world. Just like the unconscious which structures it, 'ideology is eternal'. To capture this lived tissue of ideological structures, Althusser uses the term 'ideological state apparatuses', which include schools, family, the Church, legal systems, political parties, trade unions and the mass media. It is through our day-to-day involvement with such wider social structures, according to Althusser, that ideology does its work, 'hailing' or 'interpellating' the individual as a subject of society. Moreover, the consequences of such interpellations are material, as ideology itself is deeply inscribed in social practices. A terrorist, for example, is not just someone who believes in various fundamentalist doctrines, but rather situates their beliefs in relation to specific extremist practices centred on violence and acts of destruction.

The second thesis proposed by Althusser explores the ideological nature of the individual subject's lived relationship to the world and to itself, and it is here that Lacan's ideas on the imaginary are employed by Althusser to dramatic effect. Seeking to break from the dominant tendency in Marxist thought – derived from various comments in Marx's *The German Ideology* – which casts ideology as a mere 'reflection' of the institutional structures of society, Althusser argues that ideology is not a representation of reality but rather comprises the individual subject's lived relation to their conditions of existence. Borrowing from Lacan, Althusser writes of the 'duplicate mirror-structure of ideology' in which the individual's relation to society parallels the narcissistically encircled space of the imaginary. Like the small infant before a reflecting mirror, jubilantly imagining itself to possess a unitary identity that in reality it lacks, the 'subject of ideology' similarly misrecognizes itself. This misrecognition is, above all, a *self-misrecognition*.

As in the case of the luring mirror image, the ideological sphere entraps the individual *as* a subject, although the individual does not comprehend that its subjectivity is thereby produced. From routine social interaction through mass media to party politics, ideology confers an identity upon individuals that in actuality serves as a form of subjection.

To speak in a Marxist language, if it is true that the representation of the real conditions of existence of the individuals occupying the posts of agents of production, exploitation, repression, ideologization and scientific practice, does in the last analysis arise from the relations of production, and from relations driving from the relations of productions, we can say the following: all ideology represents in its necessarily imaginary distortion not the existing relations of production (and the other relations that derive from them), but above all the (imaginary) relationship of individuals to the relations of production and the relations that derive from them. What is represented in ideology is therefore not the system of real relations which govern the existence of individuals, but the imaginary relation of those individuals to the real relations in which they live.

Louis Althusser (1971) 'Ideology and Ideological State Apparatuses', in *Lenin and Philosophy and Other Essays*, trans. B. Brewster. London: NLB, p. 155.

Althusser's writings on ideology received widespread attention throughout the 1970s, but most critics now agree that there are serious flaws in his social theory. For one thing, his account assumes that individuals are serenely subjugated through ideology and just passively adapt to processes of socialization. But what is lost by Althusser, and no less by his many followers, is any sense of the politics of ideological struggle. What is lost is an understanding of the complex, contradictory ways in which people inculcate dominant forms of ideology and established ways of doing things as well as how people come to dis-identify with, and in turn contest, existing societal arrangements. This difficulty with Althusser's social theory arises in part from his interpretation of Lacanian psychoanalysis, an interpretation which focuses almost exclusively on the imaginary and the ego. But to view ideology solely in terms of the narcissistic lures of the imaginary is to ignore Lacan's emphasis on both the symbolic and real orders of psychic life, and particularly their unconscious contradictions and fissures. These are problems to which we will return when reviewing problems with Lacanian theory in the next section of this chapter. For the moment, I simply note that the tendency to present the human subject as a 'cultural dope' in Althusserian social theory was a key reason for the fading of influence of this perspective on ideology in the social sciences.

The screen as mirror: ideologies of visual pleasure

Lacan's postulation of a 'mirror stage', which provides for a novel psychoanalytic reformulation of the ego and the imaginary, has been influential not only in social and cultural theory; it has also impacted considerably upon media and film studies. The point of such Lacanian-inspired readings of cinema is less an interpretive or evaluative statement on the particular content of a film, and rather an examination of how cinematic representations position our sense of identity or construct our subjectivity. For just as the images of the latest Hollywood blockbuster may be an interesting diversion from the pressures of daily life, so the projection of 'life on the screen' structures our way of looking at the world and at ourselves in deeply unconscious ways.

Lacanian film criticism may be seen as a kind of *metacriticism* then, with cinema cast as a process of ideological production. What is studied is not the latent associations or repressed ideas of movie spectators, but rather the ideological codes and models through which cinema works. From this angle, a cinematic work may be seen as constructing what has been called a 'subject position' in which individuals are, as Jean-Louis Baudry has argued, 'chained, captured or captivated'. Baudry (1970), in a pioneering essay on the relation between Lacanian psychoanalysis and film theory, interprets the process of cinematic identification as analogous to the mirror stage. As with the imaginary, the mirror screen of cinema reflects back to spectators a consolingly unified series of images with which to identify. Baudry seems to assume that cinema grants a primacy to the narcissistic visual function, to the construction of an 'ideal self'. Yet if it is easy to spot how we might interpret films such as *Meet the Fockers* or *The Stepford Wives* in these terms, it is rather less obvious how the avant-garde cinema of Jean-Luc Godard or Wim Winders might be read as a kind of metaphor of the Lacanian imaginary order.

There are, however, other interesting ways of understanding the ideological effects of cinema upon identity with the help of Lacan's ideas. Christian Metz, while questioning Baudry's equation of cinematic identification with the imaginary order, argues that Lacanian psychoanalysis is valuable for understanding the voyeuristic nature of film. As Metz puts it: 'More than the other arts, or in a more unique way, the cinema involves us in the imaginary: it drums up all perception, but to switch it immediately over into its own absence, which is nonetheless the only signifier present' (1982: 45). Metz's reference to absence here refers to the manner in which film represses the production of its own making, the way in which it passes itself off as natural, the presentation of complex image constructions as simply the reality of day-to-day life. In this respect, the psychoanalysis of cinema is an attempt to decode the ideological images produced in film, and to trace out how these images construct the spectator subject. The construction of the subject in film, however, is not a fixed or stable affair. Instead, it is suggested that films *order and reorder* the subject in relation to cinematic images. Whether we are watching the evening news, or the fantasy exploits of *Batman*, the point is that we are always caught up within a complex process of ideological framing, linked to the implicit assumptions and ways in which reality is being shaped before our eyes.

The role of ideological framing, though ambiguous, functions in two central modes. The first is *structurally closed*. Imagine a typical Hollywood film which dramatizes its narrative through the reality of the image, recording action as the simple unfolding of what is happening. Here spectators are invited, as it were, to identify with actors in a closed imaginary space, something akin to the mirror stage. Cinema, in this sense, is fully imaginary, constructing spectators as unified, centred subjects who 'control' the image object before their eyes. Yet cinema in this structurally closed mode can only present such symbolic scenarios by bracketing off its active involvement in narrative construction. That is, film represses its own framing and selective definition of social reality. The second mode of film is *structurally reflexive*. Imagine a film, perhaps an avant-garde film, which constantly frustrates spectator subject identification; a film in which actions and events are presented always from different cinematic angles, including an incorporation of the role of the camera itself in the shooting of the narrative. Through such reflexive techniques, the spectator subject is made aware of the active role of cinema itself in ideological representation.

Žižek: beyond interpellation

Althusser's social theory, deeply influenced as it was by the thinking of Lacan, was a powerful attempt to demonstrate that social change is never the simple unfolding of economic or institutional contradictions in society. Since Althusser's appropriation of Lacan's ideas, social upheaval must necessarily be seen in terms of an *imaginary crisis* of human relationships. This may seem a self-evident truth in today's world, in which ideologies of extreme nationalism, racism, ethnic hatred and xenophobia proliferate, and yet one might easily underestimate the extent to which mainstream social theory in the English-speaking world for many years bypassed or ignored the volatility and vulnerability of cultural relations and societal arrangements. One influential figure in social theory who has emphasized the deeply unconscious dimension of social antagonisms and cultural traumas, with the implicit aid of Althusser's social theory of ideology, is the Slovenian critic Slavoj Žižek. For Žižek, as for Althusser, ideology implies an imaginary relationship to socio-symbolic forms of class, race and gender. In contrast to Althusser, however, Žižek contends that ideology always outstrips its own social and political forms; it is a realm *beyond* interpellation or internalization. Ideology, he says, is not something which just magically goes to work on individuals, assigning identities and roles in the act of producing itself. Rather, ideology should be conceived as an overdetermined field of passionate attachments. 'The function of ideology', writes Žižek, 'is not to offer us a point of escape from our reality but to offer us the social reality itself as an escape from some traumatic, real kernel' (Žižek 1989: 45).

The Lacanian thesis is, on the contrary, that there is always a hard kernel, a leftover which persists and cannot be reduced to a universal play of illusory mirroring. The difference between Lacan and 'naïve realism' is that for Lacan, the only point at which we approach this hard kernel of the Real is indeed the dream. When we awaken into reality after a dream, we usually say to ourselves, 'it was just a dream', thereby blinding ourselves to the fact that in our everyday, wakening reality we are nothing but a consciousness of this dream. It was only in the dream that we approached the fantasy-framework which determines our activity, our mode of acting in reality itself.

It is the same with the ideological dream, with the determination of ideology as a dreamlike construction hindering us from seeing the real state of things, reality as such. In vain do we break out of the ideological

According to Žižek, politics is that public field of activity that vainly tries to build upon a melancholy loss at the core of desire – those deeply entrenched, threatening passions that people find too painful to acknowledge. In this sense, ideology provides a 'lining' or 'support' to the lack or antagonism which lies at the core of the self. Ideologies of nationalism, racism or sexism are the very stuff of cultural fantasy – with the result that displaced, unconscious forms of libidinal enjoyment periodically erupt in violent waves of killing and 'ethnic cleansing'. Žižek sees the various eruptions of neo-nationalism and ethnic xenophobia across Europe during the 1990s in precisely these terms. Racism in his sense is an outer displacement of that which people cannot accept within. The projection of what he calls a 'surplus of enjoyment' onto denigrated others, the dumping of distressing and painful affect on socially dehumanized objects of antagonism, lies at the heart of the psychic dimension of political exclusion. This eruption of excess enjoyment, directed at the Other, represents an unbearable kernel of desire. Such excess is alleviated solely through its translation into an ideological symptom. Thus the collapse of Soviet totalitarianism in Eastern Europe unleashed a surplus of fantasy. It involved the projection of pain onto something perceived as strange and Other.

It is possible to criticize Žižek's radicalization of Althusser in various respects. It may be argued, for example, that if loss, lack and absence are ideological anchors for desire, their many forms and changing circumstances would seem more politically differentiated than Žižek recognizes. Žižek sees ideology in terms of a fantasy scenario, the sole purpose of which is to fill in or cover over painful elements of lack. Yet there is a problem with this view insofar as it tends to flatten out the complex, variable reception of ideological forms by individuals and groups. Žižek sees no significant difference between whether one is in the grip of identity politics, reading philosophy or classical literature, or watching a TV talk-show host such as Oprah Winfrey. These are all equally to be seen as pieces of ideological fantasy, aimed at effacing the sour taste of lack, gap and antagonism. In this respect, what is lost is the connection between self-identity, ideology and politics. For Žižek tends to pass over the complex ways in which people come to challenge political ideologies, and to treat the very worst and most sinister ideological formations on the same level as other relatively progressive formations. These problems in Žižek may to some degree be traced back to his engagement with Althusser, and in particular the project of using Lacan's ideas to develop a resolutely negative critique of culture. For the Althusserian and Lacanian linkage of the 'subject of the unconscious' to the idea of the arbitrary nature of the sign tends to give an inadequate account of how some political meanings and established ideologies predominate over others in personal and social life. This brings us back to Lacan's essential contribution to social theory, as well as a consideration of problems associated with Lacan's Freud.

Appraisal of Lacan

Lacan's 'return to Freud', as we have seen, has powerfully influenced the direction and development of social theory. Any theory as complex and difficult as Lacan's post-structuralist rewriting of Freud is, however, inevitably the source of fierce debate. Lacanianism has been enthusiastically applauded and critically attacked on a great number of grounds, and in what follows here I want to briefly consider some of the more important of these points. To begin with, Lacan's account of the imaginary constitution of the ego has served as a corrective balance against other social theories and particularly versions of orthodox social science which place the self at the centre of rational action, agency and autonomy. By contrast, Lacan emphasizes that the subject is necessarily alienated from its own history, formed in and through an interpersonal field haunted by otherness, and inserted into a symbolic network which decentres. Equally significant is that in emphasizing that the 'I' is an alienating screen or fiction, a medium of misrecognition which masks the split and fractured nature of unconscious desire, Lacan debunks certain traditional theories of meaning. For such theories, there is a presumption that mind and reality automatically fit together. But not so, says Lacan, who not only powerfully questions the view that signs can be explicated in terms of corresponding features of the social world, but raises the issue of whether meaning can ever be immediately present in speech and language. This issue applies not only to meaning but equally importantly to identity itself. For on Lacan's theory of the ego and imaginary, the subject can never be fully present to itself. The self is an illusion, a narcissistic mirage, and every attempt to represent identity is always somehow dispersed, displaced and decentred.

One criticism of Lacan sometimes heard in political circles is that his understanding of culture and social relations is too pessimistic. To say, with Lacan, that we are prisoners of lack, caught within the distortions of the imaginary, and trapped by laws of the symbolic is surely to undermine that sense of resistance and utopianism which is central to the radical political imagination. Whether this is true or not, the variety of contemporary approaches in social theory indebted to Lacan would seem to indicate that a sense of political resignation and cultural pessimism has been important to recent contestations of the established social order. From Althusser to Žižek, Lacan's pessimistic doctrines have been marshalled to assault such notions as truth, freedom, liberty and meaning. In Lacanian terms, to believe that these terms might hold some absolute value necessarily involves accepting the world as it is. By contrast, Lacanian cultural criticism is out to probe the 'naturalness' of the signs by which women and men live, and in so doing attempts to subvert dominant structures of language. Here it is not too fanciful to detect similarities between Lacanian social theory and the psychoanalytic-influenced social theory of the Frankfurt School, as discussed in Chapter 2. For like Lacan, Frankfurt School theorists such as Adorno and Marcuse drew from Freud to uncover the repressive forces at work in the construction of the self. In contrast to Lacan, however, the recovery of the repressed unconscious for these authors is also said to hold out a promise for autonomous social relations. In Lacanian and post-Lacanian social theory, however, a radically different tack is taken. Lacanian-inspired social theorists such as Althusser and Žižek do not so much evaluate society in terms of psychoanalysis, but rather explore the logic of desire (as revealed by the master, Lacan) as an index of society itself. That said, one of the less fortunate legacies of much social theory indebted to Lacan – especially those forms of social theory as represented by Althusser and Žižek – is an impoverished conception of the relation between the self, creativity and autonomy. Let us turn to consider three major limitations of Lacanian-inspired social theory.

First, there are problems with the Lacanian proposition that the imaginary dimension of self-identity is a product or construct of illusions or misrecognitions. Lacan, as we have seen, viewed the imaginary as a *distorting trap*. The mirror constitutes a narcissistic self through consoling images of unity and thus screens out the dismal truth that subjectivity is, in fact, fractured. But the argument that the 'mirror' distorts fails to specify the psychic processes which make any such misrecognition possible. For example, what is it that leads the infant to (mis)recognize itself in its mirror image? How, exactly, does the individual cash in on this conferring of self, however deformed or brittle? Surely for an individual to begin to recognize herself in the 'mirror' she must already possess a more rudimentary sense of self-organization. Cornelius Castoriadis (1997), an acclaimed European social theorist, has argued convincingly that Lacanianism fails to account for how the 'mirror', or indeed the other person as a reflecting mirror, is perceived as *real* by the individual. By contrast with Lacanian-orientated social theory, Castoriadis argues that a radical psychoanalytic approach must engage with the capacity of the self to 'gather meaning and to make of it something for him/herself'.

Second, and equally serious, is the complaint that Lacan actually suppresses the subversive implications of Freudianism by structuralizing the unconscious and reducing it to a chance play of signifiers. This criticism engages Lacan's reading of structuralist and post-structuralist theory, specifically his claim that the unconscious is coterminous with language. Many critics – including Paul Ricoeur, Jean-François Lyotard, Julia Kristeva and Jean Laplanche – have argued the Freudian point against Lacan that the unconscious is resistant to ordered syntax. These critics, in focusing on different threads of Lacan's work, rightly argue, in my view, that the unconscious *precedes* language. According to this account, the unconscious – as Freud emphasized throughout his writings – twins meaning and energy, representation and affect. The unconscious may thus intrude upon language, as in slips of the tongue or pen, and yet cannot simply be equated with it. Malcolm Bowie (1991: n.p.) has expressed this well:

> It is our lot as speaking creatures to rediscover muteness from time to time – in rapture, in pain, in physical violence, in the terror of death – and then to feel a lost power of speech flowing back. One may be ready to grant that these seeming suspensions of signifying law are themselves entirely in the gift of the signifier, yet still wish to have them marked off in some way as events of a special kind. A long gaze at the Pacific may be taciturn at one moment and loquacious the next. Language offers us now a retreat from sensuality, now a way of enhancing and manipulating it. Yet to these differences Lacan's theory maintains a principled indifference.

The unconscious, for Freud, is completely unaware of contradiction, time or closure. With Freud, we are the biographers of ourselves but not in the manner of our conscious choosing. Constructing self-identity is a project that emerges out of family, interpersonal and historical narratives, and is thus intricately interwoven with language. And yet our deeper sense of who we are is fashioned beyond the borders of language, as emotions, drives and memories are linked together in the specific ways that people develop as individuals.

To emphasize the pre-linguistic, unconscious character of the self is also to bring into view important social-theoretical considerations concerning Lacan's assimilation of the unconscious with language as a fixed structure. These considerations pertain to the agency of the individual subject. One influential interpretation of Lacan holds that, in presenting a model of desire as disembodied and pre-structured linguistically, the individual subject is effectively stripped of any significant capacity for lasting identity, emotional change or personal autonomy. This complaint is, however, more appropriately levelled at those post-structuralist thinkers who champion the 'death of the subject' instead of at Lacan. Rather than celebrating the disappearance of the human subject, Lacan posits a 'subject of the unconscious', a subject located in the *spacings of language*. Another widespread reading of Lacan is that, in conceptualizing the 'subject of the unconscious' in terms of difference and specifically oppositions that are structured linguistically, no theoretical room is given to practical agency, emotional literacy and the capacity for personal resistance to external social forces. In my view Lacanianism does indeed face a problem in this respect, casting off the most vital questions of self and identity onto an abstract theory of language.

All of this carries particular implications for the account of culture developed in post-Lacanian social theory. For one thing, Lacan's equation of language with cultural domination seriously downplays the importance of power, ideology and social inequalities in the reproduction of institutional life. For writers influenced by Lacan, individuals are transformed into subjects who act in accordance with the symbolic structure of society which is determined in advance. This is obviously a strongly deterministic interpretation of Lacan, but such a reading has powerfully shaped the contours of much contemporary social theory. Whether we turn to Lacan's subsequent explorations of the dislocating force of imaginary, symbolic and real orders, or indeed whether we simply reject Lacanianism altogether and approach the issue of selfhood from an alternative theoretical approach, this deterministic reading of Lacan's work is surely open to dispute. For while language certainly pre-exists us as individual subjects, it is surely implausible to suggest – as Lacanian-orientated social theory does – that the symbolic constitution of the human subject is singular, authoritarian and pre-structured in advance. It is crucial to emphasize here that identity is not constituted as 'self-divided' simply because of the insertion of the subject into language. The traumatic divisions and emotional fissures which people experience in today's world are replete with the conditions and consequences of asymmetrical relations of social power. To understand this requires, I argue, a theoretical framework more sensitive to the articulation of identity in relation to social context. This requires attention to the multiple forms in which identity is constituted in deeply unconscious ways, specifically in relation to globalization and multinational capitalism but also to the mass media and new information technologies. It remains the case, of course, that such constructions of the self – at once conscious and unconscious – will be filtered through modes of discourse. And yet the specific criticism here is that Lacan's work fails to consider what the cultural and political determinants of such codes might be.

Finally, these issues involve broader dilemmas relating to knowledge. The Lacanian narrative which we have traced – that the self is narcissistic, the imaginary a specular trap, the law omnipotent, and the symbolic a mask for 'lack' – risks coming undone at the level of social theory. For surely any political project concerned with enhancing freedom must be caught in the same imaginary networks of illusion as the Lacanian account of the self/society nexus? But if this is so, then perhaps the whole Lacanian framework might be deconstructed. For example, how can Lacan's discourse evade the distorting traps of the imaginary domain? Surely Lacan does not seriously believe that the only way of overcoming imaginary distortion is through comic word play, puns and irony? In failing to grasp that human subjects are capable of critical self-reflection and self-actualization, the issue of individual and collective autonomy remains repressed in Lacan's work.

Derrida: difference and deconstruction

Lacan's 'return to Freud' may well be seen as another instance of grand theory, revolving around such concepts as a universal mirror stage and the symbolic order of language, whereas Jacques Derrida is more concerned with the intricate productivity of chains of signification, as revealed in language in general and writing in particular. To do this, Derrida develops in an early trilogy of books – *Of Grammatology* (1976), *Speech and Phenomena* (1973) and *Writing and Difference* (1978) – first published in 1967 (the year just prior to the student and worker rebellions in France) the concept of *différance*, by which he means the spacing inherent in the system of differences governing discourse. This may at first sound like a continuation of Saussure's theorem that meaning in language is a product of difference, but it is in fact a radicalization of structuralism. This radicalization is to do with a fundamental stress on the never-ending process of difference which *unsettles* signification, and it is this stress which in many ways lies at the heart of the shift from structuralism to post-structuralism. For Derrida, as for Lacan, meaning is always necessarily unstable, as it is relayed through an endless chain of signifiers. Yet unlike Lacan, Derrida refuses the philosophical concept of subjectivity in general and rather proposes an ingenious critique of decentring, difference and discourse in *exclusively linguistic terms*. In various forms of social theory, particularly among feminist, queer, post-colonial and Afro-American critics, Derrida's application of linguistic models in the context of post-structuralism has powerfully influenced the explication of social and cultural phenomena. We will consider these developments in social theory later in the chapter, but first we must briefly consider Derrida's work to see how post-structuralism and linguistics are interrelated.

In discussing Derrida's key ideas, we are considering a form of criticism that has become widely known as *deconstruction*. This is a term which has suffered from various abuses in the hands of sympathizers and critics alike, and indeed Derrida often sought to distance himself from the more purely gestural uses of the term – especially in American deconstructive criticism. According to many critics of Derrida, deconstruction is notable for its belief that meaning is random, truth a fiction, and the human subject a mere metaphor. As we will see, this widespread view of Derrida as a subversive nihilist is in various respects inaccurate. Deconstruction, the philosophical method Derrida promoted, means not destroying Western philosophical ideas, but pushing them to their limits, to the point where their latent contradictions are exposed and criticism can press beyond them. To 'deconstruct' ideas then is to reconstruct and resituate meaning within broader structures and processes. Nevertheless, as Derrida argued, the deconstruction of language must necessarily have recourse to terminological innovation if it is to adequately subvert established categories of meaning. This is one significant reason why Derrida's work seems to many to be bafflingly opaque, as he deployed various stylistic ironies to question modernity and its distinctive language of a 'metaphysics of presence'. By placing 'under erasure' or drawing an erasing X through the pivotal ideals of Western culture – the primacy of speech over writing, the presumption that meaning is fully transparent or present in communication, the foundational belief in some alternate centre to social affairs – Derrida unearths the endless process of transformation which underlies all signification.

Derrida may be said to have fashioned a whole new style of philosophical writing, and this is nowhere more evident than in his deployment of the neologism 'différance'. In French, the words *différence* and *différance* sound the same when spoken, but the 'a' in Derrida's idiosyncratic concept cannot be heard. In this distancing from established categories of language through deliberate misspelling, 'différance' – as Derrida uses the term at any rate – refers to 'the act of deferring'. This is quite a complicated point and I shall to return to it in a moment, but here it is important to note that 'différance' indicates that you will never arrive at a final signified of social differences which is not in itself *deferred*. In emphasizing the 'différance of difference', Derrida at once continues and transgresses the tradition of Saussurian linguistics. Meaning, for Derrida as for Saussure, is created by the play of difference in the process of signification. For Derrida as against Saussure, however, signification is always deferred through potentially endless tissues of difference; our communications with ourselves and others can never reach an ultimate destination point or scoop up the idea or object they represent.

Nothing – no present and in-*different* being – thus precedes *différance* and spacing. There is no subject who is agent, author, and master of *différance*, who eventually and empirically would be overtaken by *différance*. Subjectivity – like objectivity – is an effect of *différance*. This is why the *a* of *différance* also recalls that spacing is temporization, the detour and postponement by means of which intuition, perception, consummation – in a word, the relationship to the present, the reference to a present reality, to a being – are always *deferred*. Deferred by virtue of the very principle of difference which holds that an element functions and signifies, takes on or conveys meaning, only by referring to another past or future element in an economy of traces. This economic aspect of *différance*, which brings into play a certain not conscious calculation in a field of forces, is inseparable from the more narrowly semiotic aspect of *différance*. It confirms that the subject, and first of all the conscious and speaking subject, depends upon the system of differences and the movement of *différance*, that the subject is not present, nor above all present to itself before *différance*, that the subject is constituted only in being divided from itself, in becoming space, in temporizing, in deferral.

Jacques Derrida (1981 [1972]) *Positions*, trans. Alan Bass. Chicago, IL: University of Chicago Press, pp. 28–9.

In fashioning the term 'différance', which he says is 'literally neither a word nor a concept', Derrida underscores that thought itself necessarily turns slowly (Derrida 1982: 3, 7). Language is not a transparent medium, but an opaque domain of traces or inscriptions whose content and rhetoric must be questioned (to be put, as Derrida says, 'under erasure') and thus resituated in a new register. Here we return to the spatial and temporal dimensions of Derrida's social theory. I say *social theory* because it is Derrida's emphasis on the displaced, deferred aspects of signification which has prized open conventional understandings of the relation between society, culture and history. One of the ways, according to Derrida, that social differences are ignored or repressed is through the act of delay. To differ for Derrida is to defer. Think about it. The present moment, once grasped, has passed. When I hear someone speaking or when I read a sentence, the meaning of what is conveyed is always somehow suspended. Each marking or inscription is shaken up, as it were, by the trace of other signifiers – again and again without end. 'Différance', writes Derrida, 'is thus a structure and a movement which can only be grasped in relation to the opposition of

contemporary social theory

present/absent. Différance is the systematic play of differences, or traces of differences, of the *spacing* whereby elements are connected to one-another' (Derrida cited in Giddens 1979: 31).

One way in which we might pursue Derrida's ideas on the repressed logic of différance in the structuring of a centre of meaning in more concrete terms is by reconsidering aspects of self-experience and identity. I might, for example, persuade myself that – as the author of this book – I am fully in control of the arguments developed and meanings conveyed, that I am as it were at the centre of arranging, explaining and explicating the social theories reviewed in these pages. In some obvious ways, much of this is of course the case; yet there are other powerful forces, at once intra-linguistic and extra-linguistic that function to decentre my authorship. For one thing, since meaning is an endless play of signifiers, it is an illusion for me to believe that I can ever completely get to the nub of Derrida's thinking about deconstruction. Sure, I might use various modish deconstructive terms – différance, logocentrism, trace – and yet, on Derrida's account at any rate, these words are themselves always somehow differentiated – dispersed, divided, displaced. The endless circularity of the process of différance is thus reproduced and destabilized by the constant transformations of signification itself. Still more, another thing that decentres my authorship of this book is that I am not at the centre of my own subjectivity. For Derrida as for Lacan, the conscious self is always decentred in relation to the unconscious. In Derrida, this is less an appeal to some pre-linguistic substratum of the subject than a critical focus on the binary oppositions that situate identity, subjectivity, authorship. Thus the oppositions of self–other, conscious–unconscious and identity–difference are at the core of how discursive practices structure our whole system of thought and experience of ourselves.

Another concrete way of grasping Derrida's argument that meaning is always dispersed, displaced and deferred is by considering the political oppositions of centre and periphery in the history of Western colonialism. The West in various political incarnations – the British, the French, the Dutch, among others – has historically represented itself as the centre of world order. Imperial designs have thus been fashioned through the construction of linguistic, social and political hierarchies – of a centre of civilization, culture and reason on the one hand, and a periphery of bar-barism, philistinism and unreason on the other. Constructions of social and political identities have likewise occurred within the organizing linguistic frames of nation, state, race, ethnicity and gender, all of which have served to reinforce an ideology of the West versus the rest. Yet such political hierar-chical oppositions are far from being fully secure, as the slow decline of the American imperium in our own times graphically indicates. Deconstruction in such a political context aims to displace political hierarchy, not only by examining how the West depends on its Others to constitute itself as centre, but by tracing the ongoing, deferred significations through which the West as centre is decentred by political peripheries.

Rereading psychoanalysis: Derrida's critique of Lacan

Derrida's post-structuralist social theory uses language to call attention to meanings, and in particular sees the process of naming as central to what is named in any classificatory system. The theory or edifice of psycho-analysis in this sense is no different to any other classificatory system from the standpoint of deconstruction, and in fact Derrida engaged at various points throughout his career with the writings of Freud and Lacan – most notably in his book *Resistances to Psychoanalysis* (1998).

Difference, says Derrida, is always a moment of deferral, a delay in which internal contradictions and conflicts impede the search for the identity of an individual or group, derail the full realization of a structure or centre, and displace the final moment in which ideals and illusions might be confronted. Developing a series of close readings of psychoanalytic theory in *Resistances of Psychoanalysis*, Derrida deconstructs Lacan's texts and teachings within the broader frame of post-structural linguistics. He questions, in effect, what people think they might know about Lacanian psychoanalysis by pointing to the complex structures of this body of theory and practice – all of which is only available to us as seminars, tape-recorded archives, texts, transcripts, quotations and slogans. Against this backcloth, Derrida argues that it is impossible to speak of 'Lacan in general – who does not exist'. In developing this viewpoint, Derrida insists on the power of resistance. There is an unavoidable ambiguity, he says, between Lacanian theory and that to which it lays claim – the thought of Lacan. But if resistance is understood as structural limit, not in the psychological but rather rhetorical sense, where exactly does this leave psychoanalysis?

Returning to classical psychoanalytical theory, Derrida finds 'resistance' at the heart of Freud's ideas, including the unconscious, repression and the Oedipus complex. He understands resistance not in the psychoanalytic sense of repression of defence, but rather in terms of a linguistic distortion or failure, of something that resists the identity of author and meaning. In a kind of lifting of psychoanalysis to the second power, Derrida con-tends that resistance arises from the structure of psychoanalysis itself. In short, Freud's dream machine is, for Derrida, continually on the brink of bringing itself undone.

Derrida contends that psychoanalysis is itself inscribed in an infinite tissue of differences. Freud's legacy is best approached as a product of numerous texts, histories, institutions and processes of inscription. There is no such thing as psychoanalysis in general, only various theorists, concepts, quotations, teachings, schools and factions, all of which exist as socially structured differences. This seems to me to be an interesting and useful angle on the place of psychoanalysis as a discourse and practice within our culture. The scope of psychoanalytic theory is extremely wide today, ranging from classical to postmodern approaches in therapeutic settings, and with an equally broad range of theory (object relational, clinician post-Lacanian) that circulate within the social sciences and the humanities.

However, there are limitations to Derrida's critique of Lacan as well as his deconstructionist recycling of Freud. To say of a particular school of psychoanalysis that its structure arises in and through 'difference' is interesting only up to a point. Why, for example, did Lacanian theory fail for so many years to establish its legitimacy in Anglo-American psychoanalysis? Why, for example, is Slavoj Žižek's reading of Lacan so popular in the academy at the current time, and why is it preferred over Derrida's Freud? Derrida is unable to satisfactorily address these issues, I believe, since they require an in-depth examination of the political context in which psychoanalytic theory operates. Derrida himself has hardly been noted for his political and institutional as opposed to his linguistic and discursive critiques.

Appraisal of Derrida

Derrida's writings in particular and deconstruction in general, it is often suggested, have provided a vital stimulus to social theory. Given the experimental, enigmatic qualities of post-structuralist criticism, it is perhaps not surprising that some have viewed this stimulus in a negative light. Very often, though, assessments of Derrida in social theory have been positive. Derrida's debunking of totality and transparency, of uniform linguistic patterns and absolute truth claims, and of grand organizing principles and final solutions has powerfully influenced many if not all post-structuralist sociologies and versions of postmodernist social science. The radical credential of this deconstructive assault on official or mainstream thought is said by its advocates to stem from attention to the multifarious ways in which language invades meanings, values and all 'naturalized', ideological forms of experience. The result of this philosophical appreciation of difference has been a new kind of social critique, one in which language is understood to exist on its own terms, self-generative and self-validating in equal measure. Derrida was one of the first French theorists in the aftermath of the political explosion of May 1968 to grasp the extent to which culture and politics revolves around the violent suppression of difference, the paranoid insistence of exclusive linguistic oppositions: inside/outside, truth/falsity, reality/illusion, good/evil. His deconstructive style, which in a dramatic performative sense enacted the post-structuralist fascination with undecidability, was thus an attempt to give free reign to the ambiguous, open-ended play of signification.

This aesthetics of language, however, is also for many enthusiasts of Derrida's work a *politics of discourse* – and it is here that deconstruction is of most direct relevance to social theory. Insofar as Derrida demonstrates that meaning is indeterminate and that language is unstable and ambiguous, he may be seen to be speaking up for the dispossessed, the marginal and the voiceless. To the extent that deconstruction is a critical technique opposed to linguistic, social and political closure, it is an attempt to recover – to put back into words – excluded narratives and alternative histories which have been repressed. In more sociological terms, Derrida has provided social theorists with a richly textured battery of terms (différance, trace, inscription) for rethinking action in a dynamically open field of social differences. The application of deconstructive techniques to social theory in this way has been successfully deployed to reconstruct and resituate the narratives of people – oppressed women, blacks, gays and subalterns of various kinds – excluded by mainstream political hierarchies and institutional frameworks.

Post-structuralism and post-colonial theory: Bhabha's *The Location of Culture*

Post-structuralism, especially the deconstructive theory advanced by Derrida, has exerted considerable influence over the development of post-colonial analyses of identity, culture, race, gender and the broader struggles of the Third World against the oppressions of our modern age. Harvard University's Homi Bhabha is one of the most influential post-colonial theoreticians of diasporic culture and multiculturalism, and has sought to deconstruct various narratives of nationality that serve to naturalize Third World countries as subordinate to the West.

To do this, Bhabha draws extensively from psychoanalysis – in particular Lacan, but also the post-Lacanian theories of Julia Kristeva (examined in Chapter 7). But it is Jacques Derrida who perhaps most influences his thinking. In *The Location of Culture* (1994), Bhabha argues that racism is never fixed or frozen; race is a 'liminal' category, always in process, shifting, transformational. For Bhabha, colonial identities (for example, the British in India or Africa) are always defined in relation to a marginalized, excluded Other – the colonized or colonial territories. Colonial identity thus both draws upon and represses the black Other; indeed, denigration and denial of the Other is fundamental to the imagined survival of the colonizer. Repression may well be essential to the West's existence, but Bhabha contends that psychic exclusion of the excluded Other never fully succeeds. The repressed unconscious returns to derail Western orderings of power, and this for Bhabha is nowhere more evident than in colonial strategies of 'hybridization' and 'mimicry'. The attempt to imitate, copy or blend racialized identities must necessarily come unstuck according to Bhabha, because colonized subjects are in fact different from those who advance the strategies of colonial power. Against this backdrop, Bhabha situates racial stereotyping in relation to the psychoanalytic notion of repetition. The repetition of racial insults, for example, indicates that the relation between colonizer and colonized is radically ambivalent. The racial slur or denigration is always for Bhabha in danger of coming unstuck, and this is one reason why social actors must work overtime in the making and remaking of relations of domination and submission. This 'ambivalence of colonial rule' enables a capacity for resistance throughout colonized cultures; through performative 'mimicry' of the colonizer, the colonized are able to preserve some hidden or pure aspect of themselves under the sign of an authorized identity. Discussing writers such as Nadine Gordimer and Toni Morrison, Bhabha hunts the 'location of culture' in the marginal, displaced, haunting spaces between Western Enlightenment values and its excluded others.

Bhabha, a product of Elphinstone College, Bombay and Oxford University, has sometimes been rebuked by his critics for preaching the rights of native peoples, migrational groups and marginal cultures from the lofty heights of European post-structuralism. Whatever one makes of this charge of elitism and elitist language, there can be little doubt, in my view, that Bhabha has powerfully engaged psychoanalysis with the rapidly changing social and demographic movements unleashed by the forces of globalization. Moreover, following in the footsteps of Fanon, Bhabha has fashioned a very particular politically informed psychoanalytic critique of post-colonialism, one that deploys concepts of hybridity, liminality and mimicry to challenge neo-colonial forms of political power over the colonized Third World and to deconstruct imaginary constructions of national and cultural identity. He forcefully argues against the colonial tendency to essentialize Third World cultures as homogeneous, the bearers of historically continuous traditions; rather, he suggests that relations between First World metropolitan and Third world cultures are constantly changing and evolving, involving creative hybrid interactions of various cultural identities. The theme of equal respect for cultures has emerged in his more recent writings, drawn in part from Derrida's speculations on the centrality of hospitality to justice and freedom.

Notwithstanding the significant impact of deconstruction upon social theory in particular and the social sciences in general, however, there are a number of critical objections that have been made against Derrida's work. Derrida's account of différance and the deconstructive technique of close reading that this entails, according to some critics, leads social theory to ignore the social and cultural context in which dialogue and debate take place. The criticism is that deconstruction produces a retreat into linguistic codes. In this sense, a major limitation is that Derrida's approach inherits and compounds Saussure's failure to explicate the *social dimensions* of language and of the arbitrary sign. This is an issue of considerable importance to sociological post-structuralism, as compared with, say, post-structuralist literary criticism, because it concerns those hidden or underlying political variables that shape and structure the ways in which speakers deploy language in specific social situations. Critics have argued, for example, that while deconstruction supposedly excavates processes of signification as productivity, Derrida's work tends to dismiss the issue of reference altogether and instead concentrates on the play of pure differences, of codes themselves. But does not the internal identity of codes, separated by Derrida from any connotation of reference, actually derive from the social and political context in which it is embedded? What shapes the 'identity' of codes if not the social context or the semantic aspects of forms of life in which such codes are expressed?

Related to the foregoing complaint is the charge that Derrida rewrites everything social as linguistic or discursive. This is problematic, some argue, because it reveals deconstruction as elitist. The strong version of this criticism is that deconstruction is little more than a trivial play on words, a kind of embroidered academicism. For such critics, the playful self-irony of deconstruction is itself apolitical. A disengagement with the world of structured social differences is not in my view necessarily implied by Derrida's social theory, although it is the case that deconstruction has been interpreted too crudely at times, especially in the United States. The more moderate version of this critique questions the fruitfulness of approaching social practices as exclusively linguistic. This critique draws attention to the pre-discursive, the non-linguistic, of what cannot be said in language – and powerfully questions whether such fundamental aspects of social life are really best captured through an exclusively linguistic notion of social differences.

Summary points

1   Post-structuralist social theory represents not so much a break with structuralism as a radical extension of its key ideas – especially concerning the notions of difference and the arbitrary nature of the sign.
2   In structuralism, language was treated as a reliable measure for the analysis of other signifying systems. In post-structuralism, the structuralist account of language as a structured system is powerfully critiqued.
3   Post-structuralist social theory questions the structuralist prioritization accorded to signified over signifiers in the constitution of meaning. In Lacan, this is part of an attempt to link the insights of Saussure and Freud, giving priority to the signifier over the signified. In Derrida, it is part of a reversal of the priority usually given to speaking over writing; writing for Derrida is the best illustration of difference.
4   In Lacan's post-structuralist reading of Freud, the individual subject emerges as radically split between the narcissistic illusions of the ego and the repressed desires of the unconscious. This further involves a series of claims that the unconscious exemplifies certain features of language as a systemtic structure.
5   In Derrida's critique of the Saussurian version of difference, a temporal element is introduced into the critique of meaning: to differ is to defer.
6   There have been many criticisms made of post-structuralist social theory, including that it represents a further 'retreat into the code' initiated by Saussure's structural linguistics. This is problematic for social theorists, since post-structuralism – notwithstanding its radical insights into cultural difference and decentred identities – has generally failed to generate an adequate account of reference, that is, the *reality* of social things.

Further questions

1 What is problematic for identity about the image a mirror reflects back?

2 Is Lacan's mirror stage helpful for a critique of contemporary popular culture – pop music, television soaps, the Internet?

3 Can words ever adequately represent your desires?

4 Fundamentalist ideologies – racism, nationalism, xenophobia – are all-embracing and all-consuming. For people in the grip of such ideologies, what are they seeking to escape?

5 According to Derrida, the deferral and spacing of language is essential to the generation of meaning. But beyond language, what role might social context play?

6 Thinking of current examples, how do you see the politics of difference at play in the recovery of excluded narratives and histories of individuals and groups?

Further reading

Jacques Lacan

Ecrits: A Selection (Tavistock Press, 1977).
The Four Fundamental Concepts of Psychoanalysis (Penguin, 1979).
The Seminar of Jacques Lacan, Vol. 1: Freud's Paper on Technique 1953–54 (Cambridge University Press, 1988).
The Seminar of Jacques Lacan, Vol. 2: The Ego in Freud's Theory and in the Technique of Psychoanalysis 1954–5 (Cambridge University Press, 1998).
The Ethics of Psychoanalysis 1959–60: The Seminar of Jacques Lacan (Routledge, 1992).

Jacques Derrida

Of Grammatology (Johns Hopkins University Press, 1976).
Writings and Difference (Routledge, 1978).
Dissemination (Athlone Press, 1981).
Margins of Philosophy (Harvester-Wheatsheaf, 1982).
Resistances of Psychoanalysis (Stanford University Press, 1988).

Some useful introductions to Lacan are Shonana Felman's *Jacques Lacan and the Adventures of Insight: Psychoanalysis in Contemporary Culture* (Harvard University Press, 1987), David Macey's *Lacan in Context* (Verso, 1989), Elizabeth Grosz's *Jacques Lacan: A Feminist Introduction* (Routledge, 1990), and Shaun Homer's *Jacques Lacan* (Routledge, 2005). An excellent biography of Lacan is Elizabeth Roudinesco's *Jacques Lacan* (Polity Press, 1997). In addition, for an interesting discussion of the relationship between Lacan and Derrida see John Forrester's *The Seductions of Psychoanalysis: On Freud, Lacan and Derrida* (Cambridge University Press, 1990).

Some useful introductions to Derrida and deconstruction are Christopher Johnson's *System and Writing in the Philosophy of Jacques Derrida* (Cambridge University Press, 1993), Marian Hobson's *Jacques Derrida: Opening Lines* (Routledge, 1998), and Christina Howells' *Derrida: Deconstruction from Phenomenology to Ethics* (Polity Press, 1998). Other useful commentaries include Jonathan Culler's *On Deconstruction: Theory and Criticism after Structuralism* (Routledge & Kegan Paul, 1983), John M. Ellis' *Deconstruction* (Princeton University Press, 1989), and Simon Critchley's *The Ethics of Deconstruction* (Blackwell, 1992).

Internet links

Jacques Lacan

http://www.textetc.com/theory/lacan.html
http://www.colorado.edu/English/courses/ENGL2012Klages/lacan.html

Louis Althusser

http://www.marxists.org/reference/archive/althusser/index.htm

Slavoj Žižek

http://www.lacan.com/zizekchro1.htm

Jacques Derrida

http://prelectur.stanford.edu/lecturers/derrida/index.html

chapter 5

Theories of Structuration

Contents

In the dreamy routines of daily life, we seldom think of ourselves as accomplished individuals using various skills to negotiate the social things about us. We seldom think of ourselves in this way partly because most of us, most of the time, adopt a 'natural attitude' to the world and to others around us, and partly because daily life does indeed exhibit various dream-like qualities. To say that daily life is oftentimes dreamy is to say that much of what we do, as well as why we do what we do, is *mysterious*. One of the mysteries of our daily or habitual behaviours is that our skills or accomplishments seem to be governed by forces out of the immediate reach of consciousness. Perhaps nowhere is this dreamy not-quite-consciousness of everyday life better dramatized than in the routines we all follow first thing in the morning, after raising from our dream-filled slumbers.

Like every household throughout cities of the West, my own family has developed its own internal rhythms – a richly crafted tapestry of routines – which comprise our morning happenings. If it is a weekday, I rise to skim the morning newspapers, check my email, get ready for work at university, and otherwise attend to helping my children prepare for the day ahead at school. If my own morning routine has a degree of unremarkable consistency to it, this is easily countered by the intricate routines followed by my young children. My eldest daughter, who is in the early years of primary school, starts the day gently – requiring much encouragement to get out of bed. Breakfast is her favourite meal of the day, and she prefers to take her time, sampling from a range of breakfast cereals and other foods. My 5-year-old son, by contrast, tends to scoff his breakfast – in order to get on with the demanding ritual of staging dinosaur battles. Meanwhile, my youngest daughter at only 6 months enjoys the attentions of her mother for an hour or so and then her routine dictates that she returns to bed for further sleep.

Routines of this kind are, as I say, unremarkable and yet run deep throughout society. Routines are very often considered by people as merely private – expressive of only individual preference. Routines are surely this – a central part of our private make-up as individuals – but they are also something else. From a sociological perspective, routines might be regarded as the 'social glue' that holds together the regular flow of daily life. How routines become established over time and well sedimented in daily life has long attracted the attention of social theorists. From this angle, if routine emerges as a sociological concept and not simply a psychological dispo-sition, this is because the term is fundamental to the question of the relation between the individual and society, selfhood and culture. Social theorists are thus preoccupied, among other things, with the issue of how the mundane routines of our daily life affect, and are affected by, the organization of whole societies.

Recent social theory has moved to centre stage the question of how our daily routines, habits and competencies serve to shape our social worlds. This chapter introduces the work of two famous social theorists – England's Anthony Giddens and France's Pierre Bourdieu.

Anthony Giddens: structuration and the practical routines of social life

In helping us to think about the various ways in which practical life and social relations interweave, social theorists have focused attention on the knowledge and competency that individuals routinely display in negotiating the broader social structures around them. Very broadly speaking, there have been two major approaches to explaining the relationship between the individual and society (see Chapter 1 for a more detailed discussion of these approaches). In what we might call society-dominated accounts, a view is advanced that common culture, socialization and general social structure generate individual practices. The core idea is that individuals serve as 'supports' for, or 'bearers' of, bigger social processes. This society-dominated theory has been given various colourings and inflections, ranging as we have seen from certain emphases of the Frankfurt School to versions of structuralism and post-structuralism. By contrast, in what one might call individual-dominated accounts, it is individuals who are treated as the source of broader social relations. The general idea is that people – through their personal strivings, cultural creativity or competition with others around them – are the source of actions that produce wider social patterns and cultural relations. How individual action generates collective social habits has also been the topic of many different conceptual articulations, from psychoanalysis to some strands of feminism.

Thinking about the relation between people and social things thus sharply divides in social theory, revolving on either the systemic force of impersonal structures or the individualistic capacities of people. By contrast to each of these approaches, Anthony Giddens is more concerned to grasp how individual action is structured within the mundane practices of social life, while simultaneously recognizing that the structural and organizational features of contemporary societies are reproduced by individual action. This way of phrasing things may at first appear simply academic, but Giddens insists it is a fundamental advance for social theory to break from the individual/society dualism. For to continue to define the relation between the individual and society in strictly oppositional terms is to misunderstand what goes on within the intricacies of practical social life. To approach the issue differently, therefore, Giddens develops in his book *The Constitution of Society* (1984) the concept of *structuration*, by which he means to account for the production of habitual practices as simultaneously the force of systemic structures and the individual accomplishments of agents. The starting point of his analysis is not society as fixed and given, but rather the active flow of social life.

Giddens' work is, in one sense, very much inspired by the *linguistic turn* in social theory. We have seen in previous chapters how, beginning with

Saussurian linguistics, social theory becomes increasingly preoccupied during the twentieth century with language – especially in the traditions of structuralism and post-structuralism. Like various structuralists, Giddens' argument is that we fashion ourselves as individuals and societies in and through language. Society, according to this view, is therefore clearly 'structured' in some sense or other by language. Yet Giddens is also very critical of structuralism and post-structuralism. He rejects, for instance, the structuralist argument that 'society is like a language'; his reasons for holding to this view will be examined in some detail later in the chapter. The point to note at the outset is that, in contrast to the structuralist standpoint, Giddens contends that social action is similar to language primarily in the sense that it is 'rule-following'. As we go about our daily activities – thinking and talking about our worlds and, thus, in some sense helping to make and remake these very worlds – we use all sorts of 'rules' to do so. These rules are sometimes explicit or formal, as when someone driving a car follows traffic rules and stops at a red light. More often than not, however, the 'rules' we draw from to do the myriad things we do in social life derive from *common sense* – the 'taken-for-granted' knowledge of a society. But the crucial point for Giddens, as we will see, is that while social action is rule-governed it is not preset by such rules. There are many ways of following and applying rules to social situations – many of which are appropriate, some less so. When Giddens talks of social practices as 'rule-governed', then, he means to emphasize the creativity of human action – the capacity of actors to apply rules in transformative, perhaps even novel, ways. Rules at once serve to shape social doing and action and also contain the possibility of acting otherwise.

Action, according to Giddens, cannot be adequately sociologically understood by looking at the discrete 'acts' of individuals. Rather than dissolve action into individual particles – intentions, motivations, reasons – Giddens contends that human action is a *continuous flow*. Whereas acts are discrete segments of individual doing, action refers to the ongoing flow of social practices, as people monitor or reflect on the social world of which they are part. On a general plane, Giddens advances a 'stratification model' of the human subject comprising three levels of knowledge or motivation: *discursive consciousness*, *practical consciousness*, and the *unconscious*. He explains this stratification model of agency in *The Constitution of Society* as follows:

> Human agents or actors – I use these terms interchangeably – have, as an inherent aspect of what they do, the capacity to understand what they do while they do it. The reflexive capacities of the human actor are characteristically involved in a continuous manner with the flow of day-to-day conduct in the contexts of social activity. But reflexivity operates

only partly on a discursive level. What agents know about what they do, and why they do it – their knowledgeability *as* agents – is largely carried in practical consciousness. Practical consciousness consists of all the things which actors know tacitly about how to 'go on' in the contexts of social life without being able to give them direct discursive expression. The significance of practical consciousness is a leading theme of the book, and it has to be distinguished from both consciousness (discursive consciousness) and the unconscious.

(1984: xxii–xxiii)

Discursive consciousness thus refers to what agents are able to say, both to themselves and to others, about their own action; as Giddens repeatedly emphasizes, agents are knowledgeable about what they are doing, and this awareness often has a highly discursive component. *Practical consciousness* also refers to what actors know about their own actions, beliefs and motivations, but it is practical in the sense that it cannot be expressed discursively; what cannot be put into words, Giddens says following Wittgenstein, is what has to be done. Human beings know about their activities and the world in a sense that cannot be readily articulated; such practical stocks of knowledge are central, according to Giddens, to the project of social scientific research. Finally, the *unconscious*, says Giddens, is also a crucial feature of human motivation, and is differentiated from discursive and practical consciousness by the barrier of repression.

Giddens, as I have already mentioned, repeatedly emphasizes 'what people know' is important – both to social action itself and to social analysis. This underscoring of individuals as knowledgeable agents refers, in the broadest sense, to the capacity of people to explain – both to themselves and to others – why they act as they do. Discursive consciousness is the ability of people to *put things into words* – articulation of the reasons for social action. But Giddens also recognizes the limits of language: *talk* takes us so far, but it is not all. Much of what people know about the social world, and of their reasons for acting in the ways that they do, cannot be articulated. To refer to some part of our human capacities as 'preconscious' or 'practical consciousness' is simply to say that there are some things we cannot put into words. Much of human conduct, in other words, is practically guided or steered.

Practical social life, especially the rules we follow (whether we know it or not) as we go about our everyday activities, might thus be recast as the terrain of *mysterious accomplishments*. Consider, for example, the morning routine of which I wrote at the beginning of this chapter. Accessing email in the morning seems a relatively straightforward affair, provided all is fine with my computer. However, if asked to recite the technical specifications of the computer or explain how I am able to retrieve email from the network,

I would very quickly exhaust my working knowledge of the topic. That is to say, I can operate the computer program to a certain level of skilled accomplishment, but have next to no idea of how to explain the technical aspects of electronic communication. The same holds true, for that matter, of language – in this case, the talk I engage in with my children and wife as we conduct our morning routine. While we are engaged easily in talking, I would still be hard pressed to explain the finer rules of grammar which govern our linguistic exchanges in the morning. Of course, if I were a professional linguist and not a sociologist, I would presumably be able to detail more about the grammatical rules governing our conversation. But even then that is a matter of degree and not kind, and the point is that our conscious understandings of the world around us continually fluctuate between discursive articulations and practical accomplishments.

But what of social structure? What of social power, political authority, common culture? The first thing to emphasize about Giddens' social theory, in this respect, is that 'social structure' is not something that exists externally. Society is certainly 'structured' or 'textured' for Giddens, but not as a result of the intrusion of 'out there' social forces such as capitalism or bureaucracy into the inner realms of our lives. Rejecting the sharp division between the individual and society in social theory, Giddens instead argues that social structure, or 'society', is a constant product of our social activities – of our talk, our practices, our doings. Such a conception of social structure contrasts powerfully with more mainstream sociological accounts. Sociologists have tended to conceptualize structure in terms of institutional constraint, often in a quasi-hydraulical or mechanical fashion, such that structure is likened to the biological workings of the body or the girders of a building. Giddens strongly rejects functionalist, biological and empiricist analyses of structure. Following the 'linguistic turn' in twentieth-century social theory, Giddens critically draws upon structuralist and post-structuralist theory, specifically the relationship posited between language and speech in linguistics. He does this, not because society is structured like a language (as structuralists have argued), but because he believes that language can be taken as exemplifying core aspects of social life. Language, according to Giddens, has a virtual existence; it 'exists' outside of time and space, and is only present in its instantiations as speech or writing. By contrast, speech presupposes a subject and exists in time/space intersections. In Giddens' reading of structural linguistics, the subject draws from the rules of language in order to produce a phrase or sentence, and in so doing contributes to the reproduction of that language as a whole. Giddens draws extensively from such a conception of the structures of language in order to account for structures of action. His theorem is that agents draw from structures in order to perform and carry out social interactions, and in so doing contribute to the reproduction of institutions and structures. This analysis leads to a very specific conception of structure and social systems. 'Structure', writes Giddens (1984: 26), 'has no existence independent of the knowledge that agents have about what they do in their day-to-day activity.'

Giddens' theoretical approach emphasizes that structures should be conceptualized as 'rules and resources': the application of rules which comprise structure may be regarded as generating differential access to social, economic, cultural and political resources. In *The Constitution of Society* Giddens argues that the sense of 'rule' most relevant to understanding social life is that which pertains to a mathematical formula – for instance, if the sequence is 2, 4, 6, 8, the formula is $x = n\ \&\ 2$. Understanding a formula, says Giddens, enables an agent to carry on in social life in a routine manner, to apply the rule in a range of different contexts. The same is true of bureaucratic rules, traffic rules, rules of football, rules of grammar, rules of social etiquette: to know a rule does not necessarily mean that one is able to explicitly formulate the principle, but it does mean that one can use the rule 'to go on' in social life. 'The rules and resources of social action', writes Giddens, 'are at the same time the means of systems reproduction' (1984: 19). Systems reproduction, as Giddens conceives it, is complex and contradictory, involving structures, systems and institutions. Social systems, for Giddens, are not equivalent with structures. Social systems are regularized patterns of interaction; such systems are in turn structured by rules and resources. Institutions are understood by Giddens as involving different modalities in and through which structuration occurs. Political institutions, for example, involve the generation of commands over people in relation to issues of authorization, signification and legitimation;

economic institutions, by contrast, involve the allocation of resources through processes of signification and legitimation.

Routines and rules are different to be sure. But for Giddens they both enable or guide the practical conduct of social life. Social rules and routines, amazingly, are learned and nurtured by us in a largely semi-conscious way. We know how to apply countless rules to the conduct of our social life – we know 'how to go on', as Giddens says – even though we may not be able to explicitly formulate those rules. Taking my children to school, for instance, involves me in all sorts of conversational exchanges with other parents. For the most part, these exchanges are of a routine nature – mostly involving talk about our respective children, organizing play-dates and such like. Following the school run, I then drive to university to give some lectures or seminars in my area of specialism – social theory. What is curious, when viewing this routine through the lens of Giddens' structuration theory, is that things work well enough when I apply the 'rules' of social interaction – not that I am often aware of doing so – to these practical situations. Parents talk to me at school about matters to do with my children; students talk to me at university about matters to do with social theory. But try imagining what might happen if I got mixed up in this routine, and applied the wrong rules. Talking about the social theory of 'structuration' itself in the school grounds is something unlikely to win me few friends, and certainly not the approval of my children. If I were to keep talking the abstract language of social theory in the school grounds, as opposed to the university classroom, it is likely something that would have the school headmaster contact the local authorities and report me as a nuisance. Fortunately, social rules are usually applied to the appropriate social situation. Rules, remember, form part of our practical consciousness – and that for Giddens involves knowing 'how to go on', how to apply the right rules to particular social contexts.

The constitution of agents and structures are not two independently given sets of phenomena, a dualism, but represent a duality. According to the notion of the duality of structure, the structural properties of social systems are both medium and outcome of the practices they recursively organize. Structure is not 'external' to individuals: as memory traces, and as instantiated in social practices, it is in a certain sense more 'internal' than exterior to their activities in a Durkheimian sense. Structure is not to be equated with constraint but is always both constraining and enabling. This, of course, does not prevent the structured properties of social systems from stretching away, in time and space, beyond the control of any individual actors.

Anthony Giddens (1984) *The Constitution of Society.* Cambridge: Polity Press, p. 25.

Giddens' structuration theory, which powerfully distinguishes practical from discursive consciousness, thus yokes a sociological appreciation of the generative power of structures (albeit 'virtual') to a phenomenological conception of common-sense, taken-for-granted knowledge. When we talk about, or act on, the world, we do so by mixing together rational accounts of our actions (the discursive) and a general awareness of taken-for-granted knowledge without being aware of it at any particular moment (the practical). From this angle, practical consciousness is the capability of actors to use a range of rules and methods that are taken for granted – which means, roughly, that in our heads we are not usually conscious of them. We speak language to varying levels of grammatical proficiency, and yet for the most part we are unable to detail the grammatical rules we use. Many of the practical codes governing daily life operate in a similar manner. Men may, depending on when and where they were brought up, accord priority to women in entering and exiting social gatherings – without knowing exactly why.

Another way of putting this point is to say that social theory trades equally with that which we know on the one hand, and that which we intuitively grasp (but cannot explicitly formulate) on the other. However, there are other, subterranean forces at work within people's lives – although these are not readily accessible within the language of sociology. To that end, Giddens turns to psychoanalysis in order to account for more primitive elements of human agency. Drawing from a range of psychoanalytic perspectives, and most notably from Lacan's Freud in some of his earlier writings, Giddens argues that there are some things of which we will never know – due primarily to the 'barrier of repression' which is imprinted upon the unconscious mind during childhood. This is an important insight into the emotional dimensions of our lives as human agents acting in the world, although it is not one that Giddens focuses upon in any particular detail. Rather than thinking through the repressed unconscious for an account of human action, Giddens for the most part limits the disruptive force of the unconscious to that which erupts only at crisis points. Except for the 'critical moments' of social upheaval or political crisis, Giddens contends that unconscious anxiety is – by and large – held in check by our habitual routines. The routine, he says, brings emotional security. From this angle, he draws especially from psychoanalyst Erik Erikson's account of 'ego-identity' to understand how early childhood routines help to establish a sense of emotional security and faith in the durability of the social world.

In the last few paragraphs I have noted how Giddens approaches issues of human action, agency and subjectivity. It is important to link these more subjective aspects of his social theory back to issues of social practices and structures in order to grasp his emphasis upon duality in structuration theory. Agents, according to Giddens, draw on the rules and resources of structures, and in so doing contribute to the systemic reproduction of institutions, systems and structures. In studying social life, says Giddens, it is important to recognize the role of 'methodological bracketing'. Giddens argues that the social sciences simultaneously pursue *institutional analysis*, in which the structural features of society are analysed, and the *analysis of strategic conduct*, in which the manner in which actors carry on social interaction is studied. These different levels of analysis are central to social scientific research, and both are crucial to structuration theory. Connected to this, Giddens argues that the subjects of study of the social sciences are concept-using agents, individuals whose concepts enter into the manner in which their actions are constituted. He calls this intersection of the social world as constituted by lay actors on the one hand, and the meta-languages created by social scientists on the other, the 'double hermeneutic'.

Giddens on modernity and the self

None of the outline of structuration theory so far casts specific light on the sociological issue of what may be distinctively *new* to our own age of, among others, intensive globalization, hi-tech finance and new information tech-nologies. It was not until the early 1990s that Giddens turned his sociological attention to consider this acceleration of social change, most notably in his books *The Consequences of Modernity* (1990) and *Modernity and Self-identity* (1991). Here Giddens set out a powerful account of the tensions and contradictions of contemporary societies – ranging from current anxieties affecting identity and intimacy to high-intensity global risks, such as nuclear war. His basic thesis is that modernity heralds dramatic social trans-formations – the kind of which social theory today stands unable to adequately confront. Rejecting Marx's equation of modernity with corrosive capitalism, and wary of Weber's portrait of the modern age as a bureaucratic iron cage, Giddens instead presents an image of modernity as *juggernaut*. Giddens' juggernaut is a world certainly beyond control, but one which none the less offers immense personal opportunities and political possibilities, even though its menacing dark side – the high-consequence risks of ecological catastrophe, political totalitarianism or nuclear destruction – threatens to bring all this undone. He argues that our experience of the mod-ern world is one always divided – split between security and risk, intimacy and impersonality, reassuring expert knowledge and disorientating cultural relativism. As with the stress on the open-ended nature of social relations in his earlier work, Giddens sees modernity as unpredictable. 'To live in the "world" produced by high modernity,' writes Giddens (1991: 28), 'has the feeling of riding a juggernaut. It is not just that more or less continuous and profound processes of change occur; rather, change does not consistently conform either to human expectation or to human control.'

A fundamental feature of modernity for Giddens is the *reflexivity of social life*. Reflexivity, as we have seen, is regarded by Giddens as an essential aspect of all human activity. How people think about, monitor and reflect on what they do, according to Giddens, is crucial to how society constitutes itself. In our own age, however, there is a radical intensification of reflexivity, such that self-monitoring and social relations become increasingly interwoven. Giddens (1990: 38) defines this intensification thus: 'The reflexivity of modern social life consists in the fact that social practices are constantly examined and reformed in the light of incoming information about those very practices, thus constitutively altering their character.' In current times, we can see a clear acceleration in processes of social reflexivity. This is obvious, for example, in the expansion of communications media and new information technologies. Recent changes in mass media and information technology have arguably made the globe more *interconnected* than was previously the case, and which in turn has led to increasing reflexivity of social things happening across the world. What happens on one side of the planet can now be relayed worldwide virtually instantly thanks to advances in media technology. In this sense, our 'social eyes' have dramatically expanded. And as our 'social eyes' take in these distant happenings, so we come to incorporate such knowledge into how we talk about, and act upon, our more local worlds.

Consider, for example, what we know of the changing social landscape of marriage and divorce. Ours is a high divorce and remarriage society. Divorce statistics in the UK and across Europe indicate that over one-third of marriages entered into today will end in divorce; in some states of the United States, the figures rise as high as 50 per cent or more. Giddens' thesis of accelerated social reflexivity emphasizes that such statistics are not merely incidental to marriage today, but influence and reshape people's understandings of what marriage actually is. When a couple walk down the aisle in these early years of the 2000s, they do so 'knowing' (in a blend of the discursive and practical) the general chances for marriage longevity. The shift from marriage till-death-do-us-part to marriage until-further-notice is, from the vantage point of Giddens' theory of modernity, the result of people reflecting on the changing cultural norms governing identity, intimacy, marriage and divorce.

> The reflexivity of modern social life consists in the fact that social practices are constantly examined and reformed in the light of incoming information about those very practices, thus constitutively altering their character. We should be clear about the nature of this phenomenon. All forms of social life are partly constituted by actors' knowledge of them. Knowing 'how to go on' in Wittgenstein's sense is intrinsic to the conventions which are drawn upon and reproduced by human activity. In all cultures, social practices are routinely altered in the light of ongoing discoveries which feed into them. But only in the era of modernity is the revision of convention radicalised to apply (in principle) to all aspects of human life, including technological intervention into the material world. It is often said that modernity is marked by an appetite for the new, but this is not perhaps completely accurate. What is characteristic of modernity is not an embracing of the new for its own sake, but the presumption of wholesale reflexivity – which of course includes reflection upon the nature of reflection itself.
>
> Anthony Giddens (1990) *The Consequences of Modernity*. Cambridge: Polity Press, p. 38.

Reflexivity for Giddens means a world of self-monitoring – of our own lives, the lives of others (both proximate and distant), and wider social happenings. Reflexivity here doesn't equate with reflective control or predictability, since much of what unfolds in daily life involves reflex-like actions and knee-jerk responses. Nor is it accurate to view reflexivity as merely personal. While reflexivity goes to the heart of how we perform the most basic tasks of our personal routines (such as catching a train or emailing a friend), it is also deeply inscribed in social processes and organizations in the broadest sense. Microsoft, British Petroleum and Calvin Klein are all companies with global reach, but the point is that these organizations could not operate in the global economy if not organizationally structured in reasonably reflexive ways. For this reason, Giddens distinguishes between *individual reflexivity* and *institutional reflexivity*. If the former is to do with self-monitoring and the ongoing observation and retracing of personal life, the latter is to do with organizational tracking, administrative surveillance as well as broader economic and market forces. His emphasis on institutional reflexivity connects closely with science and expert knowledge too. In a world of dramatic scientific advances, for instance, there is – as a result of intensive reflexivity – a rise in the questioning of science. Paths of action and scenarios of choice are undertaken against a reflexive backdrop of a variety of other ways of doing things. Giddens offers the following overview, for example, in relation to global warming:

> Many experts consider that global warming is occurring and they may be right. The hypothesis is disputed by some, however, and it has even been suggested that the real trend, if there is one at all, is in the opposite direction, towards the cooling of the global climate. Probably the most that can be said with some surety is that we cannot be certain that global warming is *not* occurring. Yet such a conditional conclusion will yield not a precise calculation of risks but rather an array of 'scenarios' – whose plausibility will be influenced, among other things, by how many people become convinced of the thesis of global warming and take action on that basis. In the social world, where institutional reflexivity has become a central constituent, the complexity of 'scenarios' is even more marked.
>
> (Giddens 1994: 59)

Written in 1994, this overview of scientific and lay opinion on global warming already looks quaint. However, Giddens' reasoning remains convincing: it is because so many people across the planet have become deeply concerned about the potential risks of climate change, and have pressed their governments to take important policy initiatives in this respect, that global warming has become the debate of our times. Giddens' argument – that the complexity of 'scenarios' is central to our reflexive engagement with the wider world – speaks directly to the global pathways we face in the early twenty-first century.

The experiential character of contemporary daily life is well grasped by two of Giddens' key concepts: *trust and risk* as interwoven with *abstract systems*. For Giddens, the relation between individual subjectivity and social contexts of action is a highly mobile one; and it is something that we make sense of and utilize through 'abstract systems'. Abstract systems are institutional domains of technical and social knowledge: they include systems of expertise of all kinds, from local forms of knowledge to science, technology and mass communications. Giddens is underscoring much more than simply the impact of expertise on people's lives, far-reaching though that is. Rather, Giddens extends the notion of expertise to cover 'trust relations' – the personal and collective investment of active trust in social life. The psychological investment of trust contributes to the power of specialized, expert knowledge – indeed it lies at the bedrock of our Age of Experts – and also plays a key role in the forging of a sense of security in day-to-day social life. Trust and security are thus both a condition and outcome of social reflexivity. Giddens sees the reflexive appropriation of expert knowledge as fundamental in a globalizing, culturally cosmopolitan society.

While a key aim may be the regularization of stability and order in our identities and in society, reflexive modernity is radically experimental however, and is constantly producing new types of incalculable risk and insecurity. This means that, whether we like it or not, we must recognize the ambivalence of a social universe of expanded reflexivity: there are no pre-ordained, nor even clear, pathways for individual or social development today.

In *The Transformation of Intimacy* (1992), Giddens connects the notion of reflexivity to sexuality, gender and intimate relationships. With modernization and the decline of tradition, says Giddens, the sexual life of the human subject becomes a 'project' that has to be managed and defined against the backdrop of new opportunities and risks – including, for example, artificial insemination, experiments in ectogenesis (the creation of human life without pregnancy), AIDS, sexual harassment, and the like. Linking gender to new technologies, Giddens argues that we live in an era of 'plastic sexuality'. 'Plastic sexuality' (1992: 2), writes Giddens, 'is decentred sexuality, freed from the needs of reproduction . . . and from the rule of the phallus, from the overweening importance of male sexual experience.' Sexuality thus becomes open-ended, elaborated not through pre-given roles, but through reflexively forged relationships. The self today, as the rise of therapy testifies, is faced with profound dilemmas in respect of sexuality. 'Who am I?', 'What do I desire?', 'What satisfactions do I want from sexual relations?' – these are core issues for the self according to Giddens. This does not mean that sexual experience occurs without institutional constraint, however. Giddens contends that the development of modern institutions produces a 'sequestration of experience' – sexual, existential and moral – which squeezes to the sidelines core problems relating to sexuality, intimacy, mortality and death (see Elliott 1992).

Giddens, in other words, adopts an idealist language of autonomy, stressing as he does the creativity of action and the modernist drive to absolute self-realization, while remaining suspicious of intellectual traditions that prioritize subjects over objects, or actors over structures. This comes out very clearly in his work on the changing connections between marriage, the family and self-identity. According to Giddens, individuals today actively engage with novel opportunities and dangers that arise as a consequence of dramatic transformations affecting self-identity, sexuality and intimacy. For Giddens, divorce is undeniably a personal crisis, involving significant pain, loss and grief. Yet many people, he argues, take positive steps to work through the emotional dilemmas generated by marriage breakdown. In addition to dealing with financial issues and matters affecting how children should be brought up, separation and divorce also call into play a reflexive emotional engagement with the self. Charting territory from the past (where things went wrong, missed opportunities and so on) and for the future (alternative possibilities, chances for self-actualization) necessarily involves experimenting with a new sense of self. This can lead to emotional growth, new understandings of self, and strengthened intimacies. Against the conservative critique of marriage breakdown, Giddens sees the self opening out to constructive renewal. Remarriage and the changing nature of family life are crucial in this respect. As he develops this point:

> Many people, adults and children, now live in stepfamilies – not usually, as in previous eras, as a consequence of the death of a spouse, but because of the re-forming of marriage ties after divorce. A child in a stepfamily may have two mothers and fathers, two sets of brothers and sisters, together with other complex kin connections resulting from the multiple marriages of parents. Even the terminology is difficult: should a stepmother be called 'mother' by the child, or called by her name? Negotiating such problems might be arduous and psychologically costly for all parties; yet opportunities for novel kinds of fulfilling social relations plainly also exist. One thing we can be sure of is that the changes involved here are not just external to the individual. These new forms of extended family ties have to be established by the very persons who find themselves most directly caught up in them.
>
> (Giddens 1991: 13)

Marital separation, as portrayed by Giddens, implicates the self in an open project: tracing over the past, imagining the future, dealing with complex family problems and experimenting with a new sense of identity. Further experimentation with marriage and intimate relationships will necessarily involve anxieties, risks and opportunities. But, as Giddens emphasizes, the relation between self and society is a highly fluid one, involving negotiation, change and development.

The manner in which current social practices shape future life outcomes is nowhere more in evidence than in the conjunction of divorce statistics, the reckoning of probability ratios for success or failure in intimate relationships, and the decision to get married. As Giddens rightly points out, statistics about marriage and divorce do not exist in a social vacuum; everyone, he says, is in some sense aware of how current gender uncertainties affect long-term relationships. When people marry or remarry today, according to Giddens, they do so against a societal backdrop of high divorce statistics, knowledge of which alters a person's understanding and conception of what marriage actually is. It is precisely this reflexive monitoring of relationships that, in turn, transforms expectations about, and aspirations for, marriage and intimacy. The relationship between self, society and reflexivity is thus a highly dynamic one, involving the continual overturning of traditional ways of doing things.

Giddens, politics and the third way

In the late 1990s, Giddens left Cambridge University to take up the high-profile Directorship of the London School of Economics. At the LSE, Giddens was not only more directly involved with the shaping of higher education in Britain, but his writings became more politically focused too. A new political approach had been detailed in his book, *Beyond Left and Right: The Future of Radical Politics* (1994). In time, Giddens termed this new political agenda 'the third way'. His best-selling *The Third Way* (1997) became hugely influential, and he became an adviser to UK Prime Minister Tony Blair. He was also much in demand as a consultant to governments throughout the world, including American President Bill Clinton. In 1999 Giddens delivered the prestigious Reith Lectures on globalization, entitled 'Runaway World'. In 2003, he was appointed to the House of Lords.

In *Beyond Left and Right*, Giddens asserts that we live today in a radically damaged world, for which radical political remedies are required beyond the neoliberalism offered by the Right or reformist socialism offered by the Left. To this end, Giddens provides a detailed framework for the rethinking of radical politics. This framework touches on issues of tradition and social solidarity, of social movements, of the restructuring of democratic processes and the welfare state, and of the location of violence in world politics. Giddens' interpretation of the rise of radical politics may perhaps best be grasped by contrasting dominant discussions in the fields of critical theory and postmodernism. Theorists of the self-endangerment of modern politics, from Daniel Bell to Jürgen Habermas, characteristically focus upon the loss of community produced by the invasion of personal and cultural life by the global capitalist system. Postmodernist social and political theorists, from Michel Foucault to Jean-François Lyotard, alternatively focus on the contemporary plurality of knowledge claims, and conclude that there are no ordered paths to political development. Giddens' approach, by contrast, takes a radically different tack. He develops neither a lament nor a celebration of the ambivalences of contemporary political processes. Instead, Giddens asks: What happens when politics begins to reflect on itself? What happens when political activity, understanding its own successes and excesses, begins to reflect on its own institutional conditions?

At issue, says Giddens, are reflexivity and risk, both of which he isolates as central to transformations in society, culture and politics. By reflexivity, as noted, Giddens refers to that circularity of knowledge and information promoted by mass communications in a globalizing, cosmopolitan world. Reflexivity functions as a means of regularly reordering and redefining what political activity is. Of central importance in this respect is the impact of globalization. Globalizing processes, says Giddens, radically intensify our personal and social awareness of risk, transforming local contexts into global consequences. Thus the panic selling of shares on the Dow Jones has implications for the entire global economy, from local retail trade to the international division of labour. At the beginning of the twenty-first century, a world of intensified reflexivity is a world of people reflecting upon the political consequences of human action, from the desolation of the rain forests to the widespread manufacture of weapons of mass destruction. In such social conditions, politics becomes radically experimental in character. People are increasingly aware of new types of incalculable risk and insecurity, and must attempt to navigate the troubled waters of modern political culture. This means that, whether we like it or not, we are all engaged in a kind of continual reinvention of identity and politics, with no clear paths of development from one state of risk to another.

It is against this backdrop of transformations in risk, reflexivity and globalization that Giddens develops a new framework for radical politics. The core dimensions of Giddens' blueprint for the restructuring of radical political thought include the following claims:

- We live today in a post-traditional social order. This does not mean, as many cultural critics and postmodernists claim, that tradition disappears. On the contrary, in a globalizing, culturally cosmopolitan society, traditions are forced into the open for public discussion and debate. Reasons or explanations are increasingly required for the preservation of tradition, and this should be understood as one of the key elements in the reinvention of social solidarity. The new social movements, such as those concerned with ecology, peace or human rights, are examples of groups refashioning tradition (the call to conserve and protect 'nature') in the building of social solidarities. The opposite of this may be seen, says Giddens, in the rise of fundamentalism, which forecloses questions of public debate and is 'nothing other than tradition defended in the traditional way'.
- Radical forms of democratization, fuelled by reflexivity, are at work in politics, from the interpersonal to the global levels. But the issue of democratization cannot be confined only to the formal political

sphere, since these processes also expose the limits of liberal political democracy itself. As the American sociologist Daniel Bell put this some years ago, the nation-state has become too small to tackle global problems and too large to handle local ones. Instead, Giddens speaks of a 'democratizing of democracy', by which he means that all areas of personal and political life are increasingly ordered through dialogue rather than pre-established power relations. The mechanisms of such dialogic democracy are already set in process, from the transformation of gender and parent–child relations through to the development of social movements and self-help groups. The rise of psychotherapy and psychoanalysis is also cast in a favourable political light by Giddens. Democratizing influences such as these also influence the more traditional sphere of institutional politics as well.

- The welfare state requires further radical forms of restructuring, and this needs to be done in relation to wider issues of global poverty. Here Giddens urges the reconstruction of welfare away from the traditional 'top down dispensation of benefits' in favour of what he terms "positive welfare'. Welfare that is positive is primarily concerned with promoting autonomy in relation to personal and collective responsibilities, and focuses centrally on gender imbalances as much as class deprivations.

- The prospects for global justice begin to emerge in relation to a 'post-scarcity order'. This is a complex idea, but it is central to Giddens' political theory. Giddens is not suggesting that politics has entered an age in which scarcity has been eliminated. On the contrary, he argues that there will always be scarcities of goods and resources. Rather, a post-scarcity society is a society in which 'scarcity' itself comes under close reflexive scrutiny. Coping with the negative consequences of industrialism, says Giddens, has led to a radical reappraisal of the capitalistic drive for continuous accumulation. This broadening of political goals beyond the narrowly economic is reflected today in the pursuit of 'responsible growth'. Several key social transformations are central here. The entry of women into the paid labour force, the restructuring of gender and intimacy, the rise of individualization as opposed to egoism, and the ecological crisis: these developments have all contributed to a shift away from secularized puritanism towards social solidarity and obligation.

Criticisms of Giddens

Giddens' work is a brilliant conjuncture of social theory and modern sociology, involving a provocative account which examines the very constitution of society through recurrent social practices. It is not, however, without its difficulties. For one thing, some critics think Giddens is gravely mistaken in his project to overcome the individual/society opposition. Sociologist Margaret Archer (1982, 1990) argues that, not only is Giddens wrong to amalgamate agency with structure, but that he fails to grasp the necessity of treating structure and agency as analytically distinct in order to deal with both methodological and substantive problems in the social sciences. At the core of Archer's critique there lies anxiety about Giddens' strong argument that structures exist only in and through the social practices of human agents. If any society were to eliminate time in the manner that Giddens' model of virtual structures actually does, according to Archer, then it would be radically impoverished in terms of its understanding of history. That is to say, structures need to be identified historically, across time, in order for sociologists to analyse how agents have acted to both reproduce and change the structures of social life. A similar point has been made by Nicos Mouzelis (1989), who questions the applicability of structuration theory to collective actors such as social movements. According to Mouzelis, Giddens' notion of structuration is more or less appropriate to our immediate, routine lives – where agents carry out their actions without undue levels of reflection. But the model is less well suited, he argues, to situations where actors consciously and conceptually reflect on the power of structures in shaping the world. Where workers take a principled stand against unfair working conditions, or where women act collectively against entrenched forms of gender discrimination, are situations that demand taking a highly reflective attitude to the world. They are situations, according to Mouzelis, that involve separating agency from structure – in order for actors to understand the power of structures in their lives and, subsequently, to try to change such determination. The contestation of economic or gender power, in this view, is not something that can be left to the routine actions of reflexive individuals.

Perhaps the most critical voice among commentators on Giddens has been John B. Thompson, who worked very closely with Giddens during the 1980s and 1990s at Cambridge University. Thompson clearly admires the scope and ambition of Giddens' social theory, but questions the adequacy of his notion of rules and resources for grasping social structure. According to Thompson, Giddens' account of rules and resources is vague and misleading. The study of the rules used to speak a language, he points out, is not the same thing as the study of social structure. Linguistic and grammatical rules, says Thompson, are important forms of constraint upon human action; however, they are not the only forms of constraint in social life. Taxation laws requiring that I pay a portion of my income to the government each year are clearly more socially important than my own imposed rule that I try to exercise three times a week. Yet to grasp that importance requires some concept of social structure. Social structures are, thus, very much about the practical ways in which individuals come to reproduce, challenge, question and transform the realities of the world. In this connection, Thompson questions Giddens' account of the transformational properties of structures, and suggests there is inadequate differentiation between the structural and institutional features of social life in his approach. A worker at the Ford Motor Company, notes Thompson, may be said to contribute to the reproduction of that institution, and may thus also be said to contribute to the reproduction of capitalism as a structure, to the extent that the worker pursues their everyday employment activities. However it is also possible that the worker along with others may undertake activities that threaten the smooth running of Ford as an institution, but without similarly threatening to undo capitalism. 'Every act of production and reproduction', writes Thompson (1989: 70), 'may also be a potential act of transformation, as Giddens rightly insists; but the extent to which an action transforms an institution does not coincide with the extent to which social structure is thereby transformed.'

Giddens is a social theorist who has done perhaps more than anyone to draw our attention to the virtual feel of structures in everyday life. Yet even in his scrupulous attention to the power of invisible structures, he always reminds us of the activities of individuals. Let us recall his formulation of structuration theory: *structures exist only in and through the social practices of human agents*. If there has been criticism of Giddens' reformulation of the concept of structure in social theory, however, there has equally been disagreement with his account of the individual or identity. The routine nature of our daily lives is a powerful sociological idea that helps account for the astonishing fact that, despite the immense complexity of social organization, there is a kind of order or regularity to the world. This may seem to be only a surface phenomenon. For while most of us know 'how to go on' in social situations, the actual detail of what goes on in social life is complex and contradictory. Many people are able to 'give off' the impression of things running smoothly, though in fact they may feel their lives to be running out of control. Even so, such personal confusion does not seem to be problematic to Giddens's social theory – at least so long as the individual is able to maintain 'role-taking' in social interaction and carry on 'business-as-usual' with the micro-situations of daily life. Certainly, Giddens makes it clear that he regards routines as essential to the production of *both* identity and society. 'Routine', writes Giddens (1984: 60) 'is integral both to the continuity of the personality of the agent, as he or she moves along the paths of daily activities, and to the institutions of society, which are such only through their continued reproduction.' This is not an expression of socio-logical determinism (in the sense that identity is pre-programmed) nor political conservatism: there is no logical reason why social reproduction demands an acceptance of *particular* habitual practices. Moreover, Giddens' more recent political writings advancing a 'third way' for social democracy plainly indicate his discontent with neo-liberalism and neo-conservativism. Rather, Giddens' stress on routinization suggests that existing, alternative and oppositional forms of life demand some sort of motivational commit-ment to the integration of habitual practices across space and time.

And yet it is precisely here that Giddens pushes the routinized nature of social life to breaking point – or so argue some critics. If the structured nature of social interaction is the ability of individuals to do what they do in a routine fashion, then what is it exactly that provides the sense of organizing consistency to such routines? How do the organized routines of daily life come into existence – from the imagination of individuals, or the complex social things of society? Suddenly, the duality proposed by structuration theory returns us to a familiar sociological opposition. But still there are other concerns. There is the question, for example, of how far down routines really go in private life – of whether they actually create identity through providing social consistency from situation to situation, or whether they instead provide a social framework for an already established emotional complexity of the self. And if routines are, in some sense, tied up with the making of identity, how might we come to understand the structured realities of individuals living their routine lives? What, in other words, makes for the social differences between routines in, say, China and North America? How might the notion of routine apply to the Third World? Is the term, as Giddens uses it, a sociologically neutral account of social interaction, or a normative image of Western living?

Finally, we may note that this account of the relation between society and the individual, for all its claims of transcending the dualism of subject and object, betrays a sociologically impoverished grasp of the emotional lives of people. At the centre of this criticism is Giddens' use of psychoanalysis. We have seen earlier that Giddens draws on Freud's account of the uncon-scious to supplement his notion of practical consciousness: like practical consciousness, the unconscious is a sector of human experience that is non-discursive; unlike practical consciousness, there is much in the unconscious that cannot be brought into language due to the barrier of repression established in early infancy. The effects of the repressed unconscious, to be sure, are disabling at moments of societal stress or crisis; but there is for Giddens a certain kind of stability to the unconscious, which is regulated by the force of daily habits and routines. Predictable routines, says Giddens, keep the unconscious at bay. It is worth pausing to ask of this standpoint, however, whether the unconscious is really 'bracketed' by routines? What of the narcissistic routines promoted by consumer capitalism, in which individuals are encouraged to obsess about their bodies, or constantly measure their physical appearance against the standards of celebrity culture? Is it meaningful to speak of a routine limiting of the unconscious within these parameters of popular culture? Similarly, some critics think that Giddens closes off the radical implications of psychoanalysis for social theory through the bulk of the vocabulary of self-organization – 'bracketing anxiety', 'ontological security' and 'emotional inoculation'. All of these terms seem to suggest an individual serenely inserted into the social order; but this is a far cry from the split and fractured individual subject of psychoanalysis.

Pierre Bourdieu: *habitus* and practical social life

Giddens' theory of structuration operates on a reasonably grand scale, revolving on such general sociological concepts as system, structure and subject, whereas the French social theorist Pierre Bourdieu is more concerned to analyse the surreptitious forms by which power inculcates itself within our personal and bodily dispositions as expressed in daily life. Like Giddens, Bourdieu is interested in the habits of whole societies – so much so that he has invented a sociological concept, *habitus*, to account for how well-practised habits bridge individuals and the wider social things of which they are part. Also like Giddens he holds that social actors exhibit intricate complex understandings of the social conditions which influence, and are in turn influenced by, their personal decisions and private lives. It may be hard to judge the exact differences between Bourdieu and Giddens on this point – for both of them are at pains to emphasize the semi-conscious reflexiveness of social actors. Bordieu's formulation is that actors possess a 'sense of the game', which is the basis from which people deploy a kind of semi-automatic grasp of what is appropriate to differing social situations. Where Bourdieu and Giddens certainly part company however – and this is a point that will be examined subsequently in the chapter – concerns the extent to which power goes all the way down – for Bourdieu, to the inculcation of bodily dispositions as well as the dramatization of personal style.

Studying how society generates particular practices in individuals is Bourdieu's way of rethinking the relation between identity and social structure in social theory. Like Giddens' blending of social structure and human action, Bourdieu wants to develop a sophisticated social theory that will neither reduce actors to mere 'supports' of social processes nor elevate them to the source of all social things. In this connection, he was attempting to steer a new direction in French intellectual culture in the early part of his career, one beyond the liberationist existentialism of philosopher Jean-Paul Sartre (arguably France's most famous public intellectual at the time) and also the equally problematic structuralism of Lévi-Strauss, Barthes and Foucault (see Chapter 3). His ambition, put simply, was the puzzle of how seemingly spontaneous individual action comes to dovetail with society's expectation that people perform appropriate practices in specific situations.

To address this puzzle, Bourdieu outlines in *Outline of a Theory of Practice* (1977) his concept of *habitus*, by which he means the moulding of a set of individual dispositions interlocking with the specific cultural characteristics of the society concerned. Here is how Bourdieu develops, in his typically dense style, the concept of *habitus*:

> The structures constitutive of a particular type of environment . . . produce the *habitus*, systems of durable dispositions, structured structures predisposed to function as structuring structures, that is, as the principle of generation and structuration of practices and representations which can be objectively 'regulated' and 'regular' without in any way being the product of obedience to rules, objectively adapted to their goal without presupposing the conscious orientation towards ends and the express mastery of the operations necessary to attain them and, being all that, collectively orchestrated without being the product of the organizing action of a conductor.

It is because individuals inculcate particular cultural dispositions that their actions are, by and large, carried out in a fashion that appears spontaneous yet structured, unregulated yet regular. You decide you want to travel somewhere new in town, but then find yourself queuing at the railway station; you decide to express the 'inner self' by painting, but first you need to visit the local arts store to stock up on paints and brushes. It is as if the very 'spontaneity' of our daily behaviour is always overwritten, as it were, with some kind of social unconscious which serves to harmonize our practices with those deeply tacit norms and values of the wider society. This is not to suggest, Bourdieu stresses, that social structures actually *determine* individual action. On the contrary, *habitus* is a flexible, open-ended structuring system, one which enables social actors to have numerous creative strategies at their disposal and thus to cope with unforeseen social structures.

A s an acquired system of generative schemes, the *habitus* makes possible the free production of all the thoughts, perceptions and actions inherent in the particular conditions of its production – and only those. . . . Because the *habitus* is an infinite capacity for generating products – thoughts, perceptions, expressions and actions – whose limits are set by the historically and socially situated conditions of its production, the conditioned and conditional freedom it provides is as remote from creation of unpredictable novelty as it is from simple mechanical reproduction of the original conditionings.

Pierre Bourdieu (1977 [1972]) *Outline of a Theory of Practice*, trans. Richard Nice. Cambridge: Cambridge University Press.

Bourdieu developed his concept of *habitus* from his anthropological studies of the Kabyle tribespeople and, in particular, from close sociological analysis of gift exchanges in Kabyle society. Bourdieu considers that structuralism is correct in its initial diagnosis that society possesses a reality that precedes the individual. This is the point, for example, that language pre-exists us as speaking agents, and will subsequently continue as a social institution long after we have left the planet. If this is so, Bourdieu supposes, then structuralism is right to claim that language has the power to regulate, even shape, our individual speech-acts – whether we realize it or not. But where structuralism is palpably insufficient, according to Bourdieu, lies in its reduction of social action to a mechanical system of rules which imposes itself upon individuals. Studying the intricacies of gift exchange in Kabyle society, Bourdieu finds that men's sense of honour is facilitated less by an application of pre-established rules than by carrying out a whole range of practices – such as 'playing with the tempo' of response and acknowledgement of a gift. An actor's response to the receipt of a gift is not therefore socially determined by the application of mechanical rules, and nor is it a matter of mere private judgement. It rather involves the creative artistry of the recipient, experimenting within a fluid structuring structure, one marked by group norms of acceptable practice, obligation, reciprocity and honour.

Habitus, in the sense of deeply ingrained dispositions, is a structuring feature of social practices, but it is more than just that. If our practical, or habitual, behaviours have a degree of consistency to them, this is because our bodies are literally moulded into certain forms that interlock with existing social arrangements. One way of thinking about how *habitus* reaches all the way down into bodily needs and dispositions is to consider the process that sociologists call 'socialization'. The notion of socialization refers, broadly speaking, to the training or regulation of children within the structure of bigger social things. The learning of good manners at home, or respect for figures of authority at school, are examples of the socialization process. Bourdieu's account of how *habitus* penetrates the body – what he calls the 'corporeal hexis' – is similar to the idea of socialization, but is much broader in scope. Socialization conveys too much the sense of active or conscious learning, and this is not how Bourdieu thinks we come to act in the world. Instead, he is interested to get at the subtle ways in which messages are relayed to people over time, such that cultural norms become routine patterns of behaviour and, thus, withdrawn from consciousness. The parent who routinely tells their son or daughter to 'sit up straight' at dinner, or who instructs them to 'always say thank you' when offered food at the home of a fellow classmate, is thus going about the business of reproducing the *habitus* of modern society. This is the sense, too, in which *habitus* bites deeply into the very bodies of individuals – structuring the ways in which people come to talk, walk, act and eat. *Habitus*, thus, is deeply interwoven with the stylization of bodies.

What has been discussed so far about social practices and bodies is central to the analysis of human action, and yet it hardly needs saying that – for regular social life to get up and running – such practices must be anchored in wider institutional contexts. Bourdieu seeks to do this by introducing the notion of 'field', by which he means the structured space of positions in which an individual in located. For Bourdieu, there are various kinds of fields – educational, economic, cultural – which contain different kinds of social properties and characteristics. A field, says Bourdieu, pre-exists the individual. It ascribes an objective place to individuals within the broader scheme of social things, and thereby serves as a relation of force between individuals and groups engaged in struggles within certain fields. As John Thompson (1984: 49) explains this social reach of the field in Bourdieu's work:

> A field may be seen synchronically as a structured space of positions, such that the properties of these positions depend on their location within the space and not upon the personal attributes of their occu-pants. However different the fields may be – whether, for example, it is a pedagogical space in which teachers transmit a form of 'knowledge' or a cultural space in which literary works are offered for consumption – there are certain general laws which commonly obtain. Thus, in every field, one may struggle between the nouveaux entrants who try to jump over the rights of entry and to alter the structure in their favour, and those established agents or groups who try to defend their monopoly and to exclude competition.

Questions of taste: Bourdieu's *Distinction*

Cultural tastes and social preferences are *habitus*, in Bourdieu's terminology, but they are also an outward expression of power and social class. In *Distinction: A Social Critique of the Judgment of Taste* (1984), Bourdieu developed a brilliant analysis of the habits and tastes of French society – which he divided into the working class, the lower middle class and the upper middle class. His argument, broadly speaking, was that while economics is the baseline of social order, the struggle for social distinction is played out with other forms of capital too – notably, cultural capital and symbolic capital.

In Bourdieu's view, the struggle for capital is more a matter of practices than ideas, which in turn brings us to core distinctions between poverty and affluence in the realm of culture as well as lifestyle practices. As Bourdieu (1984: 77) writes:

> If a group's lifestyle can be read off from the style it adopts in furnishing or clothing, this is not only because these properties are the object of the economic and cultural necessity which determines their selection, but also because the social relations objectified in familiar objects in their luxury or poverty, their 'distinction' or vulgarity, their 'beauty' or their 'ugliness' impress themselves through bodily experiences which may be as profoundly unconscious as the quiet caress of beige carpets or the thin clamminess of tattered garish linoleum, the harsh smell of bleach.

Culture then is the sense of fine living, manners, refinement or an elegant ease of social interaction that lies at the centre of how individuals demonstrate social sophistication. Such social sophistication requires certain economic capital – for example, expensive private schools. But social struggles for distinction have a cultural dimension too: cultivation of the self is also a matter of learning, aesthetics, the arts.

Bourdieu's concept of cultural capital directs our attention to the means whereby social inequalities are generated through the classifying power of taste as expressed in the consumption of culture. Bourdieu found that the possession of specific forms of cultural capital – of intellectuals and artists, for example – is used to maintain social dominance over those who do not possess such competences. This valuable sociological perspective may also be extended to the analysis of popular culture and the media.

In 'reality television', for example, new forms of symbolic violence are arguably evident as regards the public humiliation of people and their relegation to an inferior social standing within the social order. Analysing the UK television programme *What Not To Wear*, media theorist Angela McRobbie has used Bourdieu's notion of cultural capital to focus on practices of symbolic violence and forms of domination. As McRobbie (2005: 147–8) writes:

> Bourdieu's writing allows us to re-examine symbolic violence as a vehicle for social reproduction. . . . The victim of the make-over television programme presents his or her class habitus for analysis and critique by the experts. The programmes comprise a series of encounters where cultural intermediaries impart guidance and advice to individuals ostensibly as a means of self-improvement. . . . These programmes would not work if the victim did not come forward and offer herself as someone in need of expert help. On the basis of her own subordinate class habitus, the individual will have a 'feel for the game', a 'practical sense for social reality' which means in the context of the programmes, she will instinctively, and unconsciously, know her place in regard to the experts, hence the tears, the gratitude and the deference to those who know so much better than she does.

Bourdieu's ideas help us understand why people adopt certain kinds of cultural practices, and how – through habitus adjustment to dominant social classes – conformity with the requirements of consumer culture are maintained.

Criticisms of Bourdieu

Appropriately enough for a social theorist whose writings are arrestingly original, Bourdieu's work has been subjected to many – and sometimes vehement – criticisms. Critics have questioned, for example, the adequacy of the concept of *habitus* to address the complexity of social experience. The criticism here is that *habitus* overemphasizes the *containment* of cultural dispositions within social structures – thereby downgrading the capacity of individuals to negotiate or transform existing social systems through their creative actions. There may be some truth to this charge, but the criticism needs more precision. Bourdieu's *habitus* emerged as a theoretical innovation in the aftermath of structuralism and post-structuralism; it fitted well enough with a political and intellectual climate in which dissent was still possible, but now conceptualized in a fashion that fully broke with individ-ualistic ways of understanding the world. Society for Bourdieu was less the outcome of individual acts and choices than a structuring, structured field of dispositions in which individuals mobilize themselves and act to exclude others on the basis of relevant cultural capital. The *habitus*, in other words, refers to an objectivity ('society') that inscribes itself within identity. There is something about social production which is both enabling and coercive. What is most dynamic about *habitus* for Bourdieu is its status as the condition of sociality: the *habitus* prescribes the kinds of agency demanded by culture. Yet while this viewpoint was in some general sense radical, it seemed on the whole to have little of interest to say about specific issues of identity (the concrete negotiations of the self in relation to social relations), even if Bourdieu had provided a whole range of sociological enquiries, from education to aesthetics. Part of the difficulty in this respect is that Bourdieu might be said not to have broken with structuralism thoroughly enough, in the sense that structures in his work continue to confer on us our agency – to such a degree that we misrecognize our fate as our choice. In doing so, Bourdieu's *habitus* neglects the creativity of action which individuals bring to all encounters with social and cultural processes – a matter of profound significance to the question of social change. Ultimately, as Charles Lemert (1995: 146) writes, '*habitus* cannot account for change in *habitus*'.

The debate over Bourdieu's contributions to social theory has also addressed many other issues. One central criticism concerns certain *assumptions about society* Bourdieu appears to make in his various socio-logical analyses. Some critics contend, for example, that he takes the economy for granted, leaving unanalysed the role of economic forces upon social life. While Bourdieu was widely seen as sympathetic to the political Left, the politics of his social theory was somewhat oblique; he certainly distanced himself from Marx and Marxism. Against this backdrop, some have argued that he elevated cultural capital over economic capital, thus tending to skirt issues of economic oppression. A more interesting line of criticism, in my view, is that his account of symbolic violence assumes a certain kind of consensus with respect to the norms and values that are central in society. This is less a matter of assuming that people openly agree with one another about societal values than a presupposition that those who exercise cultural and symbolic capital are perceived by others as 'legitimate' bearers of social authority. That is to say, Bourdieu may be criticized for conceptualizing social practice in terms of how social stability is sustained. Such an approach allows him to develop powerful insights into how symbolic domination is wielded in contemporary societies, and yet these insights arguably come at the sociological cost of understanding how social structures – or ways of acting with cultural capital – can be changed. In short, *habitus* may not be so overwhelmingly rigid.

Finally, it is now widely agreed that Bourdieu's commitment to the political notion of resistance led him to overestimate the constraints of social domination operating within specific power structures of advanced capitalism on the one hand, while underestimating the degree to which the world really had changed as a result of the impacts of globalization on the other. Certainly, there can be little doubt that Bourdieu's attacks on globalization and the neoliberalism promoted by various French conservative governments were provocative. Notwithstanding his commitment to stand shoulder to shoulder with struggling workers, immigrants and others dispossessed from the contemporary French political system, however, Bourdieu failed to develop an outline of what a progressive politics might actually look like in our own time of accelerated globalization. French social theory has often turned on a contrast between some utopian moment of resistance to power as such and the contaminated terrain of reformist social policy, and Bourdieu is no exception in this respect. However, his disquisitions on resistance in general – when coupled to the sociological diagnosis of people's cultural *habitus* – can easily be misinterpreted as a form of defeatist politics. Here comparison between Bourdieu and Giddens is, once again, instructive. Notwithstanding the various criticisms of Giddens' theory of a radical centre or third way in contemporary politics, Giddens' work powerfully acknowledges the extent to which the political landscape of modern societies has changed in recent decades – primarily as a result of globalization and the information technology revolution. Certainly Giddens' late political writings have significantly influenced the direction of various Centre-Left governments – in Britain, Canada, Germany, Brazil, Mexico, Argentina and even France. Bourdieu's political tracts did not exert this kind of policy impact, and it is interesting to consider why this was the case. Whereas Bourdieu pitched his political critique at the level of blue skies resistance to power in general, Giddens' third way constituted a new political path, one designed in response to the realities of the global electronic economy. A dynamic economy for Giddens is essential not only to the creation of wealth but for social solidarity and social justice too. Whereas Bourdieu tended to dismiss globalization processes as intrinsically anti-democratic, Giddens recognized that globalism is a much more complex political phenomenon – one that opens out to 'depoliticized global space' and is central to the economic and political problems of our time. By contrast, globalization for Bourdieu appears as a remorseless totalization, one to which the only political counterweight is 'anti-globalization'.

Summary points

1 Structuration theories seek to comprehend how individual action is organized within the mundane activities of practical social life, while simultaneously recognizing that the structural features of society are reproduced through individual action.

2 In borrowing the term 'structuration' from French, British social theorist Anthony Giddens argues that society should be understood as a complex of recurrent practices forming institutions. The focus of Giddens' work is not society as fixed or pre-given, but rather the active flow of social life.

3 Giddens insists that the dualism of agency and structure should instead be conceived as a *duality*. In this view, social systems are at once the *medium* and *outcome* of the practices they organize.

4 Critiquing structuralist and post-structuralist thought, Giddens argues that society is not 'structured like a language', although language does exemplify core aspects of social life. According to Giddens, human agents draw from structured 'rules and resources' in order to carry out social interactions, which in turn contribute to the reproduction of society as a whole.

5 Structures for Giddens have no independent existence of the knowledge that agents have about what they do in social life. Social structures thus exist outside of time and space, and exhibit a 'virtual' existence.

6 In Giddens' late work on the 'runaway world' of modernity, reflexivity is key to the production of personal life and the complexity of society. For Giddens, reflexivity means that social practices are continually examined and re-formed in the light of ongoing information about those very practices – which thus influences the very texture of those practices.

7 There have been various criticisms made of Giddens' version of structuration theory, including that it is unhelpful to amalgamate human agency with social structure and that the notion of 'rules and resources' is limited for grasping social reproduction. Giddens' account of reflexivity has also been criticized for its individualistic bent, as well as its neglect of emotional and interpersonal factors.

8 In French sociologist Pierre Bourdieu's version of structuration, the fluidity of social life is captured by the notion of *habitus* – which refers to how bodily dispositions and well-practised habits bridge personal and social life.

9 For Bourdieu, the *habitus* of an individual or group is anchored in the institutional life of 'fields'. Fields, such as the domains of the economy or culture, refer to the structured space of positions in which individuals act.

10 Bourdieu's social theory has been criticized, among other things, for suppressing change in personal and social life, as well as over-emphasizing the rigidity of the *habitus* in which social practices are generated.

Further questions

1 Giddens distinguishes two key types of social knowledge: practical and discursive consciousness. What do you understand to be their differences?

2 How is it that our individual actions – daily habits, routines and competencies – help to 'reproduce' the structures of society?

3 Giddens says that social structures are *both* 'medium and outcome' of a social system. What he is getting at?

4 How does the modern reflexive monitoring of individual action come to alter social structures?

5 *Habitus* is both enabling and coercive. How so?

6 From clothing to musical taste, Bourdieu asserts that 'cultural capital' is at play. Make a reading of cultural capital in your own life.

Further reading

Anthony Giddens

Central Problems in Social Theory (Macmillan; University of California Press, 1979).
The Constitution of Society (Polity Press; University of California Press, 1984).
The Consequences of Modernity (Polity Press; Stanford University Press, 1990).
Modernity and Self-identity (Polity Press, 1991).

The Transformation of Intimacy (Polity Press, 1992).

Beyond Left and Right (Polity Press; Stanford University Press, 1994).

(with Ulrich Beck and Scott Lash) *Reflexive Modernization* (Stanford University Press, 1994).

Pierre Bourdieu

Outline of a Theory of Practice (Cambridge University Press, 1977).

Distinction (Routledge, 1984).

Homo Academicus (Polity Press, 1988).

Language and Symbolic Power (Polity Press, 1991).

The Field of Cultural Production (Polity Press, 1993).

The Rules of Art (Stanford University Press, 1995).

The State Nobility (Polity Press, 1996).

Weight of the World (Stanford University Press, 2000).

(with Priscilla Parkhurst Ferguson) *On Television* (New Press, 1999).

A good way to start further research on Giddens is with Christopher Pierson's interview book, *Conversations with Anthony Giddens* (Stanford University Press, 1998). There are many introductory works to Giddens. Some useful ones are Lars Bo Kasperson's *Anthony Giddens: An Introduction to a Social Theorist* (Blackwell, 2000), Ian Craib's *Anthony Giddens* (Routledge, 1992), and Ira Cohen's *Structuration Theory: Anthony Giddens and the Constitution of Social Life* (Macmillian, 1989). There are also edited critical readers on the work of Giddens including David Held and John B. Thompson's *Social Theory of Modern Societies: Anthony Giddens and his Critics* (Cambridge University Press, 1989), Christopher Bryant and David Jary's *Giddens' Theory of Structuration: A Critical Appreciation* (Routledge, 1991), and *The Contemporary Giddens* (Palgrave, 2001).

Some useful introductions to Pierre Bourdieu include R. Harker *et al.* (eds), *An Introduction to the Work of Pierre Bourdieu* (Macmillan, 1990), Jeremy Lane's *Pierre Bourdieu: A Critical Introduction* (Pluto Press, 2000), and Michael Grenfell's *Pierre Bourdieu: Key Concepts* (Acumen Press, 2008). For a more critical look at his work Craig Calhoun *et al.* (eds) have a critical collection of essays, *Pierre Bourdieu: Critical Perspectives* (University of Chicago Press, 1993). In addition, there are many critical books that focus on specific aspects of his theory including David Swartz's *Culture and Power: The Sociology of Pierre Bourdieu* (University of Chicago Press, 1998), Loic Wacquant's (2005) *Pierre Bourdieu and Democratic Politics* (Polity Press, 2005), and Bridget Fowler's *Pierre Bourdieu and Cultural Theory: Critical Investigations* (Sage, 1997).

Internet links

Anthony Giddens

http://www.edge.org/3rd_culture/bios/giddens.html
http://www.theory.org.uk/giddens2.htm
http://www.faculty.rsu.edu/~felwell/Theorists/Giddens/index.htm

Pierre Bourdieu

http://www.kirjasto.sci.fi/bourd.htm
http://www.guardian.co.uk/obituaries/story/0,,640396,00.html

chapter 6

Contemporary Critical Theory

Contents

In early 2002, the United States government identified Iraq, along with North Korea and Iran, as part of an 'axis of evil'. The argument put was that Iraq, under President Saddam Hussein, was a threat to America specifically and the world in general owing to its stockpiling of weapons of mass destruction. In addition, the United States argued that Hussein had tyrannized his own population and politically unsettled the Middle East. At a meeting of the United Nations General Assembly in late 2002, United States President George Bush urged the body to deal with the 'grave and gathering danger' of Iraq. A period of intensive political debate throughout the world about Iraq and the imminent threat it posed to global peace followed. The UN Security Council imposed new arms inspections on Iraq. Although many observers argued that Hussein's regime was cooperating with the demands imposed by international law, countries such as the United States, Great Britain and Spain remained unconvinced, warning that military action against Iraq may become inevitable. The political debate and dialogue continued through early 2003, while massive peace demonstrations were held in cites throughout the world. Eventually, however, the process of political debate and diplomatic dialogue came to an end – at which point talk transmuted into violence, dialogue into destruction. On 19 March 2003, the United States launched 'Operation Iraqi Freedom', an ongoing round of coordi- nated air strikes against Baghdad, coupled with the invasion of troops into the country. In its invasion of Iraq, the United States had in one stoke embraced unilateral militarism and brought unstuck the structure of international law.

A great deal of ink has been spilt explaining the American invasion of Iraq in 2003. Defenders argued that the United States invoked its military supremacy in order to maintain world peace – an argument that became increasingly dubious in light of the subsequent evidence that Iraq did not possess weapons of mass destruction. Critics of the war attributed the invasion to an American lust for oil. Others argued that the Iraq war was a result of widespread fear of Islamic terrorism. Some others contended that it was part of a neoconservative agenda to democratize the Middle East. Still others discerned the interests of turbo-capitalism at work: the high-pitched moral discourse of freedom and democracy was, it was argued, a cover for the profits reaped from the industrialization of war.

Whatever the precise mix of social forces at work, this disturbing episode in recent world history can help us to see the complex relation between democratic debate and political dialogue on the one hand, and the systemic institutional control of economic and bureaucratic logics on the other, in social and political affairs. In the approach of the world's leading critical theorist today, Jürgen Habermas, the deliberation over Iraq became systematically bent out of shape by extra-discursive forces (such as lust for oil profits, or the territorial ambitions of Empire) – at which point debate was replaced by the destruction of war. Rooted in the tradition of the Frankfurt School, Habermas' writings have been central to the revitalization of social theory and the progressive political imagination in recent decades. His path-breaking work on how lapses of communication and social misunderstandings are rooted in the power of invasive institutional forces has become increasingly influential, and much of this chapter is devoted to reviewing and appraising Habermas' critical social theory. Later in the chapter we will consider other developments in contemporary critical theory, notably Axel Honneth's theory of disrespect and recognition as well as theories of discursive democracy.

Habermas: the democratization of society

The ideas of reason and rationality, fundamental to the tradition of classical social theory, had come under fire through the most daring social critique with the Frankfurt School. The alleged connection between reason and progressive social change was profoundly challenged in the writings of Marcuse, Fromm, Adorno and Horkheimer. The major thrust of Frankfurt School critical theory was to explore the intricate interrelations between the textures of reason' and the dominance of techno-scientific rationalization, which from the outset was used to explicate the social barbarism and mass terror of the age, from the rise of Nazism and fascism in Europe to the degeneration of the Russian Revolution into Stalinism and the spread of technocratic societal management. In the aftermath of the Second World War, however, new political possibilities spread throughout Europe; the world, in short, looked very different to the bleak social diagnosis presented by the Frankfurt School. For example, West Germany commenced the task of developing a liberal political culture after the Allied powers had imposed a basic legal structure that provided for democratic political institutions, a development which took place against the international backdrop of growing Western economic prosperity. During this period, as discussed in Chapter 2, Marcuse remained in the United States, penning books which catapulted him to celebrity status with the New Left. Adorno and Horkheimer resettled in West Germany, and sought to defend their social critique. Yet, in various ways, the social theory elaborated by the Frankfurt School appeared somewhat out of kilter with the post-war world, and it was to fall to a new generation of critical theorists – the most prominent of whom was Jürgen Habermas – to remould the basic tenets of social theory.

If the societal backdrop to the Frankfurt School writings of Marcuse, Fromm, Adorno and Horkheimer was that of the Great Depression, Nazism and Soviet communism, the historical period in which Habermas developed his core theoretical and sociological preoccupations was very different indeed. As the nightmare of social barbarism and mass terror receded in the public mind, the world appeared to open out to different social pathways and more optimistic political possibilities. Habermas, a research assistant to Adorno in post-war Germany, developed his political sensibilities not only against the backcloth of the country's emerging preoccupation with democracy and liberal constitutionalism but also the student protests and new social movements sweeping Europe and the United States during the 1960s. Seeking to reformulate critical theory around the imperative of a radical democratization of society, Habermas believed that the basic assumptions of the Enlightenment – particularly the expansion of the spheres of freedom and solidarity – were adequate to transforming society.

Under the pragmatic presuppositions of an inclusive and non-coercive rational discourse among free and equal participants, everyone is required to take the perspective of everyone else, and thus project herself into the understandings of self and world of all others; from this interlocking of perspectives there emerges an ideally extended we-perspective from which all can test in common whether they wish to make a controversial norm the basis of their shared practice; and this should include mutual criticism of the appropriateness of the languages in terms of which situations and needs are interpreted. In the course of successfully taken abstractions, the core of generalizable interests can then emerge step by step.

Jürgen Habermas (1995) 'Reconciliation Through the Public Use of Reason: Remarks on John Rawls's Political Liberalism', *Journal of Philosophy*, 92 (3): 117–18.

Habermas conceived of his work from the outset as an attempt to reorientate social theory towards an interest in language in general and communication in particular. Like many other European intellectuals of the post-war years, such as Michel Foucault, Jacques Lacan and Jacques Derrida whose contributions we have examined, Habermas makes language a central preoccupation of social theory. But his analytical rigour and his interest in language is deployed to take critical social theory in a very specific direction, primarily as a means to understanding *the power of rationality in everyday life*. Language, communication and rationality are key themes of his revised social theory, and he insists that the heritage of Enlightenment reason is no mere projection of local tradition, preference or power. In this connection, his argument is that language is always orientated by and towards mutual agreement and consensus. This may be shown, he argues, in our most basic human capacities for speaking, hearing, reasoning and argumentation. In every act of speech, however shaped by power interests, validity claims are raised and reciprocally recognized: that what we say makes sense and is true, that we are sincere in saying it, and that there is a performative appropriateness to the saying of it. In reformulating critical theory in this way, Habermas projects from this conceptualization of language a radical approach to truth, defined as that which we ultimately come to rationally agree about through communicative dialogue. It is from our capacity for communicative reason that Habermas claims to discern a normative image of the political values of freedom, equality, mutuality and ethical responsibility.

The early Habermas: development and decline of the public sphere

A concern with the sociological distinction between the public sphere and private life has been fundamental to Habermas' social theory from his earliest published writings. *The Structural Transformation of the Public Sphere: An Inquiry into a Category of Bourgeois Society* (1989 [1962]), a detailed historical study which traces the emergence of a new kind of 'public opinion' to the eighteenth century, managed to combine Habermas' core interests in the public sphere and institutional structures, bourgeois society and social transformations, in its very title. In this early work, he traces the notion of the public sphere to the life of the polis in classical Greece. In ancient Greece, the public realm was constituted as a profoundly dialogical arena, a place where individuals came to meet to engage in a public discourse of critical reason and to debate issues of common interest. It was not until the development of mercantile capitalism in the sixteenth century, however, that the meaning of 'public opinion' began to shift away from the domain of courtly life as embedded in the traditional texture of old European societies and towards the expansion of market economies and newly defined spheres of division between the state and civil society. In the societies of early or market capitalism, individuals performed a vital role in mediating between the differentiated spheres of the state and civil society through interpersonal interaction, business dealings and civic association. Habermas argues that the essential condition for the emergence of these developments was the culture of the bourgeois family. In the intimate sphere of comfortable family life, a new individual subject emerged, one who was free to think about and probe the traditional textures of hierarchical authority. This emergent, critical attitude was transferred in time to the public domain and, consequently, the institutional structure of societies was transformed.

The emergence of the bourgeois public sphere, according to Habermas, may be traced to various forums of public discussion. Of key importance in this respect were the rise of newspapers, weekly journals and clubs throughout the cities of early modern Europe. In particular, newspapers and journals were used by various educated elites when interacting to debate and question political authority and the conduct of the state. 'Newspapers', wrote Habermas, 'changed from mere institutions for the publication of news into bearers and leaders of public opinion – weapons of party politics.' At the same time, the social basis of this emergent public realm became rooted in the coffee houses, lodges and literary salons of early eighteenth-century Europe, where individuals and groups met to exchange opinions on a dizzying array of ideas and ideologies. Under these social conditions, critical debate flourished.

> The bourgeois public sphere may be conceived above all as the sphere of private people come together as a public; they soon claimed the public sphere regulated from above against the public authorities themselves, to engage them in a debate over the general rules governing relations in the basically privatized but publicly relevant sphere of commodity exchange and social labor. The medium of this political confrontation was peculiar and without historical precedent: people's public use of their reason (*öffentliches Räsonnement*). In our [German] usage this term (i.e., *Räsonnement*) unmistakably preserves the polemical nuances of both sides: simultaneously the invocation of reason and its disdainful disparagement as merely malcontent griping.
>
> Jürgen Habermas (1989 [1962]) *The Structural Transformation of the Public Sphere: An Inquiry into a Category of Bourgeois Society*, trans. Thomas Burger with the assistance of Frederick Lawrence. Cambridge, MA: MIT Press, p. 27.

This then is a narrative of the bourgeois age in which unfettered public dialogue reigns supreme, and in which gentlemen come together in clubs and cafés to debate the key issues of the day. Habermas' account of the emergence of a debating public thus grants particular privilege to reason and rationality, logical thinking and consensus. Moreover, he sees in the rise of the bourgeois public sphere a direct parallel between the polis of classical Greek city-states and the literary salons and coffee houses of early eighteenth-century Europe, where the critical functions of dialogue and debate were celebrated as a kind of social good. This contrasts, says Habermas, very sharply with modern times. In industrially advanced mass democracies, these critical and probing aspects of the public sphere become substantially reduced. According to Habermas, the commercialization of the media begins to alter the bourgeois public sphere as a forum for the criticism of politics and public decision-making processes. In particular, there is a breakdown in the separation between the state and civil society. Under these conditions, the state comes to penetrate more and more the economy and civil society, and as such the public sphere is compressed. The rapid expansion of capitalism, and associated intensification of cultural consumption, spells the demise of the public sphere. The public sphere is shrunken, according to Habermas, as the corrosive bureaucratizing logic of capitalist society comes to eat away at the practical and civic agencies of everyday life as well as eroding the influence of broader cultural traditions.

These developments have significance, Habermas argues, not only for the relations between public and private life but also for politics in the contemporary age. The commercialization of the media and the growth of the culture industries in our own time, Habermas concludes, has produced a degradation of genuine civic engagement and the quality of public political debate. In order to understand this distortion of politics, Habermas outlines a critique in which he suggests that individuals today encounter mass communications in essentially *privatized* terms, as isolated selves obsessed with mediated spectacles. 'In comparison with printed communications,' writes Habermas,

> the programmes sent by the new media curtail the reactions of their recipients in a peculiar way. They draw the eyes and ears of the public under their spell but at the same time, by taking away its distance, place it under 'tutelage', which is to say they deprive it of the opportunity to say something and to disagree. . . . The sounding board of an educated stratum tutored in the public use of reason has been shattered: the public is split apart into minorities of specialists who put their reason to use nonpublicly and a great mass of consumers whose receptiveness is public but uncritical.

Our age of mediated conversation (TV chat shows, radio talkback) is that of politics trivialized. As Habermas concludes, 'today the conversation itself is administered'. The privatized reception of media communication is such that it may be pointless to speak of a robust public sphere at all, which in turn lies at the core of the urgency of Habermas' attempt to reconstruct critical social theory.

There are, however, various difficulties with Habermas' account of the development and decline of the public sphere. While there are many more critical points raised in the general literature on Habermas, there are three significant limitations that I think are worth noting. First, one important criticism is that Habermas' theory of the public sphere, through a series of progressive exclusions, ascribes significance to the *bourgeois* public sphere at the cost of displacing attention from other forms of popular culture and a variety of social movements. But this criticism demands immediate qualification. Habermas' work is not blind to the impact of various forms of popular culture as well as social movements upon the institutional character of modern states. Yet he does underestimate its significance. Recognition of the importance of popular cultural forms is not adequately taken into account in his theorization of the emergence of the public sphere, in the sense that these alternative worldviews and ideologies seem in no way to significantly influence, either positively or negatively, the coffee house debate and discourse that Habermas privileges.

Another, perhaps harsher, criticism of Habermas' early social theory is that it is premised upon a model of the rational human subject which has come under fire and today is widely discredited. In this connection, critics argue that *The Structural Transformation of the Public Sphere* is marred by a typically male and Western overestimation of 'reason' itself. In portraying gentlemen engaged in coffee house debate as the principal bearers of public opinion in the early modern period, Habermas arguably fails to engage with the deeper political implications of the constitution of the bourgeois public sphere as a predominantly white, male preserve. Feminist, post-feminist and post-colonial social theorists have, for example, profoundly challenged the supposed universal claims of the white, male subject to rationality, and have argued that such global claims have historically been implicated in the marginalization and oppression of minority cultures. If the white, male bourgeois figures as the principal agent of the public sphere in the early modern period, it is for structural, political reasons – the exclusion of women, ethnic minorities and others was so vital to the delineation of political life in early modern Europe, to such an extent as to be fundamental to the very character of the public sphere. It is thus that Habermas' attempt to generalize the male culture of the bourgeois public sphere is questionable, as is his argument that this model of public political life can provide a basis for freedom if successfully reinstated in the contemporary period.

Finally, Habermas' arguments concerning the demise of the public sphere are questionable. The central limitations of this standpoint are twofold. The first is that, while his account is surely correct in emphasizing the commercial character of the media as a factor in explaining the trivialization of politics and depoliticization of public life, Habermas fails to adequately consider the changing nature of the relation between the media, culture and society. Some critics argue that, while Habermas' account of the socio-economic shifts which have led to an erosion of the separation between the state and civil society as well as the emergence of a depoliticized culture is substantially valid, what he nevertheless fails to do is put those shifts into context in terms of issues of media consumption and cultural reception. Few would deny, for instance, that the commercialization of the media and cultural consumption do not impinge on many aspects of our lives. And yet it is surely too simplistic to suggest that such social developments have produced in one fell swoop a systematic degradation of public political life. The second limitation here concerns Habermas' failure to seriously engage with new forms of communication and information technology. Had he considered current developments in communications and transformations of technology, he would surely recognize the increased complexity of the public political sphere in today's media age. For the development of communications media, particularly the Internet and digital technologies, has significantly altered the relation between the public sphere and private life and – contrary to Habermas' diagnosis of the demise of the public sphere – politics is now a long way from being merely administered. Many of these developments in communications media, especially the growth of digital, decentralized technologies, may not at first sight appear to promote an extension of public political debate, but this is only the case if such developments are judged against traditional highbrow media formats. If disconnected from anachronistic assumptions about what constitutes genuine public debate, these trends might be used to make some sense of the otherwise puzzling explosion of new voices that the contemporary media ushers into existence. For many of these new media forums and formats, from talkback and talk shows to Internet chat-rooms, is where many people engage with the public sphere, defining issues of social importance which critics have too hastily defined as apolitical or trivial. The current media age is certainly not identical with Habermas' portrait of the demise of the public sphere, and it seems evident that what social theory now requires is a framework of analysis for the public sphere that is relevant to transformations of twenty-first-century social life.

Habermas on capitalism, communication and colonization

During the late 1970s and throughout the 1980s, Habermas became increasingly preoccupied with addressing the social conditions of rational decision-making and of delineating the conditions under which communicative argumentation and debate might best flourish in modern societies. In one sense, this shift away from consideration of the public sphere to the social critique of communication made his social theory more directly politically relevant. The historical reconstruction of the public sphere, its flowering and faltering, had given way to more pressing realities of social rationalization and capitalist commodification in societies of the West. Modernity was a world which combined lethal rationalization with seductive consumerism, one upshot of which for Habermas was a wholesale fragmentation of social consciousness. Against the backdrop of a dramatic rise in large corporations, as well as pervasive cultural rationalization stemming from the breakup of society into various specialized, technical processes, it was not surprising that Habermas' work from this period became more specifically sociological in orientation. If the arrival of late capitalism signalled a new phase of globalism, then so too social theory required a new analytic with which to confront the most pressing issues of the day. In Habermas' hands, this meant a return to Grand Theory.

Habermas' Grand Theory scoops up and reconfigures conceptual traditions from Marxism to the Frankfurt School, while along the way managing to incorporate the traditions of symbolic interactionism and functionalism. As far as the relationship between rationality and communication goes, however, Habermas' key reference point in *The Theory of Communicative Action* is the work of Max Weber. For it was Weber's account of purposive-rational action, according to Habermas, that paved the way for grasping the rationalization of Western culture, from science, law and politics to art, music and literature. Yet there remain various respects in which Weber's theory of Western modernization as the upshot of a universal historical unfolding of rationalization remains inadequate for understanding the production of modern society. It is against this backdrop that Habermas reassesses Weber's critique of reason. There is a key difference, Habermas contends, between believing in reason as fundamental to the attainment of the good society on the one hand and processes of rationalization on the other. You can believe in the power of reason without being committed to the social rationalization of culture. Indeed, Habermas raises the important question of whether Weber failed to consider that capitalist modernization represents only a partial attainment of the development of reason through degraded processes of rationalization.

In one sense, rationalization is inescapable, since the functional reproduction of large-scale technical systems, such as banking or pensions, is essential to the coordination of life today as we know it. Nevertheless, the coordination of such systemic mechanisms does not take place in a social vacuum. All societal structures, no matter how seemingly technical or administrative, must be anchored in the deeper symbolic textures of society. This, to be sure, requires attention to language, communication and cultural relations. It is against this backdrop that Habermas situates his social theory with reference to what he terms the 'lifeworld', that everyday space of symbolic interaction and communicative dialogue in which individuals generate particular practices and encounter social structures that become incarnate in their daily activities. In doing so, Habermas develops in his *magnum opus The Theory of Communicative Action* (1987) an account of the relations between rationality and communication that differs in many respects from the first generation of critical theory. While Habermas, like the Frankfurt School, retains many of the links between political domination, social pathologies and repression of the self, he refuses to accept that the idea of the 'administered society' provides an adequate characterization of late capitalist societies. According to Habermas, the fatalistic vision of reason as self-mutilating in early critical theory arises because of a specific theoretical assumption: namely, that technological rationality applies writ large in all spheres of social action. For Habermas, however, societies develop not only through technological modes of action but also through symbolic interaction, or what he calls 'communicative action'. If mastery of the external world is dependent upon forms of instrumental rationalization, then it is crucial to recognize that the social world is structured to its core through language, communication and symbolic exchange. For Habermas, this analytical separation indicates that there are cognitive, moral and expressive dimensions of social life. The expansion of science, morality and art in modern culture, in Habermas' view, suggests that rationality can be divided into 'three worlds': our relation to the external world, our social relations with others, and an aesthetic-expressive dimension which we bring to our own 'inner nature'.

The lifeworld for Habermas refers to certain fundamental convictions and traditions, to collectively shared commitments. These commitments are not necessarily easily articulated, but they are fundamental to the way people live. To believe that it is decent to give a friendly welcome to colleagues arriving at work, to demonstrate extra caution driving a car when children are crossing the road, to offer your bus seat to someone elderly: these are basic kinds of commitments that both preserve the cultural traditions of previous generations and contribute to the reproduction of personal identity and social integration. By contrast, there are actions to do with the functional integration of society which are only partially related to the symbolic field of the lifeworld. Functional systems, then, do not pertain to the question of having value commitments. That my bank maintains its technical support system for Internet banking is primarily an achievement of what Habermas terms 'systematically stabilized action-contexts'.

Things are different when system integration intervenes in the very forms of social integration. . . . the subjective inconspicuousness of systemic constraints that *instrumentalize* a communicatively structured lifeworld takes on the character of deception, of objectively false consciousness. The effects of the system on the lifeworld, which

> change the structure of contexts of action in socially integrated groups, have to remain hidden. The reproductive constraints that instrumentalize a lifeworld without weakening the illusion of its self-sufficiency have to hide, so to speak, in the pores of communicative action. This gives rise to a *structural violence* that, without becoming manifest as such, takes hold of the forms of intersubjectivity of possible understanding. Structural violence is exercised by way of systematic restrictions on communication; distortion is anchored in the formal conditions of communicative action in such a way that the interrelation of the objective, social, and subjective worlds gets prejudged for participants in a typical fashion.
>
> Jürgen Habermas (1987 [1981]) *The Theory of Communicative Action, vol. 2*, trans. Thomas McCarthy. Cambridge: Polity Press, pp. 186–7.

It follows from this analytical separation of system and lifeworld that one must distinguish processes of administrative and economic rationalization from distortions inflicted upon the symbolic texture of everyday life. Habermas argues that the rationalization of systems on the one hand, and that of the lifeworld on the other, follow entirely different logics. According to Habermas, the uncoupling of 'system' from the 'lifeworld' is *not* a sign of cultural domination. On the contrary, this division is intrinsic to modernity. Modern societies, in short, are highly differentiated, divided between the technical reproduction of complex systems and the communicative competence of social actors. On one side there are system domains, specializing in the material reproduction of capitalism and the modern bureaucratic state. On the other side there is the lifeworld, specializing in symbolic reproduction – involving communicative competence and dialogue as reproduced in processes of self-formation, socialization and cultural transmission. Now as far as the good society goes, this theory obviously carries significant implications. For one thing, Habermas stresses that any account of the freeing potential of rationality must recognize that the complex systems of modern social life are here to stay. The functional regulation of society, which necessarily entails the coordination of economic and administrative structures, is an essential part of modernity. Such intrinsic aspects of modernity must be carefully distinguished, however, from those insidious forces by which the rationalized logic of systems reproduction seeps into everyday communicative practice. In Habermas' view, the spheres of systems and communicative rationalization sometimes intersect in perversely damaging ways, one upshot of which is personal alienation, lack of societal direction and cultural crisis.

From this more differentiated account of rationalization, Habermas is able to return to the traditional concerns of critical theory: analysing the distorted and pathological aspects of the modern era. Like Marcuse, Fromm and Adorno, Habermas agrees that modern culture has become increasingly subjected to administrative and bureaucratic control. As the modern state becomes increasingly centralized and systematized, so too the communicative and consensual foundations of the life-world have been subjected to rationalization. In fact, systems integration in modernity has become rationalized to such an extent that Habermas speaks of an 'inner colonization of the lifeworld'. He summarizes this destruction of the resources of cultural tradition as follows:

> The analysis of processes of modernization begins from the general assumption that a progressively rationalized lifeworld is both uncoupled from and made dependent on formally organized action domains, such as the economy and state administration, which are always becoming more complex. This dependence, stemming from the mediazation of the lifeworld through system imperatives, assumes the social-pathological form of an *inner colonisation* in so far as critical disequilibria in material reproduction (that is, steering crises accessible to system-theoretical analysis) can be avoided only at the cost of disturbances in the symbolic reproduction of the lifeworld (i.e., of 'subjectively' experienced, identity-threatening crises or pathologies).
>
> (Habermas in Thompson 1984: 291)

In modernized societies, then, functional rationalization has reached the point where it threatens the very foundations of cultural transmission, socialization, and the formation of self-identity upon which it depends for its own legitimation. Having gone beyond their facilitating roles, the economic and administrative systems of the institutional order are today producing 'pathological' effects via the rationalized penetration of the lifeworld. However, the distinction between 'system' and 'lifeworld' allows Habermas to claim that processes of rationalization are not as total in character as they might at first appear. There is a deep resistance, he contends, at the core of subjectivity. The pathological effects of such cultural rationalization will often be defended against by the lifeworld. The rise of new social movements, such as ecological and anti-nuclear associations, highlights for Habermas the existence of such tendencies.

The importance of these issues becomes clear if we consider the links between the capacity to engage in social discourse and public debate and certain contemporary ideological biases which repress, privatize and displace particular interests from the dialogic process. Nancy Fraser, in a persuasive critique of Habermas' work, argues that male dominance and female subordination is a basic element of the current gender system which profoundly delimits equal sexual access to the medium of public debate (Fraser 1987). Fraser charges Habermas' model with a gender-blindness in theorizing the conditions for free communicative practice, claiming that it represses any consideration of women's institutional incapacity to bring certain issues, thoughts and feelings to light. As an example of women's incapacity to enter public discourse, Fraser points to the many legal jurisdictions in which marital rape is not sanctioned as a crime. If, in the legal domain, women are unable to refuse sexual relations, Fraser enquires, how can they possibly bring their deeper needs, aspirations and desires to a dialogic process which renders their interests invalid? If women's relationship to collective autonomy is already systematically distorted in this way – 'when a woman says "no" she means "yes"' – then surely the crucial matter of women's participation in political debate is also likely to be consistently misunderstood and devalued? The key problem, in Fraser's view, is that Habermas' model closes down consideration of the relation between the public sphere of political speech and the institutional repression of interests precisely at the point where the most pressing problems arise.

Emotional imperialism: feminist criticism of Habermas

Our present political order in the affluent West is based upon the invasion of economic forces into relationships of intimacy, care and our emotional lives as never before. Increasingly, in both the affluent West and the developing world, we witness the invasion of economic thinking into the private realm of personal identity, interpersonal relationships, family life, sexuality and intimacy.

Consider, for example, the 'outsourcing' of care for the young, sick and elderly from rich countries to the developing world. In countries such as Sri Lanka, Thailand and the Philippines, many marginalized, poor women feel economically compelled to migrate to the West in order to obtain paid employment by providing care in contexts of affluent family life. American sociologist Arlie Hochschild terms this global trend the 'care drain', a kind of asset stripping of migrant labour from the developing world.

We can better conceptualize the social forces driving this care drain with reference to Habermas' ideas on the colonization of the 'lifeworld' by the 'system'. As contemporary women and men in the work-orientated West find themselves with less and less quality time available for non-work pursuits, so the private sphere and family life – traditional spaces of care and nurturance – come under the influence of invasive economic forces. This dominance arises through the importing of care from the developing world, as traditional caring roles are replaced more and more by economic relations involving cash, credit and power inequalities.

Put this way, Habermas' social theory directly engages with how globalization is restructuring fundamental aspects of our lives. However, some feminists argue that Habermas' view of modernity as involving an uncoupling of 'system' and 'lifeworld' leaves untouched the complex connections between society and gender. That is to say, Habermas' work fails to examine the arguments and evidence concerning transformations of modernity along gendered lines.

In an influential critique, Nancy Fraser (1987) contends that Habermas' thesis of a colonization of the 'lifeworld' by the 'system' is blind to current gender inequalities. Moreover, this blindness reasserts a traditional masculine view of the relation between the public and private spheres as gender neutral. Habermas' distinction between the private realm of the lifeworld and the institutional economic system, according to Fraser,

> directs attention away from the fact that the household, like the paid workplace, is a site of labor, albeit of unremunerated and often unrecognized labor. Likewise, it does not make visible the fact that in the paid workforce, as in the household, women are assigned to, indeed ghettoized in, distinctively feminine, service-orientated, and often sexualized occupations. Finally, it fails to focalize the fact that in both spheres women are subordinated to men.

This sheds light on an unexplored dimension of the social changes affecting the public–private distinction in Habermas' social theory. Fraser highlights the gendered subtext of Habermas' theory of the modern age: the private sphere of the lifeworld, she argues, is far from gender neutral; it has fallen to women, over a long historical period, to carry out the work of domesticity and of providing the emotional labour of care, comfort and nurturance in family life. But money and power, she notes, should not be viewed as separated off from the private sphere, or as somehow only recently penetrating the world of domestic family life from the institutionalized economic system. According to Fraser, money and power have always been intricately intertwined with the internal dynamics of the family.

Habermas on globalization and post-national societies

As cultural awareness of the immense possibilities and threats of global-ization accelerated throughout the 1990s, Habermas began renewed reflection on the conditions and consequences of democracy in a world where transnational forms of liberal democratic decision-making are increasingly viable and necessary. In his more recent work, he has argued that since the nation-state is poorly equipped to deal with the extraordinary political, legal and normative challenges posed by globalization, a new 'post-national constellation' is needed at the transnational level to promote democracy and human freedom. Deeply appreciative of the immediate challenges posed by globalization to traditional conceptions of democratic self-governance, political institutions, the public sphere as well as freedom, ethics and justice, he has maintained the goal of a new society based on communicative rationality, one centred upon democratic processes of collective decision-making across territorial borders.

In his discussion of globalization and the political possibilities for new transnational institutions, Habermas explores whether in the complex societies of late capitalism the nation-state is still the central driving force in institutional politics. While acknowledging that proclamations about the supposed 'death of the nation-state' have been greatly exaggerated, he notes that there has been a perceptible change in public consciousness concerning the capacity of national states to effectively respond to, and deal with, global political problems. There are a number of persistent key themes in Habermas' late writings in this connection, and these can be summa-rized as follows. First, he argues that the disempowering consequences of globalization for national governments are increasingly evident. He writes (2001b: 80):

> The fiscal basis for social policies has steadily dwindled, while the state has increasingly lost its capacity to steer the economy via macro-economic policy. Moreover, the integrational force of nationality as a way of life is diminishing, along with the relatively homogeneous basis of civil solidarity. As nation-states increasingly lose their capacity for action and the stability of their collective identities, they will find it more and more difficult to meet the need for self-legitimation.

Second, he contends that the moral and political challenges facing the European Union cannot be met by adapting a policy of *laissez-faire*, much less by embracing neoliberal or postmodern theories of globalization processes. 'Under the changed conditions of the postnational constellation,' writes Habermas (2001b: 81),

> the nation-state is not going to regain its old strength by retreating into its shell. Neo-nationalist protectionism cannot explain how a world society is supposed to be divided back up into pieces, unless through a global politics which, right or wrong, it insists is a chimera. A politics of self-liquidation – letting the state simply merge into postnational networks – is just as unconvincing. And postmodern neoliberalism cannot explain how the deficits in steering competencies and legitimation that emerge at the national level can be compensated at the supranational level without new forms of political regulation.

Third, Habermas argues that the prospects for transnational political institutions are better than ever before, but so too our need to achieve global solidarity has never been greater. Again, he stresses that European Union institutions can significantly contribute to the furtherance of democratic political communication, and in this connection he questions the political claims advanced by Eurosceptics, Market Europeans and Eurofederalists. The growth of transnational or transboundary problems for national political communities can only be partly addressed by bureaucratic initiatives and market dynamics; we are compelled, says Habermas, to recognize both the intensity and extensity of globalizing forces, with all the radical challenges this presents for democratic political thought. Finally, he argues in favour of popular processes of collective will-formation at the global level. In short, he suggests that social solidarity, which has for so long been stabilized at the level of nation-states, must be shifted up a gear in order to produce a cosmopolitan sense of shared commitments and shared responsibilities. Such a radicalization of democracy, comments Habermas, is not necessarily abstract; the flowering of culturally cosmopolitan sentiments of belonging, inclusion and shared interests is already emerging from the weakening of the nation-state. In terms of the debate over Europe, Habermas (2001b: 103) wishes to speak up for

> a pan-European political public sphere that presupposes a European civil society, complete with interest groups, non-governmental organisation, citizens' movements, and so forth. Transnational mass media can only construct this multivocal communicative context if, as is already the case in smaller countries, national education systems provide the basis of a common language – even if in most cases it is a

foreign language. The normative impulses that first set these different processes in motion from their scattered national sites will themselves only come about through overlapping projects or a common political culture.

It is perhaps not difficult to discern parallels between Habermas' call for cosmopolitan global government and his early, path-breaking arguments concerning political transformations of publicness, as set out in *The Structural Transformation of The Public Sphere* (1962). An emphasis on the rapid expansion of political participation within the bourgeois public sphere was an essential aspect of Habermas' early social and political thought, particularly the democratic initiatives leading to new forms of public life beyond the sphere of the state. The historical emergence of a bourgeois public sphere in the eighteenth century, as represented by Habermas, signified emergent individuation, autonomy and enlightenment – even though he acknowledged that the political form of such a 'public' did not last for long. It is clear, at least in the context of the arguments developed in his essay 'The Postnational Constellation and the Future of Democracy' (Habermas 2001c), that Habermas still sets ultimate political value on public participation and the widest reaching democratization of decision-making processes. Only popular processes of communication and practical discourse, reflecting the impress of collective will-formation, will adequately generate forms of cosmopolitan solidarity geared to the pluralization of democracy emerging at the level of transnational or global social policies. Crucially, moreover, it is clear that Habermas views such democratization as central to the advancement of modernity, especially in terms of the development of post-conventional learning patterns in the realms of society, personality and culture. As he puts this (2001b: 102),

> The artificial conditions in which national consciousness arose argue against the defeatist assumption that a form of civic solidarity among strangers can only be generated within the confines of the nation. If this form of collective identity was due to a highly abstractive leap from the local and dynastic to national and then to democratic consciousness, why shouldn't this learning process be able to continue?

Towards deliberative democracy

Perhaps more than any other contemporary social theorist, Habermas' recent writings on communicative discourse and ethics are responsible for an explosion of interest in the possibilities and dilemmas of democratic politics in the current age. Since the collapse of authoritarian communism in the late 1980s throughout the former Soviet Union, in East Central Europe and the Baltic countries, along with apparent shifts from dictatorship to liberalism in countries such as Brazil, Argentina and the Philippines, a global trend towards democracy has been celebrated and critiqued in equal measure by many social scientists and intellectuals indebted to Habermas. Some of the most prominent social scientists writing on contemporary politics – such as Amy Gutmann, Seyla Benhabib and Iris Young – have drawn from Habermas' recent work not only to better understand how communicative rationality and reasoned judgements shape the contours of democracy. They have also drawn from Habermas to better understand the *processes* by which reasoned decisions are collectively framed and considered. This focus on the processes of fair and transparent communication is what many social and political theorists have termed 'deliberative democracy'. The idea of deliberation, it is argued by such authors, provides for a conception of democracy that can chart the continued spread of democratic autonomy throughout the globe, as well as critique oppositions to this democratic trend – as demonstrated in the many civil wars, ethnic and national conflicts of recent years, from the Middle East to North Africa.

What is 'deliberative democracy'? The deliberative conception of democracy is firmly grounded in the collective judgement of the people. According to proponents Amy Gutmann and Dennis Thompson (2004: 3)

> deliberative democracy affirms the need to justify decisions made by citizens and their representatives. Both are expected to justify the laws they would impose on one another. In a democracy, leaders should therefore give reasons for their decisions, and respond to the reasons that citizens give in return.

What is being underscored here is the capacity of citizens to reflect on arguments and differing points of view, the ability of individuals to deliberate on particular policy proposals and political judgements. What matters is that decisions are reached through a *process* of collective decision-making, but this should not be taken to imply that the deliberative process will always produce agreement. Disagreements between individuals and groups are an endemic feature of politics, and hence deliberative democracy must be conceived of as open-ended. It may then help to view deliberation less as a particular style of politics, than as a particular open-ended process of argument and counter-argument within politics.

Consider, once more, the invasion of Iraq in 2003. Prior to commencing military action against Saddam Hussein, the United States government sought to justify its decision to go to war before the Congress and United Nations. Various arguments were advanced by the Bush administration concerning the exhaustion of non-military options against Iraq. Secret intelligence relating to Iraq's alleged weapons of mass destruction was also cited by, among others, American, British and Australian governments as justifying the military decision to attack Iraq. But while individuals may not have had sufficient time to carefully appraise these political arguments at the time they were made, what matters from the standpoint of deliberative democracy is that individuals were subsequently able to profoundly question their original judgements. As Gutmann and Thompson (2004: 2) argue:

> the deliberation that did occur laid the foundation for a more sustained and more informative debate after the U.S. military victory than would otherwise have taken place. Because the administration had given reasons (such as the threat of the weapons of mass destruction) for taking action, critics had more basis to continue to dispute the original decision, and to challenge the administration's judgment. The imperfect deliberation that preceded the war prepared the ground for the less imperfect deliberation that followed.

How relevant do you find the deliberative conception of democracy to today's political realities? How might the idea of deliberative democracy apply in a world of 24/7 media and global information flows?

Criticisms of Habermas

Habermas' writings on communicative action, democracy and discourse ethics, as well as Europe and the post-national constellation, rank among the richest, most sophisticated contributions to contemporary critical theory. His writings have been, nevertheless, subject to a barrage of criticisms. I will concentrate upon three major weaknesses identified by critics – the first concerning his analysis of modern societies, the second concerning his model of language for social critique, and the third concerning his notion of democratic deliberation and discourse ethics.

Social theory ought to be able to provide some account of its own political positioning and historical contextualization as discourse, especially as regards the relationship between social critique and the analysis of social domination. It seems, however, that for some critics Habermas' thesis of the inner colonization of the lifeworld is simply too generalized. One complaint sometimes heard is that Habermas has replaced one top-heavy critique of the present day – that of the 'administered society' developed in early critical theory – with another top-heavy version. On this view, the thesis of the inner colonization of the lifeworld remains too indebted to the theories of social rationalization advanced by Adorno, Horkheimer and Marcuse. Society stands over and above the individual, with big social institutions ultimately controlling the actions of actors. I have already indicated that it is mistaken to see Habermas as equating processes of social rationalization with the phenomenon of administered societies traced in early critical theory. For one thing, the analytical differentiation of system and lifeworld recognizes the complexity of processes of social reproduction in a fashion that certain currents of Marxist thought cannot; for another, the interpersonal perspective deployed by Habermas for theorizing communication in the contemporary era is significantly different from the solitary subject-centred orientation to be found in Adorno, Horkheimer and Marcuse. Another charge sometimes heard against Habermas, somewhat more plausibly, is that he has taken over too much of Weber's gloomy social diagnosis and renovated it for the contemporary era. In a striking paradox, then, Habermas' criticism that Weber confined rationalization to purposive rationality is, in the final analysis, disowned in his theory of communicative action. While separating out the spheres of social rationalization and communicative rationality at a theoretical level, Habermas ends up concurring with Weber that a degraded form of rationality predominates in modern societies. In this as in other ways, the legacy of classical sociology reasserts its power over modern social theory.

However, the more pressing difficulty arising from Habermas' work, in my opinion, concerns not the top-heavy or gloomy account he provides of social rationalization and domination (for, as noted, Habermas is far too subtle and sophisticated a social analyst for these charges to have much force), but rather why actors do not perceive such threats more acutely. In effect, this is to raise the question of how might Habermas' theory of the inner colonization of the lifeworld round upon its own conditions of possibility as lived experience? John B. Thompson (1984: n.p.) puts such concerns forcefully:

Why do members of the life-world not perceive that they are threatened by the uncontrolled growth of system complexity, rooted ultimately in the dynamics of capital accumulation and valorization? Why do they not resist this growth directly and demand, in an open and widespread way, the transformation of the economic system which underlies it?

If a traumatized lifeworld threatens to bring society undone, this would appear to be a trauma that for Habermas remains blocked to consciousness – denied, displaced, disowned. But such an assessment of modern culture is surely questionable. It may be that social practices like booking a flight online, watching a DVD or listening to talkback radio are so contaminated by the functional logic of late capitalism that people cannot possibly think outside of these terms. But could the same be said for donating money to Oxfam or Save the Children, attending a community meeting on local government issues or reassessing the weekly grocery list in terms of environmental considerations? There is no easy way to understand the ideological or political differences as regards such social practices in Habermas' sociology, save for invoking the terms 'inner colonization' or 'social pathology'. Yet one might reasonably wonder how suggestive such terms are for grasping the diversity and plurality of social practices in the current age.

Second, Habermas' work has come in for some sharp criticism as regards his model of language and how he ties forms of communicative rationality to the project of critical theory. There are serious reservations, for example, about the supposedly invariable, intrinsic connections between language, rationality and the counterfactual ideal speech situation which Habermas posits. In what sense, one might reasonably wonder, does the yelling of obscenities at a football match presuppose an orientation towards mutual agreement and consensus? How might one discern in the slogans of fascist organizations, such as the British National Party or the National Front, respect for the ideals of communication and community? These are indeed serious problems, and some critics have gone so far as to suggest that Habermas' model of communicative rationality is too procedural and legalistic, unable to account in all but the most abstract fashion for how people might agree on what counts as a better argument in concrete instances of political conflict. How might the impact of colonialism, post-colonialism, race, ethnicity, sexuality and gender affect participants in debates affecting their forms of life? Part of the difficulty here, according to Seyla Benhabib, is that Habermas' model is pitched so wide as to accommodate only the 'generalized other' and not the 'concrete other'. Viewed from this perspective, we can identify the political limitations of Habermas' theory of communicative rationality more precisely. In theory, Habermas' model presumes that reason permits individuals to decide on competing perspectives and that decisions or norms can be judged fair provided that all people are equally affected. But how can such a political ideal of communicative rationality be projected from a model of language to a world in which actions, decisions, debates and norms affect millions and millions of people widely scattered in space and time?

Finally, some commentators are especially critical of Habermas' reconceptualization of the normative dimension of the public sphere in terms of the theory of communicative action and deliberative democracy. For these critics, it is not easy to see how democratic ideals can be projected from the allegedly universal structures of language. The weak version of this criticism is that Habermas' deep consensus theory of truth does not sufficiently protect liberal values such as human rights or freedom of expression (see Gutmann and Thompson 2004). The stronger version of this criticism is that Habermas' overall democratic project fails to adequately account for the grip of neurotic, compulsive patterns of behaviour – patterns that block the very grounds for deliberating rationally in modern societies. The argument, bluntly put, is that Habermas' notion of rational consensus is out of kilter with the plurality of moral, ethical and related evaluative standpoints that proliferate in contemporary societies. How might it be possible, for example, to provide individuals with equal chances to deliberate, let alone ever successfully disentangle the 'force of the better argument', on the controversial political and moral issues of our times? And quite how Habermas' vision of unconstrained communication applies to our 24/7 media and entertainment culture is not immediately apparent. Other critics note that Habermas' stress on participation in rational debate cannot cope with problems arising from the exclusionary character of the public sphere – exclusions on grounds of, say, identity, gender or ethnicity (see Fraser 1987). Ultimately, all of these criticisms appear to acknowledge that democratization requires an undoing of the systematic distortion of the communicative structures of modern societies. Where these critics part company with Habermas, however, concerns the adequacy of the notion of rational consensus as a means of confronting the moral and practical issues of our times. The problem, in other words, is that Habermas' consensual, cooperative theory of social action seems to bear little relation to the kinds of politics, cultures and lifestyles that predominate in these early years of the twenty-first century.

Honneth: the struggle for recognition

One of the more influential inheritors of the tradition of critical theory in our own time is Axel Honneth. Like Adorno, Marcuse and Habermas before him, Honneth attempts to unmask pathologies of society as rooted in the fragility and fragmentation of reason. Yet whereas Habermas connects the fitful interplay of reason and irrationality to other fundamental forces, revolving on language, communication and dialogue, Honneth is more concerned to trace our daily social conflicts in terms of moral experiences of disrespect, denigration and humiliation. To do this, Honneth focuses in *Disrespect* (2007) on the notion of recognition, drawing attention to the growing political demands today of individuals and groups for public acknowledgement of particular identities, needs, emotions and more particular ways of life. According to Honneth, demands for social recognition derive from relays or transmissions of negative, painful experiences of disrespect. From the psychological experience of humiliation to the political ramifications of injustice, social antagonisms and cultural conflicts are for Honneth associated with the attempted recovery of individual needs and desires for self-respect. Recognition, rather like the interpersonal, dynamic process of communication itself, is an open-ended affair which facilitates ceaseless explorations of, and reconciliations between, self-assertion and dependency, individualism and solidarity.

Social life contains different kinds of recognition, each anchored in different experiences of interpersonal interaction and moral claims. Honneth focuses on three forms of recognition in particular, which he seeks to connect to the normative or utopian aspirations of critical theory. These are (1) self-confidence; (2) self-respect; and (3) self-esteem. Confidence in continuity of the self derives from our primary emotional relationships with familial or significant others in childhood. These earliest experiences of love are for Honneth essential preconditions for the realization of mature ego-development. Drawing from the psychoanalytic theories of D.W. Winnicott, Honneth considers how early experiences of love contribute to the emergent individual's negotiation of social interaction – with a focus on the role of unconscious spontaneity in shaping the moral conduct of daily life. What matters in such early interactions between the infant and mother, or significant other, is not that the child learns to view itself as a fully independent being in one fell swoop; rather, a complex emotional interplay between self-assertion and attachment is established. At their emotional core, human relationships are always marked by a radical tension between connection and separation, dependence and self-assertion. It is from this interplay that individuals develop a positive emotional relation to their own identities, as well as self-confidence for acting in the wider world.

Love, in Honneth's opinion, fulfils the role of preparing individuals for the difficult emotional work of reconciling demands for recognition from others on the one hand with the desire for self-assertion on the other hand throughout life. Love is thus, one might claim, at the very root of both moral identity and political society. Indeed, Honneth contends that the experience of self-confidence which derives from love is 'conceptually and genetically prior' to other forms of identity recognition – such as respect and esteem. The demand for recognition knows no inner limit. It can be held in place only by intersubjective, reciprocal, moral, political and legal forms, which means that it is always in process rather than at some final point of destination. This is surely one reason why all demands for recognition betray a kind of personal injury or cultural trauma at their very core. The form or kind of violation in question, according to Honneth, can be of three sorts – corresponding to the earlier typology of self-confidence, self-respect and self-esteem. Because people are routinely maltreated in familial and wider social circles, the experience of self-identity often contains some degree of emotional damage. A similar logic is at work with the modern political world in general, where exclusion from certain legal rights is inseparable from harm to a person's sense of self-respect. In another sense, the fate of self-esteem hangs on how others react to, and engage with, the way of life a person has chosen.

Demands for recognition, then, always harbour certain experiences of disrespect, which they seek to recall and reconfigure in social and political terms. Feelings of shame, humiliation or rage are an emotional infinity, which can be interpreted as signs of injustice. Indeed, the desire for freedom is shaped to its core by experiences of social disrespect – there is an *internal link*, according to Honneth, between the sense of injustice and the demand for recognition. Such injustice, or the experience of disrespect, acts as a trigger for the launching of social antagonisms or cultural conflicts against the established political order. Only in this way, says Honneth, can the progressive movement towards more democratic public spheres be understood. Consider, for example, the women's movement and feminism. The emergence of the women's movement, and especially the heyday of feminism in the 1960s and 1970s, involved the critical examination of certain exclusions of women from the workforce in particular and wider society in general. The whole sensibility of feminism involved a reappraisal of women's suffering away from the narrowly psychological realm and towards social life as a whole. There was a genuinely excited sense that feminism as a social movement offered a new, enlightened understanding of women's oppression. The anxiety and depression which many women suffered in the modern age had their roots not in any emotional failings or maladjustments of women themselves, but in power imbalances and gender divisions throughout society. Using the ideas of Honneth, the exclusion of women from the public sphere and confinement to domesticity occurred as part of a patriarchal blending of control and violence, denigration and injustice. Feminism, as both social theory and social movement, thus came about as more and more people developed a new self-consciousness of these traumatic exclusions – determined as they were to initiate a societal shift from gender injustice to gender struggle.

In one sense, Honneth's reorientation of contemporary critical theory away from communication and towards recognition brings social critique closer to the bone of current political conflicts. That is to say, Honneth underwrites the sociological significance of a range of new social movements, respecting their demands for political recognition and seeing in them a radical challenge to traditional ideas about class, economy and the nation-state. For Honneth, a critical theory of recognition dovetails with the new politics of identity, culture, ethnicity and difference – which runs all the way from post-feminism and the green movement to the struggles of indigenous peoples and the politics of multiculturalism. This is not to say that recognition theory is simply an index of the contemporary political climate; it is also, vitally, a normative or utopian image of how individuals and groups might navigate the troubled waters of the twenty-first century. From this angle, for example, the fight that an organization like Amnesty International has waged against state torture may be recast as part of a 'politics of self-confidence' – the unmasking of forms of bodily violation, tied to the demand for human rights.

Honneth's theory of recognition has been important for contemporary social theory. In outlining alternative strategies for engaging the new politics of identity and cultural difference, his work has scooped up and reconfigured social theory, moral theory and political philosophy. His approach has certain affinities with other theorists of the 'politics of recognition', such as Charles Taylor and Seyla Benhabib, but arguably Honneth's is the richest in terms of social theory rather than political philosophy. For to understand social conflicts after Honneth means being able to grasp the new politics of recognition as rooted in the experience of disrespect or humiliation. From this perspective, Honneth's attempt to recover the political meanings and normative possibilities springing from displaced emotions is a return to the original Frankfurt School project of investigating the personal dimensions of social crisis and political domination. Notwithstanding this, and while also acknowledging that Honneth's work is still in the process of elaboration, there are difficulties worth noting. For one thing, it is not immediately obvious what needs to be done to conclusively prove Honneth's account of recognition correct. That is to say, how exactly might such an abstract account of human needs – manifesting as the desire for recognition – be tested against current global realities? Does the fact that only some groups in society demand special forms of public recognition invalidate the general sweep of Honneth's theory? What about the personal and social conditions under which people become aware of hurt feelings? Honneth seems to assume that the objective forms of disrespect – towards women of colour, ethnic groups, indigenous peoples and others marginalized – are always accompanied by an awareness of hurt feelings. But is this, in fact, so? What of the consequences of cultural trauma? Is it not the case that the suffering and pain inflicted upon some victims of state violence is so brutal that individuals are unable to struggle against such injustice? Part of the difficulty here is that Honneth, while attentive to the emotional dimensions of human suffering, and while selectively engaged with psychoanalysis, fails to appreciate that the *unconscious* can block the translation of hurt feelings into the public demand for recognition.

The shift from disrespect to a struggle for recognition and justice, in other words, is only likely to come about in quite specific personal and political conditions. In our own time, the rise of globalization, multinational corporations and a wall-to-wall entertainment culture is arguably such that many individuals are incapacitated to some degree in their emotional capacities as concerns the translation of private injuries into demands for political recognition. Not only is this something that Honneth is insufficiently alert to – unlike the Frankfurt School, for example, he says little about the 'culture industries' – but it leads him to overestimate the degree to which demands for recognition can actually transform social relations. In Honneth's account, the emergence of more inclusive institutional forms of recognition – which unfold through the new politics of identity and cultural difference – is intrinsically tied to the moral progress of society. But, again, why should this be so? Why should the politics of recognition result always in the progressive moral advancement of society? How, at any rate, might we adequately judge between morally valid and invalid types of identity-politics? What of the demands for recognition from neo-nationalist movements or ethnic tribal traditions? Cornelius Castoriadis (1997: 398) captures this political point well:

> I do not respect others' difference simply as difference and without regard to what they are and what they do. I do not respect the difference of the sadist, of Eichmann, or Beria – any more than those who cut off people's heads, or even their hands, even if they are not threatening me directly.

If it is true that recognition struggles lead to moral progress, the onus is on Honneth to demonstrate how this might tally with a world in which disrespect appears limitless. Like Habermas, Honneth focuses on morality to emphasize the learning capacities of individuals, groups and social institutions within society. This is a fundamental aspect of contemporary critical theory. But it is a dimension of both Habermas' and Honneth's work which at times pulls uneasily against the commitment to social critique elaborated in the Frankfurt School writings of Adorno, Fromm and Marcuse. For as the Frankfurt School demonstrated, moral discourse is around to help us realize the best of which we are capable; while it is the task of social theory to remind us of how and why, as a society, we often fall short of such lofty ambitions.

Summary points

1 Contemporary critical theory represents the systematic extension of ideas developed by the neo-Marxist Frankfurt School in order to analyse current global transformations. The leading representative of contemporary critical theory is Jürgen Habermas, Emeritus Professor of the University of Frankfurt and one of Europe's foremost public intellectuals.

2 Habermas' contributions to social theory span some five decades. But all of his contributions, broadly speaking, contest technocratic social policy and power politics in the name of a more rounded communicative approach to social life and morality.

3 Focusing on language in general and communication in particular, Habermas seeks to reconstruct the presuppositions of human communication, dialogue and debate. His essential idea is that any statement about the world raises three validity claims: that the claim

makes sense and is true, that the claim is sincere, and that there is a performative appropriateness to the saying of it. From this idea, Habermas derives a theory of truth defined as rational agreement through communicative dialogue.

4 In Habermas' studies of the public sphere, reason and rationality are traced as fundamental to the transformed relations between personal and social life in market capitalism. In advanced capitalism, however, bureaucracy, technology and the culture industries erode the quality of public political debate. Politics and social life, says Habermas, become *administered*.

5 Modern societies for Habermas are powerfully torn by conflicts between the 'lifeworld' and 'systems reproduction', so much so that the latter comes to *colonize* the former. These conflicts are between communicative action in the lifeworld (the social dialogues that remain in principle open to rational debate) on the one hand, and on the other hand capitalist culture, bureaucracy and technology that come to dominate the modern world.

6 There have been various criticisms made of Habermas' reformulations of critical theory, including that his account of the colonization of the lifeworld by large-scale technical systems is too Marxist or deterministic. A related criticism is that Habermas neglects how culture and the economy intermingle in the lives of individuals; contemporary cultural processes are simply dismissed as trivializing and, thus, Habermas ignores the vital ways in which cultural creativity may be used to contest social pathologies issuing from capitalism, bureaucracy and technology.

Further questions

1 Does public debate lead to an advancement of reason and rationality?

2 What are some modern arenas for public debate?

3 Habermas argues that freedom and solidarity are universal values that should be supported. Do you agree? Should they be supported with force?

4 What kinds of contact with the public sphere have you experienced throughout your life? How does discussion and deliberation lead to a better society?

5   Do you use Internet news sources such as blogs, chat-rooms or discussion boards to engage with political developments and news?

Further reading

Jürgen Habermas

The Theory of Communicative Action (Polity Press, 1987).
Moral Consciousness and Communicative Action (MIT Press, 2001).
The Structural Transformation of the Public Sphere (Polity Press, 1989).
Between Facts and Norms: Contributions to a Discourse Theory of Law and Democracy (Polity Press, 1996).
The Postnational Constellation: Political Essays (Polity Press, 2001).

Axel Honneth

The Struggle for Recognition: The Moral Grammar of Social Conflicts (Polity Press, 1995).
Disrespect: The Normative Foundations of Critical Theory (Polity Press, 2007).

Useful introductions to the early work of Habermas include Thomas McCarthy's *Critical Theory of Jürgen Habermas* (MIT Press, 1978) and John B. Thompson's *Critical Hermeneutics: A Study in the Thought of Paul Ricoeur and Jürgen Habermas* (Cambridge University Press, 1981). Some good overviews of Habermas' mature social theory are William Outhwaite's *Habermas: A Critical Introduction* (Polity Press, 1994) and Stephen White's *The Cambridge Companion to Habermas* (Cambridge University Press, 1995). A short introduction to Habermas' theory of society is Jane Braaten's *Habermas's Critical Theory of Society* (SUNY Press, 1991).

The literature on deliberative democracy is extensive. See, for example, Amy Gutmann and Dennis Thompson, *Why Deliberative Democracy?* (Princeton University Press, 2004); Seyla Benhabib (ed.), *Democracy and Difference* (Princeton University Press, 1996), and James S. Fishkin, *Democracy and Deliberation: New Directions for Democratic Reform* (Yale University Press, 1991).

A discussion of Honneth's early social theory may be found in Anthony Elliott, *Critical Visions: New Directions in Social Theory* (Rowman and Littlefield, 2003). A useful summary of Honneth's approach to recognition theory is Simon Thompson's *The Political Theory of Recognition* (Polity Press, 2006).

Internet links

Critical theory

http://www.cla.purdue.edu/academic/engl/theory/
http://plato.stanford.edu/entries/critical-theory/
http://www.uwec.edu/ranowlan/intr_whystudy_crit_thy.htm

Jürgen Habermas

http://www.habermasforum.dk/
http://www.uky.edu/ per cent7Ecfzurn/CZonJHLong.pdf
http://www.helsinki.fi/~amkauppi/hablinks.html

Axel Honneth

http://www.phillwebb.net/History/TwentiethCentury/Continental/Marxism
/Honneth/Honneth.htm

chapter 7

Feminism and Post-feminist theory

Contents

In a university where I worked some years ago, an email exchange among colleagues rapidly and dramatically threatened to bring some promising academic careers undone. The precise details I have long since forgotten, but the core of the matter concerned what people then called a 'gender incident' – a matter which had arisen over nothing more and nothing less than the hasty deployment of words (issuing from a colleague's email), and which then attached itself to powerful emotions throughout this university department. This served to divide and antagonize various members of staff. Along the way, several staff noted for their reconciliatory talents tried to intervene in the dispute. Yet each further email only seemed to make matters worse, as if dragging language away from whatever connections to social things and events it might once have had. Such was the play of emotional forces operating inside this heated exchange of language that confusion abounded, no one could agree or take up any single, consistent viewpoint in relation to the incident. Established patterns of meaning within this academic department were thrown into question. Furthermore, the original parties to this dispute were going through absolute contortions in order to defend themselves against certain misunderstandings and possible trans-gressions of gender politics. Each email, or at least according to memory, began: 'What I meant to say was . . .'.

When, more than thirty years ago in Europe, the psychoanalytic feminist Julia Kristeva wrote so insightfully of a pattern or play of unconscious forces at work inside language, she may have had in mind experiences of this kind, even though as a literary critic the bulk of her own work has addressed the writings of poets and novelists. Kristeva, whose contribution to feminism and post-feminist theory we will examine in some detail throughout this chapter, looks to the emotionally laden realm of the repressed unconscious – what she terms the 'semiotic' – as enabling for feminism. Like many feminist social theorists who have turned to psychoanalysis to better understand how unequal gender relations shape identities and everyday life, such as Juliet Mitchell, Nancy Chodorow, Jessica Benjamin and Judith Butler, Kristeva focuses on the repressed unconscious or 'semiotic' as a means of undermining the patriarchal sexual and social order of modern societies. Kristeva's version of feminism, as we will see, is in one sense all her own – an exotic blend of Lacan, linguistics, literary criticism and post-structuralism. In the course of this chapter, however, we will also review other groundbreaking feminist criticism, ranging across engagements with sociology, psychology, political theory, postmodernism and queer theory. In all of these approaches, feminism and post-feminist theory provide a crucial link between embodied experience and social relations, between identity and culture, between problems of identity or sexuality and problems of social organization.

Theorizing patriarchy: 1970s feminisms

The university dispute over gender I mentioned above took place in the 1980s. This was a time in which academics, feminists and political progressives of various kinds were becoming increasingly aware of multiple differences between women, between women and men, and indeed of the powers of social diversity and cultural difference in the making of identity itself. This is perhaps why, in the university gender dispute I recall, there seemed to be as many divisions between female colleagues as there were political differences between women and men. At the level of social theory, this increasing attention to both gender differences and social divisions within feminism was closely aligned with the influence of post-structuralism (see Chapter 4). Various post-structuralist emphases, from its suspicion of 'identity' to its debunking of metaphysical foundations, seemed to fit hand-in-glove with the rise of the more consumerist and individualizing 1980s. Yet deconstructing the differing styles of gender, through either post-structuralist or postmodern discursive analyses, was itself a counter-reaction to an earlier feminist sensibility. I am referring to 1970s gender theory, in which an emphasis on women's shared needs and political interests was considered key to the critique of gender.

In her classic book *The Second Sex* (1988 [1949]: 295), the French feminist Simone de Beauvoir declared: 'One is not born, one becomes, a woman.' This statement prefigured the whole cast of 1970s gender theory, with its totalizing claim that gender goes all the way down, and thus organizes the very constitution and shape of 'femininity' and 'masculinity'. Human beings are born male and female, but become men and women through a process of social construction. Seeking to give some analytical precision to this gendered process of social construction, the British feminist Ann Oakley (1972) wrote of a distinction between biological 'sex' and socialized 'gender'. This was an attempt, in effect, to overwrite the naturalization of biology with the cultural learning investigated by sociology. Gender reproduction, in this view, refers to the ways in which people are socialized into distinct gender patterns of behaviour. Gender roles of 'masculinity' and 'femininity' may be experienced by people in their daily lives as spontaneous dispositions, but are in fact deeply determined by the wider society and culture. Gender is bound up with cultural forces of socialization, role learning and gender stereotyping.

'Sex' is a biological term: 'gender' a psychological and cultural one. Common sense suggests that they are merely two ways of looking at the same division and that someone who belongs to, say, the female sex will automatically belong to the corresponding (feminine) gender. In reality this is not so. To be a man or a woman, a boy, or a girl, is as much a function of dress, gesture, occupation, social network and personality, as it is of possessing a particular set of genitals.

This rather surprising contention is supported by a number of facts. First, anthropologists have reported variation in the way different cultures define gender. It is true that every society uses biological sex as a criterion for the ascription of gender, but, beyond that simple starting point, no two cultures would agree completely on what distinguishes one gender from the other. Needless to say, every society believes that its own definitions of gender correspond to the biological duality of sex.

Culturally, therefore, one finds the same biological distinctions between male and female coexisting with great variations in gender roles. By contrast one also finds individual people whose culturally defined genders coexist with indeterminate sex.

Ann Oakley (1972) *Sex Gender and Society*. Melbourne: Sun Books, p. 158.

The claim that the whole of our lives is carried out within the frame of certain 'sex roles' or 'sex-role stereotyping' gave rise to the highly politically charged character of much feminist social theory throughout the 1970s. Whether studying the broader gender context of family life, education or the job market, feminist social theorists argued that gender and sexuality are key organizing forces of social relations and cultural domination. One valuable insight of feminism in the 1970s was the unearthing of the intricate connections between personal and family life, sexuality and culture. Gender stereotypes or norms were demonstrated to be indissociable from certain ideological forces – such as capitalist market relations or bureaucratic authority – and thus deeply bound up with issues of power and social control. If gender roles reflected patterns of sexual inequality, this is because we live in a social order in which men are dominant. On this reckoning, masculinity symbolizes power and prestige, with women recast by a sexist culture as subordinate and oppressed. The political task of feminism thus emerged as involving not only the critique of men's dominance in the social order but a particular form of politics, concerned with social justice and the transformation of gender relations in modern societies.

The rise of gender theory during the 1970s occurred when radical politics, especially liberationist movements and black civil rights protests, was in the ascendant. Feminism, as part of a multitude of liberationist social movements, was concerned to put the whole sexual and social order of modern societies into question in the name of a transformed and emancipated social organization. For some, the ambition of feminism's social critique was over-politicized; for others, the emancipatory zeal of feminism was mere utopianism. Nevertheless, the women's movement – as the political wing of feminist social theory – was stunningly successful in its impact upon both personal and political life. From the nursery to marriage, the field of gender was unmasked by feminist social theorists as social and political to its very roots. Gender was deployed in this context to refer to both the constitution of differences between men and women and the perpetuation of male domination throughout history. The upside of this political deployment of social theory is that it offered a strikingly direct account of the social dynamics of the gender – with power encircling solicited gender roles at every turn. The downside of 1970s feminism, however, is that gender binaries – dominant masculinity, subordinate femininity – seemed to become entrenched. Not only were possible similarities and points of emotional connection between women and men sidestepped, but the matter of social and cultural differences between women were theoretically and politically ignored. As feminist theorist Lynne Segal (1999: 42) observes of the limits of 1970s gender theory:

> many men have little or no purchase on the power that is supposed to be the prerogative of their sex, while a significant minority of women have access to considerable power and privilege. Gender binaries never exist in pristine form. Women and men are always already inserted in contexts of race, class, age, sexual orientation and multiple other belongings: each with their deeply entrenched connections to power and authority, or the lack of it.

Gender theory of the 1970s is now some thirty years or so behind us. Yet the social theory of gender undertaken throughout the 1970s is not all cut from the same cloth. While gender theory undoubtedly had as its prime focus issues of women's shared needs, social subordination and gender inequalities, there were countless reworkings of feminist social theory during this period. Some of the most significant theoretical breakthroughs concerned trying to understand how unequal gender relations bite deeply within the fabric of personal experience and the textures of daily life. Other innovative feminist research focused on the interplay of women's role as mothers on the one hand, and the cultural learning of gender on the other. In both approaches, gender was understood as sociologically and psychologically complex in character, and in the groundbreaking work of feminist social theorists such as Mitchell, Dinnerstein, Chodorow and Benjamin the field of gender was always conceptualized within the broader structures of society, culture and politics.

Juliet Mitchell on femininity and sexual difference

The publication in 1974 of Juliet Mitchell's *Psychoanalysis and Feminism* represented a path-breaking moment in feminist theory in the English-speaking world. This widely read book defended the importance of psychoanalysis to feminism and women's oppression, developed a powerful critique of the biological reductionism implicit in then influential feminist psychologies, and introduced Lacan to many English-speaking people. Like many other social theorists we have looked at in the course of this book, Mitchell made use of Lacan's approach in studying identity in order to grasp how modern societies perpetuate gender divisions. In emphasizing the importance of loss to the making of identity (see Chapter 4), Mitchell radicalizes Lacan's emphasis.

> The greater part of the feminist movement has identified Freud as the enemy. It is held that psychoanalysis claims women are inferior and that they can achieve true femininity only as wives and mothers. Psychoanalysis is seen as a justification for the status-quo, bourgeois and patriarchal, and Freud in his own person exemplifies these qualities. I would agree that popularized Freudianism must answer to this description; but the argument of this book is that a rejection of psychoanalysis and of Freud's works is fatal for feminism. However it may have been used, psychoanalysis is not a recommendation *for* a patriarchal society, but an analysis *of* one. If we are interested in understanding and challenging the oppression of women, we cannot afford to neglect it.
>
> Juliet Mitchell (1974) *Psychoanalysis and Feminism*. London: Penguin Books, p. xiii.

Mitchell argues that the unconscious acquisition of patriarchy in modern societies is central to women's suffering. In Mitchell's analysis of femininity, the family and sexual politics, a Lacanian-based feminism is developed to make the following points: the positioning of the human unconscious within asymmetrical power relations as men and women; the separation between biological sex and the construction of sexual difference; and the consequent interlinking of sexuality and other forms of ideology for the replication of unequal power relations. That the account of sexual difference offered by Freud and Lacan should be read as an *analysis* of the psychic roots of patriarchal social relations, and not as a justification for patriarchy, is perhaps the main contribution of Mitchell's early work to feminism. In this view, Freud's account of the central 'marks of womanhood' – masochism, penis envy, jealousy, a weak superego – are understood as a consequence of women's subjection to patriarchal law, and not as innate psychological attributes.

Femininity, for Mitchell as for Lacan, is defined by loss. Woman, in this view, is nothing outside of the various linguistic, psychological, social and cultural constructions in which identities are forged. Sexuality and subjectivity, intertwined in the unconscious, are constituted with entry into the symbolic order of language (see the discussion of Lacan's Saussurian-influenced account of language in Chapter 4). Perhaps one of the most controversial psychoanalytic claims that contemporary social theory engages with is the idea that gender identity is tied to loss – specifically, the possession or absence of the penis. When considering Lacan's theory in Chapter 4, we looked in some detail at how his 'return to Freud' involved reinterpreting certain core concepts in psychoanalysis – the Oedipus complex and castration, for example – through the lens of post-Saussurian linguistics. It is these aspects of Lacan's work on sexuality to which Mitchell is especially attentive, which now requires us to reconsider some aspects of Freud's work and its subsequent modification by Lacan. Several features of Freud's theory are relevant for understanding Mitchell's feminism. In Freud's account of the Oedipus complex, an active, masculine sexuality is attributed to children of both sexes – as Freud puts this, 'the little girl is a little man'. Biological sex difference, in this view, remains irrelevant for the child until the onset of the phallic phase, in which sexual difference becomes centred on the possession or absence of the penis. In the case of boys, said Freud, Oedipus depends upon an imagined event of the father's threat of castration; in the case of girls, castration is imagined as having already been inflicted.

Why does Freud argue that girls suffer from 'penis envy'? Many feminists reject Freudian psychoanalysis as sexist, and initially at least it is easy to see why. But Mitchell rejects this claim; she argues that Freud's claim about the little girl's 'penis envy' is, in fact, a critique of how patriarchy goes all the way down – to our emotional lives, gender and intimacy. Girls, as Mitchell rehearses Freud, respond to the discovery of genital difference through *imagining* that castration has already taken place – both upon themselves and their similarly 'castrated' mothers. Freud makes clear that this occurs at the level of *fantasy*; none the less it is a fantasy that calls into question the girl's former masculine sexuality – she realizes that she lacks the penis with which to pursue her active, libidinal desires. Rejecting her mother in fury, the girl withdraws emotionally and instead turns towards her father. But this is a kind of emotional dead-end, once the girl realizes that she cannot have her father exclusively. As such, the girl turns back – unconsciously – towards her mother, and forges an identification with her feminine gender position.

It is precisely these aspects of Freud's account of gender identity – Oedipus, the castration complex and sexual difference as the result of a painful emotional division within the child – which Mitchell feels are fruitfully extended in the work of Lacan. In Lacan's theory, as discussed in Chapter 4, the child's entry into social relations occurs at the symbolic level of language. The shift from the child's imaginary unity with the maternal body into a symbolic order of social and sexual differences requires the intervention of a third person (the father), or term (language). By prohibiting the child access to the mother's body, the symbolic order (or what Lacan calls the 'Name-of-the-Father') operates to institute the threat of castration – the *power* backing this threat being symbolized by his *phallus*. The phallus both serves to wrench the child away from desire for the mother (which must be repressed) and stands for entry into the symbolic order. That is to say, the position an individual takes up as a gendered subject within the symbolic order is necessarily tied to a fundamental loss – the loss of the maternal body. And it is because of this loss of the maternal body that human sexuality is understood as being created within a lack, leaving the phallus to stand in for the divided and incomplete human subject at the level of sexual division.

Following Lacan, Mitchell argues that the phallus – at the level of cultural fantasy – inscribes unequal gender relations at the heart of identity. One reason why gender relations are unequal, says Mitchell, is that social difference is *represented* by men. Children encounter difference through reference to the father, as representative of language and the symbolic world. Linking Lacan with structuralist emphases, Mitchell thus argues that female sexuality is not something with 'positive' content. Femininity acquires meaning only by way of its *difference* from masculinity. The category 'woman' operates as an idealized Other, entirely separate from particular females, that men and women fantasize as a potential site of desire, fulfilment, joy and wholeness. Female sexuality is thus an imaginary supplement to that lack which informs the structure of subjectivity. A radical feminist politics, for Mitchell, implies interrogating and subverting those rigid masculine, phallic phantasies that are so central to our systematically unequal gender relations.

> The girl only acquires her secondary feminine identity within the law of patriarchy in her positive Oedipus complex when she is seduced/raped by, and/or seduces the father. As the boy becomes heir to the law with his acceptance of the symbolic castration from his father, the girl learns her feminine destiny with this symbolic seduction. But it is less important than the boy's 'castration', because she has to some extent perceived her situation before it is thus confirmed by the father's intervention. She has already accepted the information that as she is not heir to the phallus she does not need to accept symbolic castration (she is already 'castrated'). But without the father's role in her positive Oedipus complex she could remain locked in the pre-Oedipal dilemmas (and hence would become psychotic), for the Oedipus complex is her entry into her human heritage of femininity. Freud always said that a woman was 'more bisexual' than a man. By this he seems to have been hinting at the fact that within patriarchy her desire to take the father's place and be the phallus for the mother is as strong as the boy's ultimate right to do so. The bisexual disposition of her pre-Oedipal moment remains strong and her Oedipus complex is a poor, secondary affair. An affair in which she learns that her subjugation to the law of the father entails her becoming the representative of 'nature' and 'sexuality', a chaos of spontaneous, intuitive creativity. As she cannot receive the 'touch' of the law, her submission to it must be in establishing herself as its opposite – as all that is loving and irrational. Such is the condition of patriarchal human history.
>
> Juliet Mitchell (1974) *Psychoanalysis and Feminism*. London: Penguin Books, pp. 404–5.

What perhaps was so striking, and ultimately so disturbing, about Mitchell's feminist engagement with psychoanalysis was its bypassing of notions of cultural learning or socialization in favour of a more complex model of both psychic experience and gender identity. This involved an in-depth feminist reading of both Freud and Lacan, and in particular grappling with the psychoanalytic claim that fathers or men – in breaking the imaginary unity of the mother-and-child unit – represent the core links between power and desire in the current gender order. Of course, one response within feminist social theory to Mitchell's work was simply to dismiss psychoanalysis

contemporary social theory

as itself sexist. However, and as already noted, Mitchell had confronted that claim directly, refocusing psychoanalysis as a *critique* of patriarchy. More interestingly, some critics asked whether fathers or men must always stand as the representative of the symbolic order of language. For if this is so, surely it seems to suggest that a non-patriarchal symbolic order is impossible, thus undercutting the feminist political project in one stroke. Such questions were obviously vital to feminist social theory, and in time served to clarify the principal shortcomings of Mitchell's approach to gender identity. Perhaps the most widely agreed limitation is that, notwithstanding her use of very complex psychoanalytic categories and concepts, Mitchell's analysis tends to exaggerate the rigidities and uniformity of gender in the current social order. If, as Mitchell claims, women entirely repress their unconscious sexuality and become symbolically fixed in relation to the phallus as the lacking Other (that is, as men's object of desire) it is extraordinarily difficult to understand what motivates feminist strategy in the first place or how a radical politics might destabilize gender categories.

Contrary to Mitchell's exploration of gender identity, still we might ask: Is the symbolic order of language, painstakingly tracked in psychoanalytic theory and post-structuralism, really so rigid and monolithic? Can femininity only be defined as the negative pole of masculinity? These are questions to which feminist social theory returns, and develops some novel answers, throughout the 1980s and 1990s. But first we must turn to some other versions of feminist social theory, which seek to shift the emphasis away from fathers or men and towards mothers or women in the constitution of gender identity.

Dinnerstein: societal nurturing arrangements

The idea that our earliest emotional experiences of family life are fundamental to the formation of gender identity has been central to many femininst interpretations of patriarchy. Dorothy Dinnerstein is one theorist who has given particular emphasis to the impact of mothering under patriarchy in the analysis of gender inequality. In *The Mermaid and the Minotaur* (1976), Dinnerstein examines the psychic impact upon the sexes of societal nurturing arrangements. Her claim is that, given exclusive female mothering in late capitalist societies, children of both sexes encounter a social context that violently deforms gender. Female mothering, Dinnerstein says, leads us inevitably to fear women. Both sexes fear the power that mothers wield over them as infants, a fear which leads children to betray the 'engulfing mother' by turning to the father in search of emotional security. Paternal authority offered by the father offers an escape route from ambivalence, involving infantile helplessness, rage and hate felt towards the mother. As Dinnerstein writes: 'It is as we leave infancy that the possibility of transferring dependent, submissive feeling to the second parent – whose different gender carries the promise of a new deal, a clean sweep – entices us into the trap of male domination' (1976: 186). In other words, patriarchy is the outcome of a denial of emotional ambivalence: unconscious anguish in connection to the mother is denied, coupled to an idealization of paternal authority. The psychic costs of this denial are severe. Men and women remain haunted by the memory of maternal dominance. For while infantile helplessness may have been repudiated, the return of the repressed continually threatens to outstrip masculinist culture. Significantly this situation, says Dinnerstein, is worse for women than for men. Associated with the power of mothering, women are doubly denigrated – as mother and as wife or lover – within the contemporary gender system.

Situating her analysis of the mother/child relationship within a Kleinian framework, Dinnerstein contends that socially predominant ideologies of gender are marked by a failure to work through persecutory and depressive anxieties about women, especially women's role as mothers. Instead of gaining a sense of the mother as an independent agent, fantasies proliferate about women as all-powerful and thus as objects of fear. In this context, Dinnerstein locates some of the most pathological features of contemporary culture: man's need to control and humiliate women; woman's collaboration in denigrating her own sex; the domination of nature; sexual violence; and the cultural denial of human fragility. The way forward to a transformation of gender, says Dinnerstein, is through shared parenting. 'So long as the first parent is a woman,' writes Dinnerstein, 'women will inevitably be pressed into the dual role of indispensable quasi-human supporter and deadly quasi-human enemy of the self.'

Dinnerstein's work offered one of the first psychoanalytic challenges to mainstream feminist accounts of gender relations. Society, for Dinnerstein, is not something external, which then 'goes to work' on people by imprinting gender power. Rather, society is a force that penetrates to the deepest emotional roots of sexual experience, engendering anti-female feelings in the very act of constituting the self. As such, her work raises important issues about the connections between sexuality, power and culture. Significant as it is, though, Dinnerstein's critique of gender is severely limited by several major flaws. She assumes, for example, that the avoidance of psychic pain in early life connects with the devaluation of women in a universal, mechanistic way. What this overlooks, however, is that motherhood is situated in a social, political and economic context – a *patriarchal* context which distorts the social organization of parenting and childrearing. In other words, what Dinnerstein's model cannot adequately accommodate is the impact of ideology: those complex, contradictory political forms through which society influences the feelings, thoughts and aspirations of individuals. This is a serious omission, and it is one which causes Dinnerstein to ignore the point that men, as well as women, can be idealized, envied, feared and hated. Moreover, Dinnerstein's account of the contemporary gender system runs into a kind of theoretical brick wall since she cannot comprehend resistances to, or transformations in, gender power. Women and men are simply deemed dependent on patriarchy as a way of side-stepping their neurotic, paranoid reactions to motherhood, childrearing and nature.

Chodorow: *The Reproduction of Mothering*

In *The Reproduction of Mothering* (1978), Nancy Chodorow argues that exclusive female mothering leads to gender oppression. In her view, women's mothering is pivotal for understanding gender development and division since it is a global feature of the sexual division of labour. Chodorow argues that, in mothering, women become primarily preoccupied with emotional and relational issues; women turn their energies to the care of their children and families. By contrast, men work in the cold and detached world of public and economic affairs. As men are less connected to their emotional lives, they develop more analytical modes of relating to others and the wider society. Chodorow says that we need to know more about this division of gender roles, and accompanying sense of self, in order to understand the cultural logic of gender hierarchy and to contest oppressive social relationships.

According to Chodorow, Freud's model of gender development – in which the mother hovers in the background – is unconvincing at best and plainly defective at worst. In situating the mother as the first emotional attachment for the child, Freudian theory opened up a fertile research area relating to the emotional consequences of maternity. Yet mothers, paradoxically, are accorded little recognition in shaping the psychology of the self in Freud's writings. Instead, the child's attachment to the mother is broken up through the intrusive impact of the father – which Freud theorized in terms of the Oedipus complex. The symbolic intervention of the father, represented by the phallus, into the mother/child dyad is fundamental to the constitution of selfhood, gender, sexuality, meaning, rationality and culture. Freud's theory is essentially father-centred; mothers do not get much recognition for their input into self or gender development. Rejecting what she sees as the patriarchal assumptions of classical Freudian theory, Chodorow turns to object-relational theories of psychoanalysis and also to theories of core gender identity. In doing so, she develops a perspective that examines not only the infant's needs and desires in its earliest years (as with classical Freudian theory), but also the desires for, and behaviour towards, the child experienced by parents. The constitution and development of self and gender, says Chodorow, involve a two-way traffic – between parents and child.

It is Chodorow's contention that the creation of self and gender depends upon the internalization – an emotional taking in or incorporation – of imagery of the mother. In the early pre-Oedipal period, where the father does not figure as a strong emotional presence, the process of gender differentiation is set in train by the mother's mode of relating to, and interaction towards, her child. This brings us to the core of Chodorow's argument: *mothers relate to daughters in a fashion that they do not to sons.* The mother, Chodorow says, relates to her daughter as an extension of herself, as a double, as belonging to the same gender. Since daughters are treated by mothers as the same, the daughter in turn finds it extremely difficult to separate from her mother, to establish a sense of personal identity and autonomy. The consequences of this are complex. Chodorow suggests that daughters are likely to grow up with a strong sense of emotional continuity with their mothers. This sense of continuity provides for intimate, relational connections throughout women's adult life, but it also results in problems of merging with others, difficulties with interpersonal boundaries, and disturbances of self and identity. All this serves to drive the daughter from the love of her mother to the security offered by her father; this subsequent and defensive identification with the father serves as an unacknowledged support for oppressive gender relations and patriarchy.

Mothers tend to experience their daughters as more like, and continuous with, themselves. Correspondingly, girls tend to remain part of the dyadic primary mother–child relationship itself. This means that a girl continues to experience herself as involved in issues of merging and separation, and in an attachment characterized

contemporary social theory

by primary identification and the fusion of identification and object choice. By contrast, mothers experience their sons as a male opposite. Boys are more likely to have been pushed out of the preoedipal relationship, and to have had to curtail their primary love and sense of emphatic tie with their mother. A boy has engaged, and has been required to engage, in a more emphatic individuation and a more defensive firming of experienced ego boundaries. Issues of differentiation have become intertwined with sexual issues. This does not mean that women have 'weaker' ego boundaries than men or are more prone to psychosis. Disturbances in the early relation to a caretaker have equally profound effects on each, but these effects differ according to gender. The earliest mode of individuation, the primary construction of the ego and its inner object-world, the earliest conflicts and the earliest unconscious definitions of self, the earliest threats to individuation and the earliest anxieties which call up defences, all differ for boys and girls because of differences in the character of the early mother–child relationship for each.

Nancy Chodorow (1978) *The Reproduction of Mothering*. Berkeley: University of California Press, pp. 166–7.

The sense of sameness imposed by mothers upon their daughters stands in marked contrast to the projection of difference and otherness on to sons. Boys, according to Chodorow, separate more easily than do girls because the mother treats the male child as different, as a member of the other gender. Here masculinity is constituted by maternal disengagement: the mother, because of the child's otherness, propels the boy towards differentiation and individuality. Boys must learn to deny their primary emotional attachment to the mother. By turning away from their emotional dependence on the mother, boys direct their energies to more active, and very often aggressive, forms of play and relationship. In doing so, boys, with the help of their mothers, begin to prepare for the sorts of emotional detachment and analytical forms of reasoning that the economic world of capitalism will demand from them in later life.

If Chodorow sometimes worries that gender identity is not as clear-cut as her theory implies – What of lesbian mothers? What influence do house-husbands wield? What impact do siblings have? – the story that emerges from her book about the emotional roots of women's mothering is forceful and compelling. Since the emotional core of feminine identity is relational – that is, there is a strong preoccupation with issues of nurturance, care, empathy and relatedness – women will tend to look for such emotional resources in other people in their adult relationships. But here women run into difficulties. Since men are very often emotionally detached and unresponsive to more reflective and caring relationships, women routinely find themselves cut off from interpersonal communication and erotic intimacy with their partners. In order to escape from this emotional deadlock, women turn instead to the prospects and challenges of motherhood. Chodorow thus suggests that the desire to mother is, in part, produced from current distortions and pathologies of gender hierarchy. Against this bleak assessment, she urges shared parenting as a means of challenging and subverting the reproduction of gender difference and hierarchy.

Chodorow's work has exercised enormous influence in feminism, sociology and social theory. Her account of core gender identity (that is, socially induced psychological constructions of femininity and masculinity) is appealing owing to its potentially wide application – from public policy issues concerning parenting to differences in the moral outlooks of men and women. Her argument that there is a basic gender identity for males and females has proved attractive to many wishing to understand the persistence of patriarchy. In this respect, Chodorow's claims about female psychology are illuminating – especially her assertion that women want to have children in order to recapture the primary bond of the mother/daughter relationship. Women's lives, she says, are potentially emotionally bereft because men are cut off from sexual intimacy and interpersonal communication. From this angle, the desire to have a child is actually rooted in the distortions of the current gender system. Conversely, the abstract traits of male selfhood described by Chodorow provide a direct purchase on men's anxieties over intimacy and love. Masculinity, says Chodorow, necessarily involves the adoption of intolerance, insensitivity and emotional coerciveness. From this angle, male sexual dominance, often involving the use of violence towards women, has its roots in the damaged, fragile and precarious nature of masculine identity.

However, Chodorow's feminism, as the reader will have gathered, is not without its problems. There is, for example, something too neat about Chodorow's claim that exclusive female mothering produces gender oppression. Chodorow presents us with a model of woman as mother, as primary caretaker, with female desire sharply constrained by this social role. Yet is mothering really so sharply constrained and constraining? For instance, what of mothers who encourage 'feminine' modes of expression in their sons? What of mothers who foster 'masculine' aims of autonomy, independence and achievement in their daughters? What of the sharp rise of single-parent, mother-led families? The difficulty is that Chodorow tends to ignore the vast complexity of familial life in modern societies, and privileges instead a traditional style of mothering rapidly in decline today. As Lynne Segal (1987: 140) notes:

I have found everywhere evidence of the amazing diversity buried within the ideology of the familial: fathers who were present and caring, 'working' mothers who were strong and powerful within the home, daughters who bonded tightly with fathers or older brothers, mothers who could not love their sons, mothers who never accepted their daughters, mothers who identified with their sons, and so on.

Other psychoanalytically oriented feminists have made some harsh criticisms too. Jacqueline Rose, for example, has suggested that Chodorow does not explain the psychodynamics of sexual identity and selfhood, but rather addresses the question of gender roles. For Rose, Chodorow's work displaces the core psychoanalytic concepts of fantasy and the unconscious in favour of a sociological notion of 'gender imprinting'. The psychic lives of women and men, Rose points out, are more contradictory or split than Chodorow's theory suggests. Likewise, Janet Sayers argues that Chodorow conflates femininity with motherhood.

These are legitimate criticisms, and can actually be pressed further. Chodorow assumes that the mother's manner of relating to her daughter or son is fairly more or less consistent with established gender norms; to the extent that she does, these patterns of relating will have very clear-cut emotional consequences at the level of self, sexuality and gender. But we need to be careful about assuming that children's emotional responses to significant others may be understood through reference to parental or cultural norms. We need to be careful because, as Freud himself and other social theorists after him argue, the child experiences others and the wider world through fantasy, as well as other cognitive modes of understanding. Chodorow rides roughshod over this psychoanalytic insight, and thus arguably her concept of 'core gender identity' returns us to a pre-Freudian understanding of identity. That mothers perceive, on a deep psychological level, their daughters as the *same* as themselves is surely evidence of the psychological importance of sexual difference and its cultural structure; the ways in which fantasy shapes, distorts or transforms this psychological and cultural structure require analysis.

Here Freud's theory of the Oedipus complex and Lacan's emphasis on language and symbolism are important. In Freud and Lacan, it is the father's phallus, as the mark of sexual difference, that separates the child from the maternal body and plunges her or him into the order of language and the world of symbolism. In this approach, desire is founded in language – the sexes are organized around linguistic shifters: 'femininity' and 'masculinity', 'woman' and 'man', 'his' and 'hers'. Chodorow, by contrast, sees the mother as playing a more central role in the establishment of gender identity, and her use of object-relations theory to analyse emotional connection and separation offers a substantial correction to the father-centred perspectives of Freud and Lacan. Yet reversing the Freudian emphasis from the father to the mother is hardly a radical political gesture unless the question of sexual difference is itself raised and problematized. Chodorow, it may be said, fails to see that the psychoanalytical theory she draws from is deeply inscribed in asymmetrical gender relations.

Benjamin: the analysis of love

Jessica Benjamin, in her widely influential *The Bonds of Love* (1988), extends Chodorow's analysis by focusing on women's and men's experience of love. Like Chodorow, Benjamin sees patriarchy as devaluing motherhood, while underwriting the symbolic power of fatherhood with agency and power. Unlike Chodorow, however, Benjamin argues that sexual identity does not simply mirror gender asymmetry. To understand why this is so, Benjamin develops the concept of 'identificatory love', by which she means a pre-Oedipal phase of *rapprochement* in which the child seeks to establish a sense of attachment and separation with parental figures. Emotional continuity is central here. Through identification, the small child is able to separate out a sense of self while remaining emotionally connected to others.

Reflecting upon contemporary culture, Benjamin argues that children must displace or disown their pre-Oedipal identificatory love with parents. Children of both sexes cannot maintain their identificatory love for the mother since she is devalued by current sexual ideology. This leads Benjamin to adopt a similar position to Chodorow. The core of her argument is that, while boys can identify with the father and his phallus to separate from the mother and establish autonomous individuality, the same path to psychic individuation is denied to girls. An alternate, empathic relationship with the exciting father, says Benjamin, is usually refused, the result being women's 'lack' of desire and its return as masochism in idealizations of male power. For Benjamin, what this means is that the tension between dependence and independence, which underpins healthy emotional relationships, breaks down within culture at large. Moreover, sexual relations between men and women grow diseased and deformed into master/slave patterns.

In *Like Subjects, Love Objects* (1995) and *The Shadow of the Other* (1998), Benjamin explores in more detail the range of multiple identifications that women and men forge or discover through sexual object choice as

contemporary social theory

well as the negotiation of personal identity. In this interpersonal feminist psychoanalysis, Benjamin elaborates upon post-Oedipal constructions in which the self accepts multiplicity and difference, owns complementary erotic fantasies or gender ideals, and tolerates oscillating and alternating identifications. Benjamin's arguments in these works are highly complex, though she starts from the relatively uncontentious position that traditional psychoanalysis has been too father- or masculine-centred. She forcefully questions Freud's construction of gender identity along the lines of splitting and polarization – masculinity versus femininity, activity versus passivity, same versus other. Oedipal theory, says Benjamin, divides the sexes too neatly around the notion of anatomical difference, foreclosing the myriad psychic paths through which individuals identify with, as well as emotionally own, both masculine and feminine ideals within the self.

Against the Oedipal construction in which object love and identification are polarized, Benjamin focuses instead on the murky, indistinct emotional identifications with both mother and father, stressing throughout that interpersonal relationships and fantasy always coexist. Perhaps what is most important here is Benjamin's stress on the bisexual or polymorphous identifications of the most primitive stage of psychosexual development, the pre-Oedipal position. According to Benjamin, pre-Oedipal bisexuality suggests that the defensive repudiation of opposite sex identifications in the Oedipal stage depends upon a denial of bisexual identifications as well as the adoption of mutually exclusive gender positions. Such substitution of paradox for polarity, argues Benjamin, may be an accurate portrayal of dominant forms of gender relationship in masculinist culture. However, her critical point is that the recuperation of the pre-Oedipal phase can be revisited throughout life, and indeed cross-identifications of the pre-Oedipal stage, with tolerance for difference and multiplicity, inform what she terms the 'post-Oedipal' configuration, in which a more playful and creative approach is taken to identity, sexuality and gender.

Benjamin's argument carries important implications for the analysis of gender, particularly as regards the development of boys. According to her, the psychological task of replacing splitting and polarization with the sustaining of psychic tension and the ability to manage opposing emotional dispositions towards self and other results from fluid boundaries between Oedipal and post-Oedipal configurations. For the boy, inclusion of denied feelings or blocked identifications depends upon regaining contact with multiple identifications of the pre-Oedipal period, in particular experience of the mother as a creative subject.

What of the possibilities for change? Benjamin differs sharply from both Chodorow and Dinnerstein in her evaluation of gender transformation. Paternal identification, Benjamin says, can play a positive role in the achievement of autonomous female subjectivity. According to Benjamin, however, any identification with the father is likely to prove counterproductive so long as the cultural devaluation of women remains in place. In this context, an alteration of parenting arrangements – as proposed by Chodorow and Dinnerstein – is itself an insufficient basis to transform gender structures. Non-repressive gender relations, Benjamin argues, depend rather on replacing the cultural split of progressive, autonomous father against regressive mother with new sexual identifications that permit a less rigid set of sexual roles. This would involve the repudiation of defensive modes of separation – that is, the father's phallus would no longer be used as the dominant medium to beat back an engulfing mother. Instead, children might construct more fluid sexual identifications – expressing both masculine and feminine aspects of identity – in relation to a socially and sexually autonomous mother and a more empathic, caring father. Two figures of love and idealization – mother and father – are thus located as necessary for the creation of non-patriarchal patterns of socialization.

Julia Kristeva: semiotic subversions

The writings of the French social theorist Julia Kristeva press the feminist critique of identity to a parodic extreme. Her post-Lacanian-inspired reading of Freud and feminism leads her to outline an emotional realm she terms 'semiotic', a residue of pre-Oedipal longings or drives that both structure and disrupt the operations of everyday speech. This notion of a semiotic process operating within the established meanings of ordinary language was given powerful expression in Kristeva's first book *Revolution in Poetic Language* (1984), of which she has said:

> What interested me was, by way of the semiotic, to further elaborate a level of psychic representation that for Freud remains extremely primitive and imprecise, which is the representation of affects that are psychic inscriptions, hence very primitive and very fragile: drives and affects that are in fact already psychic.
>
> (Guberman and Kristeva 1996: 22)

Kristeva's ambitious psychoanalytic extension of the concept of the semiotic powerfully confronted some of the central weaknesses of structuralist and post-structuralist thought, especially the theorem of the arbitrary character of the sign. Kristeva may well have formed many of her key concepts in the heyday of Parisian post-structuralism, yet the implications of her conceptual developments have not only outstripped the ideological parameters of the structuralist controversy but continue to inform the endeavours of social theorists the world over.

Kristeva's genius is certainly evident in the manner in which she questioned Saussure's model of individual and society, particularly her criticism that structuralism has no intermediate terms for connecting the affective dimensions of subjectivity, the play of signifiers at the level of subjecthood and meaning, as well as the linguistic system as a whole. Yet her supple, civilized intelligence is also evident in her style as a writer, her voice. For in attempting to show that affective pressures and primitive anxieties structure the constitution and reproduction of society, it was through her poetic and expressively crafted sentences that Kristeva uncovered how the rhythm and sound of language exerts a kind of unconscious pressure within language itself. She sees in this fluid, heterogeneous flow of affects a sort of residue of attachment to pre-Oedipal experience, specifically the ongoing impact of memory issuing from the child's contact with the mother's body. The semiotic is thus the 'other' of the symbolic, even though Kristeva insists that these two modes of signification are always intricately entwined.

For me signification is a process that I call *significance*, and to recognize the dynamism of this process, I distinguish between two registers: the register of the symbolic and register of the semiotic. By symbolic, I mean the tributary signification of language, all the effects of meaning that appear from the moment linguistic signs are articulated into grammar, not only chronologically but logically as well. In other words, the symbolic is both diachronic and synchronic; it concerns both the acquisition of language and the present syntactic structure. By semiotic, on the other hand, I mean the effects of meaning that are not reducible to language or that can operate outside language, even if language is necessary as an immediate context or as a final referent. By semiotic, I mean, for example, the child's echolalia before the appearance of language, but also the play of colors in an abstract painting or a piece of music that lacks signification but has a meaning.

Julia Kristeva (1996) 'A Conversation with Julia Kristeva', in Ross Mitchell Guberman (ed.) *Interviews*. New York: Columbia University Press, p. 21.

In her various studies of art, literary creation, motherhood, psycho-analysis and philosophy, Kristeva has time and again observed the semiotic at work in children's play and mental life, as well as in the avant-garde poet's language which she sees as highly evocative of the feminine as well as memory of the maternal body. In this linking of the semiotic so closely to the theme of femininity, Kristeva underscores the importance of her social theory to feminists in particular and the analysis of gender power in general. She explains this often questioned connection of the semiotic to feminism thus:

> In our monotheistic-capitalist societies, 'the woman effect' entails a specific relationship to both *power* and *language*, or, if you will, to the power of language. This particular relationship is based not on appro-priating power and language but on being a source of silent support, a useful backdrop, and an invisible intermediary. I have called this modal-ity of the linguistic (and social) functioning of language the '*semiotic*'. The semiotic is heard in rhythms, intonation and children's echolalia as well as in artistic practice and in discourse that signifies less an 'object' than a jouissance.
>
> (Guberman and Kristeva 1996: 104)

It is as if there is the connecting path between the semiotic and the femi-nine that works both ways – which we will shortly examine in more detail. Silence, support, invisibility, sound, inflexion, intimation: these are the terms through which the semiotic makes the body signify.

Kristeva was only in her early thirties when *Revolution in Poetic Language* became a major talking point among intellectuals on the left bank of Paris. Her doctoral training with Roland Barthes and in particular the imprint of the thought of Jacques Lacan were highly evident in this mam-moth undertaking. Yet what perhaps caused the real intellectual stir was her audacious blending of disciplinary concerns, ranging as the book did over Hegel, Husserl, Freud and Lévi-Strauss, while managing the exceptional feat of elaborating a *post-Lacanian* understanding of the complex relations between self and society.

Revolution is, as we will see, unquestionably a brilliant work of social theory. Yet as significant as it may be, it is not Kristeva's most important contribution to social thought. That honour must go to either *Tales of Love* (1987) or *Strangers to Ourselves* (1991). Where *Revolution* provides highly suggestive concepts for thinking anew about the self/society nexus, *Tales of Love* and *Strangers to Ourselves* offer illuminating workings through of Kristeva's social theory in relation to such central sociological issues as love, intimacy, gender, the psyche, cultural reproduction, immigration and global-ization. Still, in order to grasp how this influential blend of psychoanalytical, feminist and social theory comes together it is necessary to return to Kristeva's pioneering *Revolution* and briefly examine some of its central concepts.

In *Revolution*, Kristeva looks to psychoanalysis as a means of overcoming the fixed positions and binary oppositions of structural linguistics. Although her thinking was much influenced by Saussure, she is profoundly aware that the static conception of language advanced by structuralists – in which culture speaks its subjects – is 'helplessly anachronistic when faced with the contemporary mutations of subject and society'. One of these mutations that most interests Kristeva is feminism, from which during the late 1960s and early 1970s the women's movement had launched a sustained assault on the patriarchal sexual order of contemporary societies. The oppressiveness of existing sexual relations, for Kristeva as for Lacan, issues from patriarchy – symbolized by the phallus – in which subjects are accorded symbolic positions as defined by sexual difference. As we saw earlier when looking at the theories of Lacan, the evolution of Oedipal, gendered identity in the symbolic order of things provides the individual with an illusion of centredness and stability.

For Kristeva, the merit of Lacanian psychoanalysis is that it uncovers how the constitution of the speaking subject revolves around a pre-given structure of social roles and sexual relations – the individual's painful decentring within the symbolic order. However, Kristeva argues that Lacan's central blindness – notwithstanding the stress on the 'split subject' – is his overemphasis on the determining power of speech and language at the expense of pre-verbal experience. While language is the realm of meaning and its encounters with the rules of social interaction, the dynamism of self and society is sustained and nourished by deeper emotional forces. It is thus Kristeva's central project – psychoanalytical, social-theoretical and political – to elucidate the *pre-verbal sensations* which leave their imprint upon the life of the subject and of our lives in a wider social context.

The corporeal origins of the semiotic are traced by Kristeva back to the small infant's pre-Oedipal interaction with the mother, or primary caretaker. As a pre-Oedipal realm prior to the establishment of sexual difference, the infant does not yet have access to language and thus the place of pre-verbal experience is paramount. The mother's caresses, touching, rhythmic rocking, singing and general care of the child are vital to the foundation and function of the pre-verbal semiotic. For Kristeva, the sensory qualities of maternal care leave an indelible stamp upon the psychic life of the individual subject, all of which is constituted as a flow of affective sources and energetic drives. It is in a sense the virtue of the semiotic that it is geared towards others – and thus towards language – because the affective domain is interpersonal through and through. This, in itself, deconstructs the rigid determinism of Lacanism, with its insistence that the child's entry into the symbolic order of language involves an overriding or limiting of the imaginary. For it is in describing the pre-verbal semiotic as a form of language, as psychic inscriptions of sensory experience operating *inside* language, that Kristeva most forcefully challenges Lacan's objectivism as well as underscores the role of affects in psychic and social life. This is not to say, however, that Kristeva positions affect over and above the symbolic order. She is insistent, for example, that there is an ineluctable closure of the semiotic process with the child's entry into the relatively stable domain of symbolization and language. This closure, however, is not complete: the criss-crossings of the semiotic and symbolic are interestingly mobile. The semiotic, Kristeva intimates, is always 'at work' within the operations of language, threatening an identity-forming break or transformation from the imposed form and structure of symbolic processes.

Another way of putting all this is to say that, for Kristeva, we are – all of us – nine-tenths ventriloquists of the culture. We simply mouth the words of others, in gestures that express an essentially passive relation to the codes of culture and society. Yet confoundingly, every so often we may say something startlingly original. Something different. Something unique. If the imposed symbolic order of language closes us to the genuinely new and different, the semiotic reopens the psyche to complex imaginaries and the drives and affects they bring into play. For the early Kristeva of *Revolution*, the semiotic is the sight of our imaginative attempt to contest symbolic structures in the name of desire – and one noticeable place in her account where this may be seen historically is in the poetic language of various modernist writers such as Mallarmé and Lautréamont where 'semiotic transgressions' explode traditional literary discourse. Another location where Kristeva sees the semiotic at work, at least in her subsequent writings, is in psychoanalysis itself – where the unspeakable emotion unlocked through processes of regression with an analyst brings directly into play intense modulations of primitive anxiety and affect, both pleasurable and destructive.

Kristeva conceptualizes the semiotic as intimately entwined with memory of the mother's body and thus with the feminine more generally. As we have seen, however, if the semiotic is a force operating inside discourse this is far from a language exclusive to women. Noting that the semiotic is fabricated from a pre-Oedipal phase which itself is prior to the imposed Oedipal distinctions of gender hierarchy, the semiotic remains for Kristeva an affective force within language available to either sex. Thus in her work throughout the 1970s, the pre-verbal, destabilizing semiotic is detected at work by Kristeva in the writings of various male avant-garde poets and writers. Some feminists sharply criticized Kristeva for ignoring female writers in her studies of semiotic literary practice, arguing that the semiotic might in theory function as a mode of experience available to both sexes, but in Kristeva's literary criticism at least the supposed radicalism of this unconscious force appears to operate mostly in the hands of men. It is perhaps as a result of this critique that Kristeva subsequently conducted a multi-volume study on female genius, in the spheres of literature, philosophy and psychoanalysis.

Yet it is in Kristeva's writings on motherhood and maternity that the specific emotional contradictions of female identity are explored in detail. This work dates from the late 1970s and early 1980s, at which point Kristeva herself became a mother, and there can be little doubt that her suggestive theories of a 'maternal ethic' have served to stimulate developments in feminism and social theory. For the Kristeva of this period, in books such as *Powers of Horror* (1982) and *Tales of Love* (1987), motherhood represents 'the semiotisation of the symbolic'. 'A mother', Kristeva announces, 'has always been a permanent division, a division of the flesh itself, and consequently a division in language.' All experiences of pregnancy and maternity call into play powerful unconscious forces and primitive anxiety, reawakening the repressed division between flesh and word, imagination and representation, nature and culture.

Kristeva on motherhood and maternal ethics

In a series of provocative essays about mothering and childbirth – most importantly 'Stabat Mater' (1986), 'Motherhood According to Bellini' (1980b) and 'From One Identity to An Other' (1980a) – Kristeva analyses both dominant cultural representations of maternity and the psychic experience of motherhood itself. These essays contain Kristeva's argument that the psychoanalytical concept of fantasy is of core importance for grasping the complexity of maternity, and especially the complex emotional dynamic between mother and child.

Kristeva suggests that dominant scientific understandings of maternity, from the cult of the Virgin in Christian theology to media images of women in popular culture, have objectified women. In conflating femininity and maternity, she argues, the mother's desire exists only insofar as it is related to her desire to have children, to reproduce the species, to fulfil her biological function in the name of patriarchy. Kristeva focuses on *fantasies* of maternity rather than on *practices* of motherhood. In doing so, she makes explicit her debt to the Freudian conceptualization of the self. She suggests that, although maternity has been disfigured by patriarchy, motherhood is in fact associated with repressed desire.

In developing this provocative argument, Kristeva returns to classical psychoanalysis. Freud regarded maternity as a return of the repressed, a return of the daughter's buried wish to bear a child for her own father. Fundamental to Freud's view is the presumption that women's desire exists only insofar as it is directed towards the phallus – that is to say, the symbolic father of the Oedipus complex. According to Kristeva, Freud constructed maternity in wholly patriarchal terms. But this association of motherhood with the masculine logic of Oedipus prevents the woman from voicing her own desire, her own enjoyment, her own ambivalent fantasy of maternity. For Kristeva, motherhood must be approached differently, in a fashion other than that emphasized in philosophical, literary and psychoanalytic traditions, with their stress upon biological and social reproduction.

In 'Stabat Mater', a title that refers to the anguish of the Virgin Mary at the Crucifixion, Kristeva reflects on her own experience of pregnancy and birth. Dividing the essay into two discourses, she writes on one side of the page of the mythical language of Christian theology and the rationality of science, while on the other side she develops a more private and autobiographical account of motherhood. In dividing the narrative of her essay in this way, Kristeva seeks to underscore the split or hiatus between the ideal and actuality of maternity. Most importantly, she argues that splitting itself defines maternal experience. Maternity for Kristeva involves a state of radical paradox, of heterogeneity, of singularity and plurality, of sameness and difference. In Kristeva's words (1986: 178–9):

> A mother is a continuous separation, a division of the very flesh. And consequently a division of language – and it has always been so. Then there is this other abyss that opens up between the body and what has been its inside: there is the abyss between the mother and the child. What connection is there between myself, or even more unassumingly between my body and this internal graft and fold, which, once the umbilical cord has been severed, is an inaccessible other? . . . Trying to think through that abyss: staggering vertigo. No identity holds up.

The passions associated with maternity, according to Kristeva, split the woman between identity and its collapse, between consciousness of self and its erasure.

The mother's experience of transformations occurring in her own body during pregnancy reorient her away from the narrow confines of masculine logic and patriarchy. Whereas Freud sees maternity as an expression of repressed paternal longings, in Kristeva's eyes the desire to have children is itself a sublimated desire to recover the maternal body. That is to say, Kristeva suggests that there is a homosexual component implicit in women's desire to mother, or at least this is so in fantasy at any rate. 'By giving birth,' writes Kristeva, 'the woman enters into contact with her mother; she becomes, she is her own mother.' In underscoring this homosexual facet of motherhood, Kristeva rewrites psychoanalysis away from the father and the Oedipus complex and towards the (imaginary) relation between women, a relation that persists over time and across generations.

Kristeva connects the complexity and heterogeneity of maternal experience not only to women, but also to the emotional development of children. She emphasizes the importance of maternity in shaping and regulating the emerging self prior to entry into the Oedipus complex – in which the acquisition of language, rationality and sexual subjectivity occurs. This is a very important aspect of Kristeva's argument, an aspect that directly challenges the claim advanced by Freud and Lacan that it is the father alone who propels the child into an order of language and symbolism. By contrast, Kristeva argues that the mother imposes a sense of regulation and order upon the child's psychic world. Before 'the Law of the Father' (Lacan), the child constantly encounters various maternal regulations, what Kristeva terms 'the law before the law'. Whereas Freudians and Lacanians view the regulation of the self in terms of rationality or structure, Kristeva emphasizes the importance of the body to the constitution of the self. The mother, says Kristeva, regulates what goes into, and also what is evacuated from, the child's body. This maternal regulation and control of the infant's traffic with both nourishment and love provides a foundation for the emotional dealings of the self with itself, other people and the wider society.

Appraisal of Kristeva

Kristeva's suggestive work has made a considerable impact on recent social theory, especially in feminism and based on gender, no doubt in part since it is reflective of profound personal, cultural and political changes occurring in contemporary societies. Kristeva is among those public intellectuals who have contributed to a revised understanding of the relations between self and society, linked particularly to a heightened sensitivity to the intersections of the unconscious, affect, gender, sexuality and intersubjectivity. This is an understanding that foregrounds dynamism, innovation, imagination and the new in personal and political life, and so would seem to accommodate various complex processes of social redefinition – issuing from, for example, the women's movements, gay and lesbian movements as well as other new social movements – that occurred in the final decades of the twentieth century as well as at the beginnings of the twenty-first century. Particularly as the 1970s and 1980s gave way to the postmodern 1990s, and as the globalization of commerce, communication and culture became increasingly evident to all, Kristeva's powerful mapping of the emotional dynamism of the individual subject seemed suited to grappling with the social conditions of women and men in which self-reflexivity was increasingly prized and economic flexibility increasingly demanded. This is perhaps nowhere more evidently so than in gender relations, where sexual norms which engage some of the deepest emotional dimensions of social life have been powerfully transformed.

Viewed against the backcloth of Lacanian psychoanalysis, the theory of the semiotic developed by Kristeva may be seen as a means of calling into question the individual's subjection to symbolic norms. For an over-emphasis on the discursive remains, in the eyes of Kristeva, a fundamental weakness of contemporary theory and thus is at the core of the inability of Lacan and his followers to grasp how language encodes unrepresentable emotion. Notwithstanding the importance of this recovery of the role of emotion and affect in the context of childhood, maternity, the family and the private and public spheres, however, much criticism of Kristeva's work has been directed against her whole attempt to develop a theory of pre-verbal signs, in which the distribution of unconscious forces, energies and drives structure and transform processes of signification. Thus some feminists have criticized as illusory and reactionary the search for semiotic signs which might somehow function as an *alternative* to impose symbolic forms of identity or patriarchal sexual orientation. The results of such general theoretical criticism have led, in turn, to more specific concerns as regards the analysis of gender power. Some feminists, for example, criticize Kristeva for eliding the semiotic with motherhood.

Not all feminist sociology has been as critical of Kristeva as this, and yet indeed many have pointed out that her project involves rethinking the basic categories of gender in ways that mainstream social science has tended to ignore. Her examination of maternity in terms of the semiotic as a kind of internal limit to gender power does not then involve essentialism, and it is important to keep in mind that she is not proposing the semiotic as an emancipatory alternative to the symbolic order of language. Kristeva, a practising psychoanalyst, is certainly well aware that rejection of the symbolic order can only spell emotional catastrophe – namely in the form of psychosis. Yet she is rightly insistent that the symbolic order of language is not a monolithic structure. Rather, symbolic order provides an illusion of stability; social power and symbolic order are fluid and contestable, and from this angle the semiotic is at the core of our imaginative attempts to battle with and subvert dominant frames of reference.

Kristeva may thus be said to have fashioned a post-Lacanian approach to subjectivity, society and history that cuts through traditional opposition between the unconscious and the symbolic, desire and the social, the inner world and the external world. Yet however insightful her observations are regarding the semiotic as an affective source within language and public political discourse, there remain important difficulties with her account of how such primitive emotional processes relate to society as well as processes of social transformation. For one thing, it is not clear how the semiotic process – centred on the individual – might be methodologically applicable to broader social structures, particularly the workings of social power and political domination. For another, the semiotic too often appears in Kristeva's work as a kind of mini-agent, operating within or behind the back of an individual. Yet how, exactly, do individuals reflect on – become aware of – semiotic displacement of symbolic power? Are these primarily revolutions in poetic language (and thus the preserve of the critic), or are these wide disruptions to daily life? And how, in any event, are such internal transformations threaded to the power networks and technical processes of contemporary society?

Notwithstanding these criticisms, it is clear that Kristeva's influence on contemporary research into identity and culture within social theory is immense. Her reading of Freud and Lacan is bold and productive, and in an astonishingly radical interpretive stroke locates the 'subject-in-process' in the imaginative substratum of historical life, in its exquisite creativity and pure open-endedness.

Irigaray: the feminine imaginary

Luce Irigaray, a French philosopher who trained as a psychoanalyst with Lacan, argues controversially that the feminine cannot be adequately symbolized – in discourse or in theory – under patriarchy, as femininity is the repressed or hidden support structure upon which phallocentric social relations depend. Irigaray, taking her cue from Lacan, proposes the feminine as permanently excluded from language in the symbolic order. She writes of the corrosive personal consequences for women of the process of 'specularization'; women, she says, reflect back to men particular phallocentric ideals concerning masculinity, such that the feminine is defined not in its own terms, but always as mirror, reflection or object. From maternal devotion to sexual masquerade, the seductive presence of the feminine frames the illusions of masculine desire.

More concretely, Irigaray argues that the pre-Oedipal mother/daughter relationship remains on the 'outside' of symbolic boundaries – an outside that leaves women in a state of 'dereliction', undifferentiated from maternal space. As she puts this (1985: 143),

> there is no possibility whatsoever, within the current logic of socio-cultural operations, for a daughter to situate herself with respect to her mother: because, strictly speaking, they make neither one nor two, neither has a name, meaning, sex of her own, neither can be 'identified with respect to the other'.

In contrast to Lacan, however, Irigaray contends that the idea of woman as outside and Other always threatens subversion, thus transforming the dominant masculinist social order. The feminine, says Irigaray, threatens subversion to patriarchal language and culture. Here Irigaray's position has affinities with Kristeva's notion of the semiotic. However, Irigaray goes further than Kristeva as regards the disruptive impact of female sexuality, proposing a direct link between women, feminine sexuality and the body. In line with other feminists of the 'écriture féminine' movement, such as Hélène Cixous, Irigaray grounds the feminine in women's experience of sexuality and the body, an experience which is plural, dispersed and multiple. Women, says Irigaray, need to establish a different relationship to feminine sexuality, affecting a range of displacements to patriarchy through writing as a cultural practice. Speaking the feminine, says Irigaray, can transform the constricted and constricting sexed identities of patriarchy. In her more recent work, from *An Ethics of Sexual Difference* (1993) to *To Be Two* (2000), Irigaray locates the renegotiation of identities in the frame of ethical practice, specifically the recognition of the otherness of the other sex. An ethics of sexual difference, she argues, would respect the Other in her or his own right, with regard or sensitivity to finitude, mortality, creation and the divine.

Irigaray's writings have been sharply criticized as biologically essentialist. Here it is suggested that Irigaray's direct appeal to feminine specificity or the material female body assumes that there is an unchanging, trans-historical female sexuality subversive of all social contexts. This critique of Irigaray's essentialism has been forcefully developed by both Moi and Segal. Other feminists have questioned this essentialist critique, and have instead argued that Irigaray's work seeks to theorize the reproduction and transformation of feminine specificity in terms of the broader cultural force of sexual difference. While Irigaray is certainly concerned to trace the impact of distorting socio-symbolic forces upon the pre-Oedipal mother/daughter relationship, it does seem that her appeal to feminine specificity is problematic to say the least. Juliet Mitchell sums up the difficulty with this position:

> You cannot choose the imaginary, the semiotic, the carnival as an alternative to the symbolic, as an alternative to the law. It is set up by the law precisely as its own lurid space, its own area of imaginary alternative, but not as a symbolic alternative. So that politically speaking, it is only the symbolic, a new symbolism, a new law, that can challenge the dominant law.
>
> (Mitchell 1984: 291)

Judith Butler: scripts of gender performance

To see language as encoding powerful emotional, semiotic forces is a critical advance on viewing it as simply the 'neutral' expression of rational intentions. For if the pre-verbal residue of the semiotic may be seen as a form of language, this means that there are always at work powerful undercurrents of affects and anxieties in our daily social contact, and perhaps nowhere more evidently so than when we negotiate social practices of gender. Let us go back for a moment to the 'gender incident' I outlined at the beginning of the chapter, where former university colleagues of mine were caught up in a heated exchange of words over the politics of gender. I implied that much of this political heat stemmed from the issue of career advancement – that for many of my colleagues the matter of promotion was, so to speak, an outcrop of gender politics itself. Everyone, it seemed, had a view about this; and even if they didn't, colleagues were quickly accorded a 'position' in the debate: siding with the traditionalists, speaking with the liberals, or adopting the pose of radicalism. Attention to the semiotic modalities of these exchanges, at least according to Kristeva's way of viewing things, would no doubt reveal all sorts of complex unconscious forces and drives in what people actually said to each other. Such an emphasis on the disruptive power of repressed desires and primitive anxieties may indeed well account for why many of my colleagues had difficulty resuming everyday dialogues well after the incident had passed – in fact, some still don't talk to one another!

To say that interpersonal communication is routinely outstripped by powerful unconscious forces is not, however, the only way one might try to figure out what is going on here. Indeed, notwithstanding that emotional life has become a central topic in much recent sociology, there are many social theorists and feminists who would contest Kristeva's idea of the semiotic as a force inside language. Asking about the emotional dispositions as linked to gender identities in the situation I have outlined, some would argue that the idea of sexual hierarchy as enforcing deep divisions in university affairs is itself an illusion created by *repeated gender performances*. In other words, the 'taking up' of gender positions among my former colleagues was a learned, situational performance whose dramatic consequence was the production of inner feelings and disposition – the latter of which might only then be labelled disruptive or subversive of everyday life.

The notion that gender is constituted through 'repeated performance' – the 'doing' of gender roles – has been advanced by Judith Butler, one of the most influential critics within debates over sexuality and feminism in our own time. In her *Gender Trouble* (1990), Butler not only boldly questioned the ways in which feminism has invoked an identity-based theory which unintentionally serves to reinforce the binary gender hierarchy it opposes, she outlined a provocatively original theory which emphasizes the performative nature of identity and gender. *Gender Trouble* had an almost instant massive impact in feminism, sexuality studies and the formation of queer theory, and Butler's work since has continued to be at the cutting edge of developments in social theory. Part of the reason why Butler's *Gender Trouble* was so influential was due to timing: the 1990s inaugurated a shift from the era of post-structuralism to the reign of postmodernism, and Butler's work represented a critical and stylish blend of the perspective of the French historian Michel Foucault, the psychoanalytic theory of Lacan, plus the deconstructive operations of postmodern feminism.

Language or discourse is Butler's central theme in *Gender Trouble*, and in particular the post-structuralist insight that the sign is always a matter of difference. Butler will have nothing of the search for attributes of a core gender identity. Rather, her critique of the history of sexuality is derived more or less directly from an exploration of the consequences of the idea of identity as a 'discursive effect' – first as drawn from the writings of Foucault, and then as reformulated with reference to Lacanian psychoanalysis. Butler seeks to understand the relational character of identity positioning in the context of post-structuralist philosophy. In the same fashion that the subject is constituted in structuring of language through difference, so speech situates us as women or men by connecting discourse with a binary gender order. Thus, for example, identity is not immediately *present* in a sign: it is by learning to use language situationally – which is itself a matter of linguistic differences and cultural conventions – that subjects project themselves into gender roles as women or men.

So far this account of the construction of gender identity may sound like little more than a feminist reworking of post-structuralism, and there is some merit to seeing Butler's work in this way. But Butler's appropriation of post-structuralism themes is neither straightforward nor uncritical. What emerges from her radical feminist systemization of Foucauldianism is a new emphasis on how language or discourse compels our attention to inner or emotional aspects of subjectivity itself; gender performance, anchored in ordinary speech, constitutes and sediments the possible range of identities, congealing over time to create illusions of self as interiority, emotions, desires. As Butler puts this, there is 'no doer behind the deed'. Questioning the dualisms of outside and inside, externality and internality, Butler argues that people only come to see themselves as the authors of their own inner lives through a set of repeated gender performances. Such performances are regulated with reference to constraining cultural representations of masculinity and femininity, as well as the narrative scripts of gender that are told and retold within the culture at large.

> If there is something right in Beauvoir's claim that one is not born, but rather *becomes* a woman, it follows that *woman* itself is a term in process, a becoming, a construction that cannot rightfully be said to originate or to end. As an ongoing discursive practice, it is open to intervention and resignification. Even when gender seems to congeal into the most reified forms, the 'congealing' is itself an insistent and insidious practice, sustained and regulated by various social means. It is, for Beauvoir, never possible finally to become a woman, as if there were a *telos* that governs the process of acculturation and construction. Gender is the repeated stylization of the body, a set of repeated acts within a highly rigid regulatory frame that congeal over time to produce the appearance of substance, of a natural sort of being. A political genealogy of gender ontologies, if it is successful, will deconstruct the substantive appearance of gender into its constitutive acts and locate and account for those acts within compulsory frames set by the various forces that police the social appearance of gender.
>
> Judith Butler (1990) *Gender Trouble: Feminism and the Subversion of Identity.* London: Routledge, p. 33.

Another way of putting this point is to say that gender performances are always copies, imitations fashioned out of fantasies or idealization of dominant cultural representations of femininity or masculinity. Performance for Butler has a minimum of agency or voluntarism – the 'formed' nature of gender identity conceals social and political forces that constitute individuals as set subjects – and this in itself suggests that gender is a determining structure. Yet Butler shrewdly insists that constraint is the condition of possibility of sexuality and gender. In linking gender performance with a post-structuralist treatment of language and power, Butler is out to show how sexualities, bodies and desires are rendered coherent and continuous within the symbolic field and yet are also implicated in disruptions to the reproduction of gender itself. For despite the constrained and constraining aspects of dominant heterosexual norms, Butler does not consider people as 'cultural dopes'. All gender performance, she argues, involves an open process of repetition. And repetition, for Butler as for Freud, opens to possibilities of change. As Butler (1990: 137) contends,

> If every performance repeats itself to institute the effect of identity, then every repetition requires an interval between the acts, as it were, in which risk and excess threaten to disrupt the identity being constituted. The unconscious is this excess that enables and contests every performance, and which never fully appears within the performance itself.

Repetition of everyday social practices and gender norms thus secures the regularized aspects of identity formation. Yet because repetition itself operates through a temporalized reiteration of the performative, there is an *intrinsic instability* at the heart of dominant gender relations. Every performance of identity, for Butler, is at once self-reproducing of symbolic norms and potentially transgressive of those norms. The performative process of gender resignification is always potentially disruptive and disturbing, and it is against this analytical backcloth that Butler attempts to specify the explicitly political consequences of her feminist analysis. According to Butler, the parodic plane with homosexual identities evident, for example, in queer practices and politics highlights the complex ways in which sexualities, bodies and desires are reproduced and destabilized in the course of their reiteration. A transgressive edge is accorded in particular to 'drag' and 'gender bending'. 'In imitating gender,' writes Butler,

> drag implicitly reveals the imitative structure of gender itself – as well as its contingency. Indeed, part of the pleasure, the giddiness of the performance is in the recognition of a radical contingency in the relation between sex and gender in the face of cultural configurations of causal unities that are regularly assumed to be natural and necessary.
>
> (Butler 1990: 137)

Appraisal of Butler

There are several important reasons why Butler's work has been especially well received in sexuality studies, feminism and social theory. First, it provides a powerful theoretical account of various disjunctions between sex, gender and identity that chimes with key transformations of intimacy occurring in society at large. For it has primarily been questioned over the fracturing of cultural and sexual identities, routed in the actual political conditions of Western societies, which highlights the limitations of mainstream identity politics. Butler is among the first feminists to call attention to the dynamics of social life as a challenging mixture of identities, sexuality and reality; deconstructing 'women' as a category of identity, the political aim has been to demonstrate that people are not simply 'masculine', 'feminine', 'straight', 'lesbian', 'queer', or any one identity. The feminist, postmodern and post-structuralist preoccupation with the performative and reiterated aspects of identity, with subverting constructions of gender and sexuality, were responses to the cultural mood of the 1990s and especially the sense that identity cannot be reduced to any defining essence.

Second, Butler's view of gender as enacted in repeated cultural performances has proved attractive to intellectuals and activists dismissive of traditional political strategies for combating experiences of exclusion and domination. Postmodernists especially have welcomed Butler's refusal of identity politics, finding in her stress on the performative a means to contextualize a series of profound social changes in the relation of globalization, media, information technology, identity, culture and representation. Some have appropriated Butler to subvert the liberal politics of contesting social exclusion in the name of fairer participation in institutional life, pointing out that such single-interest politics is a thing of the past. The world can no longer be adequately understood according to traditional notions of representation in politics and the public sphere; in conditions of globalization, it is the logic of performance which is most appropriate for grasping disjoinings of sex and gender, the private and public spheres, as played out in mass media. Others have drawn upon Butler to argue for new social alliances and forms of political contestation, as have sociologists associated with cultural studies, critical race theory and post-colonial theory.

However, there are various problems with Butler's work, both in terms of social theory and as a model of gender critique. Many of Butler's critics worry about the notion of 'performance', claiming that it seems to suggest a voluntarist process of choosing a gender at will. This criticism involves in my view an inaccurate reading of *Gender Trouble*, and indeed Butler herself has empathized that gender performativity involves not so much choice as it does a forced repetition of sexual norm. If anything, she stresses the structuring rather than the agency of the human subject. Gender identities for Butler take on what stability and coherence they have through the performative reiteration of discourses, all of which she locates at the structural level of the 'heterosexual matrix'. Seen in this light, Butler's theory of the subject is perhaps best recast as one of *involuntary performance*. Even so, however, it is not clear that such a perspective can avoid reproducing the deterministic emphasis of Foucault, insofar as Butler privileges the moment of constraint in her account of repeated gender performances. What is arguably missing from Butler's theoretical framework is, among other things, a reflexive notion of agency – particularly as this pertains to the relation between gender identity and social structure.

Related to this is the considerable criticism and debate which has followed on from Butler's account of dissident sexual performances which make trouble for established gender categories. Butler's theory of gender trouble emphasizes, as we have seen, the potentially disruptive power of marginalized or non-normative sexualities, an undoing of the heterosexual matrix which secures sexual binaries and gender hierarchy. From lipstick lesbians to drag queens, every performance of gender bending may potentially weaken, disrupt or transgress normative gender framing. However, Butler's invoking of the transgressive theatrics in perverse or queer gender performances gains its rhetorical force primarily in relation to routine or mainstream enactments of gender identity. In the final analysis, some critics find this division of performativity into mainstream and transgressive unduly restrictive. As Lynne Segal (1999: 61) notes:

> Icons of mass culture, from Mae West to Madonna, Valentino to Michael Jackson, have always thrived on forms of sexual ambiguity which suggest the seductive appeal of a transgressive or perverse dynamic at the very heart of heterosexist culture. But with drag and queer display as popular (or unpopular) with reactionary as with radical audiences, its ability to unsettle and subvert normal structures of gender and sexuality seems no more powerful than its ability to mirror and to legitimate them.

Ultimately, the criticism of Butler's underwriting of drag or gender bending is that this represents a trivial response to the complexities of fashioning alternative sexed, sexualized and gendered forms of identity in the contemporary age.

Queer theory

The affirmation of self-identity can sometimes be as much limiting as it can be freeing. Controversies over the personal and cultural problems involved in identity politics, especially in respect of asserting a common identity and community, have frequently plagued those committed to progressive sexual politics. The dilemma is primarily one of how to redress social exclusion and political oppression by creating a new sense of self, solidarity and community while avoiding the confinement of fixed identities and categories. Most of us, most of the time, make sense of identity by telling stories about our experience, shared understanding, sense of communal belonging, and so forth. We want the interrelationship between personal and cultural life to be open-ended in this complex and pluralistic world; we seek to avoid simple generalizations about our identity, and none of us want our experience coded as stereotype. A preoccupation with the relation between personal identity and social difference has been increasingly central to sexual politics over the past few decades, especially as developed by the lesbian and gay movement and also in queer theory and politics. The core challenge for the self, as defined by such standpoints, is to find some balance between the need for identity and the recognition of cultural diversity and social difference. In the remainder of this chapter, I shall chart some of these changes in the intimate texture of social life, paying special attention to conceptions of the self that have arisen from contemporary sexual politics. Contemporary feminist and gay studies in particular have developed powerful ideas about the historical formation of sexual identities, with the social impact of the science of sexuality a key theme. This research represents, in many respects, an alternative history of the self and sexual identity, and it is worth noting briefly some of the more salient aspects of such perspectives on sexual identity and the self.

There are various ways of denoting sexual orientation. At various historical points, in various cultures, the terms 'homosexual', 'gay', 'lesbian' and 'queer' have been deployed to refer to same-sex sexual desires and practices. The word 'homosexual' was coined in 1868 by the German-Hungarian journalist Károly Mária Kertbeny (born Karl Maria Benkert) in a letter to the German legal reformer Karl Heinrich Ulrichs, and was used by them as a scientifically neutral term in their campaign against criminalizing sexual relations between men. Neither man claimed to be a physician, but their term slowly entered the medical literature. Yet it was not until the end of the nineteenth century that the word became commonly used in English, and indeed a public culture involving core distinctions between homosexuality and heterosexuality as distinctive identities did not fully emerge until some point in the 1920s or 1930s. Prior to this, homosexuality was – for the most part – thought of as a particular kind of behaviour; the law punished illegal activity (sodomy), not deviant identity. The slow filtering through of the medical/expert term 'homosexual' into public discourse and common culture changed all this, and it is a good example of the intrusion of expert knowledge into the fabric of daily life that I have emphasized in preceding chapters. For it was in and through this invasion of social-scientific knowledge that homosexuality came, in time, to be established as a unique identity, a specific psychological disposition, a particular sense of self, and thus as separated or marked off from the heterosexual mainstream. This in turn opened a path to the coercive idea that psychological health depends upon a normalized sense of personal identity, something to which homo-sexuality was from the beginning excluded in the view of the medical establishment. For homosexuality, in the majority of medical discourses, was treated as a pathology. But it also opened a path for the ongoing interrogation of identity – in this context, a problematization of the idea that homosexuals have a specific sexual nature and sense of self. *Coming Out* (1977), by gay studies theorist Jeffrey Weeks, accounts for homosexual identity as just such a cross between social and historical event on the one hand and the absorption of social-scientific ideas governing sexuality by the wider public on the other. In charting the role of science, especially sexology, in the historical making of a specific homosexual identity, Weeks tells a compelling story of how these historical forces have shaped identity-based gay liberation in both progressive and constraining ways.

Throughout the 1960s and 1970s, the rise of gay liberation in many Western countries was closely associated with an ongoing interrogation of dominant conceptions of sexuality, self and identity. Some gay writers argued that homosexuality was psychologically and socially the equal of hetero-sexuality; this standpoint, in one stroke, embraced all in the mainstream who viewed the homosexual as a distinct type of person, but with the crucial inversion that homosexuality was now cast as just as morally worthy as heterosexuality. According to this approach, which in one version or another was extensively adopted in the gay movement, the notion of a distinctive sense of personal and sexual identity should be deployed to defend gays against the homophobia of the wider culture, and thus to advance gay rights.

There are a number of important criticisms of the political radicalism of gay liberation. I shall only note in passing those that directly relate to the topic of the self. It is sometimes argued, particularly by postmodern sexual theorists, that gay liberation rode roughshod over race, ethnic and class differences. There is some accuracy to this charge, since the desire to legis-late an affirmative gay identity was often pursued at the cost of awareness of wider social issues – especially ignorance of the emotional damage that other social and historical forces have had upon the self. However, this argument can be overstressed; there is always a danger of oversimplification when discussing the gay movement as a unified entity, and in fact many gay activists shared a strong political commitment to other issues of discrimina-tion (such as the black and union movements). Perhaps more importantly, and no doubt ironically, the gay liberation movement has been criticized by many for reinforcing the divide between homosexual and heterosexual cultures, positing essentialist identities, and carving the world into majority and minority experience.

In time, the identity framework of the gay movement gave way to a different sort of politics concerned with sexual identities, preferences and activities, one connected with the new social theories of post-structuralism and postmodernism. In the late 1980s and 1990s, the term 'queer' was used by theorists and activists alike to attack identity politics, to interrogate sexuality and decentre the self, and to construct alternative political geographies for the heterosexual/ homosexual divide that shapes our communities and cultures. Queer theory represents a sexual politics sensitive to our new era of transnational capital, globalized technology and postmodern culture. The social and historical forces influencing the shift from identity to queer politics are located in the fragmentation of social identities and political alignments associated with globalization. Queer politics is pluralistic, multidimensional and open-ended, especially at the level of addressing experience of the self and sexuality.

The writings of Diana Fuss are important in this context. Reflecting upon the widespread discontent with identity politics in the 1980s, Fuss developed an influential critique of the ways in which gay and lesbian liberation discourses unwittingly reinforced heterosexual norms; her critique, in turn, shaped the politics of subversion advocated by queer theorists. Describing configurations of sex, gender and sexuality in terms of our culture's obsession with notions of sameness and difference, Fuss contended that the opposition between homosexuality and heterosexuality reinforced the social imperative to divide the world between norm and pathology, inclusion and exclusion, identity and otherness. The hetero/homosexual logic of identity is one premised on difference. Such forms of sexual orientation, however, are in fact constantly crossing into each other. It is only through psychological exclusion and repression that homosexuality is rendered subordinate to heterosexuality. Part of the problem here, according to Fuss, is that we are lost in identity, its logic and categories. Questioning identity categories, Fuss asks (1989: 100):

> Is politics based on identity, or is identity based on politics? Is identity a natural, political, historical, psychical, or linguistic construct? What implications does the deconstruction of 'identity' have for those who espouse an identity politics? Can feminist, gay, or lesbian subjects afford to dispense with the notion of unified, stable identities or must we begin to base our politics on something other than identity? What, in other words, is the politics of 'identity politics'?

Fuss asks us, in effect, to consider what our lives might be like without the anxious grip of identity categories. She questions what the self can do without, a challenge taken up and developed in queer theory and politics in the 1990s.

The best-known and most influential author associated with the queer critique of feminist theorizing is Eve Kosofsky Sedgwick, routinely described as 'the mother of queer theory'. A professor of English with an uncanny gift for grappling with the sexual politics of language, Sedgwick stresses the experiential significance of discourses on homosexuality not only for the self and identity, but for the production and distribution of knowledge in the wider society. In her most important book, *The Epistemology of the Closet* (1990), Sedgwick describes the hetero/homosexual opposition as our culture's 'master term', a term that structures not only self, identity and sexuality, but also social conventions, modes of thought, and cultural knowledge to its core. The normative regulations and sanctions governing homosexuality have never applied, and never will, to gays and lesbians alone; rather they cut to the heart of heterosexual identity, which maintains itself in opposition to homosexual experience. But what is repressed returns. Heterosexuality and homosexuality are intimately, hysterically intertwined; homosexual identifications, for Sedgwick as for Butler, are contained within heterosexual relationships, just as heterosexuality is gathered up and transfigured in gay and lesbian relationships.

Sedgwick has perhaps done more to interrogate the political limits of self, identity and sexuality than any other scholar associated with contemporary gay and lesbian studies. Her version of queer theory is out to demonstrate that homosexuality is integral to the culture of heterosexuality which hysterically repudiates same-sex desire. Not surprisingly, given her predilection for language as at the centre of social life, Sedgwick worries away at the cluster of keywords that betray the dreads of heterosexist culture. Thus 'the closet' turns out to ground knowledge of sexuality and gender in ways that pathologize. Bluntly put, Sedgwick argues that 'the closet' – as representation, metaphor, desire, fantasy – is installed at the heart of both homosexual and heterosexual identity, experience and definition. Consider, for example, the experience of coming out. Coming-out stories have long been a common part of gay experience. 'It's OK to be gay': this is one of the better-known slogans promoted by the gay and lesbian movement to assist young people to negotiate the difficulties of coming to terms with their homosexuality. Yet for the most part, asserts Sedgwick, coming-out stories have the capacity to disturb and damage dominant conceptions of sexuality. Because of the erotic energy and anxious fear associated with the closet and coming out, we can never know the truth about the self, sexuality or gender. The closet is the underside of 'normal sexuality', always threatening to open or be opened.

The apparent floating-free from its gay origins of that phrase 'coming out of the closet' in recent usage might suggest that the trope of the closet is so close to the heart of some modern preoccupations that it could be, or has been, evacuated of its historical gay specificity. But I hypothesize that exactly the opposite is true. I think that a whole cluster of the most crucial sites for the contestation of meaning in twentieth-century Western culture are consequentially and quite indelibly marked with the historical specificity of homosocial/homosexual definition, notably but not exclusively male, from around the turn of the century. Among these sites are, as I have indicated, the pairings secrecy/disclosure and private/public. Along with and sometimes through these epistemologically charged pairings, condensed in the figures of 'the closet' and 'coming out,' this very specific crisis of definition has then ineffaceably marked other pairings as basic to modern cultural organization as masculine/feminine, majority/minority, innocence/initiation, natural/artificial, new/old, growth/decadence, urbane/provincial, health/illness, same/different, cognition/paranoia, art/kitsch, sincerity/sentimentality, and voluntarily/addiction. So permeative has the suffusing stain of homo/heterosexual crisis been that to discuss any of these indices in any context, in the absence of an antihomophobic analysis, must perhaps be to perpetuate unknowingly compulsions implicit in each.

Eve Kosofsky Sedgwick (1990) *The Epistemology of the Closet*. Berkeley: University of California Press, pp. 72–3.

The political implications of such an assault on identity categories, in the recent history of queer theory at least, are highly ambiguous. In the work of Fuss, Sedgwick and others, legitimating forms of cultural identity as something coherent, unified or fixed are progressively called into question by a subversive critique that interrogates the oppressive fusing of sex, gender and sexuality at the level of the self. As a kind of anti-identity politics then, queer theory advocates and celebrates a coalition of alternative, subversive and transgressive sexual identities. Queer politics embraces not only lesbian, gay and bisexual identities, but also fetishists, sadists, drag queens, transsexuals, butches and gender benders. The mobilization of identities as queer is potentially indeterminate, as the assessment of queerness depends on a self-identification with forms of sexuality that question or subvert 'the normal' within patriarchal power relations. Like much postmodernist culture, queer theory and politics is unashamedly open-ended, plural and multiple; the transgression of sexual norms is the key that defines queerness. But how transgression constitutes a progressive politics is not altogether clear. Jeffrey Weeks makes this criticism well (1995: 115):

> In the long perspectives of history, queer politics may well prove an ephemeral ripple rather than a refreshing wave. Queer politics has all the defects of a transgressive style, elevating confrontation over the content of alternatives. Although it seeks to deconstruct old rigidities, it creates new boundaries; although it is deliberately transgressive, it enacts dissidence through the adoption of a descriptive label which many lesbians and gays find offensive, often seeking enemies within as much as enemies without.

Much like Butler's notion of subversive performance, the slant towards transgression in queer theory is perhaps geared more towards fashion than the fine detail of concrete political transformation.

It is against this backdrop that some commentators have suggested that queer theory is unable to provide a progressive basis for politics. The emphasis upon literary deconstruction in queer theorizing is, for some critics, intellectually interesting but politically shallow; the whole style of queer theory, with its relentless droning of sexual transgression, is said to be apolitical, with little analytical concern for the realities of social institutions, economic development or the policies of government. In postmodern culture, the language of transgression is sometimes only an inch away from anti-political irrationalism – or so some argue. Others, however, welcome queer theory's dismantling of social science and literary criticism as distinct fields of study, and see in the queer critique of identity a radical revaluation not only of self-experience and social relationships, but also of knowledge and politics. Indeed, as Patricia Clough has argued, the style of queer theoretical interrogations of the self, identity and sexuality suggests that style itself is political, always overdetermined with cultural assumptions and sexual ideologies. In particular, the style of mainstream social science, with its patriarchal longing for certitude, structure and order, is rendered dubious in this respect.

Similar doubts hang over the question of the self in queer theory. Is queer theory's ongoing interrogation of selfhood radical or reactionary? Certainly the focus of queer theory upon, say, transvestite performance or gender-corrective surgery dramatizes the incoherence of our culture's obsession with stable selves, identities, sexualities and genders. But it is far from obvious that, in its relentless debunking of the self and identity politics, queer theory can provide any psychological analysis of self. It is one thing to decentre or deconstruct the autonomous, rational, masculinist self of Enlightenment culture; yet it is quite another to imagine that self as a category can be conveniently done away with altogether. The critique of identity I have described in the foregoing pages, from Butler to Sedgwick, does not, in my opinion, attempt to transcend the realm of individuality and the self in such a manner. It remains the case, however, that the exuberance and idealism of queer theory, however intellectually invigorating the call to sexual transgression might be, does underestimate the considerable personal and emotional difficulties involved in cultural change and political transformation.

Summary points

1   Feminism views the relation between gender and identity as a core political issue. In 1970s gender theory, the fundamental distinction is that between biological 'sex' (viewed as innate) and socialized gender (viewed as constructed socially). In the 1970s and early 1980s, gender theory was eclipsed by a feminist interest in the complexity of women's role as mothers as well as the psychodynamic intricacies of femininities and masculinities.

2   The psychoanalytic theories of Freud and Lacan, according to feminists such as Juliet Mitchell, offer crucial critiques of how unequal gender relations come to be emotionally experienced by women and men. According to Mitchell, it is through language that the child is subjected to the law of the Name-of-the-Father, which operates to institute repression, sexual difference and gender identity by the threat of castration.

3   Mitchell's feminism has been widely criticized for exaggerating the rigidities and uniformities of gender hierarchy.

4   Exclusive female mothering, according to feminist Nancy Chodorow, is central to gender asymmetry in modern societies. It produces social relations split between connected, empathic female identities on the one hand, and isolated, instrumental male identities on the other. Masculine identity is built on a denial of primary maternal identification resulting in a fragile sense of self, defensively structured by an abstract attitude to the world. Feminine identity is grounded in a strong sense of gender, but is limited in capacity for autonomy and individuality. The only viable route out of contemporary gender asymmetries, says Chodorow, is through shared parenting.

5   In various French feminisms, there is an engagement with Freud and Lacan to critique the patriarchal sexual order of contemporary societies. In Kristeva, this is represented through the notion of the 'semiotic' – a pre-Oedipal realm of intense affect associated with the

imprint of the mother's body. In Irigaray, the subversive 'feminine' is grounded in relation to women's plural, multiple experience of sexuality and the body.

6 For Judith Butler, gender identity is a 'discursive effect'. Sexuality is shot through with psychological and cultural illusions created by the *repeated performance* of gender.

7 The term 'queer' has been used by social theorists from the late 1980s and 1990s to critically interrogate sexualities and the decentring of identity. Queer theory is a politics affirming the plural, multidimensional and ambivalent.

Further questions

1 In the light of this chapter's discussion of feminism and post-feminism, what do you understand the sex–gender distinction to denote?

2 In what ways do you think psychoanalysis has either enhanced or constrained the feminist critique of unequal gender relations?

3 Has feminism been eclipsed by the advent of a post-feminist sensibility?

4 How might the repressed 'feminine' be politically mapped in contemporary masculinist society?

5 What are some of the political ramifications of the queering of sexualities?

Further reading

Juliet Mitchell

Psychoanalysis and Feminism (Penguin Books, 1974).
Mad Men and Medusas (Basic Books, 2001).

Nancy Chodorow

The Reproduction of Mothering (University of California Press, 1978).
Feminism and Psychoanalytic Theory (Polity Press, 1989).

Femininities, masculinities, sexualities: Freud and beyond (University Press of Kentucky, 1994).

Jessica Benjamin

The Bonds of Love: Psychoanalysis, Feminism, and the Problem of Domination (Pantheon Books, 1988).
Like Subjects, Love Objects: Essays on Recognition and Sexual Difference (Yale University Press, 1995).
Shadow of the Other: Intersubjectivity and Gender in Psychoanalysis (Routledge, 1998).

Julia Kristeva

Powers of Horror: An Essay on Abjection (Columbia University Press, 1982).
Revolutions in Poetic Language (Columbia University Press, 1984).
Tales of Love (Columbia University Press, 1987).
Strangers to Ourselves (Harvester Wheatsheaf, 1991).
Black Sun: Depression and Melancholia (Columbia University Press, 1989).

Judith Butler

Gender Trouble: Feminism and the Subversion of Identity (Routledge, 1990).
Bodies that Matter: On the Discursive Limits of Sex (Routledge, 1993).
The Psychic Life of Power: Theories in Subjection (Stanford University Press, 1997).

Eve Kosofsky Sedgwick

Between Men: English Literature and Male Homosocial Desire (Columbia University Press, 1985).
The Epistemology of the Closet (University of California Press, 1990).
Tendencies (Duke University Press, 1993).

There are a number of excellent introductions to and critiques of post-feminism in recent social theory. See, among others, Lois McMay, *Gender and Agency* (Polity Press, 2000); Drucilla Cornell, *Transformations: Recollective Imagination and Sexual Difference* (Routledge, 1993); Lynne Segal, *Why Feminism?* (Polity Press, 1999); Sarah Gamble, *The Routledge Companion to Feminism and Postfeminism.* (Routledge, 2001); Carole R. McCann and Seung-Kyung Kim, *Feminist Theory Reader: Local and Global Perspectives* (Routledge, 2002); Ann Brooks, *Postfeminisms: Feminism,*

Cultural Theory, and Cultural Forms (Routledge 1997), and Tania Modleski, *Feminism Without Women: Culture and Criticism in a Postfeminist Age* (Routledge, 1991).

Internet links

Feminism and post-feminism

http://www.marxists.org/subject/women/feminists.htm
http://www.cddc.vt.edu/feminism/psy.html
http://bailiwick.lib.uiowa.edu/wstudies/l (feminist theory)

Juliet Mitchell

http://www.jesus.cam.ac.uk/contacts/fellows/profiles/mitchell.html

Nancy Chodorow

http://cyberpsych.org/homophobia/chodorow.htm (Chodorow on homophobia)

Jessica Benjamin

http://nyih.as.nyu.edu/object/JessicaBenjamin.html

Julia Kristeva

http://www.msu.edu/user/chrenkal/980/JKRIST.HTM
http://www.egs.edu/resources/kristeva.html

Judith Butler

http://www.theory.org.uk/ctr-butl.htm
http://sun3.lib.uci.edu/indiv/scctr/Wellek/butler/

Eve Kosofsky Sedgwick

http://web.gc.cuny.edu/English/fac_esedgwick.html

Queer theory

http://www.queertheory.com/
http://www.theory.org.uk/ctr-quee.htm

Postmodernity

Contents

In the course of this book so far we have examined a number of perspectives and problems in contemporary social theory. The theoretical perspectives surveyed – post-Marxism, structuralism, feminism – have been considered in terms of their different preoccupations in approaching the critique of society. And yet all of these social theories have been united by their concern to put into question a whole form of social life in order to entertain possible alternative futures. That is, the social theories reviewed in previous chapters display a certain totalizing bent, indebted as they are to the modernist assumption that the whole definition, constitution and transformation of society may be comprehensively mapped at the level of theory. The Frankfurt School had revealed that the culture industries are intricately interwoven with the organizing logics of advanced capitalism, manipulating personal life in terms of surplus repression and reorganizing public life in terms of intensified consumerism. Structuralism had showed that the signs and structures that frame personal and social life, popular and high culture, are governed by the systemic processes of language. Feminism had probed the interlocking of sex and gender, and made its appeal to emancipation in the form of autonomous identity unencumbered by the oppressive weight of patriarchy.

For those social critics who found themselves less than impressed with the programmatic, synoptic ambitions of modernist social science, one way out from these conceptual conundrums and political deadlocks lay in displacing and decentring the operations of social theory as a whole. Why go on trying, the sceptics asked, to locate single drivers of social repro-duction and political domination – capitalism, language, gender – when it is more and more obvious that we live today in a multidimensional world that continually escapes the powers of theory? Why continue with the act of conceptual house-tidying, dividing the world into neatly segmented subsystems, micro-processes and deterministic identities, when it is evident that theory practised in this fashion is a form of repressive political closure? In short, why scratch where it doesn't itch? Dispense with the totalizing ambitions of social theory – which are, in any event, ill-conceived, a hangover from the Enlightenment – and grasp what most people today intuitively recognize: that human experience is multiple, dispersed, fragmented, complex, contradictory? In the announcement of this novel cultural mood, we have entered the troubled waters of postmodernism.

Postmodernism was a response in the 1980s to the waning of radical politics and of theory, the outsourcing of manufacturing from the West to various Second and Third World countries, the spread of a seemingly unstoppable universal consumerism, the development of new information technologies as well as the emergence of new forms of identity politics. There are already several accomplished surveys of the history of the term 'postmodernism' in the critical literature (Anderson 1998), which readers may wish to consult. More interesting than its conceptual history, however, is the speed with which the term 'postmodern' has entered the lexicon of popular culture. Everything from MTV, Madonna and mobile phones to irony, information culture and iPods has attracted the label 'postmodern'. In this sense, postmodernism – as suggestive of a fresh cultural mood and novel aesthetic styles – scandalizes identity, society and politics, with its levelling of hierarchies, its interpretive polyvalence, its dislocating sub-version of ideological closure, its self-reflexive pluralism.

In introducing the main parameters of postmodern social theory in this chapter, I shall concentrate on the central ideas developed by various social theorists in their visions of postmodernity. These visions may be labelled, for our purposes at any rate, as follows: (1) postmodernity as schizoid desire; (2) postmodernity as simulated media culture; (3) postmodernity as global capitalist transformations; and (4) postmodernity as liquid sociality. In describing postmodernity in these ways, I have in mind the work of Gilles Deleuze, Félix Guattari and Jean-François Lyotard as belonging to the first category; the French sociologist Jean Baudrillard to the second category; the American cultural theorist Fredric Jameson to the third category; and the European sociologist Zygmunt Bauman to the final category. The writings of Deleuze, Guattari, Lyotard, Baudrillard, Jameson and Bauman are of crucial significance for any sustained critical reflection upon postmodernity. Each of these authors has developed an immensely powerful aesthetic, cultural or sociological understanding of the conditions and consequences of postmodernity. Yet each author has also expressed reservations about the very notion of the postmodern, and each in their own way has attempted to keep some distance from the so-called 'postmodern turn' in social theory. This makes their respective ideas of key importance for appraising the char-acteristics of postmodernity, and throughout this chapter I shall interweave other important studies on postmodern transformations of identity, culture and society.

Deleuze and Guattari: postmodernity as schizoid desire

The work of Gilles Deleuze and Félix Guattari emerged in the context of post-1968 libertarian Left politics in France. Deleuze, a philosopher who committed suicide in 1995, and Guattari, a psychoanalyst who was very active in the anti-psychiatry movement of the 1960s, worked together to produce some arrestingly original books expounding what they termed 'the philosophy of desire'.

In their celebrated work *Anti-Oedipus* (1977), a book widely hailed in postmodern and radical political circles, Deleuze and Guattari detailed a vision of schizophrenic desire as the basis for an account of social transformation. *Anti-Oedipus*, which scandalized French psychoanalysis and the academy, developed a postmodern vision of desire from two main perspectives. First, Deleuze and Guattari use psychoanalytic theory against itself, launching a polemical assault against the tenets of classical Freudianism. Second, they outline a multiple, depersonalized account of desire, which they term 'schizoanalysis'. Deleuze and Guattari invoke schizophrenia as a model for understanding the nature of desire in contemporary times – that is, the emerging social landscape of postmodernity. They propose a celebration of the fluid and multiple intensities of schizophrenic desire, primarily in order to oppose the repressive functioning of social norms under capitalism. To this end, they develop the notion of a 'subjectless machine', a kind of schizophrenic overflowing of desire that produces and reproduces itself in aimless circulation. Against the Oedipalizing logic of capitalist discourse, where desire is channelled into prescribed pathways under the sign of the commodity form, Deleuze and Guattari speak up for the impersonalized flows of schizoid desire, a productive network of libidinal articulations which potentially short-circuit capitalism.

In this view of postmodern social transformations, the world is seen as a mix of libidinal and symbolic forms that continuously displace one another. The historical development of capitalist production is interpreted by Deleuze and Guattari in terms of the injurious traumas of repression. In its early stages, capitalism is said to have severed the economic realm from symbolic forms such as kinship systems, customs, religious beliefs and the like. Capitalist production, at this historical point, was embedded in a form of collectivism, with pre-given social roles and identities. The emergence of monopoly capitalism, however, radically transformed the social world: it swept away traditional social forms, as economic forces bite deeply into the symbolic textures of society itself. The creation of an international capitalist system and of world markets, it may be said, breaks down the symbolic framework of the local community and of tradition. Deleuze and Guattari refer to this process as the 'deterritorialization' of social codes. Capitalism ruthlessly dismantles bourgeois cultural forms and moral codes, replacing these with the exchangeability and anonymity of commodities. Deleuze and Guattari argue that the logic of capitalist economic relations is deeply interwoven with the discontinuities of schizophrenic desire. Like the indifference of the commodity itself, schizophrenia knows no symbolic limit, no constraint of reality, no high-minded guilt born of the superego. Instead, schizoid desire produces itself in fragments of pleasure, slicing capitalist temporality into the fluidity of the moment. 'The order of desire', write Deleuze and Guattari, 'is the order of *production*; all production is at once desiring production and social production.'

Capitalism, however, not only 'deterritorializes' but constantly 'reterritorializes' in radically new ways. Against capitalism's dismantling of pre-existing social boundaries, Deleuze and Guattari point to a proto-fascist, paranoiac tendency at the heart of modernity, a tendency that restructures schizoid flows into oppressive norms and which thus functions as ingrained pathologies. What is being emphasized here is the oppressive nature of late capitalist society, its recoding of desire into the ordered, conventional world of international banking, stock markets and insurance companies. Schizophrenic and paranoiac desire: both forms of production are to be found at work within the social system. Global capitalism produces a profound deterritorialization of social forms into schizoid flows on the one hand, while simultaneously recoding these flows into the symbolic circuit of culture on the other. From iPods to the International Monetary Fund, the schizophrenic signals of desire are endlessly recoded to support the economic logics of capitalism.

The decoding of flows and the deterritorialization of the socius thus constitutes the most characteristic and the most important tendency of capitalism. It continually draws near to its limit, which is a genuinely schizophrenic limit. It tends, with all the strength at its command, to produce the schizo as the subject of the decoded flows on the body without organs – more capitalist than the capitalist and more proletarian than the proletariat. This tendency is being carried further and further, to the point that capitalism with all its flows may dispatch itself straight to the moon: we really haven't seen anything yet! When we say that schizophrenia is our characteristic malady, the malady of our era, we do not merely mean to say that modern life drives people mad. It is not a question of a way of life, but of a process of production. Nor is it merely the failure of codes, such a parallelism is a much more precise formulation of the relationship between, for example, the phenomena of shifting of meaning in the case of schizophrenics and the mechanisms of ever increasing disharmony and discord at every level of industrial society.

Gilles Deleuze and Félix Guattari (1983 [1977]) *Anti-Oedipus: Capitalism and Schitzophrenia*, trans. Robert Hurley, Mark Seem and Helen R. Lane. Minneapolis: University of Minnesota Press, p. 34.

As with the creative destruction of capitalism, similar contradictions are at work within psychoanalysis itself. Desire prior to Oedipus, Deleuze and Guattari contend, is multidimensional, discontinuous and shifting. Desire just *is* the production of 'machine parts', spilling out across libidinal surfaces, pluralized in its operations through contact with other human 'machines'. 'The breast', they write, 'is a machine that produces milk, and the mouth a machine coupled to it.' Desire is schizoid to its roots, subjectless through and through, an impersonal force of production. Not so, however, after the impact of Oedipalization. The impersonal force of schizoid desire, according to Deleuze and Guattari, is repressively codified through Oedipus. For Deleuze and Guattari, the Oedipus complex works to *personalize desire*, referring all unconscious productions to the incestuous sexual realm of family life. Oedipus, then, is a prime instance of the capitalist recoding of desire. Deleuze and Guattari argue that psychoanalysis functions as a repressive force which projects desire into the personalized, neurotic structures of 'daddy-mummy-me'.

The process of capitalist reterritorialization is in this view paranoid to its roots; such social pathologies however, while deeply entrenched, do not go all the way down. For Deleuze and Guattari, the schizoid nature of desire constantly *escapes* the well-ordered structures of capitalist production. The schizoid tribulations of desire, argue Deleuze and Guattari, are transgressive, polymorphous, fragmenting. In its anarchic, heterogeneous lines of libidinal intensity, schizophrenic desire offers, paradoxically, to outstrip the centralized, unified organization of capitalist production in which it is encoded. 'Schizophrenia', write Deleuze and Guattari, 'is desiring production at the limit of social production.' Like the Surrealist avant-garde, then, Deleuze and Guattari are fascinated by the idea of transgression, the breaking of limits and undoing of rules. Smashing through the boundaries of ordinary life, schizoid desire is pure production: desire turning back upon itself to further the production of desire.

Deleuze and Guattari's celebration of the transgressive edge of desire lies in stark contrast to the Lacanian model of the unconscious, as discussed in Chapter 4. Whereas Lacan ties the unconscious to loss, Deleuze and Guattari conceive of schizoid desire as pure affirmation. Moreover, they view Lacan's Freud as essentially conservative in political orientation. Psychoanalysis, both traditional and Lacanian, constructs desire as loss for the purpose of adapting human subjects to the social order. From this angle, psychoanalysis deciphers and reinscribes Oedipal compulsions for identification which are essential to the ego-centred, neurotic structures of subjecthood in late capitalism. In this manner, the signs of power constitute us as individual subjects through and through. In contrast, Deleuze and Guattari emphasize the multiple paths of desire – schizoid proliferations, openings, zigzags and flows. To designate this, they propose 'schizoanalysis', which interprets unconscious desire hydraulically as a desiring machine; unconscious flows of libidinal energy at once anchor and destabilize the social process. For Deleuze and Guattari, schizophrenia is revolutionary since it defies identification, categorization and differentiation. According to this view, unconscious desire represents nothing, neither representation nor the sign. Desire simply is. Desire floats in the social field as indeterminate, impersonal production. Hence the factory metaphor, 'desiring machines'.

Deleuze and Guattari's arguments have provoked a barrage of critical responses. Some critics lampoon the suggestion that schizophrenia is naturally rebellious and subversive. In celebrating the mind-shattering flux of schizoid desire, so critics argue, Deleuze and Guattari sidestep the issue of how personal and social change interweave. Clinical portraits of schizophrenia are said by various critics to belie the celebratory gloss provided by Deleuze and Guattari. What clinical studies reveal is a world, not of euphoric celebration, but of disintegration, fragmentation, terror and emotional devastation. Some defenders of Deleuze and Guattari have argued that to anticipate how the world might be radically altered from the standpoint of the schizophrenic *process* is not the same as promoting schizophrenia itself. Yet as regards social theory, it certainly seems doubtful that schizoid processes offer a fruitful basis for the rethinking of social organization. Even if it is granted that schizoid processes break apart received social meanings in potentially productive ways, who would seriously put forward such a case for social change given the pain, emptiness and terror of schizoid experience? Perhaps most limiting of all, however, is the failure of Deleuze and Guattari to distinguish between different forms of social organization. In defending the 'schizo' against the repressions of modernity, Deleuze and Guattari appear to slide into an indiscriminate rejection of politics as such. All social systems become, in effect, 'terroristic' irrespective of their modalities of power. But what of the vital political differences between liberal democracy and fascism? What about the impact of ideologies, such as religious fundamentalism, nationalism and political militancy? In lamenting the 'terror of norms', Deleuze and Guattari are left without any secure footing to elucidate the revolutionary political agency to which they attach key importance. Instead, Deleuze and Guattari are left with a romantic, idealized fantasy of the 'schizoid hero'.

The postmodern condition: Lyotard

Alongside the work of Deleuze and Guattari, the social theorist whose name is most closely associated with postmodernism is the French philosopher, Jean-François Lyotard. Like Deleuze and Guattari, Lyotard wishes to talk up a postmodernism with strong political commitment.

Abandoning the claims of the Enlightenment and universal theories of knowledge, Lyotard offers an original analysis of today's transformed connections between libidinal desire and social differences.

Whereas Deleuze and Guattari interpret society in terms of schizoid desire against repressive desire, revolutionary against fascist desire, Lyotard in *Libidinal Economy* (1974) sees the social as itself secretly libidinal, with sociality inscribed on the 'inside' of desire. Society, though dependent on a repression of desire, is traversed by 'libidinal intensities'. Yet interestingly, Lyotard rejects the libertarian view that transgression is inherently good, repression bad. All societies, he argues, are complex networks of discourse and desire. Instead of prioritizing desire over signification, as in Deleuze and Guattari's *Anti-Oedipus*, Lyotard highlights different modalities of desire and the structures of their production. Highlighting ambivalences in Freud's account of the unconscious, Lyotard discerns two aspects of desire: desire-as-wish (fantasy) and desire-as-force (libido). Desire-as-wish, the figural component of the unconscious, is the representational form impressed upon lost objects. Here the individual subject fantasizes images of the self, of others and of the world as a compensation for various lacks or exclusions. In this regime, desire operates under the sign of lack, absence and negativity. By contrast, desire-as-force, the energetic component of the unconscious, is pure energy, libido and primary process. In this regime, desire functions through the act of its own production, endlessly reproducing itself in some transcendental process of repetition.

Lyotard wishes to claim desire-as-force as inherently positive and affirmative. He advocates, in Nietzchean fashion, a celebration of libidinal intensities. Libidinal intensities consist of a flux of desire, energy in a state of continuous nonlinear movement. Lyotard refers to a rotation of a 'libidinal band' that constantly disrupts all intersections of self and other, of internal and external, of the differentiation of 'this' from 'not-this'. The whole notion is somewhat like the 'action painting' of Jackson Pollock, in which figural lines interweave without end. For Lyotard, libidinal intensities are an unconscious force prior to representation and conscious knowledge.

If the libidinal intensities of which Lyotard writes constitute symbolic representation, however, it is not his political aim to oppose the libidinal to the social. Rejecting as politically naive proclamations about the 'truth of desire', Lyotard turns instead to the dissolution of symbolic representation as a *medium* of the libidinal band itself. The dominant ideological forms of the Enlightenment, including doctrines of truth and freedom, self-determination, reason and universality, are thus recast as inseparable from a libidinal poetics. Knowledge itself is just one mode of libidinal intensity among others. Here we reach the core of Lyotard's political analysis in *Libidinal Economy*: contemporary social theory must reject the view that desire does not flow freely enough in contemporary society – as Deleuze and Guattari contend. For Lyotard, by contrast, desire circulates endlessly around objects, surfaces and bodies. In this connection, late capitalism is an immense desiring system. He describes late capitalist society as a culture swamped with flashy commodities and signs, in which all social forms are colonized by the economic logic of exchange. Yet the implications of this for radical politics are not necessarily bad news. According to Lyotard, the exchangeability and anonymity of contemporary capitalist processes parallels the aimless flux of the libidinal band itself. He advocates embracing the fragmentation of desire as a way of intensifying the lived experiences of postmodern culture. The challenging and exhilarating task for postmodernism is to recognize that desire is always already realized, to extract pleasure from the fragments and surfaces in which identities are constituted.

In *The Postmodern Condition* (1979), the work for which Lyotard is most widely celebrated and which helped ignite the debate over postmodernism, the distinction between modern and postmodern models of knowledge is examined. Lyotard views the defining features of the postmodern condition as involving a rejection of the 'grand narratives' of the Enlightenment, such as Truth, Freedom, Justice and Reason. Modernity, for Lyotard as for some other postmodern theorists, is characterized by the grounding of knowledge and science in appeals to 'master or metanarratives'. The seductive, rhetorical force of epic narratives, such as the Enlightenment's story of human progress or the Marxist story of the coming of socialist utopia, has helped legitimate oppressive social hierarchies and political domination. For example, the political terror unleashed in the former Soviet Union under Stalin throughout the 1940s and 1950s was made possible with ongoing reference to the epic narrative of Marxism. This was not necessarily the result of any in-built fault of Marx's work itself, something which Lyotard – a former socialist militant – is at pains to emphasize. But Marxism, just like all political ideologies, has involved a synthesizing of its worldview with various epic Enlightenment narratives, which in turn has given rise to the tragic consequence of a terroristic Reason. Grand narratives for Lyotard are intrinsic to the social repression and political domination of modernity.

But not so the postmodern condition, which finds a novel way of con-textualizing knowledge. 'I define postmodern,' announces Lyotard, 'as incredulity towards metanarratives.' In conditions of postmodernity, knowledge is fragmented into multiple disciplines, diverse sites and par-ticular paradigms. Following the philosopher Wittgenstein, Lyotard posits that knowledge today is more and more 'grounded' in contextualized 'language games', with each game conducted within a locally agreed, tentative specificity. Abandoning the universal categories of modernist science, the postmodern universe of knowledge is perspectival and incomplete in its self-ruling singularity. From Einsteinian relativity theory and quantum mechanics to paralogical science and black holes, the purity of perspectival, provisional knowledge is key. Social conflict, symbolic violence and political injustice occur in postmodern societies when one language game is ruthlessly imposed upon another.

Lyotard's vision of the postmodern condition has had a considerable impact upon social theory. At the centre of his postmodernism lies a political concern with grasping the development of knowledge and science in the era of new information technologies, and specifically with highlighting the decentring of society in non-essentialistic ways. Any understanding of society which reduces knowledge multiplicity into unity, or which freezes identities and cultural meanings with reference towards an epic narrative, is no longer credible according to Lyotard. What becomes of science and knowledge in conditions of postmodernity is a turning back upon their own linguistic practice and self-legitimating language games. Struggles over knowledge always take place in singular spheres which are dispersed, fragmented and heterogeneous. One impor-tant upshot of Lyotard's standpoint, therefore, is that any attempt to fix, close or stabilize the meanings we attach to, say, identity, sexuality, gender, ethnicity or social class is unjust and politically dangerous.

There are, however, problems with Lyotard's account of the postmodern condition – of which two will be briefly mentioned here. The first is the criticism that Lyotard celebrates pluralism as a good in itself, without any broader political content. Multiplication of small, singular language games: this is, in short, Lyotard's rallying cry for a postmodern politics. Yet there are difficulties in assuming that small revolts against large authorities are always politically progressive. What of the resurgence of neo-fascism in Europe? What of the British National Party? Fortunately, the numbers of members of fascist political parties remain gratifyingly small in the West, but the point is that such social practices surely constitute a 'small language game' in Lyotard's terms. It seems doubtful that the affirming of a pluralism purged of political substance can promote social differences, especially the recovery of rights for marginalized and excluded groups, in the manner desired by Lyotard. The second problem arising from Lyotard's account is that some have criticized his dismissal of the link between rational knowledge on the one hand and a meta-view of society on the other. According to critics, Lyotard fails to appreciate that all language games – no matter how provisional and tentative in formulation – implicate assumptions about the shape of society. Ecological discourses, for example, proceed from an awareness of, and desire to transcend, the environmental ills of industrial production. To that extent, such discourses certainly adopt elements of a 'meta-view' of society, and necessarily so in order to engage with and confront the risks of global environmental degradation.

What do you see as the gains and losses of Lyotard's postmodern perspective on knowledge? Is Lyotard's approach to contemporary living more or less convincing than that offered by Deleuze and Guattari?

Baudrillard: postmodernity as simulated media culture

To see culture in terms of signs and spectacles, not as a symptom of deeper economic contradictions but as a productive constituent of daily life, is to cast the postmodern as a dehistorized affair, depthless, decathected and disfiguring – for which, as Jean Baudrillard has argued, 'simulations' are all that exist. In his early works such as *The System of Objects* (1968), *The Consumer Society* (1972), *For a Critique of the Political Economy of the Sign* (1972) and *The Mirror of Production* (1973), Baudrillard appeared as a semiological structuralist, analysing the signifying systems of mass media, advertising, packaging and fashion with effortless theoretical panache. In reinterpreting Marx's theory of capitalist exchange value through a Freudian lens that emphasized the fetishizing of commodities, he sought to demonstrate how objects are encoded within a system of symbolic exchange that is fast transforming consumer societies of the West. The early Baudrillard's social semiotics, while not in any sense postmodernist, none the less drew from an extended array of other theories – including his sociology teacher Henri Lefebvre's 'critique of everyday life', the work of Guy Debord and the Situationists, Jacques Lacan's reading of Freudian psychoanalysis and George Bataille's theory of expenditure and symbolic exchange. Indeed, the stylish, playful, satiric prose of Baudrillard's sociology even at this relatively early juncture entered into conflict with the scientific rigours of structuralist semiotics, and in a sense already prefigured the mature Baudrillard's characteristic blend of post-structuralism and postmodernism – what he subsequently termed 'fatal theory'.

Signs and symbols are Baudrillard's key themes, and in particular his early work draws from both Saussure's structural linguistics and Roland Barthes' semiological analysis of signifying systems (see Chapter 3 for discussion of the structuralism of Saussure and Barthes). He was deeply influenced by the structuralist emphasis on the arbitrary character of the sign, with its problematization of the relations between images and things, language and reality. Signs, for Baudrillard as for Saussure, are primarily constituted through differences within the structures and rules of signification of any given society. Yet the radical impulse behind his early work lies in his attempts to situate the arbitrary character of signifiers and what they signify both critically and historically. In Baudrillard's view, advanced capitalism inaugurates a new structure of signs, one in which the forces of consumption outstrip the logic of production that organized industrial societies. 'The social logic of consumption', writes Baudrillard, 'is not at all that of the individual appropriation of the value of goods and services. . . . It is a logic of the production and manipulation of social signifiers.' For Baudrillard, the 'signifier' is less a particular seductive message or enticing representation, which manipulates the masses into unthinking or unwanted acts of consumption, than a kind of super-object that defies all attempts at classification, an erasure and overcoming of the product simply by mediating it, and in turn structuring the consumer's fascination with the signifier as central to the process of consumption. In this sense, the signifier is the 'real of desire'. Whether through the purchase of a Mercedes, an Apple iPod or Nike trainers, individuals make their identities through the signs they consume and display to others. In the ideological code of consumerism, identities are fashioned primarily through the exchange of symbolic differences.

From the vantage point of Marxism as well as Baudrillard's association with the French political Left throughout the 1960s, this was an unsettling perspective. In placing economic productivism at the core of social life, says Baudrillard, Marxism had functioned as a mirror to bourgeois society. The early semiological Baudrillard rejects the Marxist critique of commodities in terms of exchange value as economistic; it is *sign value*, as he comments, that shapes expressions of style, power and prestige in the age of consumer society. Moreover, he trusts to the possibility of a semiological critique of society's structured code, suggesting that the critic might establish a sufficient analytical distance from the capitalist order of symbolic exchange in order to play a role in its dismantling and reconstruction. Yet as Baudrillard came to recognize in *Simulation and Simulacra* (1981), the world of culture and critique is constituted to its roots in the depthless, fragmented surfaces of postmodernist society, and thus the idea that critical discourse can be cut loose from the play of signs that constitutes media and consumer societies is itself just metaphysical nostalgia.

This led Baudrillard to pay much more attention to transformations in media culture, particularly the role that communication media plays in shaping the world in which we live. The era of hi-tech capitalism, as he explains, transmutes social reality to a mediascape of floating signifiers and codes, as images and spectacles proliferate endlessly. Baudrillard is genuinely fascinated by these details of global information culture, and considers it essential to craft a self-parodying, scrupulously stylized language capable of addressing the sublimely promiscuous and polymorphous terrain of popular entertainment, information and communication technologies. In *Simulation and Simulacra*, he addresses the issue of communicative exchange in a world dominated by the media. Unlike many major postmodernist theorists, for whom modernity is a discredited project of political domination and oppression, Baudrillard isolates the critical rigour of classical social theory as concerned with both the powers and limits of that social order's production and consumption of commodities. Such analytical attention towards commodity production and political economy, however, has now been rendered outmoded, he contends, as postmodern societies are organized increasingly through the production of signs, images and codes. The more postmodern culture develops, the more people come to define their identities based on media images and signs.

Indeed, Baudrillard's *Simulation and Simulacra* is at its most subversive and scandalous in its critique of 'hyperreality', a kind of outstripping of reality by the logic of media simulations. Media simulations, thanks to their brilliant hallucinogenic excess, are the ruin of all structured realities, bringing low modernist distinctions between object and representation, original and copy, thing and idea. Hyperreality is itself self-referential, a free-floating world of signs in which transgression, self-expansiveness and implosion are central. The scandal of postmodernity for Baudrillard lies in its conversion of codes, models and signs into seductive excess, a rendering up of radically ambiguous simulations that at once cut to the core of common experience and yet somehow remain aesthetically distant from everyday life. Reality is thus made foreign, perverse, uncanny. Yet in a strange reversal, what is produced out of this non-reality, or hyperreality, is one of the most imaginative forms of cultural production of the current era. For simulacra, in Baudrillard's eyes, have no grounding in any 'reality' except their own production. TV news creates information streams only to narrate them, crude notions of 'sex' are raised to the nth degree in pornography and politics is raised to the second power in terrorism. From this angle, postmodernism is less a microcosm of societal forces than a world which operates independently of the culture it draws upon and transfigures.

> In this passage to a space whose curvature is no longer that of the real, nor of truth, the age of simulation thus begins with a liquidation of all referentials – worse: by their artificial resurrection in systems of signs, which are a more ductile material than meaning, in that they lend themselves to all systems of equivalence, all binary oppositions and all combinatory algebra. It is no longer a question of imitation, nor of reduplication, nor even of parody. It is rather a question of substituting signs of the real for the real itself; that is, an operation to deter every real process by its operational double, a metastable, programmatic, perfect descriptive machine which provides all the signs of the real and short-circuits all its vicissitudes. Never again will the real have to be produced: this is the vital function of the model in a system of death, or rather of anticipated resurrection which no longer leaves any chance even in the event of death. A hyperreal henceforth sheltered from the imaginary, and from any distinction between the real and the imaginary, leaving room only for the orbital recurrence of models and the simulated generation of difference.
>
> Jean Baudrillard (1994 [1981]) *Simulacra and Simulations*. Ann Arbor, MI: University of Michigan Press, p. 167.

In the age of the satellite and digital technology it is a mistake to imagine that what occurs on the surface is merely the level of the superficial. On the contrary, postmodern culture glitters at the edge of its surfaces, in media simulations, computational signs and globalized codes, and such surfaces for Baudrillard encode particular forms of political power. Baudrillard's vision in this connection might be described as Nietzschean, in that he holds to the view that there is nothing but surface. *Pace* modernity, with its hidden organizing logics and surreptitious systematic forces, postmodern society does not lend itself easily to interpretation or critique by inherited modernist traditions. This leads Baudrillard to launch a full-blooded assault on the hermeneutics of suspicion in *Seduction* (1990b), where Marxism, structuralism and psychoanalysis come under attack for their metaphysical rationalizations and intellectual deceptions. The modernist notion that the manifest operations of bourgeois society may be critiqued in terms of latent functions or hidden structures is dismissed as deterministic. Postmodernism itself expresses no hidden, determining essence.

The condition of postmodernity is itself just a fleeting appearance, the transient moment, sensuous surface. Baudrillard's strategy for confronting this autonomy of the postmodern, a world cut loose from all relationship to modernity, lies with mapping the terrain of symbolic exchange, today's ever-proliferating network of images, signs and codes. In *Seduction* he urges the importance of hallucination, self-referentiality, simulation. Contemporary society, he says, is dominated by the logic of the sensuous surface – in a play of seduction which he sees as the very life-blood of the postmodern.

It is evident that Baudrillard's position, at the period of *Simulation and Simulacra* and *Seduction*, underscores the misalliances between self and world, the individual and social, in contemporary social conditions. Indeed, Baudrillard explicitly states that postmodern consumer society positions the individual in a state of fragmented multiplicity, denoting a psychic frame of never-ending seduction and mesmorization, such that the contemporary self is increasingly unable to differentiate itself from the informational blizzard of global media culture. In his subsequent writings, this objectivist strand of post-structuralist theory about the fate of subjectivity feeds further into his postmodernism. In *Fatal Strategies*, in which the contours of 'fatal theory' are contrasted to critical theory, Baudrillard contends that the self-constituting, self-authorizing subject of modern philosophical thought no longer provides an adequate reference point for interpreting the world; indeed, in the aftermath of the 'death of the subject', the object is to be privileged *over* subjects, such is the limitless control that the world of things now exerts over our senses. It is the object – specifically the hyperreal object, the simulated object – which for Baudrillard produces postmodern 'ecstasy' and an aesthetic hallucination of culture. What fascinates Baudrillard is the incessant productivity which lies at the core of hyperreal objects, the sense of euphoria, seduction and ecstasy which is instilled in subjects, and the endless multiplication and proliferation of images, messages and codes as reproduced through media spectaculars and the transnational culture industry.

Postmodernism is the moment at which the proliferation of hyperreal objects and alluring commodities becomes obscene, and this, too, carries profound implications for the emotional capacities of individuals to process both information and thought itself. Postmodern media culture, with its glimmering surfaces, its hallucinogenic intensities and its interpretive polyvalence is a world of seduction and stupefacation. 'Things have found a way', writes Baudrillard (1990a: 185),

> to elude the dialectic of meaning which bored them: it is to proliferate to infinity, to fully realize their potentialities, to surpass their essence in going to extremes, in an obscenity which henceforth takes the place for them of an immanent finality and of an insane rationality.

The obscenity is that global information culture is so compelling, so intoxicating and so seductive that it all but cancels out, as media simulations float free from the play of objects encoded. This is the world of CNN and Sky News, where the 24/7 proliferation of disasters, tragedies, political scandals and world catastrophes surpasses all attempts to historically contextualize or relocate in a broader frame of common meanings.

What have been the consequences of this postmodern *ob-scene* for the experience of subjectivity? Baudrillard, like many other major postmodernists, likens postmodern mentalities to schizophrenic fragmentation. A schizoid incapacity to distinguish between inside and outside, surface and depth, becomes culturally common. Here the postmodern subject, according to Baudrillard, lives in 'a state of terror which is characteristic of the schizophrenic, an over-proximity of all things, a foul promiscuity of all things which beleaguer and penetrate him, meeting with no resistance, and no halo, no aura, not even the aura of his own body protects him. In spite of himself the schizophrenic is open to everything and lives in the most extreme confusion' (Baudrillard 1988: 27). In a culture of virtualization, hallucination and seduction, the most one can do is channel-hop, surf the Net or absorb the inanities of American-dominated popular culture, such is the overloading of images and information upon the human mind. Baudrillard thus casts the postmodern subject in a wilderness of hyperreal mirrors; the subject is 'a pure screen, a pure absorption and resorption surface of the influence networks' (Baudrillard 1988: 27).

Baudrillard's non-event: the Gulf War did not take place

The arrival of the 1990s witnessed one the largest deployments of military arsenal by the United States in the history of warfare. The target was Iraq and its President Saddam Hussein. War was in the air: mass media were predicting it was only a matter of time until President Bush gave the green light for air strikes and a ground offensive. Meanwhile, on 4 January 1991, the French newspaper *Liberation* ran an article by Jean Baudrillard, 'The Gulf War will not take place'. On 16 January, America launched air strikes against Iraq. In February, this was followed by a three-day ground offensive. Astonishingly, however, Baudrillard stuck firm to his line. On 29 March 1991, he penned another article for *Liberation*, 'The Gulf War did not take place'.

Baudrillard's claim unleashed massive controversy. Many inside and outside of academia were offended by these articles. Critics lampooned the 'absurdity' of Baudrillard's postmodernism, finding abhorrent his alleged denial of human suffering on a massive scale. But forgotten in all the intellectual anxiety over Baudrillard's claims was his underscoring of our hi-tech media world, of televisual wars and of moral indifference generated through virtual violence. For what Baudrillard did – notably in focusing on the 'place' of war in this technological programming of military violence at the Gulf – was to question our cultural assumptions about what it means for an event to 'take place' and to suggest, scandalously, that simulation drains reality from the world. Baudrillard thus sees the spectacular visibility of the Gulf War as a dubious non-event, or pseudo-event, of uncertain left-over issues by virtue of its instant transformation into the media and their hyperreal appropriation. There are two key aspects to this analysis. First, the culture of militarism; and second, the media's hyperrealization of reality as 'truer than true'.

For Baudrillard, the Gulf War was a non-event in the sense that combat was written out of the military scripting in advance. What happened in the Gulf was rather a military simulation of war – prescripted, programmed and produced by the US administration. Baudrillard's 'The Gulf War did not take place' is filled with technical discussion of how a non-event materializes its signs and excludes anything not scripted for the programme, but the core political points can be well-enough summarized: US military processing meant that the enemy appeared only as a computerized target, with little or no possibility of reaction; the deployment of America's superior military hardware meant that the enemy was, in effect, already dead in advance; the programming of precision bombing at a distance from the site of conflict effectively excluded any exchange of munitions and arms, thus guaranteeing a one-sided war. This for Baudrillard was not war but the theatre of war.

The military scripting of the war, premised upon the coalition's technological superiority, was in turn intensified by the media's production of the conflict as a TV event. The media produced a virtualization of war through its 24/7 coverage, endless commentary, consultation with experts, ongoing speculation. Paradoxically, such attempts to represent the war in real time transformed it into its opposite, into a whirl of pure information. 'War,' says Baudrillard, 'implodes in real-time.'

Baudrillard's claims offer a novel perspective on the illusions of war. To the extent that his articles were published to astonished condemnation in Paris, and in time to global denunciation, this reminds us that

Baudrillard's arguments must be viewed in the wider context of his social theory of simulation. There are of course many limitations to Baudrillard's social theory and, in the context of his articles on the Gulf War, critics are certainly right to be concerned about his often excessive claims as to how media simulation outstrips the force and power of reality in our daily lives. Yet whatever the precise import of such criticisms, Baudrillard's claims concerning the Gulf War should not be seen as a denial of human suffering. It has been estimated that over 100,000 Iraqis lost their lives in the conflict, with many more seriously injured and wounded. This was but one of the terrible social costs of the West engaging the Third World in a First World War. But if Baudrillard is right, then ultimately the terror of the war was even more evil than this – since, in the end, the conflict was processed, produced and packaged as deathly simulation in advance.

Do you agree with Baudrillard's thesis regarding the virtual construction of wars? Is simulation the face of new wars for the coming century?

Jameson: postmodernity as global capitalist transformations

In the narrative of social theory, the development of modernity in Europe is, in broad terms, linked to the political and cultural penetration of what became market capitalism into many other countries of the world. This diffusion of an emergent capitalism, as I have already noted, was funda-mental to the logic of production and utility that organized modern societies and spread laboriously outward from 'the West' until the main organizing principles of society were rewritten by the primacy of post-industrial production and the arrival of new information technologies. One of the main attractions of the theory of postmodernity as simulated media cul-ture, associated especially with the work of Baudrillard, is its specific delineation of new social processes that no longer operate according to the laws of industrial capitalism. Since Baudrillard's main preoccupation is with signs and their impact upon the rest of society, there is a sense in which materialism dissolves into the background in this version of postmodernist culture. If this is indeed the case, we are now in a new era dominated by symbolic reproduction, from information processing to digital high-tech. In Baudrillard's eyes, the postmodern spells the 'end of political economy'.

There may, nevertheless, be some way of working across from – or cross-referencing – the information society or spectacles of consumerism to money markets and the incessant flows of speculative finance. It is just this kind of project that has been taken up by Fredric Jameson, the doyen of American cultural theorists, who argues the case for a full-blooded, systematic materialist conceptualization of postmodernity as part of a new stage of multinational capitalism. His magisterial *Postmodernism: or, The Cultural Logic of Late Capitalism* (1991) is a sprawling, interdisciplinary book, which gives particular emphasis to the discontinuity between modernity and postmodernity and manages to link postmodernism, culture and capitalism in its very title. What Jameson calls theories of 'postmodernism in culture' have displayed a repressed historical periodization as well as an implicit or explicit political stance on the conditions of advanced capitalism. In an age which has fetishized culture, Jameson develops his theory of global capitalist transformations in conscious contrast to accounts of the postmodern that displace or bury the movements of capitalism itself or alternatively render the postmodern as merely a kind of incipient materialism.

Jameson is critical of those authors who have sought to coin new terms, like post-industrial society or consumer society and the rest, for explicating contemporary cultural transformations. According to him, rather than terminological innovation it is necessary to look again at the nature of capitalist modernity itself, particularly the ways in which the consequences of capitalism are becoming both more global and abstract in scope. Rather than entering a period beyond political economy, Jameson stresses that we can perceive the contours of a new and 'higher' stage of capitalism. In advancing this position, he draws from the economist Ernest Mandel's periodization of 'long waves' of capital expansion, as set out in Mandel's benchmark book *Late Capitalism* (1975), for grasping the disorienting consequences of new forms of social organization. As Jameson (1991: 35–6) puts this,

> there have been three fundamental moments in capitalism, each one marking a dialectical expansion over the previous stage. These are market capitalism, the monopoly stage or the stage of imperialism, and our own, wrongly called postindustrial, but what might be termed multinational, capital. . . . Mandel's intervention in the postindustrial debate involves the proposition that late or multinational or consumer capitalism, far from being inconsistent with Marx's great nineteenth-century analysis, constitutes, on the contrary, the purest form of capital yet to have emerged, a prodigious expansion of capital into hitherto uncommodified areas.

For Jameson, this purest form of capital, witnessed in the global spiralling of multinational capitalism, has dramatically compacted both space and time with its instant electronic communications and digital flows, thereby ushering in the first genuine global cultural ideology. Understood in this way, postmodernism represents a new ideological form of capitalism, a 'cultural dominant' truly worldwide in scope.

Jameson is a pluralistic theorist in many senses, drawing from (and reconfiguring in the process) the discourses of structuralism, post-structuralism, phenomenology, hermeneutics and psychoanalysis. If his theoretical comprehensiveness can sometimes appear too accommodating of competing idioms, it is partly because he is so insistent that intellectual discourses and political ideologies must be situated within the broader economic and structural conditions of the current historical moment. Certainly, the Jameson of *The Political Unconscious* (1981) establishes just such a placement of contemporary social theory within the broader dynamics of the economy and society at large, insisting as he does that post-structuralism and deconstruction must be contextualized within the Marxian conceptualization of history. In his writings on postmodernism and late capitalism, Jameson similarly argues that the ascendancy of the category of space over time and hence our contemporary experience of cultural fragmentation and dispersal intimates that there are now profound trans-formations occurring at the level of personal identity and psychic structure. Indeed, as we will see, such are the spatio-temporal dispersions and liquidizations of postmodernity and its cultural logic that human subjects can only barely struggle to hold their inner and outer worlds together, as the imaginary has become almost entirely subordinated to signifiers of the global.

In a remarkably probing analysis of this lifting of global technologies into the operations of the mind itself, Jameson proposes a detailed check-list of the pervasive emotional climate of postmodern culture. These include 'The Waning of Affect', 'Euphoria and Self-Annihilation', 'Loss of the Radical Past', 'The Breakdown of the Signifying Chain' and 'The Abolition of Critical Distance'. Such is the intensification of reification – primarily under the operations of the service, finance and communications sectors – that postmodern living becomes a kind of cynical parody of modernist manners and orientations, flowing from a Deleuze-like readiness to abandon Enlightenment rationalities as a false path and instead savour the delicious sensuousness of erotic intensities.

Conventionally, postmodernism denotes a transmutation of the aes-thetic, detected by critics principally in the fields of literature, architecture, the plastic arts and philosophy. Much the same is true of Jameson's analysis of the transition from modernism to postmodernism in the arts, humanities and culture at large. Yet from Jameson's own Marxist standpoint, it is critical to connect the terrain of postmodern culture to structural transformations occurring within the economic operations of capitalism itself. This is a vital conceptual and political move, as we will see, allowing Jameson to open the debate over postmodernism beyond the spectrum of the arts to the domains of both the economy and society. The postmodern for Jameson is totalizing, discontinuous, expansive – a new world economic system. At the centre of this radical transformation from modernity to postmodernity lies the revolution in electronics and the societal impact of new information technologies. Here Jameson points to the vastly expanding role of the communications sector in capitalist innovation and profit.

As the force-field of globalization came to restructure international flows of trade, investment and culture during the 1980s and 1990s, so the entire capitalist system was to extend its operational hold over whole regions, communities and continents. For Jameson, this was nowhere more evident than in the organizational dominance of transnational corporations and their outsourcing of manufacturing to cheap-wage locations in the developing world. Meanwhile, in the polished, expensive cities of the West, speculative finance moved away from industrial manufacture and towards the service and communication sectors. Media conglomerates such as Time Warner and News Corporation, now wielding unprecedented power across national boarders, altered the connections and relations between peoples and communities. With communications revolutionized – due largely to the increasing use of digital methods of information processing – the economy became cultural as never before, ever more dependent on image and information.

Cultural sensibility is one of Jameson's principal themes, and in particular he reworks the Marxist proposition that social experience is in the end a matter of multiple economic and historical determinations. This is much more, in Jameson's hands, than an attempt to relate post-Marxism to the subtleties of post-structuralism, and nor is it simply a matter of relating culture to the economy. Rather, there is a complex interplay for Jameson between the social and economic fields. What exactly are the cultural consequences of postmodernity, he asks, for the experience of subjectivity? As the countercultural 1960s and 1970s gave way to a profound sense of political defeatism in the 1980s and 1990s, a new depthlessness came to afflict individuals at an emotional level. Among the characteristics of this postmodernization of subjectivity, in Jameson's view, is the collapse of any active sense of historical memory, in the sense of either enabling pasts or oppressive traditions. It is one of the functions of history to give 'narrative shape' to social experience, to link past, present and future. Yet with the waning of history, narrative and memory, the psychic experience of identity becomes disconnected and empty – locked on the images, codes and messages of digital media and the information superhighway.

Late capitalism for Jameson is saturated to such a degree with signifiers, codes and messages – routed in a multi-billion-dollar culture industry and media spectaculars – that what is unfolding is 'a new and historically original penetration and colonization of Nature and the Unconscious'. This lifting of the logics of commodification into the psychic texture of experience is, for Jameson, akin to the fragmentation of schizophrenia. This dislocating, dispersed flux of unconscious intensities disrupts modernist relations between self and others, desire and discourse; it also leads to a breakdown of the signifying chain itself, to structures of meaning. Such an image of subjecthood is one in which the imaginary is regulated by the symbolic as never before, with individuals taking their cultural cues from media messages while mindlessly surfing TV channels. More than another Marxist cultural lament over the powers of commodification, however, Jameson impressively extends his analysis of the postmodern to encompass the insights of Lacanian psychoanalysis, and in particular Lacan's theorization of schizoid fragmentation as deeply interwoven with a derailment of the symbolic order of language. Following Lacan, Jameson argues that the depthlessness of postmodern media culture produces a snapping of the signifying chain, a 'schizophrenia in the form of a rubble of distinct and unrelated signifiers'. In the age of mass consumption and transnational corporations, it is specifically the euphoria of the subject that captures Jameson's analytical attention. And perhaps not surprisingly for a Marxist theoretician, it is the libidinal pleasures of consumerism – 'the commodity rush' – that Jameson isolates as pivotal to the reproduction of postmodernity.

Consumerism is nowadays the duty of the newly affluent professionals and yuppies who emerge as a result of the take-off of the service and communication sectors of the economy, and personal freedom is increasingly defined in terms of access to markets and the shopping mall. Yet how to assess the possibilities of autonomy when postmodernization of the subject involves both the spread of consumerism and the rise of pseudo-individualism? For Jameson, the problem is only compounded by the vast networks of corporate power and production, whose high-tech operations criss-cross the globe and wreak havoc upon both the cognitive and emotional capacities of human subjects to grasp the links and disjunctions of the new global capitalism. As a radical, Jameson believes that change remains possible and contends that the task of the Marxist project is to critically trace the intermediate forms linking experiential or subjective responses to the postmodern on the one hand and regional, national and global institutional developments on the other. This he terms, borrowing from the urban studies of Kevin Lynch, the postmodern aesthetic of 'cognitive mapping'. Grasping the multinational system of postmodernism from within, cognitive mapping involves for Jameson a reimagination of the relations between identity and culture; it unfolds, as he explains, through sustained, systematic reflection upon the intertwining of the local and global, identity and non-identity, the present and the past. Cognitive mapping is thus presented as an emancipatory principle necessary to confront the disorder of global capitalism, a kind of counter to postmodern forms of fragmentation, dispersal and dislocation.

An aesthetic of cognitive mapping – a pedagogical political culture which seeks to endow the individual subject with some new heightened sense of place in the global system – will necessarily have to respect this now enormously complex representational dialectic and invent radically new forms in order to do it justice. This is not then, clearly, a call for a return to some older kind of machinery, some older and more transparent national space, or some more traditional and reassuring perspective or mimetic enclave: the new political art (if it is possible at all) will have to hold to the truth of postmodernism, that is to say, its fundamental object – the world space of multinational capital – at the same time at which it achieves a breakthrough to some as yet unimaginable new mode of representing this last, in which we may again begin to grasp our positioning as individual and collective subjects and regain a capacity to act and struggle which is at present neutralized by our spatial as well as our social confusion. The political form of post-modernism, if there ever is any, will have as its vocation the invention and projection of a global cognitive mapping, on a social as well as spatial scale.

Frederic Jameson (1991) *Postmodernism, or, The Cultural Logic of Late Capitalism*. Durham, NC: Duke University Press, p. 54.

Bauman: postmodernity as modernity minus illusions

The story of what this wholesale aestheticization of culture will do to society in more general terms, as contemporary women and men find themselves increasingly seduced by the fetish of surface and style as well as the cult of hedonism and libidinal intensities as promoted by late capitalism, belongs to a more properly sociological critique of postmodernity. For it is the sociology of postmodernity, rather than the elaboration of a postmodern sociology, which seeks to understand the global transformations that have shaped the society in which we live today – and it is just this project which acclaimed sociologist Zygmunt Bauman takes up and develops to brilliant effect. It is hard to imagine an analyst of the postmodern condition more theoretically sophisticated and consistently innovative than Bauman. His is a voice cautioning that our new globalized world is one of uncertainty, unpredictability and ambivalence. In his view, postmodernization creates radical new patterns of power and inequality, from which fresh opportunities and risks arise for everyone. During the past twenty years or so, Bauman has published an astonishing series of books that offer a trenchant sociological critique of postmodernity, from his highly acclaimed study *Legislators and Interpreters* (1987) to his more recent visionary arguments detailed in *Liquid Modernity* (2000) and *Liquid Love* (2003). Certainly the great strength of this research is his tenacity in pursuing the idea of the postmodern through its every shifting guise and mutation, from the economy to entertainment. He tracks cultural pressures, emotional torments and political dilemmas with a uniquely agile understanding, helping us to glimpse, if not the solutions, then at least the complexities of global postmodern transformations.

Bauman's interest in postmodernity and global culture has come increasingly to the fore, but he was a leader of the cultural turn in sociology as far back as the 1970s. His first book published in English, *Between Class and Elite* (1972), took the British labour movement as its field of investigation. In the following years, in books such as *Culture as Praxis* (1973), *Socialism: The Active Utopia* (1976) and *Memories of Class* (1982), he established himself as a dazzlingly erudite analyst of the interconnections between class and culture. Bauman's fame, however, rests upon his more recent writings on modernity and postmodernization. *Modernity and the Holocaust* (1989), his masterpiece, is a dark, dramatic study of the deathly consequences of Enlightenment reason. Auschwitz, in Bauman's eyes, was a result of the 'civilizing' mission of modernity; the Final Solution was not a dysfunction of modern rationality but its shocking product. The Holocaust, according to Bauman, is unthinkable outside the twin forces of bureaucracy and technology. In subsequent work, including *Modernity and Ambivalence* (1991) and *Postmodernity and Its Discontents* (1997), Bauman moved from a concern with the historical fortunes of the Jews as victims of modernity to an analysis of the complex ways in which postmodern culture cultivates all of us as outsiders, strangers, others.

Bauman sprang from a marginalized position in post-war Poland; indeed, in many ways, his analysis of the dreads and dislocations of modernity and postmodernization may be read as a series of intellectual concerns developed from biographical experience. He is both Polish and English, sociologist and social theorist, modernist and postmodernist, high theoretician and anthropologist of the *Lebenswelt* of postmodern society. Born in 1925 in Poland and educated in Soviet Russia, Bauman became a soldier with the Red Army and fought against the Germans in the Second World War. His promising career in the military came undone in 1953 when he was summarily dismissed, a victim of an anti-Semitic purge. In going virtually overnight from insider of the Communist Party to marginalized outsider, Bauman found – through his emergent dedication to sociology – an intellectual space for radical doubt within a society obsessed with ideological certainty. Indeed, the groundwork for Bauman's sociological fascination with ambivalence, ambiguity, difference and otherness stems in various senses from his Polish background and the visceral anti-Semitism he encountered.

Bauman adopts a postmodernist language stressing ambivalence and ambiguity, while being thoroughly suspicious of the whole terrain of post-modernism. Sociologically speaking, his work analyses the fissures between modernist cultural practices on the one hand and postmodern global trans-formations on the other, with particular emphasis on the deregulation and privatization of all things social. Any compressed reconstruction of the main arguments of Bauman's sociology of postmodernity cannot possibly do justice to it as a whole, such is its sheer imaginative sweep and intellectual breadth of concerns. These include a liquid mode of experience – experience of the self and others, of space and time, of life's possibilities and risks – that is shared by women and men the world over; the separation of power and sovereignty from the politics of the territorial nation-state; the collapse of 'society' as a bounded complex, or set of structures, and thus the eradication of sociology's disciplinary self-evident client; and the outsourcing of public political functions to non-political, deregulated market forces. This last is a central theme, and gives his work a highly radical political edge. Privatization and deregulation, according to Bauman, becomes a vital preoccupation of the postmodern age for a whole host of reasons. In the neoliberal epoch, the drastically shrinking world of public political space may seem (and in various respects is) an upshot of transnational capitalism. Yet at the same time, privatization of life experience and life politics is pretty much policed and regulated by culturalist and subpolitical processes that follow a kind of Weberian logic all their own, an institutional development which the discipline of sociology has been too slow to recognize. As Bauman (2002: 68) develops this:

> Governments are today no less, if not more, busy and active than ever before in modern history. But they are busy in the TV Big Brother's style: letting the subjects play their own games and blame themselves in the event that the results are not up to their dreams. Governments are busy hammering home the 'there is no alternative' message, the 'security is dependency' and the 'state protection is disempowering' messages, and enjoining subjects to be more flexible and to love the risks (read: erratic and unpredictable) life-settings is fraught with.

(An influential critique of Bauman's interpretation of bureaucracy is Paul du Gay (2002).) Notwithstanding his suspicion of traditional institutional politics, Bauman is in various senses a collectivist thinker, the product of his training in the Polish sociological tradition with its affinities to Weberian-Marxism. What is striking about Bauman's sociology from the earliest texts is the scrupulous exactness with which he maps not just class power or social hierarchy, but social oppression and political domination in general. There were after all no ruling capitalists throughout Central Europe following the Second World War, and this is undoubtedly one reason why Bauman became so peculiarly attuned to various modes of 'ordering action' and forms of repression. Socialism, in the post-individualist sense of affective solidarity, may be seen as the collective unconscious motivating resistance to capitalism, a kind of 'counterculture of modernity', as he puts it in *Socialism – The Active Utopia*.

Modernity is an obsessive project, marked by desire for constant change. Whatever is seen as old must be replaced by the new – always, and in itself, a sign of progress. Science and its technological offshoots are the central drivers of assigning an object, event or person to ever-new systems of rational classification; and in this way rationalization and science consequently merge in curious ways to further modernity's obsessive urge to control. Modernity is thus a highbrow, abstract affair, concerned above all with constant rationalizing and the logics of classification, at once distant and dismissive of the messiness and unpredictableness of the everyday. In fact, if modernity takes an interest in the dynamics of everyday life, this is driven primarily out of its obsessive quest for order, stability and consistency. If modernity and modernism in their various guises are interested by the everyday details of human ambivalence and ambiguity, the point of this interest is to strengthen the impulse for order. To keep things neat and tidy, with all glimmerings of ambivalence safely disowned, is key.

Bauman himself demonstrates something of an obsession with ambivalence, from *Modernity and Ambivalence* to *Wasted Lives*, but he is able to connect this contemporary cult of the unpredictable to radical political ends. For Bauman, as for Sigmund Freud, ambivalence is essential to human subjectivity, at once enriching the affective texture of interpersonal experience and multiplying the complexity of social life itself. The more we become aware of ambivalence, undecidability and uncertainty as intrinsic to human life and forms of association, the more dense networks of social dependencies become. And yet modernity is the moment at which ambivalence becomes prohibited, constructed as both aberrant and abject. The modernist impulse to order is a regime governed by intolerance, inflexibility and symbolic violence, with regulating patterns of classificatory inclusion and exclusion serving less as a transparent rational medium than as a surreptitiously hegemonic form of repression.

Postmodern ethics: the global moral gap

A global moral gap defines today's world in which 1.2 billion people live on less than $1 a day. The moral gap further arises in a world where 46 per cent of the world's population lives on less than $2 a day, and in which 20 per cent of the world's population enjoys over 80 per cent of its income. How do we cope with this global moral gap, and how might we begin to respond to it without feeling overwhelmed? That global inequalities spark conflict and contestation is hardly very surprising given the pervasiveness of mass media today, and especially the visibility of Western lifestyles in the globalization of communication. How the Other lives is known to us, and vice versa. Those in the West know how the world's poorest live; the poor also know how those in the polished cities of the West live.

Today's global realities make for vulnerability and disconnection in equal measure, and one powerful approach to the impact of globalization on moral responsibility may be found in Zygmunt Bauman's analysis of postmodern ethics. In an age of intensive globalization marked by ever-widening gaps between rich and poor, asks Bauman, what chance morality and ethics? For what is it that binds us together in a world where social relations are increasingly liquid and shifting?

The fundamental ethical problems today, according to Bauman, spring from the ever-widening gap between moral responsibly on the one hand, and the consequences of rampant technology and globalization on the other. As Bauman (2001c: 1) puts this:

> While our hands have not grown any longer, we have acquired 'artificial eyes' which enable us to see what our own eyes never would. The challenges to our moral conscience exceed many times over that conscience's ability to cope and stand up to challenge. To restore the lost moral balance, we would need 'artificial hands' stretching as far as our artificial eyes are able to. . . . Our sensitivity is assaulted by sights which are bound to trigger our moral impulse to help – yet it is far from obvious what we could do to bring relief and succour to the sufferers. Moral impulse won't be enough to assure that the commitment to help will follow the sight of suffering.

The global challenge for Bauman is how to activate individual moral responsibility in a world where our daily actions potentially affect, sometimes lethally, millions of people.

In *Postmodern Ethics* (1993) and *Life in Fragments* (1995), Bauman integrates sociological and philosophical analysis of how modern and postmodern social orders react and respond to problems of morality and ethics. His starting point is ambivalence. There is, says Bauman, an intrinsic ambivalence at the heart of our moral conditions, which itself is excruciatingly painful to tolerate. No wonder then that much of history has been dedicated to designing ways of sidelining awareness of this pain. Modernity, in large part, was such an exercise in depersonalizing the ethical urge; modernity sought to universalize morality by legislating an ethical code that would fashion a world free from the stain of moral ambivalence. The moral world of modernity, as organized and organizing, offers direct escape from a lot of anxious groping in the dark over ethics, precisely because its coded rule-book of dos and don'ts gave practical help in achieving a sense of moral certitude.

Not so the postmodern. Today there is little widespread belief in the possibility of a foundational moral code. In the disordered and increasingly risky world of postmodern discontent, there are no clear-cut answers to ethical problems; people have to face moral ambivalence all over again, by design or by default. This terrain is what Bauman terms 'postmodern ethics', and his analysis proceeds partly through an appropriation of the works of the phenomenological philosopher Emmanuel Levinas. According to Levinas, the ethical urge is more a matter of intuition than of cognition and it arises well before people are socialized into 'rules' and 'responsibilities'. In Levinas' vision, being for the Other, which he sharply distinguishes from being with others, is an unlimited ethical urge: there is no rest or hiding place from the disturbance of ethics, no position from which the self might feel safe or secure in the knowledge that responsibility has been discharged. The ethical self is hostage to the Other: our natural inclination to care for others places the Other as asymmetrical and hierarchical in relation to the self.

Adapting Levinas' philosophy to the current climate of globalization, Bauman suggests that the condition of postmodernity contains a potential movement towards a repersonalization of ethics. The collapse of the hard-and-fast moral rules of modernity means that, in postmodern conditions, each individual must decide for themselves on how to cope with ethics, as well as how to respond to human suffering, vulnerability and frailty. 'Choices between good and evil', writes Bauman,

> are still to be made, this time, however, in full daylight, and with full knowledge that a choice has been made. With the smokescreen of

centralized legislation dispersed and the power-of-attorney returned to the signatory, the choice is blatantly left to the moral person's own devices.

This is not to say, however, that the postmodern represents anything more than a chance for ethics. Bauman considers in detail the myriad ways in which moral dilemmas are shifted back to the marketplace in conditions of postmodernity. Expert promises of how to lead a life free from the strains of ambivalence are today bought and sold, in matters concerning ethics as much as in any other area of life. Bauman calls this the privatization of morality, which involves the renunciation of ethical freedom for the intoxications of consumerism. Against this backdrop of privatization, moral reasoning and evaluation becomes little more than responding to the task at hand; we attempt to clear up the mess of yesterday's actions, but only in order to get on with tomorrow. And we act without giving ourselves enough time to think of the long-term effects of our actions on others or on society at large.

Such a privatization of morality seems to suggest that we are all in unbelievable trouble, condemned to inhabit a social universe without ethical meaning, commitment or value. Yet Bauman insists that the postmodern does not represent a twilight for ethics; his argument is that today we are left with questions where once there appeared to be answers – and that this is the postmodern enigma of morality. Against the backdrop of globalization and new information technologies, we have seen the emergence of new kinds of moral questions. Questions which span the enormous space-and-time dislocation opened up by postmodernity. What, for instance, will be the several-generations-long social effects of artificial insemination and *in vitro* conception? Or the long-term social consequences of global warming?

Postmodern ethics for Bauman represent a chance, although a slim one, for a better world. While the ills of present-day society may be beyond the scope of humanity to cope with, his analysis of postmodernity powerfully discloses that what finally comes to pass will be a question of ethics and not simply politics itself.

There is a sense in which Bauman initiates a postmodern recasting of the ordering ambitions of modernity, preferring to cobble together fragments of various modernist and postmodernist mentalities, orientations, dispositions and worldviews. He is certainly no enthusiast of post-structuralist or postmodernist versions of postmodernity, of what he terms 'the preachers and enthusiasts of the postmodern bliss' (Bauman, 2000: 339). 'It is simply,' he says, 'a salutary decision to speak of post-modernity, rather than late modernity, without necessarily accepting every rubbish written in the name of postmodern theory' (Bauman et al. 2001: 20). For him, everything postmodern is fashioned out of something modern. There is no definitive line of separation between the modern and the postmodern, as postmodernity is itself 'a self-conscious stage in the development of modernity' (ibid.). In the end, Bauman rejects pronounce-ments of the 'end of modernity' and yet – retaining the enthusiasm of some postmodernists – declares the postmodern a 'chance of modernity', a chance for tolerance, solidarity and autonomy. This sense of potential transfiguration, deriving from reflexive self-consciousness of the temporal and spatial flux of contemporary life, is what gives Bauman's portrait of the postmodern age its sociological distinctiveness.

This tension in Bauman's writing – between embracing and rejecting certain elements of the discourse of postmodernism – is the sign of a familiar sociological dilemma. If the postmodern is a cultural phase beyond modernity, it is granted a peculiar stamp of autonomy which is somehow free of ambivalence; if postmodernity represents a break with the modern, it displaces the modernist surgical ambition of social engineering, but – in pluralizing the social and cultural pursuit of order – runs the risk of 'anything goes'. It is for this reason that Bauman resists the widespread tendency to historically periodize the modern and postmodern, and indeed the point of his sociology is to have it both ways: modernity and postmodernity mix, and necessarily so in various overlappings and criss-crossings. 'Postmodernity', writes Bauman, 'is modernity that has admitted the non-feasibility of its original project. Postmodernity is modernity reconciled to its own impos-sibility – and determined, for better or worse, to live with it. Modern practice continues – now, however, devoid of the objective that once triggered it off.' It is in this way that Bauman can simultaneously proclaim the energizing dimensions of the postmodern, opening a space for the imaginative plural-ization of structures of meaning, and critique the cultural consequences of modernity. Contemporary women and men aspire to power, to modernist dreams of certitude, order and structure; yet they equally seek to live without guarantees, trading yesterday's road-maps for the sudden lurches of mood generated by today's hi-tech blend of lifeworlds and experiences. We are neither one nor the other, but potentially both, modern and postmodern.

If for Jameson postmodernism is a cultural dominant tendentially global in scope, it is for Bauman a more unstable affair, often on the brink of bringing itself undone. Indeed the postmodern, which for Bauman repre-sents not transcendence but a societal turning back on the consequences of modernity, is everywhere evident (especially in popular culture, the plastic arts and new communication technologies) but nowhere supreme – such is the ruthless colonizing logic of modernist desires for homogeneity, control, order and certitude. At once akin and estranged, both inside and outside each other's culturalist or ideological range, modernity and postmodernity share in common the crisis of identity that afflicts life in the contemporary West. Yet if the postmodern worldview – permeated with a sense of the ambivalence of existence – is premised upon a compact with reflexivity, it also involves a thoroughgoing dismantling of the normative force of standards, ideals and truths. This, one might immediately hasten to add, is not necessarily bad news – as the following passage from Bauman regarding postmodern wisdom plainly indicates.

> What the postmodern mind is aware of is that there are problems . . . with no good solutions, twisted trajectories that cannot be straightened up, ambivalences that are more than linguistic blunders yelling to be corrected, doubts which cannot be legislated out of existence, moral agonies which no reason-dictated recipes can soothe, let alone cure. The postmodern mind does not expect any more to find the all-embracing, total and ultimate formula of life without ambiguity, risk, danger and error, and is deeply suspicious of any voice that promises otherwise. The postmodern mind is aware that each local, specialized and focused treatment, effective or not when measured by its ostensive target spoils as much as, if not more than, it repairs. The postmodern mind is reconciled to the idea that the messiness of the human predicament is here to stay. This is, in the broadest outlines, what can be called postmodern wisdom.
>
> Zygmunt Bauman (1993) *Postmodern Ethics*. Oxford: Blackwell, p. 245.

Bauman's postmodernism here is close to a celebratory affair, but in a manner that sociologically delineates between postmodern worldviews (seen as potentially subversive) and postmodernity (a mix of opportunity and risk). There is, at any rate, a force at work in the postmodern habitat making for autonomy, even if, sociologically speaking, this movement towards autonomy collides with the more oppressive features of post-modernity as a social system.

Criticisms of postmodernism

Postmodernism no longer enjoys the cultural and political cache it once did. Indeed, the postmodern celebratory cult of endings – of history, meaning, ideology and identity – may itself now be outdated. The pioneering work of the leading figures ordinarily associated with postmodernism, such as Lyotard, Baudrillard and Deleuze, is already many years past. Such is also the case for the debate that raged in social theory over modernity and postmodernity in the writings of Jürgen Habermas, Anthony Giddens, David Harvey, Fredric Jameson, Seyla Benhabib and Zygmunt Bauman. This passing of time since the postmodern constellation first took off on the radar screens of social theory in the mid-1980s has served to highlight not only that the so-called radical credentials of postmodernist thought are highly ambiguous, but that postmodernism occurred in the context of a specific social history. For one of the central claims of this book is that a social theory alert to social differences and cultural ambivalences cannot simply be limited to a concern with the exhaustion of Enlightenment reason – sweeping though the epistemological issues to be addressed may be in this connection – but has to investigate a range of personal and political dynamics which are increasingly reconfigured through transformations associated with modernity, globalism and postmodernization.

The powers and limits of postmodernism in both political and sociological terms are by now well-trodden terrain. Intellectual assessments of the adventures of postmodernity as a concept have been launched from almost every conceivable perspective, from critical theory to psychoanalysis, from feminism to post-colonialism. For many, principally the hard-core devotees of Baudrillard or Lyotard, postmodernism could do no wrong. Media theorist Arthur Kroker celebrated digital culture and technology as the exemplar of postmodernism, revelling particularly in its unleashing of commercial flows and libidinal intensities, while the post-structuralist historian Mark Poster raised some interesting-sounding questions about the status of historical truth in an age that has almost altogether sidelined discourses of Truth, Freedom and Meaning. For others critical of this wholesale aestheticization of culture and critique, postmodernism was much more politically troubling. At one end of the spectrum, luminary critical theorist Jürgen Habermas criticized postmodernism as an element of neoconservative cultural criticism. The other end of the spectrum witnessed more diverse responses, with Marxist sociologist Alex Callinicos offering the platitude that postmodernity was only a 'theoretical construct' (and one which he felt, obviously enough for a Marxist, lacked comprehension of the economic operations of capitalism) and Sara Ahmed lamenting that an ascendant postmodernism now dictated the contemporary feminist agenda. On an altogether different register, others penned – at astonishing speed and in suitably postmodern style – introductory primers on the lexicon of postmodernism – with titles from the strait-laced *Introducing Postmodernism* to the DIY-styled *Teach Yourself Postmodernism*. In between much of this academic noise there was the occasional genuine critical insight – such as Terry Eagleton's *The Illusions of Postmodernism* (1997) or Perry Anderson's *The Origins of Postmodernity* (1998).

The four versions of the postmodern examined in this chapter are not easily separable, though each contains quite distinct preoccupations and concerns. If postmodernity as simulated media culture is to be exact about the organizing logics of contemporary social experience, it must identify an epochal rupture with modernity, one which bids farewell to productivism and political economy, and embraces instead ever-expanding and spiralling cycles of signs and codes. By disconnecting the modern and postmodern in this way, advocates of postmodernity as simulated media culture can euphorically celebrate the play of signs, spectacles and simulacra, cut loose communication technologies, entertainment and information from any relation to an external 'outside', and dissolve the concepts of the political and society as mere metaphysical nostalgia. Baudrillard, as we have seen, has more than a touch of Nietzchean nihilism about him, as when he speculates about 'fatal strategies' of melancholy, passivity, silence. In giving priority to the depthless, fragmented surfaces of postmodernist culture in this way, Baudrillard's suggestion is that critics must learn to view silence, apathy and passivity as signs of a potentially productive vitality of social life against its drive for seductive domination in an age of simulation and virtuality. For followers of Baudrillard's account of postmodernity as simulated media culture, there is nothing but pure surface.

Postmodernity as global capitalist transformations takes something from this emphasis on simulations and hyperreality, but mixes it with analytical attention to the worldwide economy, finance capital and new structural forces generating exploitation, repression and the like. From postmodern aesthetics, this critique adopts an emphasis on blendings of high and mass cultures, the dissolution of art into everyday life and the acceleration of schizoid or fragmentary elements of self-constitution as such, but crosses this with a modernist impulse to unearth generalized structures of socio-economic domination as well as the search for political justice and human autonomy. This response to the global crisis of postmodernization, as we have seen, is crystallized in Jameson's notion of 'cognitive mapping' – the working through for a resourceful critique of the subject's inability to mentally represent or locate themselves in the global postmodern, with a view to rewriting possible intermediate forms of connection between the conditions of identity on the one hand and the global economy on the other. In an age of image, information and identity, Jameson's breathtakingly audacious project is to refloat the question of the postmodern so that it may be considered as a historical-ontological condition from which deeper structural antinomies may be assembled, critiqued and transfigured.

Alternatively, rather than posit some intolerable conflict between modernity and postmodernity, it is possible to establish a two-way traffic between these two modalities of culture and critique. In bracketing off the issue of historical periodization, what is at stake here – under a response to the crisis of postmodernity as generalized social systems – is nothing less than the pluralization or liquidization of human ambivalence. What links modern and postmodern orders for Bauman is that for both, though in very distinct ways, ambivalence is key to social life and its reproduction. Modernity is no longer a description of a particular historical period than a kind of social practice seeking the erasure or prohibition of ambivalence by rationalizing classifications, an essentially permanent cultural possibility within which hegemonic patterns of compulsory inclusion and exclusion are rehearsed daily by women and men. The postmodern here is the reverse lining of modernity and takes the other way out as regards ambivalence. If ambivalence is here to stay then the postmodern response seeks to fully acknowledge this, embracing ambiguity, difference and otherness as the basis for, or any result of, human creativity. Postmodernity is thus symptomatic of a ruthless and episodic existence, one in which thick global flows of cash and credit unleash staggering new possibilities and risks, novel forms of polarization between rich and poor and the globalization of a whole way of life in which structures of reflexivity and self-experimentation become increasingly dominant.

My own inclination is to argue for a more complex relation between modernity and postmodernity than has been grasped in the social sciences hitherto, and to focus on the importance of such concepts as human agency, societal complexity as well as transformations of emotion in contemporary global affairs. Since the postmodern – aesthetic, cultural and political – is always and in advance an approach to human affairs from the perspective of the post-contemporary or post-traditional, it is not easy to imagine what a stage beyond the postmodern would look like exactly. That said, the transformation of global affairs today presents social theory with fresh challenges, opening personal and political alternatives to the postmodern orthodoxy. Notwithstanding the emancipatory promise of fractured, fluid and multiple perspectives as developed in much postmodernist theory, such standpoints have failed to adequately engage with a range of vital new political issues concerning the multiple ways in which a sense of personal identity is constituted in contemporary societies, as well as the growing sense many of us live with of our mutual interconnectedness and vulnerability in the changing structure of the global order. Of course, this is not to say that these issues do not bear upon postmodernism, nor that postmodernism cannot be deployed to think about such developments in interesting and fruitful ways. The contribution of postmodernism to social theory – with its levelling of hierarchies, its interpretive polyvalence, its dislocating subversion of ideological closure, its self-reflexive pluralism – is of immense value. And yet since the attack on the World Trade Center and the Pentagon of 9/11, and the follow-up war against Iraq in 2003, there is undeniably a growing societal sense that crises in contemporary culture are so deep and so pervasive that they demand new forms of political thinking, indeed a wholly fresh approach. It is in this sense that we might speak of the current generation as coming *after postmodernism*, most specifically as concerns the formulation of a new political agenda for tackling today's most pressing global problems.

Summary points

1   Postmodernism represents, for some social theorists at least, the end of modernity. The postmodern, at a sociological level, consists in profound social transformations associated with the transcendence of the modern. From the rise of transnational corporations to identity politics, from the 24/7 dominance of media culture to a new cultural aesthetic of pastiche and parody: postmodern virtual reality portrays a world that is doubtfully real.

2   The postmodern confounds modernist hierarchies – with its dislocating subversion of ideological closure, its interpretive polyvalence, its self-reflexive pluralism.

3   In postmodern social theory, there is a marked focus on the deconstruction and fragmentation of the human subject. In Deleuze and Guattari, this dispersal is theorized in terms of 'desiring machines'. In Lyotard, it is part of the logics of libidinal intensities. In Lyotard, it consists of a series of enquiries into 'hyperreality'.

4   For Fredric Jameson, postmodernity represents the cultural logic of late capitalism. This is the idea that the postmodern ushers into existence such spatial dispersion and temporal liquidization that human subjects can no longer effectively map their place within the social system.

5   Contrasting the sociology of postmodernity with a postmodern sociology, Zygmunt Bauman argues that the postmodern is modernity reconciled to its own limitations.

1   Postmodernism has been explained as involving fragmentation, dislocation and dispersal. How do you see the postmodern reflected in popular culture?

2   From iPods to cars, it seems that we are always desiring some new product. How is it that capitalism interacts with our desiring processes and how might this be overcome according to Deleuze and Guattari?

3   What does Baudrillard mean by hyperreality? Evaluate the claim that media representations are more seductive, powerful and 'real' than reality.

4   How does postmodernism represent a new form of capitalism? What are some tangible examples of the new economy?

5   How might postmodern ambivalence and ambiguity open up new moral questions?

Further reading

Gilles Deleuze and Félix Guattari

Anti Oedipus: Capitalism and Schizophrenia (Viking Press, 1983).
A Thousand Plateaus: Capitalism and Schizophrenia (University of Minnesota Press, 1987).
On the Line (Semiotext(e), 1983).

Jean-François Lyotard

The Postmodern Condition: A Report on Knowledge (University of Minnesota Press, 1984).

Jean Baudrillard

The Mirror of Production (Telos, 1975).
For a Critique of the Political Economy of the Sign (Telos, 1981).
Simulacra and Simulation (Semiotext(e), 1983).
In the Shadow of the Silent Majority (Semiotext(e), 1983).
America (Verso, 1988).

The Ecstasy of Communication (Semiotext(e), 1988).
Seduction (Macmillan, 1990).
Fatal Strategies (Semiotext(e), 1990).
The Transparency of Evil (Verso, 1993).
The Illusion of the End (Polity Press, 1994).
The Gulf War Did Not Take Place (Tower Press, 1995).

Frederic Jameson

The Political Unconscious (Cornell University Press, 1982).
Postmodernism, or, The Cultural Logic of Late Capitalism (Duke University Press,1991).

Zygmunt Bauman

Modernity and Ambivalence (Polity Press, 1991).
Intimations of Postmodernity (Routledge, 1992).
Postmodern Ethics (Blackwell, 1993).
Life in Fragments (Blackwell, 1995).
Liquid Modernity (Polity Press, 2000).
The Individualized Society (Polity Press, 2001).
Society under Siege (Polity Press, 2002).
Liquid Love (Polity Press, 2003).
Wasted Lives: Modernity and Its Outcasts (Polity Press, 2004).

There are many introductory works on postmodernism. In particular, Terry Eagleton's *The Illusions of Postmodernism* (Blackwell, 1997), Perry Anderson's *The Origins of Postmodernity* (Verson, 1998) or Charles Lemert's *Postmodernism is Not What You Think* (Paradigm Publishers, 2005) are very good. Also of note is Stuart Sim's (ed.) *The Routledge Companion to Postmodernism* (Routledge, 2005).

Some good sources for reading Deleuze and Guattari are Ronald Bogue's *Deleuze and Guattari* (Routledge, 1989), Brian Massumi's *A User's Guide to Capitalism and Schizophrenia: Deviations from Deleuze and Guattari* (MIT Press, 1992), Eugene Holland's *Deleuze and Guattari's Anti Oedipus: Introduction to Schizoanalysis* (Routledge, 1999), and Ian Buchanan's *Deleuze and Guattari's Anti-Oedipus: A Reader's Guide* (Continuum, 2008).

Some of Baudrillard's writings may be found in Mark Poster's (ed.) *Jean Baudrillard: Selected Writings* (Polity Press, 1992) or Douglas Kellner's (ed.) collection *Baudrillard: A Critical Reader* (Blackwell, 1994). Kellner also has a comprehensive critical introduction, *Jean Baudrillard: From Marxism to Postmodernity and Beyond* (Polity Press, 1989). Another good author to look at for Baudrillard introduction and commentary is Mike Gane and his books

Baudrillard: Critical and Fatal Theory (Routledge, 1991) and *Baudrillard's Bestiary: Baudrillard and Culture* (Routledge, 1991).

For a critical overview of Frederic Jameson, see Steven Helmling's *The Success and Failure of Frederic Jameson* (SUNY Press, 2000).

A critical introduction to Bauman with selections from his writing is Anthony Elliott's (ed.) *The Contemporary Bauman* (Routledge, 2007), and Peter Beilharz edited a good reader of Bauman's work, *The Bauman Reader* (Blackwell, 2000). Some good introductions to his work are Dennis Smith's *Zygmunt Bauman: Profit of Postmodernity* (Polity Press, 1999), Keith Tester's *The Social Thought of Zygmunt Bauman* (Palgrave, 2004) and Tony Blackshaw's *Zygmunt Bauman* (Routledge, 2005).

Internet links

Postmodernism

http://www.as.ua.edu/ant/Faculty/murphy/436/pomo.htm
http://carbon.cudenver.edu/~mryder/itc_data/postmodern.html
http://wv.nv9.georgetown.edu/faculty/irvinem/theory/pomo.html
http://www.infed.org/biblio/b-postmd.htm

Gilles Deleuze and Félix Guattari

http://www.langlab.wayne.edu/CStivale/D-G/index.html
http://www.affinityproject.org/theories/guattari.html

Jean-François Lyotard

http://www.iep.utm.edu/l/Lyotard.htm#Libidinal per cent20Philosophy

Jean Baudrillard

http://carbon.cudenver.edu/~mryder/itc_data/postmodern.html#baudrillard
http://www.stanford.edu/dept/HPS/Baudrillard/Baudrillard_Simulacra.html

Frederic Jameson

http://www.marxists.org/reference/subject/philosophy/works/us/jameson
    .htm
http://www.mun.ca/phil/codgito/vol4/v4doc2.html

Zygmunt Bauman

http://www.leeds.ac.uk/sociology/people/bauman.htm
http://www.eurozine.com/articles/2002-11-08-bauman-en.html

Networks, Risks, Liquids

Contents

In early 2008, the credit markets and global economy started haemor-rhaging. Share markets around the world went into freefall as the value of many stocks plummeted. Against a backdrop of growing economic uncer-tainty, things quickly went from bad to worse – with write-offs by various large international banks and a further decline in the asset value of many leading companies and firms. Horror sessions unfolded on Wall Street. Banks reported multi-billion-dollar losses. Fears of a recession in the United States were quickly overshadowed by talk of global economic meltdown. One indication of the seriousness of this economic crisis was that the price of gold – a traditional safe haven for investors – became volatile. Another was the announcement that the Bush administration would provide a massive stimulus package of up to US$150 billion to resuscitate the ailing economy.

At the hub of the 2008 credit crunch was the subprime mortgage crisis – which came to light towards the end of 2007 and pretty soon thereafter went global in its economic consequences. Spurred by the US banks' years of cheap credit to borrowers, the subprime mortgage crisis was a striking illustration of how dodgy financial practices come back to haunt economic institutions. What happened, in the briefest of outlines, was that more than six million people living in America with no money or regular source of income borrowed in excess of 100 per cent of the value of a house they wished to purchase. It doesn't take an economic degree to figure out what happened. The hard economic landing for these subprime borrowers was made all the worse because most of them had purchased houses right at the top of the market – which subsequently fell very sharply. Still the banks, arrogantly, thought they would be immune to the risks of such lending. Why? Because the banks had the crafty idea of rolling these subprime mortgages into bonds or securities, which were then sold around the world to other financial institutions. Eventually however, as we now know, not even the banks could keep the lid on the corrosive economic consequences of the subprime phenomenon – one consequence of which was the 2008 International Monetary Fund warning of the onset of a global economic recession.

Consider, in this context, how these fearful and uncertain economic times might impact upon Gemma – a 36-year-old financial adviser living and working in London. Gemma set up her own financial services firm in late 2006, after a period of having worked as a futures trader on Wall Street. The challenge for Gemma in returning to London from New York was to identify a niche market in the financial services sector in order to branch out and go it alone. This she did by concentrating specifically on financial services for women – selling management and investment strategies to relatively wealthy women who wanted to become even more wealthy but were too 'time-poor' to go about planning financial strategies for themselves. The result was a small financial services firm in London that showed spectacular growth and a promising future – or, at least, it did until the 2008 global credit crunch.

Gemma's financial services firm saw dramatic cuts in its profitability with the global slide of the credit markets and international economy. This she expected, primarily because much of her business focused on helping women 'unlock' funds tied up in existing investments – say, their homes – in order to make investments elsewhere in the market. Most of her clients, fortunately, had reinvested their funds in long-term wealth-creation projects. But some had put their recently unlocked funds into very short-term liquid investments, such as shares – and thus were now being held to account to banks making margin calls as a result of the subprime crisis. Consequently many of these investments were at risk, and most of Gemma's energies were spent trying to keep hold of these clients' assets by renegotiating existing loans. In doing so, Gemma was not just relying on her own instincts. For she has very good business contacts – drawing on networks she was part of in New York to access the latest information on when the share market was expected to bottom out. Late-night Skype conference calls linking London, New York and Tokyo were a regular part of Gemma's financial briefings. However, she was still mindful of the cautious attitude of her clients, and of the immense risks that remain in playing the market in short-term liquid investments.

What does Gemma's experience of the credit crunch tell us abut the impact of the global economy on our lives? In what ways might her attempts to survive the global economic downturn of 2008 serve as a guide to understanding the changing social forces of the twenty-first century? One answer might centre on *social networks*. Clearly, Gemma derives all sorts of economic and social advantage by accessing information from the global financial networks – through information technology – of which she is also part. Another answer might focus on *risks*. The risks of short-termist invest-ment strategies have clearly carried major consequences for the global economy, and assessing clients' appetite for economic risk is a core aspect of Gemma's working life. Still another answer might focus on *social liquids*: the increasing liquid investments spurred by the credit markets, but also the liquidity of identity, time and space in a global world that now spins on mobile communications. Networks, risks and liquids: these are some of the key trends of contemporary social processes, and in this chapter we review these topics by examining the social theories of Manuel Castells, Ulrich Beck and Zygmunt Bauman.

Manuel Castells: *The Network Society*

Gemma, like countless people successful in business, relies on social networks to significantly enhance the power, influence and impact of her financial services firm. Fond of the old adage 'It's not what you know, it's who you know', Gemma understands the importance of having 'good connections' in the business world. From this angle, it may be said, networks have been an essential part of doing business since time immemorial and remain unchanged right through to the present day. Not so, says the Spanish social theorist Manuel Castells, who holds that advances in information technology and especially the rise of the Internet are fundamentally transforming the core structure of networks in our own time. In his massively influential three-volume study *The Network Society* (2004a), Castells charts the rise of global informational networks and a network economy. He argues that the rise of information technology has unleashed networks that can process information in almost any part of the world. As a result, society has been transformed into a different kind of space – according to Castells, 'a space of flows that is made up of networked places'. Timeless flows and networked spaces: these notions, as we will see, are at the heart of Castells' social theory and are fundamental to its powerful account of social change. To Castells, the enormous advances in communications technology of recent decades – especially the Internet and spread of mobile telephony – have unleashed decentralized networks that facilitate communications on the move and desequenced social interaction at great distances from the physical places in which social actors are embedded. The rise of the network society, in short, accounts for how Gemma – working the Skype conference calls in the wee small hours of the night – can re-engineer her enterprise to be more flexible and responsive to customer's needs.

Castells develops his social theory by contrasting many of his key claims about the direction of contemporary society to the classical sociological writings of Max Weber, particularly his influential interpretation of the 'iron cage of bureaucracy', and Karl Marx's theories of capitalism. Weber identified bureaucracy as crucial to all large-scale modern organizations, and argued that the boundaries of bureaucratic organizations are tightly defined – in a pyramid structure, with authority stretching down from the top to the bottom of the organization. According to Castells, the rapid growth of technologically advanced, information-rich networks has undermined the explanatory power of Weber's account of formal organizations. Decentred and flat, rather than pyramidal and hierarchical, are the new boundaries without borders in the network society. Similarly Castells is equally, if not more, critical of Marx's critique of society – which is especially interesting given that Castells began his sociological career as a Marxist. Yes, says Castells, today's global economy is capitalist. But Marxism is quite wrong, he thinks, in seeing manufacture and material goods as at the core of the capitalist economy. By contrast, Castells argues that communication, computers and information technology are at the centre of global production networks.

> The culture of virtual reality associated with an electronically integrated multimedia system . . . contributes to the transformation of time in our society in two different forms: simultaneity and timelessness.
>
> On the one hand, instant information throughout the globe, mixed with live reporting from across the neighborhood, provides unprecedented temporal immediacy to social events and cultural expressions. To follow minute by minute in real time the collapse of the Soviet state in August 1991, with simultaneous translation of Russian political debates, introduced a new era of communication, when the making of history can be directly witnessed, provided it is deemed interesting enough by the controllers of information. Also computer-mediated communication makes possible real-time dialogue, bringing people together around their interests, in interactive, multilateral chat writing. Time-delayed answers can easily be overcome, as new communication technologies provide a sense of immediacy that conquers time barriers, as much as the telephone did but with greater flexibility, with the communicating parties able to lapse for a few seconds, or minutes, to bring in other information, to expand the realm of communication, without the pressure of the telephone, ill-adapted to long silences.
>
> Manuel Castells (1996, 2000, 2nd edn) *The Rise of the Network Society, The Information Age: Economy, Society and Culture*, vol. I. Cambridge, MA; Oxford, UK: Blackwell, p. 461.

The notion of network society has been among other things Castells' way of keeping social theory up-to-date, an underwriting of the period of massive social and technological change in which we are living. In some ways, especially from today's vantage point, this rewriting of social theory around networks and information technology may all seem fairly self-evident. From SMS texting to satellite television, we now live in a world that spins increasingly around the structures of communications technology. From Sydney to San Diego, Beijing to Bangkok, communication networks rule. But Castells is himself interesting not only because he was one of the first social theorists to notice these large-scale shifts from industry to information, but because he systematically analysed the global structures through which the economy became networked. This he did by becoming a truly global social theorist, lecturing and conducting research surveys in, among other cities, Paris, Hong Kong, Moscow, Amsterdam, Mexico and Montreal. As the economy became networked throughout the 1980s, shifting away from industrial manufacture to the communications, service and finance sectors, Castells sought to underscore the changing dynamics of *space* in the constitution of identity, power and society.

For a long time, social theorists tended to equate space with the operations of national societies. Space was fundamental to society, and both were theorized in terms of strictly defined boundaries, borders, territories and maps. As the 1970s gave way to the 1980s, and as manufacture was 'outsourced' to cheap wage spots around the globe and the West made the transition to an informational economy, space was up for grabs in social theory once more. Anthony Giddens wrote of 'time-space distanciation' – the stretching of social relations across space and time. David Harvey theorized 'time/space compression' in conditions of postmodernity. And Paul Virilio spoke of the 'annihilation of space' in our age of computational speed. All of these ideas were to become highly influential in social theory. And yet to define space in purely virtual terms – stretching it all the way to the point of the death of distance – meant that social theory ran the risk of ignoring those functional logics and social contexts in and through which spatialized social relations are organized. Castells, highly attuned to these dilemmas, instead defined *space as flows*, and insisted in his own way on the interwovenness of identity and power, the personal and the political. To grasp today's space of flows in our networked societies, Castells argues, means identifying the 'purposeful, repetitive, programmable sequences of exchange and interaction between physically disjointed positions held by social actors'. Purpose, repetition, programmes, sequenced interaction and disjointed identities: this is roughly Castells' position on transformations of space induced by the network society. We cannot describe what is going on in the world today, says Castells, if we fail to factor in the impacts of 'timeless time' and 'placeless space'. In the network society, identities, organizations and cultural life – whether in marketing, technology, biomedicine or higher education – are increasingly restructured by an accelerated space of flows, particularly in the major metropolitan centres.

There are three core features that comprise Castells' account of the space of flows. The first is the *informational circuits and communication infrastructures* that permit individuals and organizations to connect with each other in real time on a global scale. Castells devotes considerable sociological attention to the technological infrastructure of networks, underscoring that such circuits or conduits always operate from certain locations (and thus are territorially anchored) – even though such infrastructure organizes a global space of flows (that is, social practices without geographic contiguity). Technological infrastructure is therefore the hardware of global networks, an indispensable medium organizing the cables, computers, airports and automobilities which connect people, places, goods and information in the space of flows. In this network paradigm, enterprises and corporations fundamentally rely on instantaneous digital information to coordinate the linking of demand and supply. Through the sharing of electronic information, networked organizations are able – and now at the touch of a button – to track inventory, check budgets, contact customers, recruit staff, extend product development and revise project management. Through the computational loading, updating and integration of system software programs, firms and large-scale organizations schedule the supply of goods and services to customers. To do this, networked corporations rely on high-speed transportation links through land, sea and air.

The second feature of Castells' account focuses on the *nodes* in and through which networks are organized. Nodes facilitate the growth of network relations through the efficient processing of information, permitting communication connections between people and organizations across large distances. Nodes are thus shorthand for the uprooting of human action and social relations from local contexts and cultures when organizations become interwoven with information and communication technologies. For example, multinational corporations, in breaking up the local organization of their production processes, have reorganized production chains through nodal links in many different countries throughout the world. Nodes thus come to be identified with specific places – although these anchored locations remain fluid and depend largely on the cost advantages to specific companies and organizations. Interlocking nodes of computational, administrative and financial services thus create forms of delocalization – the shifting of social activities away from local contexts and cultures and reconstituting them within distant networks. For example, manufacturing nodes throughout the 1990s and early 2000s have been increasingly located in China and Malaysia, customer support in India and the Philippines, engineering in Russia and the US, design in Taiwan, and so on. In a networked world, multiproduct companies use interconnected nodes in order to outsource, offshore and generally expand the supply chain of their operations.

The timeless and placeless logic of nodes equates with a trend towards decentralized networks. This, again, differentiates the network society from industrial society. For Castells, we have left the industrial world of solid structures – hierarchical, formal and centred – well and truly behind. Network enterprises in which information, communication and people move freely within and across nodes is now fundamental to social life.

Networks, says Castells, decentre power – transforming it as diffuse, shifting, and spatially fluid. 'By definition,' writes Castells (2000: 15–16),

> a network has no centre. It works on a binary logic: inclusion/exclusion. All there is in the network is useful and necessary for the existence of the network. What is not in the network does not exist from the network's perspective, and thus must be either ignored (if it is not relevant to the network's task), or eliminated (if it is competing in goals or in performance). If a node in a network ceases to perform a useful function it is phased out from the network, and the network rearranges itself – as cells do in biological processes. . . . Thus, the relevance, and relative weight of nodes does not come from their specific features, but from their ability to be trusted by the network with an extra-share of information. In this sense, the main nodes are not centres, but switchers, following a networking logic rather than a command logic, in their function vis-à-vis the overall structure.

A Network is a set of interconnected nodes. A node is the point at which a curve intersects itself. What a node is, concretely speaking, depends on the kind of concrete networks of which we speak. They are stock exchange markets, and their ancillary advanced services centers, in the network of global financial flows. They are national councils of ministers and European Commissioners in the political network that governs the European Union. They are coca fields and poppy fields, clandestine laboratories, secret landing strips, street gangs, and money laundering institutions, in the network of drug traffic that penetrates economies, societies, and states throughout the world. They are television systems, entertainment studios, computer graphics milieu, news teams, and mobile devices generating, transmitting, and receiving signals, in the global network of the new media at the roots of cultural expression and public opinion in the information age. The topology defined by networks determines that the distance (or social positions) is shorter (or more frequent, or more intense) if both points are nodes in a network than if they do not belong to the same network. On the other hand, within a given network flows have no distance, or the same distance, between nodes. Thus, distance (physical, social, economic, political, cultural) for a given point or position varies between zero (for any node in the same network) and infinite (for any point external to the network). The inclusion/exclusion in networks, and the architecture of relationships between networks, enacted by light-speed operating information technologies, configure dominant processes and functions in our societies.

Networks are open structures, able to expand without limits, integrating new nodes as long as they are able to communicate within the network, namely as long as they share the same communication codes (for example, values or performance goals). A network-based social structure is a highly dynamic, open system, susceptible to innovating without threatening its balance. Networks are appropriate instruments for a capitalist economy based on innovation, globalization, and decentralized concentration; for work, workers, and firms based on flexibility, and adaptability; for a culture of endless deconstruction and reconstruction; for a polity geared towards the instant processing of new values and public moods; and for a social organization aiming at the supersession of space and the annihilation of time.

Manuel Castells (1996, 2000, 2nd edn) *The Rise of the Network Society, The Information Age: Economy, Society and Culture,* vol. I. Cambridge, MA; Oxford, UK: Blackwell, pp. 470–1.

But how, exactly, does trust operate in the network society? This brings us to the third feature of Castells' account, which focuses on *people* dispersed and interconnected within networks. Here Castells' principal concern is the managerial elite. This is an emergent global force of gold-collar class professionals – cosmopolitans who roam the planet feeling 'at home' in all the major cities. They may work for major corporations, live in gated communities, travel business or first class, belong to exclusive social clubs and eat at the most expensive restaurants. These are individuals with a sharp sense of the centrality of information and communications technology to the expanding reach of business today. What is important about this elite, for Castells, is not simply the vast sums of money they earn – which sharply marks them off from the 'network have-nots'. It is rather, as winners from the revolution in communications, such individuals inhabit an *exclusive shared culture*. This is a culture that transcends both time and geographic location. For these are generally people who have attended the 'right' schools, gone to the top universities (such as Harvard or Cambridge), are fluent in several languages, shop in designer stores (Gucci, Prada, Armani) and so on. For Castells, this cosmopolitan global elite are sociologically significant to the network society because their shared culture supersedes the specific geographic environments in which such individuals live. That is to say, managerial elites make decisions and process information about networks from a global perspective.

contemporary social theory

To speak, therefore, of a network society is to speak of high-speed infrastructures of communications and mobilities, of nodes clustered in specific cities or regions for the advanced processing of information and production, and of professional elites that make decisions and reproduce the culture of advanced network societies. But if networks, nodes and nomadic lifestyles are in one sense identical for Castells, they are not in another. Networked enterprises for Castells do not produce a trend towards social uniformity. For one thing, networks do not result in global sameness. Castells is wary, for example, of Marshall McLuhan's much celebrated announcement during the 1960s that modern communications have rendered the world a 'global village'. Because networks impose both a forced globalization and individualization, Castells rejects outright the idea of a global village. By enabling people and organizations who are geographically scattered throughout the world to interact through new communication technologies and automobilities, networks instead suggest to Castells the image of a 'global network of individual cottages'. For another thing, Castells specifically warns that it is a fundamental mistake to view network societies as framed upon one economic or cultural model. All the facets of economic networks today – the infrastructure, nodal size and complexity, as well as the interconnections of the movements of information, people and goods across the globe – are enormously different as one moves from country to country. He quotes as an example the case of Russia. Some aspects of Russian society have very highly developed information networks and are globally connected to world markets. But much of the Russian economy is disconnected. Indeed, Castells views countries such as Russia as characterized by the predominance of disconnection over connection from global networks.

None the less, if networks are internally tied to globalization processes, then they will tend to exert a dominant force over the relations between identity and society in general. This, no doubt, is what Castells seeks to underscore when he describes the global network economy as an 'automaton'. Global networks for him are now a medium of domination, and thus threaten to uproot the world from human control. 'Humankind's nightmare of seeing our machines taking control of our world,' writes Castells (2000: 56), 'seems on the edge of becoming reality – not in the form of robots that eliminate jobs or government computers that police our lives, but as an electronically based system of financial transactions.' This is Castells in apocalyptic mode, in which the global network economy – apparently beyond the reach of social actors – appears to run on autopilot.

Criticisms of Castells

Castells' work is a suggestive conjuncture of social theory, communications studies and network-analysis, involving an enriched critique of globalization which examines the uprooting of identities and social relations in networks, nodes and cosmopolitan-inspired nomadic lifestyles. Castells' trilogy *The Network Society* has been compared in scope and impact to Max Weber's *Economy and Society*, and from that angle its seminal importance consists in underscoring the centrality of networks to that fast, fluid world of the twenty-first century. Certainly, one of the major breakthroughs is Castells' concept of the space of flows in general, and of 'timeless time' in particular. The shift from the uniform and linear mode of industrial clock time to the multiple temporal rhythms and flexible time regimes of global networks is Castells' major contribution to thinking about the way people live today. This aspect of Castells' social theory is most obviously relevant to Gemma's experience of the global financial markets. The global money markets do not equate neatly with global production or trade; they are instead a virtual financial economy superimposed on the actual economy. As Castells notes (2000: 11):

> The firm continues to be the legal unity of capital accumulation. But since the value of the firm ultimately depends on its valuation in the stock market, the unit of capital accumulation (the firm) itself becomes a node in a global network of financial flows. In this economy, the dominant layer is the global financial market, where all earnings from all activities and countries end up being traded. This global financial market works only partly according to market rules. It is shaped and moved by information turbulences of various origins, processed and transmitted almost instantly by tele-communicated, information systems, in the absence of the institutional regulation of global capital flows.

Moreover, with transactions in global money markets running in excess of $1.5 trillion a day (which is over fifty times the level of world trade), time is compressed – or, as Castells says, 'annihilated' – into split-second decisions to buy and sell. As Gemma knows only too well, the timeless time of global financial markets breeds a desequencing of life – as past, present and future blur into an electronic supertext.

Notwithstanding its brilliant insights, however, Castells' social theory is not without its difficulties. One major concern is that the role of 'networked communications' in social life is unduly inflated. Castells claims that the network society is constituted by the knowledge-based information of new technologies and the communications revolution. In saying this, he is surely correct. The new global economy is networked. And networks do, in various senses, reconstitute the social relations in which we live. Still, we might question Castells's obsession with networked communications. The ubiquity of networks can be profitably questioned because, when expanded in the manner of Castells, they appear to become coterminous with lived experience itself. But are identities and social relations really as fully permeated by networks as Castells suggests? What, for example, is the social difference between someone who only occasionally uses the Internet at the local library, and someone (like Gemma) who spends much of their working life online? If working in finance involves wall-to-wall networks, then what of the local fish shop or second-hand fashions outlet? The idea that they might all be described as networked is surely dubious. As Urry (2003: 11–2) develops this criticism:

> The term 'network' is expected to do too much theoretical work in the argument. Almost all phenomena are seen through the single and undifferentiated prism of 'network'. This concept glosses over very different networked phenomena. They can range from hierarchical networks such as McDonalds to heterarchic extremely inchoate 'road protest movements', from spatially contiguous networks meeting every day to those organized around imagined 'cultures at a distance', from those based upon strong ties to those based on very important and extensive 'weak ties', and from those that are pretty well purely 'social' to those that are fundamentally 'materially' structured. These are all networks, but they are exceptionally different in their functioning one from the other.

The point is that, notwithstanding the occasional acknowledegment that networks vary across cultures, Castells expands the notion of 'networked communications' to breaking-point. The concept thus loses sociological precision, and Castells is unable to adequately capture the complex interplay between more traditional, bureaucratic structures on the one hand, and those contemporary fluid and diffuse processes on the other, that comprise networked identities and organizations today.

A related concern is that, while Castells presents a general theory of networks with universal application, the approach is arguably a highly specific account of certain informational transformations affecting life in the expensive, technologically sophisticated cites of the West. One way of expressing this criticism is to argue that Castells' social theory of networks is at its most relevant to those who inhabit the techno-worlds of Microsoft, Apple or Google, while it seems to struggle in grasping the poverty and suffering of those in the Third – or, what some now call Fourth – World. This criticism raises complex issues about some of the unexamined assumptions in Castells' social theory. Being blithe about the ubiquity of networks can quickly become a way of neglecting the many millions disconnected from our age of informationalism. This may not, however, be a wholly accurate charge against Castells: he notes in various aspects of his writings that network societies produce new forms of social exclusion and cultural polarization. That said, he has welcomed the communications revolution as heralding a culture of networked consciousness – at least among the cosmopolitan cultural elite. How far down in society this ethos of the global network economy penetrates remains an open question, however. Why do the immediate images that spring to mind for the network society consist of investment bankers on Wall Street or software innovators in Silicon Valley? By contrast to Castells' undifferentiated account of new times, it may be plausibly argued that we have transcended neither modernist nor industrial-age power hierarchies, although their ideologies have undeniably been subject to considerable upheavals as a result of information technology and the spread of flexible networks. But the critical point is that global networks produce both discontinuities and continuities with earlier social practices, and this in turn raises questions about the adequacy of Castells' theorization of identity.

Global networks and fluids: Urry on mobilities

Like Castells, many social theorists have sought to capture the decentred, diffuse and fluid aspects of contemporary networked societies. Deleuze and Guattari talk of the non-hierarchical rhizomatic proliferation of signs and space. DeLanda argues for the metaphor of 'assemblages' to grasp the multiple transformations of current social life. White (1992) sees the unpredictable fluidity of social life as shaped by 'gels and goos'.

The British social theorist John Urry defines current social processes in terms of increased *mobilities*. The bewildering speed of our mobile lives today consists in the fact that people, images, information, signs, money, power and risks are 'on the move' as never before.

Like Castells, Urry argues that networks – from mobile phones to electronic stock exchanges – generate new mobilities of astonishing speed. Unlike Castells, however, Urry seeks to differentiate between different kinds of networked relationships. To do this, he distinguishes between *globally integrated networks* (GINs) on the one hand, and *global fluids* (GFs) on the other. Globally integrated networks are complex, predictable networked connections between people, technologies and objects that span the globe. Examples include global enterprises such as McDonald's, Coca-Cola and Microsoft. By contrast, global fluids, which are much more mobile in character than GINs, are self-organizing and self-transforming boundaries that form 'heterogeneous, uneven, unpredictable and unplanned waves'.

Urry gives as an example of global fluids the rise of the Internet. Invented for the purpose of military communication in the event of a nuclear attack, the Internet was transformed into a global technology by the millions of computer users, hobbyists and hackers that used the network to communicate with other web users. Resulting in massive waves of networked activity, one estimate states that the Internet recorded 16 million users in 1995, 400 million in 2001 and now exceeds 1 billion. 'The Internet', writes Urry (2003: 63),

> can be seen as a metaphor for social life that is fluid, involving thousands of networks, of people, machines, programmes, texts and images in which quasi-subjects and quasi-objects mix together in new hybrid forms. Ever-new computer networks and links proliferate mostly in unplanned and mixed patterns. Such a fluid space is a world of *mixtures*.

Do you think that Urry's analysis of global fluids is a useful development of Castells' social theory of networks? Do you agree with Urry that increased mobilities shape today's global realities?

Ulrich Beck: organized lives in a world of risk

Like Gemma, we are all trying to cope with a runaway world of social things in our daily lives. The lives we live are lived against a dimly perceived, but finally unknowable, backdrop of societal risks. Many worry, as Gemma does, about economic risk. The possibilities of a global economic recession, or perhaps a meltdown of the financial markets, threaten not only jobs but personal and family life as we know it. The parameters of economic risk today are truly staggering, if only because many believe national societies are powerless to control the global economy. We all encounter economic risk, and yet there are other kinds of risk that are equally – if not more – worrying. In our day-to-day lives, no one – not even the most privileged – can truly control the cluster of risks which arises today in a world of advanced technology, science and multinational organizations. This 'risk cluster' is not only personally and socially challenging, but mind-boggling. From our daily dietary concerns to stock market crashes, from worries about polluted air to terrorist attacks: the risk climate of our world today is one of endless proliferation and multiplication, bound up as it is with increasingly specialist knowledge and self-proclaimed experts in risk management, with our own counterfactual guesswork, and, above all, with our deep-seated anxieties about the future. Risk, it is now widely agreed by social theorists, has become a central organizing category of both the personal and public domains. Life, as a consequence, has become more and more about carving out ways of coping and managing risk – sometimes through active engagement, some-times by resigned acceptance, or even confused denial. Coping with risk is now the way we live, yet – ironically – every attempt to 'manage' risk seems to breed only further risks. Consideration and calculation of risk-taking, risk-management or risk-detection can never be fully complete or secure, since there are always unforeseen and unintended aspects of risk environments. This is especially true at the level of global hazards, where the array of industrial, technological, chemical and nuclear dangers that confront us grows, and at an alarming rate. Indeed the German social theorist, Ulrich Beck, defines the current situation as that of 'world risk society'. The rise of risk society, Beck argues, is bound up with the new electronic global econ-omy – a world in which we live on the edge of high technological innovation and scientific development, but where no one fully understands the possible global risks and dangers we face.

World risk society, according to Beck, is about many, many things – as any cursory glance at a newspaper or television news bulletin reveals. Beck is himself interesting in the pantheon of contemporary social theory not only because he singularly put risk on the intellectual agenda during the late 1980s in Europe with his best-selling book *Risk Society: Towards a New Modernity* (1992), but because – perhaps more than anyone today – he has been exploring the multiple and nuanced ways in which risk affects all aspects of our lives. This he has done by dividing his time between the University of Munich and the London School of Economics, the latter university involving him in many current debates in social theory with such key figures as Anthony Giddens and David Held. Influenced by Giddens' account of reflexivity (as discussed in Chapter 5) and Held's approach to globalization (reviewed in the next chapter), Beck has traced in detail the many, inescapable ways in which risk both presses in on our lives and reorganizes the ways in which we live as a result. He has devel-oped powerful analyses of the ways in which the rise of what he calls 'risk society' is transforming societies, nature and the environment, sexuality and intimate relationships, politics and democracy. (For discussion of Beck's late writings on global cosmopolitanism see Chapter 11.) Whether one actively embraces or defensively repudiates the dangers, hazards and terrors of the world today, Beck's central claim is that *the notion of risk is increasingly fundamental to global social life*. For Beck, modernity is a world that introduces global risk parameters that previous generations have not had to face. Precisely because of the failure of industrial society to control the risks it has generated, such as the ecological crisis, risk today rebounds as a largely defensive attempt to avoid new problems and dangers.

Beck is careful to introduce some key sociological distinctions into his analyses of risk society, and it is important to keep these in mind when thinking about his claim that risk today changes qualitatively our experience of the world. In this connection, Beck contends that it is necessary to separate the notion of risk from that of hazard or danger. The hazards of pre-industrial society – famines, plagues, natural disasters – may or may not come close to the destructive potential of technoscience in the contemporary era. Yet for Beck this is not in any event key, since he does not wish to suggest that daily life in today's risk society is intrinsically more hazardous than in the pre-modern world. What he does suggest, by contrast, is that no notion of risk is to be found in traditional culture: pre-industrial hazards or dangers, no matter how potentially catastrophic, were experienced as *pre-given*. They came from some 'other' – gods, nature or demons. With the arrival of the modern age and scientific designs of social control, particularly with the idea of steering towards a future of predictable security, the consequences of risk become a political issue. This last point is crucial. It is societal intervention – in the form of decision-making – that transforms incalculable hazards into calculable risks. 'Risks', writes Beck (1997: 30), 'always depend on decisions – that is, they presuppose decisions.' The idea of 'risk society' is thus bound up with the development of instrumental rational control, which the process of modernization promotes in all spheres of life – from individual risk of accidents and illnesses to export risks and risks of war.

The historically unprecedented possibility, brought about by our own decisions, of the destruction of all life on this planet ... distinguishes our epoch not only from the early phase of the Industrial Revolution but also from all other cultures and social forms, no matter how diverse and contradictory. If a fire breaks out, the fire brigade comes; if a traffic accident occurs, the insurance pays. This interplay between before and after, between security in the here-and-now and security in the future because one took precautions even for the worst imaginable case, has been revoked in the age of nuclear, chemical and

In support of the contention that protection from danger decreases as the threat increases in the contemporary era, Beck *et al.* (1994) discuss, among many other examples, the case of a lead crystal factory in the Federal Republic. The factory in question – Altenstadt in the Upper Palatinate – was prosecuted in the 1980s for polluting the atmosphere. Many residents in the area had, for some considerable time, suffered from skin rashes, nausea and headaches, and blame was squarely attributed to the white dust emitted from the factory's smokestacks. Due to the visibility of the pollution, the case for damages against the factory was imagined, by many people, to be watertight. However, because there were three other glass factories in the area, the presiding judge offered to drop the charges in return for a nominal fine on the grounds that individual liability for emitting dangerous pollutants and toxins could not be established. 'Welcome to the real-life travesty of the hazard technocracy!' writes Beck, underlining the denial of risks within our cultural and political structures. Such denial for Beck is deeply layered within institutions, and he calls this 'organized irresponsibility' – a concept to which we will return.

The age of nuclear, chemical and genetic technology, according to Beck, unleashes a destruction of the calculus of risks by which modern societies have developed a consensus on progress. Insurance has been the key to sustaining this consensus, functioning as a kind of security pact against industrially produced dangers and hazards. (Beck draws substantially from the work of François Ewald in developing the idea that society as a whole comes to be understood as a risk environment in insurers' terms. See Ewald 1986, 1993.) In particular, two kinds of insurance are associated with modernization: the private insurance company and public insurance, linked above all with the welfare state. Yet the changing nature of risk in an age of globalization, argues Beck, fractures the calculating of risks for purposes of insurance. Individually and collectively, we do not fully know or understand many of the risks we currently face, let alone attempt to calculate them accurately in terms of probability, compensation and accountability. In this connection, Beck emphasizes the following:

contemporary social theory

- Risks today threaten irreparable global damage which cannot be limited, and thus the notion of monetary compensation is rendered obsolescent.
- In the case of the worst possible nuclear or chemical accident, any security monitoring of damages fails.
- Accidents, now reconstituted as 'events' without beginning or end, break apart delimitations in space and time.
- Notions of accountability collapse.

Beck on reflexive modernization

Like Anthony Giddens, Beck is deeply immersed in European traditions of social theory and has come to accord considerable importance to the idea that human agents know a great deal about the world around them. This is why they both stress the notion of *reflexivity*, emphasizing the ways in which observation of, and reflection upon, the social world by human agents comes to reshape the very forms of life instituted by society. This is an appealing sociological idea, partly because it deftly traces how processes of change unfold – sometimes subtly, sometimes dramatically – in both personal and social life. The idea is that human knowledge – of the self, of others and of the wider world – is not simply incidental to the ways in which we live; such knowledge is actually constitutive of what we do and of how we live our lives. One of Giddens' many lasting contributions to social theory – as discussed in Chapter 5 – was not only the foregrounding of reflexivity to all processes of social life, but demonstrated that – in our own time of advanced modernization and globalization – reflexivity plays an increasingly central role in both practical and public life. This is Giddens' thesis that people constantly look back at the circumstances of their lives to understand how social life is affected to its roots by knowledge itself. One can hardly imagine an aspect of social life today that is not powerfully influenced by reflexivity in the sense that Giddens has highlighted. From changing our plans when talking to friends and family via mobile phones to the ongoing monitoring of credit card use by the banking sector, reflection on existing knowledge to generate new knowledge is fundamental to the ordering of our social lives today. Beck agrees in large part with Giddens' thesis of reflexivity. But he also extends the idea of reflexivity to encompass other aspects of social experience – to do with less conscious knowledge of the world. Reflexivity for Beck, as we will see, is partly about reflection but also partly about reflexes, or knee-jerk reactions. This is a point of key difference between Beck and Giddens.

Beck believes that the era of industrial modernization has, in effect, come to a close – and much of his work may be read as an extended medita-tion on what has replaced it. The progressive, progress-obsessed dimension of the modern age is for Beck among other things a response to the sweeping, dramatic impact of large-scale industrial manufacture on previously traditional societies. In mainstream sociology, and perhaps in sociology alone, we witness this thoroughgoing blending or merging of modernity with industrial society. From Marxism to functionalism, sociology's language – centred as it was on adaptation, differentiation and rationalization – was the most telling index of its preoccupation with industrial achievement. Indeed, the tone of modern sociology was, for the most part, buoyant: industrial society appeared as simply the best of human civilization. Industrial, newly modernizing society was a world constantly changing, expanding and transforming itself. Notwithstanding this exuberance, however, the modern age remained haunted by apocalyptic nightmares of social collapse. Images of the end of society abounded. If modernizing society was the most progressive ever, with industrial capitalism cast as the end-point of human history, the story of what the dark side of modernity would mean for humanity was altogether sidelined in mainstream sociology. Beck has in his sociological sights here, perhaps above all else, the consequences of the using up of natural resources, a matter of the utmost importance of course to the reproduction of any society.

The implication of all this is that society is a much more conflictive, split, ambiguous and plural phenomenon than classical social theorists had considered. Instead of being a well-defined, clearly demarcated structure containing modernizing triggers of economic and moral advancement, society for Beck is radically divided between different kinds of social and cultural logics – constantly tangling and endlessly circulating. To capture this shift, Beck argues that society today is torn between industrial society and advanced modernity, between simple modernization and reflexive modernization. It is the autonomous, compulsive dynamic of advanced or reflexive modernization which, according to Beck, propels modern men and women into 'self-confrontation' with the consequences of risk that cannot be adequately addressed, measured, controlled or overcome, at least according to the standards of industrial society. Modernity's blindness to the risks and dangers produced by modernization – all of which happens automatically and unreflectingly, according to Beck – leads to societal self-confrontation: that is, the questioning of divisions between centres of political activity and the decision-making capacity of society itself. 'Within the horizon of the opposition between old routine and new awareness of consequences and dangers,' writes Beck, 'society becomes self-critical' (1999: 81).

The prospects for arresting the dark side of industrial progress and advanced modernization through reflexivity are routinely short-circuited, according to Beck, by the insidious influence of 'organized irresponsibility'. Irresponsibility, as Beck uses the term, refers to a political contradiction of the self-jeopardization and self-endangerment of risk society. This is a contradiction between an emerging public awareness of risks produced by and within the social-institutional system on the one hand, and the lack of attribution of systemic risks to this system on the other. There is, in Beck's reckoning, a constant denial of the suicidal tendency of risk society – 'the system of organized irresponsibility' – which manifests itself in, say, technically orientated legal procedures designed to satisfy rigorous causal proof of individual liability and guilt. This self-created dead-end, in which culpability is passed off onto individuals and thus collectively denied, is maintained through political ideologies of industrial fatalism: faith in progress, dependence on rationality and the rule of expert opinion.

Individualization

Risk restructures the globe, says Beck. But it also cuts to the core of our lives. Risk bites deeply today into how we fashion our sense of personal identity and most intimate relationships. Beck calls this 'individualization'. The arrival of advanced modernization is not wholly about risk, however; it is also about an expansion of choice. For if risks are an attempt to make the incalculable calculable, then risk-monitoring presupposes agency, choice, calculation and responsibility. In the process of reflexive modernization, Beck argues, more and more areas of life are released or disembedded from the hold of tradition. That is to say, people living in the modernized societies of today develop an increasing engagement with both the intimate and more public aspects of their lives, aspects that were previously governed by tradition or taken-for-granted norms. This set of developments is what Beck has in mind when he writes of 'individualization', by which he means to underscore the interplay of dissolution and reinvention in everyday life. For example, the disappearance of tradition and the disintegration of previously existing social models – fixed gender roles, inflexible class locations, masculinist work models – force people into making decisions about their own lives and future courses of action. As traditional ways of doing things become problematic, people must choose paths for a more rewarding life – all of which require planning and rationalization, deliberation and engagement. An active engagement with the self, with the body, with relationships and marriage, with gender norms, and with work: this is how the risk society is lived in everyday terms.

The idea of individualization is the basis upon which Beck constructs his vision of a 'new modernity', of novel personal experimentation and cultural innovation against a social backdrop of risks, dangers, hazards, reflexivity, globalization. Yet the unleashing of experimentation and choice which individualization brings is certainly not without its problems. In personal terms, the gains of today's individualization may be tomorrow's limitation, as advantage and progress turn into their opposite. A signal example of this is offered in *The Normal Chaos of Love* (1995), where Beck and Elizabeth Beck-Gernsheim reflect on the role of technological innovation in medicine, and of how this impacts upon contemporary family life. Technological advancements in diagnostic and genetic testing on the unborn, they argue, create new parental possibilities, primarily in the realm of health monitoring. However, the very capacity for medical intervention is one that quickly turns into an obligation on parents to use such technologies in order to secure a sound genetic starting point for their offspring. Individualization is seen here as a paradoxical compulsion, at once leading people into a much more engaged relationship with science and technology than used to be the case, and enforcing a set of obligations and responsibilities that few in society have thought through in terms of broad moral and ethical implications. It is perhaps little wonder therefore that Beck (1997: 96), echoing Sartre, contends that 'people are condemned to individualization'.

How would you assess the relevance of Beck's individualization thesis to today's world? Do you agree with Beck that we are 'condemned to individualization'?

Criticisms of Beck

The relevance of Beck's ideas on risk to social theory is clearly evident on a global scale. In the wake of various nuclear disasters, such as Chernobyl, as well as new social anxieties over global warming and environmental pollution, Beck's social theory powerfully confronts the institutional forces which threaten to undo the world as we currently know it. Mixing the political and the personal in equal measure, Beck reviews how human agents and modern institutions organize the social world in terms of changing human-made biological, chemical and technological hazards. From this angle, risk is an idea whose time has arrived. Indeed, in a world which could literally destroy itself, risk-managing and risk-monitoring increasingly dominate both the constitution and calculation of social action.

Even so, there are problems with Beck's social theory, both in itself and as a sociological critique of risk. It is not clear, for example, that Beck's approach can withstand historical scrutiny as to the parameters and depth of death-dealing risks that wiped out entire populations in previous eras. The sociological focus of Beck's analysis, as he says, depends on contrasting the contemporary risks of the global era with the hazards and dangers of pre-modern societies; but Bryan S. Turner (1994) has shown that such a distinction may well be merely scholastic. From bubonic plagues and epidemics of syphilis to environmental and political catastrophes of earlier civilizations, such human devastation involved mixtures of impersonal, unobservable, democratic and global risk. That is to say, these were dangers and risks which functioned in much the same manner as Beck claims for today's supposedly 'new' risk phenomena. It is true that Beck does distinguish first-order hazards and second-order risks – that is, between traditional and modern societies – and it might be conceded that his analysis of risk society is thus best read as a provocative political engagement with the current era of advanced technoscience and globalization. But it is surely questionable to upgrade 'risk' as a social category to the point where it becomes the exclusive worry in the plight of contemporary women and men. Are we all really so worried about risk? And, whether we know it or not, are we all really making the kinds of cost/benefit calculations about risk that Beck claims? More disturbingly, is the means–end rationality of risk spreading into personal and intimate spheres of life (such as marriage, friendship and childrearing) in the unified ways that Beck contends? Does the concept of risk actually capture what is new and different in the contemporary social condition?

To see the relation between risk and society in the means–end, instrumentally rational fashion as described by Beck is to adopt a strongly objectivist account of how social relations are reproduced – this is not the naive structuralist notion that structures operate behind the backs of actors, but it is one that ascribes a *dominant rationality* to contemporary women and men. To that extent, it may be argued that Beck's otherwise provocative social theory displays a lack of curiosity in how people perceive, engage or disengage with the risks they encounter in daily life. It is from this angle that the American sociologist Jeffrey C. Alexander (1996: 135) criticizes Beck for outlining an 'unproblematic understanding of the perception of risk' – one that is utilitarian, objectivist and emotionally shallow. The criticism is, in effect, that risk may be the new catch-cry of contemporary political life, but that Beck's rendition of it was too simplistic, even reductive. It is perhaps ironic that Beck should make such a great deal out of risk, given that he ignores the aesthetic and emotional dimensions of embodied experience from which contemporary women and men deal with risk (see Lash and Urry 1994; Hollway and Jefferson 1997; Elliott 2004). Beck has also been criticized for divorcing the cultural politics of risk assessment from its interpersonal contexts.

'Risk' is of course a fluid term, which can be either personal or global, and arguably both. This is, in fact, one important reason why it is crucial for social theorists to attend to the complex, myriad ways that people figure out and reflect on risk. But such explorations require consideration too of the socio-political contexts in which it is evaluated, managed and calculated. The anthropologist Mary Douglas (1986, 1992), for example, argues that advanced industrial risks are primarily constructed through the rhetoric of purity and pollution. For Douglas, what is most pressing in the social-theoretic analysis of risk is an understanding of how human agents ignore many of the potential threats of daily life and instead concentrate only on selected aspects. Interestingly, Beck fails to discuss in any detail Douglas' anthropology of risk. Where Beck comments on Douglas, the concentration is typically upon the schism in sociology between the analysis of traditional agrarian and modern industrial societies (See Beck 1997: 57–8, 87). This would seem peculiar not only since Douglas' path-breaking analyses of risk appear to have laid much of the thematic groundwork for Beck's sociological theory, but also because her work is highly relevant to the critique of contemporary ideologies of risk – that is, the social forms in which risk and uncertainty are differentiated across and within social formations, as well as peculiarly individuated.

Beck's theory of risk has also come under heavy criticism for its narrow or unproblematic understanding of power and domination (see Elliott 2002). According to Beck, reflexive modernization combats many of the distinctive characteristics of power, turning set social divisions into active negotiated relationships. Traditional political conflicts – centred around class, race and gender – are apparently superseded by new, globalized risk conflicts. 'Risks', writes Beck (1992: 35), 'display an equalizing effect.' Everyone is threatened by risk of global proportions and repercussions; not even the rich and powerful can escape the new dangers and hazards of, say, global warming or nuclear war. Equally so, risk today erodes class-consciousness (personal difficulties and grievances no longer culminate into group or collective causes) and also, to some considerable degree, class-in-itself (contemporary social problems are increasingly suffered alone). In short, class as a community of fate or destiny declines steeply. With class solidarities replaced by brittle and uncertain forms of individual self-management, Beck finds evidence for a 'rule-altering rationalization' of class relationships in new business and management practices, as well as industrial relations reforms. He contends that new blendings of economics and democracy are discernible in the rise of political civil rights within the workplace, a blend which opens up the possibility of a post-capitalistic world – a 'classless capitalism of capital', in which 'the antagonism between labour and capital will collapse'.

There is considerable plausibility in the suggestion that class patterns and divisions have been altered by rapid social and political changes in recent years. These include changes in employment and the occupational structure, the expansion of the service industries, rising unemployment, lower retirement ages, as well as a growing individualization in the West together with an accompanying stress upon lifestyle, consumption and choice. However, while it may be the case that developments associated with reflexive modernization and the risk society are affecting social inequalities, it is surely implausible to suggest, as Beck does, that this involves the transfiguration of class as such. Why, as Scott Lash (Lash and Urry 1994) asks, do we find reflexivity in some sectors of socio-economic life and not others? Against the backdrop of new communication technologies and advances in knowledge transfer, vast gaps in the socio-cultural conditions of the wealthy and the poor drastically affect the ways in which individuals are drawn into the project of reflexive modernization. These tensions are especially evident today in new social divisions between the 'information-rich' and 'information-poor', and of the forces and demands of such symbolic participation within the public sphere. What Beck fails to adequately consider is that both risk and individualization (while undoubtedly facilitating unprecedented forms of personal and social experimentation) may directly contribute to, and advance the proliferation of, class inequalities and economic exclusions. That is to say, Beck fails to give sufficient sociological weight to the possibility that individualization may actually embody systematically asymmetrical relations of class power.

Taken from a broader view of the ideals of equal opportunity and social progress, Beck's arguments about the relationship between advanced levels of reflexivity and the emergence of a new subpolitics do not adequately stand up to scrutiny. The general, tendential assertions he advances about business and organizational restructuring assume what needs to be demonstrated – namely, that these new organizational forms spell the demise of social class, as well as the viability of class analysis. Moreover, it seems implausible to point to 'subpolitics', defined by Beck only in very general terms, as symptomatic of a new socio-political agenda. When, for example, have the shifting boundaries between the political and economic spheres not played a primary role in the unfolding of relations between labour and capital? Is decision-making and consciousness really focused on a post-capitalistic rationalization of rights, duties, interests and decisions? A great deal of recent research shows, on the contrary, that income inequality between and within nations continues to escalate (Braun 1991; Lemert 2005a); that class (together with structures of power and domination) continues to profoundly shape possible life chances and material interests (Westergaard 1995); and that the many different definitions of class as a concept, encompassing the marginal, the excluded as well as the new underclass or new poor, are important in social analysis for comprehending the persistence of patterns of social inequality (Crompton 1996).

Living with liquidization: Bauman

In addition to Castells and Beck, many other social thinkers have influenced how we should conceive of life in these early years of the twenty-first century. One of them is Zygmunt Bauman, whose account of postmodernity we reviewed in Chapter 8. The dilemmas of the contemporary world – ranging from the rise of networks to the spread of high-consequence risks – are of such magnitude, however, that the concept of postmodernity is rejected by Bauman in his more recent writings in favour of the notion of 'liquid modernity'. With the benefit of hindsight, it is not difficult to see why Bauman retreated from using the term 'postmodernity' to define certain aspects of contemporary social experience. By the late 1990s, the label 'post-modern' had everywhere – from academia to popular culture – become coterminous with a form of cultivated relativism in which 'everything goes'. It was, ironically, this very flattened and generalized view of the postmodern that Bauman wished to distance himself from with his new idea – outlined in the early 2000s – of 'liquidity'.

Liquids, says Bauman, do not keep any shape for long and are constantly prone to alteration. Liquids, unlike solids, undergo continuous changes of shape. Liquids make salient the fractured, brittle nature of human bonds today: there are compelling reasons, writes Bauman (2000: 2), 'to consider "fluidity" and "liquidity" as fitting metaphors when we wish to grasp the nature of the present, in many ways *novel*, phase in the history of modernity'. What is important in the social dimension of liquidity is not its specific gravity but rather the looseness fluids possess. 'What is a truly novel feature of this social world, and makes it sensible to call the current kind of mod-ernity "liquid" in opposition to the other, earlier known forms of modern world,' argues Bauman, 'is the continuous and irreparable fluidity of things which modernity in its initial shape was bent on solidifying and fixing' (Bauman 2004: 19–20).

L iquids, unlike solids, cannot easily hold their shape. Fluids, so to speak, neither fix space nor bind time. While solids have clear spatial dimensions but neutralize the impact, and thus downgrade the significance, of time (effectively resist its flow or render it irrelevant), fluids do not keep to any shape for long and are constantly ready (and prone) to change it; and so for them it is the flow of time that counts, more than the space they happen to occupy: that space, after all, they fill but 'for a moment'. In a sense, solids cancel time; for liquids, on the contrary, it is mostly time that matters. When describing solids, one may ignore time altogether; in describing fluids, to leave time out of account would be a grievous mistake. Descriptions of fluids are all snapshots, and they need a date at the bottom of the picture. . . . The extraordinary mobility of fluids is what associates them with the idea of 'lightness'. There are liquids which, cubic inch for cubic inch, are heavier than many solids, but we are inclined nonetheless to visualize them all as lighter, less 'weighty' than everything solid. We associated 'lightness' and 'weight-lessness' with mobility and inconstancy: we know from practice that the lighter we travel the easier and faster we move.

This focus on liquidization provides a conceptual plank from which Bauman reformulates some of the central preoccupations of social theory, particularly accounts which focus on the production and reproduction of modernization. Many key features associated with modernization and industrialization are recast as instances of what he calls, provocatively and poignantly, 'heavy modernity'. This notion of modernity as 'heavy', or 'hardware modernity', appears throughout his recent writings in different contexts, depending upon the topic under discussion, although its central attributes can be spelt out as follows. Modernity as 'heavy' assumes a dominant role with the development of industrialization and the intensification of modernization throughout the West. Vast machinery, huge factories, massive workforces: economic success defined in terms of size, and symbolic power defined in terms of volume, are central to the contours of heavy modernity. 'Heavy capitalism', writes Bauman (2000: 58), 'was obsessed with bulk and size, and, for that reason, also with boundaries, with making them tight and impenetrable.'

The heavy version of modernity appears, in the view of Bauman, as a certain type of society subsumed to a specific organization of space and time. The conquering of space was fundamental to the ordering ambitions of heavy modernity: spatial expansion was deeply interwoven with the logic of social control and the logic of symbolic power. Space was to be tamed, colonized, domesticated – indeed, devoured. Referencing the work of Daniel Bell, Bauman writes of the 'space-devouring' monstrous cage of General Motors' 'Willow Run' plant in Michigan. This infamous General Motors site measured some two-thirds by a quarter of a mile, with all factory workers and plant machinery contained under the one gigantic roof. Bauman interprets General Motors' colonization of space as reflective of the modernist ideology that 'bigger means more efficient'; but he also argues that such spatial expansionist logic which informed activities of large economic enterprises became inscribed in daily social practice itself. The 'Fordist factory' was heavy modernity's ideal model of engineered rationality. 'Fordism', writes Bauman (2000: 57), 'was the self-consciousness of modern society in its "heavy", "bulky", or "immobile" and "rooted", "solid" phase.' This socially engineered delineation of space existed, argues Bauman, through a concomitant regularization of time: 'It was the routinization of time that held the place whole, compact and subject to homogeneous logic. . . . In the conquest of space, time had to be pliant and malleable' (Bauman 2000: 115). This space/time binding of heavy modernity produced, in turn, the immobilization of labour and capital. 'The frozen time of factory routine, together with the bricks and mortar of factory walls,' writes Bauman (2000: 116), 'immobilized capital as effectively as it bound the labour it employed.'

However, heavy modernity, paradoxically, contained the seeds of its own failure. The era of heavy modernity for Bauman was slowly but steadily undermined by an intrinsic contradiction: the social ordering ambitions, ethical ideals and economic and political goals of heavy modernity were presented as foundational, transcendent and eternal, but were in fact counterproductive and corrosive. This spelt the beginning of the end for heavy modernity. Bauman consequently introduces the notions of 'light modernity' and 'software capitalism' as superseding those of 'heavy modernity' and 'hardware capitalism': he refers to the unprecedented power of *liquidization* in objective alterations of the private and public domains of contemporary societies. The alteration in question springs from, among other social forces, the technological explosion of new information systems; the rise of multinationals and transnational conglomerates; the outsourcing of manufacturing operations from the West to the 'developing world'; and the large-scale shift in investment from industrial manufacture to the communications, finance and service sectors. These developments, according to Bauman, have produced a new 'weightlessness of capital' and concomitant 'liquidization of life' – in business cycles, employment patterns, family relationships, communal fates, political horizons.

Where 'heavy modernity' was the era of instrumental rationality, concerned as it was with the cultivation of seemingly endless spatial expansion and the management of time, 'light modernity' signifies a 'new irrelevance of space' and killing off of time. 'In the software universe of light-speed travel,' writes Bauman (2000: 117), space may be traversed, literally, in "no time"; the difference between "far away" and "down here" is cancelled. Space no more sets limits to action and its effects, and counts little, or does not count at all.' Liquidization assumes different forms across the space/time zonings of contemporary institutional life, from twenty-four-hour finance markets to media-ridden culture. Yet liquidity for Bauman may be said to be culturally dominant to the extent that social life is organized in and through the 'insubstantial, instantaneous time of the software world' (2000: 118).

T he era of hardware, or heavy modernity – the bulk obsessed modernity, 'the larger the better' kind of modernity, of 'the size is power', 'the volume of success' sort. That was the hardware era; the epoch of weighty and ever more cumbersome machines, of the ever longer factory walls enclosing ever wider factory floors and ingesting ever more populous factory crews, of ponderous rail engines and gigantic ocean liners. To conquer space as the supreme goal – to grasp as much of it as one could hold, and to hold to it, marking it all over with the tangible tokens of possession and 'No trespassing' boards. . . . Heavy modernity was the era of territorial conquest. Wealth and power as firmly rooted or deposited deep inside the land – bulky, ponderous and immovable like the beds of iron ore and deposits of coal.

. . . 'Fluid' modernity is the epoch of disengagement, elusiveness, facile escape and hopeless chase. In 'liquid' modernity, it is the most elusive, those free to move without notice, who rule.

Zygmunt Bauman (2000) *Liquid Modernity*. Cambridge: Polity Press, pp. 113–17.

The concepts of heavy and light modernity, which are deeply inter-related, comprise the key dimensions of Bauman's theory of societal liquidization. The transition from hardware societies of social engineering based on industrialization, of ever-expanding accumulation and its management of heavy machinery and massive workforces, to liquid societies of light modernity based on the instant flight of ex-territorial capital and socio-economic deregulation, is the conceptual backcloth from which Bauman specifies processes of the reproduction of asymmetrical relations of power. The maintenance of domination in heavy modernity, according to Bauman, was Panoptican-like – factory routine, rooted on-site management, immo-bile capital. As he puts this (2000: 57), 'capital, management and labour were all, for better of worse, doomed to stay in one another's company for a long time to come, perhaps for ever'. This no longer holds for our own time. As Bauman contends (2000: 58): 'Nowadays capital travels light – with cabin luggage only, which includes no more than a briefcase, a cellular phone and a portable computer.' In his more recent political tracts, including *Globalization: The Human Consequences* (2000), *Community* (2001) and *Society Under Siege* (2002), Bauman deploys this conceptualization of liquidity as domination in order to confront current debates surrounding global order.

This is more, however, than just an underwriting of the spread of ambivalence – in everything from body-politics to the body-politic – however important that may be. It represents rather an underwriting of the uncertainty that haunts the *political* itself. Politics in an age of liquidization, like everything else, is discontinuous: politics, and here Bauman includes the politics of governmentality, is about responding to problems as they happen; deployments of power increasingly take the form of problem solving in the short term (trading on the knowledge that public attention will have moved elsewhere by tomorrow); political forces appear today as a multitude of happenings, with little in the way for linking academic and public discourse, or indeed of personal and communal concerns (precisely for the reason that governments everywhere are deregulating and privatizing the activity of political living).

Bauman on liquid lives, loves and fears

Liquid modernity does not only reshape social institutions; it also penetrates to the core of the self and the fabric of everyday life. These are issues that Bauman addresses directly in a number of recent works, including *Liquid Love* (2003), *Identity* (2004) and *Liquid Life* (2005). Life and identity in conditions of liquid modernity are for Bauman increasingly fluid, fractured, flexible and frail. As he develops this perspective:

> Liquid life is a precarious life, lived under conditions of constant uncer-tainty. The most acute and stubborn worries that haunt such a life are the fears of being caught napping, of failing to catch up with fast-moving events, of being left behind, of overlooking 'use by' dates, of being saddled with possessions that are no longer desirable, of missing the moment that calls for a change of tack before crossing the point of no return. Liquid life is a succession of new beginnings – yet precisely for that reason it is the swift and painless endings . . . that tend to be its most challenging moments and most upsetting headaches. Among the arts of liquid modern living and the skills needed to practise them, getting rid of things takes precedence over their acquisition.
>
> (Bauman 2005: 2)

Small wonder that in such circumstances the newly constituted terrain of 'privatized identity' comes to bear a heavy burden of expectations, hopes and fears in a world where traditional social bonds are loosening their hold.

In formulating his account of 'liquid life' through an analysis of the ways in which a pervasive sense of uprootedness, anxiety and insecurity become increasingly global in scope, Bauman relies on recent social theories of individualization. In this context, and at various points of his writings, he cites the work of Beck and Giddens. He tries to elucidate some of the basic assumptions of the individualization thesis, in particular the complex ways in which identity is becoming disembedded from social structures, as well as the disengagement of individual actions and choices from collective ways of doing things and community projects. It is Bauman's view that the privatizing of life strategies transforms identity 'from a given into a task' (2001: 144), with social responsibility for self-determination now falling 'primarily on the individual's shoulders' (2000: 7–8). Bauman does not only 'apply' the individualization thesis, however; he also tries to tease out the kinds of reasoning which are increasingly taken for granted by individuals today. According to Bauman, the uncanny frailty of individualized society, particularly the feelings of insecurity generated by societal liquidization, promotes desperate attempts by men and women to shore up what is missing in their private and public lives. Experiencing ever-weaker social bonds, individuals must constantly negotiate the 'until-further-notice' of today's social relations. People now drift from one episodic encounter to the next, seeking to nail down a sense of identity – however provisional or fleeting. Such anxiety-provoking activity Bauman sees everywhere in the individualizing societies of the West: individuals reaching for mobile phones, addictively texting; surfing the Net, flitting from one chat-room to another; speed dating, moving ever faster between relationships. Yet as Bauman notes, 'the union only goes so far as the dialling, talking, messaging. Stop talking – and you are out. Silence equals exclusion. *Il n'y a pas dehors du texte*, indeed – there is nothing outside the text – though not just in the sense meant by Derrida.'

Consumer capitalism, with its ideology of 'want-now' consumption and the ever new, plays a basic role in furthering individualization. In particular, Bauman is troubled by the societal rush towards market solutions for private dilemmas. In an age defined increasingly by a cultural obsession with youth, sex and the frantic urge to consume, individuals want from relationships that which they derive from shopping at the mall: variety, novelty, disposability. Accordingly, 'lovers' are reclassified as 'sexual partners', and in turn assessed as potential risks to an individual's 'emotional investment' through cold, calculating, cost/ benefit analysis. Bauman searches high and low in obscure corners of both academia and the media for telling clues of such trends. From marriage guidance journals, he tracks the rise of 'top-pocket relationships' – those you can use when you need to and dispose of just as easily. From the Sunday newspaper supplements, he monitors the highly compartmentalized worlds of SDCs (semi-detached couples), those postmodern romantics who maintain separate pads and separate lives. On and on run the contemporary examples.

Criticisms of Bauman

Few today would dispute the importance of Bauman's writings to social theory. He discusses the notion of liquid modernity not as a systematic grand theory, but rather as sociological fragments or prefigurations – looking at developments in, among other areas, morality, ethics, individualization, love, sexuality, human rights, social exclusion, globalization and terrorism. The sociology itself is concrete – directed at the social and spatial strat-ifications of power, poverty, persecution and the public political sphere – yet rich in theoretical intensity as well as demonstrating an overriding faith in the possibility of alternative social futures. This takes us to the core of Bauman's contemporary relevance, which consists in the connection of abstract issues of social theory with concrete sociological issues and contemporary political concerns. From this angle, his works on, say, social marginalization, exclusion and human waste as well as on love, intimacy and sexuality – when viewed through the theoretical lens of liquid modernity – are surely of enduring significance to social theory.

Bauman's recent social theory has the outstanding merit of highlighting the political significance of the demise of the 'long term', now recast as liquidization or liquefaction, in contemporary social processes. There are, however, various problems with Bauman's social theory. One criticism most forcefully made against Bauman's account concerns the *adequacy* of his sociological diagnosis of liquid modern times. There are both *strong* and *weak* versions of this critique. The strong version of this criticism rests upon the misgiving that a liquidization of human bonds cannot provide a generalizable model for the sociological analysis of global institutional change, as well as forms of sociality in contemporary societies. For example, Ray (2007) rejects the plausibility of Bauman's recent work on such grounds, arguing that the theory of liquid modernity 'illustrates a tendency within sociology to view theories as metaphors to be judged on grounds of appropriateness rather than truth claims judged on grounds of explanatory power'. What one sees in this strong critique is a suspicion of developing social theory from the putative experiences of people's interactions in social contexts, as well as an implicit assumption that concepts, theories and frameworks are really only of use to sociologists when empirically grounded in observable processes of human agency and institutional patterns. There is then disagreement not only over what liquid modernity is, but over whether the term 'liquid' is relied upon to do too much conceptual work in Bauman's argument. Like almost every other general social theory, accord-ing to this strong critique, Bauman analyses current social phenomena through an undifferentiated prism – that of liquidization – and as a con-sequence must write off whatever fails to conform to this theoretical orientation. Bauman, in short, fails to specify how to tread a sociological line from the analysis of very diverse phenomena (work, love, identity) that suggest liquidity to the specific global properties of liquid modernity.

Perhaps the more difficult issue suggested by this strong critique of Bauman's theory of liquid modernity, namely that the theory does not provide an adequate general account of the complexity of Western modernity, is this: even if liquidization is an apt metaphor for the social processes spawned by globalized capitalism, how might the notion serve to help sociologists rethink global order and particularly the relations between North and South, core and periphery, the First and Third Worlds? While the criticism to date is nowhere developed in detail, one might reasonably question Bauman's account along these lines by invoking the discourses of multiculturalism and post-colonialism. For post-colonial critics, Bauman's portrait of liquid modernity – like most sociologies of a predominantly Western orientation – might be interpreted as highlighting certain developments and processes prevalent throughout the First World and projecting them worldwide, including onto the distinct geopolitical space of the Third World. As a result, or so the argument might run, the hard political differences of geopolitical space are diminished and the 'modernity differential' between the First and the Third World is erased (Chesneaux 1992: 57). Such a line of criticism may well suggest that the appeal of liquid modernity in the West proceeds from its streetwise, sceptical culture – a culture of irony which is far from evident in, say, sub-Saharan Africa. For example, Paolini (1999) has provocatively suggested that modernity, in all its heterogeneity, produces a very different set of experiences and demands in the Third World from that of the West; one reason this is so, he argues referencing Third World critiques of modernity, are the ongoing attractions of old-style modernization to vast numbers in Third World populations. From the standpoint of the theory of liquid modernity, however, it is hard to speak, let alone interpret, such Others of the capitalist world system: Bauman's diagnosis, so it might appear, better captures what is occurring in London than in Lisbon, in Melbourne than in Mozambique. A foregrounding of liquidization, plasticity, dismantling, destabilization – all this, it may be argued, smacks of a distinctively Western worldview and culture.

There is, however, a weak version of this criticism of Bauman's theory of liquid modernity – a criticism which I have developed at length elsewhere (Elliott 2007). The weak criticism is that, by focusing attention on the liquidization of the self, social relations and everyday life in a globalized world, Bauman tends to neglect the ongoing significance of more structured, solid forms of sociality. To a great extent, Bauman's many examples of our liquid modern times are drawn from daily experiences familiar to inhabitants of, say, North America or Europe – that is, of life lived in societies of high divorce and remarriage, of relationships structured with reference to mobile telecommunications, and of intimacy guided by therapy culture. Yet what

Bauman possibly neglects are the many ways in which liquid modern societies still depend on traditions, worldviews, regimes of discourse, modes of power as well as structures of feeling that are characteristic of organized or 'hardware' modernity. Why, for example, do we find the forces of liquid modernity more at work in some sectors of the economy – say, finance and the communications sectors – than in others? The ordering ambitions of modernity – centred upon structure, classification, hierarchy and control – remain vital to various private life strategies and social practices of the contemporary era. That the organizing and organized impulses of modernism have been squeezed to the sidelines by liquidized forms of social life in more recent years does not preclude the ongoing force of modernist worldviews from exerting an impact upon the contemporary era.

The sociological significance of liquidization can, in short, be exaggerated. Consider, for example, marriage once more. Smart and Shipman (2004), who criticize Bauman, have studied the lives of various transnational families living in Britain whose values and practices do not fit easily with ideas of liquid modern relationships. The analysis set out by Smart and Shipman of the ongoing power of marriage as a cultural ideal, and of the complex ways in which self-control and interpersonal commitment are negotiated across generations, differs substantially from the liquid frame of 'until-further-notice' relationships of which Bauman speaks. So too, Gross (2005) distinguishes between 'regulative' and 'meaning-constitutive' traditions of the social field governing intimacy. While acknowledging that the regulative tradition of lifelong marriage as an ideal has declined in strength across the West in recent years, Gross argues that the organizing tradition of romantic love (and its ideology of coupledom) remains central to current social arrangements throughout the West. In this context, liquidization is viewed as only a *partial* transformation of social life. Whatever the force of these criticisms, it would be quite misleading to suggest that Bauman simply overlooks or ignores the impact that traditional ideologies or worldviews still play in the shaping of social life. Indeed, arguably, the thesis of increasing societal liquidization only makes sense if it is interpreted against the backdrop of the diversity of lifestyles, forms of life and evaluative standpoints from which individuals engage with others in contemporary societies.

The other major criticism of Bauman's recent social theory concerns his account of identity. In particular, Bauman's contention that liquid life is an inherent subjective corollary of liquid modernity has been sharply questioned. Some critics dispute the details of Bauman's account of the relations between consumerism, popular culture and identity; in doing so, these critics have expressed serious reservations with the idea that consumer culture results in the production of only liquidized or privatized identities (cf. Paterson 2006). Other critics have raised important concerns about Bauman's predominantly negative interpretation of identity formation in the current age, suggesting that the idea of 'privatized identity' fails to do justice to the exciting opportunities generated by today's identity politics – particularly the rich complexity of gay, lesbian, queer, ethnic and racial identities (Gane 2004). Still others have raised doubts concerning the adequacy of Bauman's portrayal of liquid lives, pointing out that the stress on 'manic individualism' in this account jostles uneasily with other aspects of personality development in mania and narcissism as portrayed in psychoanalysis (Sayers 2007; see also Clarke and Moran 2003).

Liquidized forms of experience and identity, with their emphasis on short termism and relentless self-transformation, are undoubtedly characteristic of large areas of contemporary cultural life – particularly through the world of commodified images in the media and new information technologies. However, it is also important to recognize that contemporary social life permits the development of various critical, cosmopolitan identities, many of which contain possibilities for transcending the rigid determinations of identity – class, gender, race – associated with industrial capitalism (du Gay and Hall 1996; Habermas 2001b; Beck 2006). Recent social theories highlight the extraordinary diversity of modes of identity constitution in the global age (Taylor 1991; Giddens 1992). Against this backdrop, we might ask in a critical spirit: Is 'liquid life' only a means of adjusting narcissistic individuals to the dictates of late capitalism? Is the liquidization of identity always a defensive closure at the level of private life, against the range of possibilities and perils inaugurated by globalization? What of identities that are resistant to the short-term temper of liquid modernity, of those individuals who reject cultural pressures towards change and flexibility? Due to the generality and sweep of the theory of liquid modernity, what threatens to recede into the shadows is the point that all of us have multiple identities, some overlapping, some contradictory, and that at any moment these identities are interacting with – incorporating, resisting and transforming – broader social values and cultural differences, shaping and being shaped by contemporary societies.

Summary points

1   Recent social theories have focused attention on the increasingly networked, risk-laden and liquid character of advanced modernity. In Castells, this is traced as a shift from the age of industry to informationalism. In Beck, the shift is from first modernity (in which economic growth and security were organized through the nation-state) to second modernity (in which, for example, economic risks and

ecological crises become fully globalized). In Bauman, the shift is from the age of hard or heavy modernity to soft or liquid modernity.

2   In Castells' approach, networks are open structures, defined as centreless and as decentring established forms of power. In the new network society, power is transformed as diffuse, shifting and spatially fluid.

3   Castells argues that space today is best conceived in terms of global flows. Such flows – people, money, ideas, information, services – comprise three components: (a) informational circuits and communication infrastructures; (b) the advanced processing of production and information through nodes clustered in specific cities or regions; and (c) professional elites reproducing the culture of network societies.

4   In Beck's social theory, the contention is that humanity faces risks of a global scale and magnitude that previous generations have never faced. Risk today threatens devastating global consequences (for instance, ecological catastrophe or nuclear disaster) which cannot be limited in time and space and in which notions of individual or organizational accountability collapse.

5   According to Beck, the rise of risk society brings with it the emergence of 'individualization' – in which individuals, monitoring the risks of life, become more directly involved in the self-design of their own biographies.

6   In Bauman's late work, society is presented as continuously and irreparably fluid or liquid in its essential social coordinates. In the 24/7 world of the global electronic economy and mass media, we see the emergence of *instantaneous time* and *insubstantial space*.

7   For Bauman, the world of heavy modernity – of heavy industry and massive workforces – has been displaced by light or liquid modernity, based around economic deregulation and the instant global transfer of capital.

8   The social theories of Castells, Beck and Bauman have all been criticized for, in a sense, exaggerating the novelty of transnationalism, mobile capital and precarious forms of life associated with globalization. The criticism is that what these social theorists present as wall-to-wall in contemporary societies is, in fact, localized to specific sectors of the economy – for example, finance, media and service.

Further questions

1   What networks do you belong to?

2   To what extent are the networks to which you belong an active community?

3   From sex to air-travel, how do you judge if something is risky today?

4   Given today's global risks, what are your own ways of coping? How do these coping mechanisms fit with the wider society?

5   Is your life more fluid than that of your parents? How so? What is the significance of this?

Further feading

Ulrich Beck

Risk Society: Towards a New Modernity (Sage, 1992).
The Reinvention of Politics (Polity Press, 1997).
Democracy and Its Enemies (Polity Press, 1998).
With A. Giddens and S. Lash, *Reflexive Modernization: Politics, Tradition and Aesthetics in the Modern Social Order* (Polity Press, 1994).
With E. Beck-Gernsheim, *The Normal Chaos of Love* (Polity Press, 1995).

Zygmunt Bauman

Liquid Modernity (Polity Press, 2000).
The Individualized Society (Polity Press, 2001).
Society under Siege (Polity Press, 2002).
Liquid Love (Polity Press, 2003).
Wasted Lives: Modernity and Its Outcasts (Polity Press, 2004).
Identity (Polity Press, 2004).
Liquid Lives (Polity Press, 2005).

Manuel Castells

The Rise of the Network Society, The Information Age: Economy, Society and Culture, Vol. I (Blackwell 1996, 2000, 2nd edn).
The Power of Identity, The Information Age: Economy, Society and Culture, Vol. II (Blackwell, 1997, 2004 2nd edn).

The End of the Millennium, The Information Age: Economy, Society and Culture, Vol. III Blackwell, (1998, 2000 2nd edn).

With M. Ince, *Conversations with Manuel Castells* (Polity Press, 2003).

With G. Cardoso (eds), *The Network Society: A Cross Cultural Perspective* (Edward Elgar, 2004).

'Communication, Power and Counter-power in the Network Society', *International Journal of Communication*, 1 (2007): 238–66.

Internet links

Ulrich Beck

http://www.ualberta.ca/~cjscopy/articles/leiss.html
http://www.lse.ac.uk/collections/sociology/whoswho/beck.htm

Zygmunt Bauman

http://www.culturewars.org.uk/2004-02/identity.htm
http://www.culture.pl/en/culture/artykuly/os_bauman_zygmunt

Manuel Castells

http://annenberg.usc.edu/Faculty/Communication/CastellsM.aspx
http://www.manuelcastells.info/en/
http://globetrotter.berkeley.edu/people/Castells/castells-cono.html

---

Globalization

Contents

Jenny reclines on a couch at home, alongside members of her family, watching satellite television. Surfing the channels, she wanders from an American soap to a British documentary to a Japanese music video. As her family tires of her incessant channel hopping, Jenny relinquishes the remote control and turns her attention to her mobile phone and incoming text message. Opening the inbox, she reads a message from her friend Carmel. Jenny got to know Carmel at university in London, before the latter embarked on a gap year in Australia. The text tells of Carmel's good news: she's been accepted into a doctoral programme at an ivy-league university in the USA. Jenny responds to Carmel's text immediately, and is drawn into an intimate exchange of ongoing texts with her friend on the other side of the world. Her family, meanwhile, still sitting in the same room as Jenny, now drift into the emotional background.

Another typical evening for a prosperous London family enjoying the technological paraphernalia – satellite TV, mobiles, texting – of contemporary life in the West? Perhaps. What can be said with some confidence is that communication networks are at the centre of this episode from modern family life. As noted in previous chapters, we now live in a world in which much of practical social life, not to mention the operations of business and organizations, is conducted through email and the Net. There is more going on here, however, than simply the endless spinning communications of new information technologies. For the information networks and communication systems that Jenny and her friend Carmel deploy in their texting 'bite' deeply into the fabric of personal and emotional life. For one thing, this texting is clearly of sufficient emotional gravity that it brings Jenny into closer contact with her friend Carmel (who, remember, is on the other side of the world) than with those sitting in the same room – namely, her family. For another, it reorientates and restructures perceptions of social space, as well as of time, in the flow of daily life. As if by magic, what is on the 'other side' of the world – in this case, Australia – is now brought centrally within Jenny's world in London. Such a redrafted, spinning world is referred to in sociology as the world of globalization – the main theme of this chapter.

Globalization has become one of the key buzz-words of our times. One needs to be careful when assessing arguments about the consequences of globalization, however, as what people call 'globalization' has many different meanings – not all of them coherent, few reconcilable. One central part of what globalization means for many critics is advanced capitalism in its broadest sense, and thus by implication the term has come to revolve around Americanization. This is the view that globalization is a central driver in the export of American commerce and culture, of the vast spread of mass consumerism, of the unleashing of US-controlled turbo-capitalism. Others view globalization through the lens of a much longer historical perspective, beginning with the age of discovery and the migrations from the Old to the New World.

We will consider these differing accounts of globalization throughout this chapter, focusing especially on the main theories of globalism which have come to dominate social theory, the social sciences and public debate in recent years. It is perhaps worth noting at the outset, though, that communications media and new information technologies play a vitally significant role in many accounts of the conditions and consequences of globalization. Indeed, it is probably fair to say that recent transformations in communications are uppermost in people's minds when talking about what is truly new about globalization. Political theorist David Held (1991: 206) captures this point well when he contends:

> What is new about the modern global system is the chronic intensification of patterns of interconnectedness mediated by such phenomena as the modern communications industry and new information technology and the spread of globalization in and through new dimensions of interconnectedness: technological, organizational, administrative and legal, among others, each with their own logic and dynamic of change.

Certainly the notion of globalization, many agree, captures something about the ways the world in which we live is now continuously changing. Hence, the preoccupation in globalization theory with, among others, forces of multi-layered political governance, shifting patterns of post-industrial production, global financial flows and exchange rates. Each of these clusters is a subject of intense debate in academic circles, and it is telling that such debates are played out globally or at least throughout the contemporary West, in universities and government think-tanks from San Francisco to Sydney. Yet globalization as a concept involves considerably more than academic debate alone. Reference is made here not only to the globalized protest strategies of anti-globalizers in Seattle, Genoa, Porto Alegre and elsewhere but also the myriad ways in which the forces of globalism impact upon both the personal and social aspects of everyday life. Today, there is good reason to think that the world really has changed, and profoundly. For anyone wanting to understand these changes, it is necessary to get to grips with what globalization is, with what it is doing to our societies, and with the profound consequences it carries for our personal and emotional lives.

The globalization debate

In recent years, the term 'globalization' has fast become a central organizing category in academic disciplines from economics to international relations, from cultural studies to sociology. Some argue that the globalization debate is maddeningly abstract, with all its talk of 'borderless worlds', 'turbo-capitalism' and 'transgovernmental networks'. Others contend that globalization is now invoked to describe so many things – from the spread of AIDS to the war on terrorism – that it is in danger of losing all meaning. One of the amazing facts about globalization, though rarely commented upon, is just how quickly it has come to dominate academic and public debate. Fifteen or so years ago, the preferred terms for analysing worldwide change were those of 'internationalism' or 'internationalization'. Talk of the global didn't much figure. Today, by contrast, and in that relatively short period of time, the term 'globalization' has pretty much gone global. The term is now everywhere – in the newspapers, business magazines, radio and television, and throughout our universities.

In order to contextualize this debate, we will now examine three different accounts of globalization. Each of these standpoints has substantially influenced the debate over globalization. These three theoretical approaches to globalization turn on distinct interpretations of the changing nature of organizations, economics, society, the nation-state and personal life. Later in the chapter we will consider criticisms of the globalization debate, as well as ways in which this debate has influenced contemporary sociology and the social sciences.

Global sceptics

When various public intellectuals and academics during the 1990s pointed to the term 'globalization' to explain the major social changes going on around us, many reacted in a sceptical fashion. The sceptics in the globalization debate questioned the idea that we were witnessing an overall shift towards world integration. Pointing to trade and investment statistics from the late nineteenth century, they argued that worldwide economic flows had intensified as regards interaction between nations during the course of the twentieth century – but that, otherwise, the world was not particularly different from the recent past. Arguing against proponents of the globalization thesis (see below), the sceptics contended that there is not much new to the world.

An especially interesting version of the case put by global sceptics was that of Paul Hirst (1999). What, Hirst asked, was actually 'global' about globalization? His answer, disarmingly direct, was 'very little'. In this connection, Hirst rejected nearly every claim associated with the globalization thesis. While acknowledging that there is today more cultural and communicational contact between nations than in previous periods, Hirst and his colleagues contended that such contact did not amount to a truly globalized economy. Studying the period from 1890 to 1914, for example, they argued that trade and investment flows were higher for that period than for today, that national borders were not as restricted and that, consequently, there were higher levels of transnational immigration. In a related fashion, Hirst and his colleagues questioned the scope of one of the key institutional emblems of globalization: the multinational corporation. So-called global transnational corporations (TNCs) were not really 'global' at all they said; they were instead nationally based companies at the centre of international networks of subsidiaries. In contrast to the notion of 'footloose capital' in flight around the globe seeking out ever greater profits, the majority of economic activity across the international economy occured primarily in the OECD countries. Regionalization rather than globalization, it was said, defined the shape of the worldwide economy: because of the heavy regionalization of such trading blocs as the European Union and North America, the world economy was becoming less, not more, global. Moreover, nation-states were not becoming progressively less sovereign – on the contrary, international-ization was regarded as fundamentally dependent on the regulatory control of national governments.

The strong concept of a globalized economy . . . acts as an ideal type which we can compare to the actual trends within the international economy. This globalized economy has been contrasted to the notion of an inter-national economy in the above analysis in order to distinguish its particular and novel features. The opposition of these two types for conceptual clarity conceals the possibly messy combination of the two in reality. This makes it difficult to determine major trends on the basis of the available evidence. These two types of economy are not inherently mutually exclusive: rather in certain conditions the globalized economy would encompass and subsume the inter-national economy. The globalized economy would rearticulate many of the features of the inter-national economy, transforming them as it reinforced them. . . .

It is our view that such a process of hybridization is not taking place, but it would be cavalier not to consider and raise the possibility. Central in this respect is the evidence we present later for the weak development of TNCs [transnational companies] and the continued salience of MNCs [multinational companies] and also the ongoing dominance of the advanced countries in both trade and FDI [foreign direct investment]. Such evidence is consistent with a continuing inter-national economy, but much less so with a rapidly globalizing hybrid system. Moreover, we should remember that an inter-national economy is one in which major nationally based manufacturers and the major financial trading and

contemporary social theory

Alongside the sceptics of globalization were to be found the anti-
globalizers. The anti-globalization brigade, in all its manifestations from
anti-capitalist protesters to policy think-tanks, put forward a list of powerful
charges cataloguing the sins of globalization. Globalism was allegedly
empowering multinational corporations and speculative finance, compounding inequality and eroding democracy, promoting Western imperialism
and the Americanization of the world, destroying environmental standards,
as well as brutalizing the public sphere and the state governmental structures
through which it operates. The emergence of a planetary-scale global market
with ever-decreasing tariffs, ever-greater international production, as well as
more integrated financial markets with higher trade flows, had unleashed a
turbo-charged capitalism of unprecedented forms of economic exploitation
and political oppression. Or so argued the anti-globalizers.

The link between global Westernization or Americanization on the one
hand and turbo-capitalist exploitation on the other in the anti-globalization
discourse is sometimes explicit, sometimes implicit. A neo-Marxist con-
viction that capitalism exhibits a pathological expansionist logic, one which
now expands the geographical reach of Western corporations and markets
to the nth degree, informs this argument. The imperial West, it is suggested,
has carved up and redivided the world into exclusive trade, investment and
financial sectors and flows, with new institutions – such as the G8 and World
Bank – exercising global surveillance and domination. As a result, globalization is seen as a top-down process, its effects uniform. The weakness
of this case, however, it that it cannot adequately justify the grounds of its
own social critique: if globalization were really so omnipotent, all-powerful
and manipulating, how would the social theorist ever find a position from
which to launch an objective critique? In any event, the assumption that the

globe is always geared to perfectly integrated markets is certainly deficient. That is to say, such critics have reductively equated globalization with an economistic version of world markets. Yet, as we will see, concentrating solely on processes of economic integration, and thus neglecting current social, cultural and political transformations, leads to an impoverished understanding of how globalization is constituted, contested and shaped.

Radical globalists

Radical globalists are generally upbeat about globalization, sketching an optimistic view of the rise of free trade and open markets. The radical globalist account emphasizes the benefits to democracy and alternatives to centralized power arising from global financial markets, the growth of multinational corporations and the worldwide diffusion of popular culture. This does not mean that radical globalizers are unperturbed by current distributions of wealth and economic power, but advocates of this case do see globalization as generally beneficial and historically inevitable.

Globalization, argue radical globalists, cuts across national borders. In doing so, the forces of globalization initiate new forms of social life and world order based upon altered patterns of economic globalization, of power and of territory. One of the best-known radical globalists, the Japanese business analyst Kenichi Ohmae (1990, 1995), describes globalization as heralding a 'borderless world' – a world in which capital circulates in search of the highest investment returns irrespective of systems of national governance. According to Ohmae, the emergence of, and rapid growth in, the global economy spells the demise of the nation-state – as individual countries no longer have an effective fiscal means to control their economies. In a world where more than a trillion dollars a day are turned over on global currency markets, national governments are increasingly under strain in responding to transitional issues that cross their borders – from currency speculation to illegal immigrants to environmental risks. This challenge to sovereignty is so great that, according to Ohmae, nations are fast becoming mere 'fictions'. The fiction is that sovereignty is still vested in political leaders, but for the most part politicians have lost their capacity to shape socio-economic outcomes in our intensive age of globalization.

T he global economy follows its own logic and develops its own webs of interest, which rarely duplicate the historical borders between nations. As result, national interest, as an economic, as opposed to

For Ohmae, it is regions rather than states that are the key drivers of globalization. The current world economy, based upon unprecedented finance and capital flows, takes its cue from new regions and economic zones with large populations. Most of the giant multinational companies now focus their activities on 'region states' – 'the globe's natural economic zones' – rather than single countries.

Global transformationalists

In contrast to the global sceptics and radical globalists, a third-way position has emerged within the globalization debate – that occupied by global transformationalists. The transformationalists argue that globalization inaugurates a 'shake-out' within the realms of economics, politics, culture and personal life. This is less the heralding of a completely new age (as argued by radical globalists), than an adjustment to a world that transforms previous structures, a world that shakes up distinctions between domestic and international, internal and external affairs.

One of the most sophisticated proponents of the transformationalist position is David Held, who has tackled head-on the critics, both sceptics and anti-globalizers. Held, a professor at the London School of Economics, has quickly emerged as a leading global expert on globalization. He powerfully argues that the critics are wrong on almost all the major points. Globalization as the driver of Americanization? Yes, says Held (2004), the US is the major player in shaping economic markets; but globalization is not just an American phenomenon. As he points out, American companies account for around only one-fifth of world total imports, and approximately one-quarter of total exports. The compounding of inequalities? Individual income differences in the wealthiest and poorest countries are greater than ever, but perhaps the most significant development is that those living in the very poorest conditions appear to the on the decline worldwide. Global markets triumphant over national governments? In the West, government expenditure and taxation levels have generally risen. Globalization, says Held (2004: 6), 'has not simply eroded or undermined the power of states; rather it has reshaped and reconfigured it'. The globalizing of communications threatening national cultures? The diffusion of instant communication across large parts of the world cannot be doubted, but Held argues that available evidence indicates that local and national cultures remain robust.

In their path-breaking work *Global Transformations* (1999), Held and his associates delineate, with considerable precision, what is truly 'global' about globalization. In order to say anything meaningful about patterns of contemporary globalization, and particularly of how today's world order differs from previous historical forms of globalization, Held sets out four analytical dimensions of analysis:

- The extensity of global networks
- The intensity of global interconnectedness
- The velocity of global flows
- The impact propensity of global interconnectedness.

For Held, globalization certainly involves a *stretching* of social relations. What he means to underscore with this notion of stretching or extensity is that decisions or events occurring in one part of the world come to have ramifications for people living elsewhere. From global labour markets to global warming, it is nearly impossible today not to live with the consequences of the widening reach of networks of social activity and political power. But still there is more. For globalization implies not only a stretching of activities across frontiers, but also a rapid *intensification of interconnectedness* between peoples, institutions and states. Here the networked world of high-speed telecommunications is the most obvious example. Stretching and intensity of social relations are thus key for Held; but there are also two other forces at work in the play of global things. One is velocity, by which Held seeks to underscore the *speeding up of social life*. This refers to the emergence of a 24/7 media culture, in which breaking news – from terrorist attacks to the fighting of wars – is relayed virtually instantly around the globe. But it also refers to the speeding up of transport, travel and the global communication of information. The other concerns impact, in particular the magnification of local events or decisions into issues of global import.

> lobalization is not simply a monolithic process that brings in its wake wholly positive or negative outcomes. It is formed and constituted by complex processes with multiple impacts which need to be carefully dissected and examined. But one thing is already clear: globalization does not simply lead to the 'end of politics' or the demise of regulatory capacity. Rather, globalization is more accurately linked with the expansion of the terms of political activity, and of the range of actors involved in political life. Globalization marks the continuation of politics by new means operating at many levels.
>
> David Held (2004) *Global Covenant: The Social Democratic Alternative to the Washington Consensus*. Cambridge: Polity Press, p. 10.

Such global transformations spell, in turn, major changes for the nation-state. Held and his associates provide some dramatic statistics to prove that the growth of transnational organizations alters the dynamics of both state and civil society. At the beginning of the twentieth century there were only 37 intergovernmental organizations (IGOs) and 176 international non-governmental organizations (INGOs) in force. Today, in addition to the many millions of private firms doing business across state borders, there are an estimated 7000 IGOs and some 50,000 non-governmental, non-for-profit organizations operating around the globe. These bodies – from Amnesty International and Christian Aid to the International Red Cross and Transparency International – make up a vast, multi-layered structure of global civil society. To this pattern of extensive non-governmental inter-connectedness may also be added a thick web of key global policy-making bodies, including the United Nations, IMF, G8, World Trade Organization, European Union and Asia Pacific Economic Cooperation.

Wither the nation-state? Not necessarily according to Held, and in this connection he outlines a highly nuanced theoretical position – one which puts him at some distance from those radical globalists for whom the state is, more or less, finished. Held certainly recognizes that many traditional domains of state activity have been eroded. As he develops this point (Held and McGrew 2002: 23), 'individual states on their own can no longer be conceived of as the appropriate political units for either resolving key policy problems or managing effectively a broad range of public functions'. But he thinks it is a mistake to deny the ongoing relevance of the state to world affairs – witness, for example, the ongoing power of states such as the United States and China in global politics. Globalization in this sense is less about an erosion than a reshaping of the nation-state. 'The modern state', suggest Held and McGrew (2002: 23), 'is increasingly embedded in webs of regional and global interconnectedness permeated by supranational, intergovernmental and transnational forces, and unable to determine its own fate.'

Global cosmopolitanism

One of the confusions arising from the globalization controversy is that social theorists disagree over its possible benefits and costs to democratic politics. Some take a very pessimistic view on the political and cultural consequences of globalization, seeing a deterioration in both the quality of democracy and the public sphere. We will examine some of these arguments in more depth later. Other social theorists see alternative political possibilities stemming from globalization, and in this connection the spectre of a *global cosmopolitanism* looms large. Such social trends, some analysts argue, may be discerned in the debates of the European Commission concerning the possibilities for a new kind of supranational justice, replete with regional police force (Europol) and magistracy (Eurojust). Or they may have gleaned from the global spread of human rights movements, protesting the suffering of children and civilians in, say, Iraq, Africa, Israel or Palestine. Or it might be inferred from the cultural ties of, say, Chinese or Korean migrants living in Sydney or San Francisco, whose working lives embed them in global networks.

All are expressions – or so it has been suggested – of a vital new cosmopolitan outlook, the global refashioning of a centuries-old tradition that rejects nationalism in favour of the wider embrace of humanity. It could be argued that modernity was ever thus. Certainly since thinkers such as Goethe, Kant, Humboldt or Marx, the challenges of international politics have been associated with a transformation from narrow nationalism to universal governance. In this connection, the achievements of multi-lateralism – since the Second World War particularly – have been notable, from the founding of the United Nations system to the development of the EU. From this angle, 'cosmopolitanism' may simply be a new word for what used to be called 'internationalism'.

Ulrich Beck, the Beck whose social theory of risk we examined in a previous chapter, thinks cosmopolitanism today is radically different from old-style internationalism. In recent books such as *The Cosmopolitan Vision* (2006) and *Power in the Global Age* (2005), Beck has argued that the influence of today's cosmopolitanism is reconstructing the world order afresh, replacing provincialism and nationalism with a mature moral outlook capable of responding to contemporary global crises. Beck, whose social theory of risk we examined earlier in the book, has been writing for some years of a new European consciousness and beyond that of global cosmopolitanism. Broadly speaking, his aim is to extend the poltics of cosmopolitanism into a polemical engagement with neoliberalism throughout the consumerist, post-imperialist West.

Cosmopolitanism for Beck is an answer to the question of what we owe strangers by virtue of our shared humanity. The political form of this ethic is known as globalization, for which, as Beck comments, the living of life is carried out in a milieu of blurring national distinctions and cultural ambiguities. Cosmopolitanism thus means acceptance of cultural mixture, which Beck believes is not always to the liking of authoritarian neoliberal regimes. Beck's key contention is that neoliberalism as a political system is self-contradictory and self-mutilating. A vision of universal freedom which presupposed for its triumph the gains of Western modernity – material wealth, the rule of law, civil society – became instead the repressive mantra that we can live together only if nations are alike. In international relations, this is the view that only countries that practise democracy and value human rights can be legitimate – a view invoked by the governments of America and Britain in launching the 2003 attack on Iraq.

Beck packs a considerable punch against the neoliberal creed. With a formidably stinging intelligence, he equates neoliberalism with a US global dictatorship. As he writes (2006: 160), 'Americans are now exporting American pessimism by infecting everyone else with their terror phobia.' But Beck's sociology is more than merely the latest form of anti-Americanism. As he argues at length, the new cosmopolitanism must deal with a whole host of emergent global risks – xenophobic nationalisms, religious fundamentalisms, multinational monopolies.

Contextualizing these global changes within a broader social theory, Beck distinguishes two kinds of relation between politics and power in our time of transnational interdependencies. There is what he terms the 'national outlook', or 'methodological nationalism', which holds that politics should be principally concerned with the assertion of sovereignty, the policing of local or regional borders and the maintenance of exclusive identities. The national outlook, says Beck, is premised upon a full-blooded essentialist sociology that squares the circle between national and universal society, squeezing to the sidelines incommensurability in people's attitudes, beliefs, values and orientations. By contrast, Beck speaks of the emergence of 'cosmopolitanization', or 'methodological cosmopolitanism', by which he means to underscore internal processes of transformation affecting societies across the globe. Cosmopolitanism for Beck involves a positive pluralization of national borders, a deter-ritorialized society, a mushrooming of globalism from within the nation-state. From international students and transmigrants to multi-national global businesses and transnational criminal networks, Beck sees everywhere the influence of an ever-expanding cosmopolitanism.

Beck's main arguments against 'methodological nationalism', as well as the more programmatic aspects of his case for cosmopolitanism, are illuminating, but some important criticisms have also been made of his theory of global cosmopolitanism. For one thing, it is surely a pity that he feels the need to carry so much anti-American ideological baggage. This seems to mar an otherwise careful and judicious appraisal of global politics. Yet it is not just his distaste for American unilateralism that detracts from his otherwise vigorous case for cosmopolitanism. For all his insights regarding emergent politics of cosmopolitan openness to cultural diversity, Beck's work is in various ways depressingly *au courant*. Whatever Beck's intellectual reservations about postmodernism, the conceptual architecture of his approach is relentlessly modish in ways that clearly parallel postmodern theory – impeccably post-national, post-metaphysical, post-societal, post-internationalist and post-teleological. To the extent that Beck theorizes his own position, he occasionally acknowl-edges that various postmodernists have trodden this terrain before: perhaps the best known is Jean-François Lyotard's *The Postmodern Condition* (1984), where the argument was put that 'one listens to reggae, watches a western, eats McDonald's food for lunch and local cuisine for dinner, wears Paris perfume in Tokyo and "retro" clothes in Hong Kong'. *Pace* Lyotard, the constructive side of Beck's cosmopolitanism is that there are compelling sociological reasons – not simply cultural ones – for believing that the world really is heading in a more post-national direc-tion. However, according to some critics, if Beck really wanted to put some distance between himself and postmodernism, he should stop to consider whether nation, state, region and the rest, defined in a less ahistorical fashion than proponents of postmodernism insist on, might not be a good deal more politically relevant to today's transformed global realities than he assumes.

Other critics bemoan the lack of political depth to Beck's analysis, which at times threatens to sag into ideological naivety. For in rhapsodizing this century's brave new cosmopolitanism, Beck sometimes appears unaware of its more virulent forms. If cosmopolitanism combines cultural openness with a cavalier disregard of place, this is because it is arguably a manifestation of the mentality of the upper middle classes. In this view, cosmopolitanism functions as the ideology of advanced capitalism. It allows white Westerners to jet around the globe, effortlessly living the transnational lifestyle, crossing national borders as easily as money flows between multinational corporations. This supposedly universal and classless doctrine screens from view those excluded from the privileges and wealth of global capitalism. Although Beck himself is by no means suggesting that cosmopolitanism is a purely positive category, there are more troubling issues: what of the millions (such as refugees and trans-migrants) less well off than Beck's global cosmopolitans? Undoubtedly the world is becoming increasingly transnational, especially for those in the expensive cities of the West. But the point is that for the vast swathe of humanity, from rural Chinese peasants to women and children in Central Asia, the transnational capitalist system doesn't usually bring about cosmopolitan consequences.

This point connects with other political difficulties to which Beck may be insufficiently attentive. Beck's language for capturing cosmopolitanism – ranging, as it does, across terminological innovations such as 'individualization', 'reflexivity' and 'cosmopolitan nationalism' – is conceptually very highly inflected. This labour of the theoretician, however, still doesn't get around the fact that there are those who have access to cosmopolitan culture on the cheap, just as there are those excluded from its benefits. The relevant conflict here is between the politics of transnationalism and the politics of cosmopolitanism. Yet Beck's sociology betrays an incipient idealism in its heavily cosmopolitan bias. Tellingly, he passes over in silence the whole issue of how transnationalism and cosmopolitanism intertwine, and instead simply conflates the two. It remains, however, an intellectual sleight-of-hand to imagine that transnational activities always and everywhere lead to exactly the same process of cosmopolitanism. To suggest, for example, that someone watching satellite TV necessarily also moves within the culture of cosmopolitanism may sound peculiarly idealist, patronizing or politically naive.

Beck stands for a reflexive style of sociology – what he terms a 'sociology of sociology'. Somewhat like Theodor Adorno's notion of 'constellations', with its avant-garde analyses of social forms, Beck's weaving of reflexive sociology is self-critically experimental in design. At his best, Beck's writing is high-minded and inspired; yet, occasionally, the sociology appears to overreach itself, as if one were on a roller-coaster of ideas, concepts and theories. Given his grand claims for an emergent global cosmopolitanism, it is surely a defect of his work that he offers scarcely any detailed discussions of, say, Africa, East and South Asia or the Islamic diaspora. In the end, Beck is less interested in culture than in society, and particularly how cosmopolitanism has assumed a new sociological significance. While Beck's brand of cosmopolitanism is more concerned with transformations and transnational interdependencies than it is by nationalist politics or contemporary capitalism, this is because it is one of the most utopian of political ideologies – and, for that reason alone, provides fertile ground for alternative political futures.

Globalization since 9/11

The debate over globalization, according to many, was irrevocably transformed on 11 September 2001 – the day the planes brought down the Twin Towers in New York. This was the day the world changed for ever – or, at least, this was how the globe was represented by the mass media in the days, weeks and months following the New York terror attacks. Looking back with hindsight, and notwithstanding the catastrophic consequences of 9/11, it is arguable that much of the political debate at this time was blown out of all historical proportion. Not only does 9/11 fail to rank in comparison with genocides and wars such as Auschwitz, Hiroshima and Vietnam, but equally it has been surely eclipsed by the more recent catastrophes of conflict and war in Afghanistan and Iraq. In terms of numbers alone, approximately 3000 lives were lost on 9/11, a comparatively small number when set alongside recent political conflicts. That said, however, 9/11 did signal – in a profound and no doubt indiscriminate way – that the world in which we find ourselves in these early days of the twenty-first century is significantly different not only to the eighteenth- or nineteenth-century but also the late twentieth-century world. The differences are of course to do with global terror and new forms of warfare, but also much more than that. It is estimated that in the time between the first and second tower collapsing on the morning of 9/11 a global audience of some two billion people watched the catastrophe unfold in real time. This takes us to the heart of issues to do with the globalization of communications and cultures, as well as to the heart of debates concerning global governance and global civil society.

The 9/11 terrorist attack on the World Trade Center and the Pentagon revealed, in a most shocking and disturbing way, the new global power of *networks* (see the discussion of networks in the social theory of Castells in Chapter 9). From one angle, 9/11 showed us the ultimate interconnections and conflicts of our lives in an age of globalization. 9/11 and its aftermath certainly spelt terror, but it was also inextricably bound up with media, communications, information, signs and spectacles. It was, in short, a *global media event*, with all that entails as concerns communications networks. '9/11', as Douglas Kellner (2003: 41) writes,

> could only be a mega-event in a global media world, a society of the spectacle, where the whole world is watching and participates in what Marshall McLuhan called a global village. The 9/11 terror spectacle was obviously constructed as a media event to circulate terror and to demonstrate to the world the vulnerability of the epicentre of global capitalism and American power.

The technological terror of 9/11, to be sure, involved the use of airlines and buildings as instruments of mass destruction; but the deployment of such technologies of mass destruction only became truly global through the mediatization of 9/11.

From another angle, there was an even deeper affinity between networks and globalization issuing from the 9/11 attacks. If networks were vital to the spread of communication in which people around the globe watched 9/11 and its aftermath unfold on TV screens, radio and the Internet, they were also essential to the very orchestration of the attacks, since the use of global networks was part and parcel of the strategy and methods of Al-Qaeda. Indeed, from fund-raising to new technological bomb detonation, Al-Qaeda emerges as a kind of 'global network of networks'. Robert J. Holton (2008: 189) explains these links between globalization and terrorist networks thus:

> Al-Qaeda is a truly transnational global network. Its leaders and key personnel have been drawn from a range of societies including Saudi Arabia (bin Laden), Egypt (al-Zawahiri) and Jordan (al-Zarqawi), but are also strikingly mobile across a range of societies. . . . The appeal of Al-Qaeda is global and trans-contextual. This is linked ideologically with the outreach of Islam, and organizationally through the idea of a decentralized network of networks. These networks are differentiated according to key functions such as planning or training, and involve key figures such as al-Zawahiri and al-Zarqawi, each of whom brought key associates into the network of networks. They are also decentralized not so much to

particular localities as to translocal spheres of operation. The Al-Qaeda presence in each country is not limited to locals, and draws on those from other countries.

Global terrorist networks such as Al-Qaeda are formidably hard to track for the reasons Holton identifies – their organizational base is transnational, their activities cut across national boundaries, their terror is obscenely excessive in its indiscrimination between combatants and civilians. By and large, global terrorism is also unlike traditional forms of terrorism in that targets are transnational and beyond the locale of grievance. The World Trade Center was attacked because it was a global icon of American economic power.

What political forms of globalization, then, do such terrorist networks represent? And how, exactly, have our everyday understandings of globalization changed since the terror attacks of 9/11? Social theorists have undertaken considerable study of terrorist networks and the changing contours of globalization since 9/11, though curiously some of the major conceptual reference points for debate pre-date the attacks. One such work is Samuel Huntington's polemical *The Clash of Civilizations and the Remaking of the World Order* (1996), which grabbed the attention of various neoconservative Republicans within the Bush administration. According to Huntington, global conflict in the post-Cold War era becomes increasingly motivated by religion and takes place between 'civilizations'. The modern political order for Huntington is a cross between different cultures and religions, with the latter outstripping and reorganizing the former and thereby mobilizing potential conflicts between civilizations. The potential conflicts in an age of globalization are multipolar, and include Islam, China, Africa, Russia, Asia and the West. But the real challenge in Huntington's eyes remains Islam, and the argument soon shifts from multi-polar conflict to the issue of the supremacy of Western modernity and the maintenance of its military-industrial complex. Thus the future shape of politics, says Huntington, is likely to involve ongoing clashes between 'the West and the Rest'. A similar line of analysis is developed in Benjamin Barber's influential book *Jihad vs. McWorld* (1996). Barber sees the world as radically split, between a globalizing West geared towards ceaseless modernization as driven by multinational corporations on the one hand, and pre-modern tribalism and religious fundamentalism opposed to the modernist idea of progress on the other. This fundamental cleavage is the only global conflict which really counts.

contemporary social theory

In the emerging world, the relations between states and groups from different civilizations will not be close and will often be antagonistic. Yet some intercivilization relations are more conflict-prone than others. At the micro level, the most violent fault lines are between Islam and its Orthodox, Hindu, African, and Western Christian neighbors. At the macro level, the dominant division is between 'the West and the rest,' with the most intense conflicts occurring between Muslim and Asian societies on the one hand, and the West on the other. The dangerous clashes of the future are likely to arise from the interaction of Western arrogance, Islamic intolerance, and Sinic assertiveness.

Alone among civilizations the West has had a major and at times devastating impact on every other civilization. The relation between the power and culture of the West and the power of the cultures of other civilizations is, as a result, the most pervasive characteristic of the world of civilizations. As the relative power increases, the appeal of Western culture fades and non-Western peoples have increasing confidence in and commitment to their indigenous cultures. The central problem in the relations between the West and the rest is, consequently, the discordance between the West's – particularly America's – efforts to promote a universal Western culture and its declining ability to do so.

Samuel Huntington (1996) *The Clash of Civilizations and the Remaking of the World Order*. London: Simon & Schuster, p. 183.

The advent of global terrorism has undoubtedly cast a shadow over previous polarizations of globalization, particularly the debate of those 'for' and 'against' – that is, 'radical globalists' against 'global sceptics'. Against this backdrop, recent social theory has sought to engage more critically with the consequences of globalism in terms of such issues as democracy, cosmopolitanism, social justice, militarism and terrorism. The recent work of Beck to develop a social theory of globalization around cosmopolitanism is a signal example – see discussion above. Among other attempts to analyse and critique contemporary globalism is Dennis Smith's *Globalization: The Hidden Agenda* (2006). Smith seeks to redefine the political stakes of globalization away from the struggle between the West and terrorism, and instead towards the possible catastrophic consequences of countries at war with each other *within* the West. In our own time of network terrorism, writes Smith, globalization is one name for the traumatic, shattering, excessive and uncontainable forces of multinational capitalism that dissolve traditional society and shake identities and communities to their roots. While terror and the problem of evil moves centre stage throughout the world in the wake of 9/11, it is for Smith the shapeless immensity of socio-economic contradictions within the West that remain of the utmost significance. As Smith (2006: 1) writes,

> On one side, there are supporters of decent democracy, delivering substantial benefits, such as dignity, freedom and fair treatment, to all citizens; on the other, proponents of liberated capitalism, enforced by the domineering state, excluding many from its benefits. The outcome of this struggle will shape the world for the rest of the twenty-first century.

From the collapse of communism to 9/11, Smith asserts that the world as we know it is disintegrating. Yet if the world is really coming apart, and in particular if America's global dominance has now entered into terminal decline, what political shape will the globe now take? Smith advances the following points on the 'hidden agenda' of globalization: the emerging collapse of the US as global monarch; a massive buildup of Europe's military strength to match its pervasive economic powers; the rise of China and India as 'global superpowers'; and a sociological vision of increasing millions throughout the globe subjected to social exclusion, poverty and humiliation. It is around this last theme that Smith argues globalization *wounds*. A 'dynamics of humiliation' is part and parcel, he says, of the expansionist logic of globalization.

If the West abandons decent democracy as a genuine option, if it abandons the duty of care, if it says the market will cure all ills, what will happen then? Who then will make the case for embedding decent democracy and human rights in the working practices of strong global-regional and global institutions of governance? Probably no-one.

In that case, our global city-dwellers will be left with the choice between liberated capitalism and the domineering state, each offered to them by a different set of local politicians. They are likely to favour the latter. It offers them the chance to avoid being victimized while turning some other group into victims.

However provocative this account might appear, there are good reasons to be cautious about such far-reaching political claims. It seems unlikely, for example, that the EU will seek to replace the US as the world's moral guardian via a massive buildup of its military strength. As Anthony Giddens (2006) has recently argued, the EU is not an emergent superpower but, rather, an elastic regional community. Or, as Timothy Garton-Ash (2004) has argued, Europe is the world's Not-America. Similarly, while China may now have surpassed Japan as the world's second largest economy, it will not necessarily seek to become the next global monarch. Indeed, the whole notion of a world as structured by a single dominating power has been eclipsed; global power floats away from centres, dispersed throughout overlapping regions. For what the controversy over globalization demonstrates is that patterns of social relations, power and identity are breaking down into forms that are increasingly fluid, irregular, even liquid.

I would define the EU [European Union] as a democratic association (or community) of semi-sovereign nations. I don't regard 'semi-sovereign' as a contentious term. Far from sovereignty being indivisible, it is always partial, internally and externally. The union is an association, because any member state can leave (although this right was only formalized in the constitution). The EU is not a post-national entity, because the component nations do not disappear, and they retain large capacities for the independent action. The EU differs from the UN, however, because formal sovereignty has been pooled, such that each member takes on board decisions handed down in EU courts. It is democratic, but primarily in the sense of deliberative democracy.

Anthony Giddens (2006) *Europe in the Global Age*. Cambridge: Polity Press, p. 217.

Criticisms of the globalization debate

The debate over globalization, as we have seen, covers many issues. From the globalization of finance and the economy to the shopping mall and consumerism, and from the environment, pollution and global warming to civil society and the emergence of new global forms of cosmopolitanism: it appears there is no aspect of the structure of social life that globalization does not reach. That said, and while global sceptics may have lost much intellectual and political ground to radical globalists, a number of forceful criticisms have been made of the globalization debate. There is the question, for example, of how far down these global networks, flows and processes really go – of whether they are actually 'global', or whether they are for the most part Western. Though globalization denotes a number of socio-economic and technological developments in cities such as Sydney and Singapore, it is arguably a more open question as to what globalization actually means in Sofija, Skopje or San'a. How might globalization apply to societies of the Third World? Is the term a culturally neutral description of geo-political realities in the twenty-first century, or a normative image of a certain form of life?

Globalization, work and the new economy

Notwithstanding the foregoing criticisms of the globalization debate, there has been a widespread appreciation – in both the social sciences and public political debate – that the economy, employment market and our working lives have undergone significant changes in recent years due to the impacts of globalization. The transnational activities of multinational corporations, able to export industrial production to low-wage spots around the globe, and to restructure investment in the West away from manufacture to the finance, service and communications sectors, has in particular spelt major changes in the ways people live their lives, how they approach work, as well as how they position themselves within the employment marketplace. While employment has become much more complex than in previous periods as a result of the acceleration of globalization, one key institutional fact redefining the contemporary condition has been the rapid decline of lifetime employment. The end of a job for life, or of a career developed within a single organization, has been interpreted by some critics as heralding the arrival of a 'new economy' – flexible, mobile, networked.

If downsizing, flexibility and job insecurity have become the mark of our times, how might these changes affect people's working lives? How do such economic changes impinge upon people's sense of identity? And how can long-term personal goals – that is, the self as an ongoing

contemporary social theory

project – be pursued in a world devoted to the short term? Richard Sennett, an American sociologist, has shown just how difficult the imperatives of flexibility and risk-taking can be in our new globalized world of work. He has also shown how damaging an economy without long-term commitments or larger meaning can be for self-identity and the self. Sennett's argument, bluntly put, is that we have moved from a work world of rigid, hierarchical organizations, in which self-discipline shaped the durability of the self, to a brave new economy of corporate re-engineering, innovation and risk, in which the fragmented or dislocated nature of self-experience moves to the fore.

In *The Corrosion of Character* (1998), a book that has had a significant impact upon the debate over work in the era of globalization, Sennett contends that a

> change in modern institutional structure has accompanied short-term, contract, or episodic labor. Corporations have sought to remove layers of bureaucracy, to become flatter and more flexible organizations. In place of organizations as pyramids, management wants now to think of organizations as networks. . . . This means that promotions and dismissals tend not to be based on clear, fixed rules, nor are work tasks crisply defined; the network is constantly redefining its structure.

For Sennett, the rise of flexible capitalism, however much flexibility and risk-taking are said to give people more freedom to shape the direction of their lives, actually leads to crushing new burdens and oppressions. Flexible capitalism is 'flexible' insofar as its workers and consumers accept the dictates of a post-hierarchical world, accept that it is they and they alone who must strive to be ever more flexible, and accept the abandonment of traditional models of work as well as standard definitions of success.

'Who needs me?' is a question of character which suffers a radical challenge in modern capitalism. The system radiates indifference. It does so in terms of the outcomes of human striving, as in winner-take-all markets, where there is little connection between risk and reward. It radiates indifference in the organization of absence and trust, where there is no reason to be needed. And it does so through reengineering of institutions in which people are treated as disposable. Such practices obviously and brutally diminish the sense of mattering as a person, of being necessary to others.

The flexibility demanded of workers by multinational corporations, according to Sennett, promotes a dominant conception of individuals as dispensable and disposable. It is against this sociological backdrop that he cites statistics indicating that the average American college student graduating today can expect to hold twelve positions or jobs in their lifetime, plus which they will be required to change their skills base at least three times. From this viewpoint, yesteryear's job for life is replaced today by short-term contract work. No wonder flexible capitalism has its discontents, who find to their dismay that the alleged benefits of free markets are less and less apparent. In a subsequent work, *The Culture of the New Capitalism* (2006), Sennett spells out the deeper emotional consequences of such major organizational changes thus: 'people fear being displaced, sidelined, or underused. The institutional model of the future does not furnish them a life narrative at work, or the promise of much security in the public realm.' Today's corporate culture of short-termism is producing a thoroughgoing erosion of loyalty and trust that employees vest in their workplaces. 'Work identities', writes Sennett, 'get used up, they become exhausted, when institutions themselves are continually reinvented.' In a corporate world where people are always thinking about their next career move, or preparing for major change, it is very difficult to remain loyal to any one company or organization.

Sennett's sociology speaks directly to the practical difficulties of living in a globally interconnected world. He is especially attentive to the personal dimensions of global change, and uses much biographical material in his work to chart the impacts of globalization upon the lives of working people. At the heart of his book *The Corrosion of Character*, for example, is the story of Rico – a materially successful businessman with a very high income, who none the less feels a sense of discontent with his high-pressured lifestyle. What most surprises Sennett about Rico is the degree to which his personal sense of identity is shaped by the dictates of work. For, after graduating from university and marrying a fellow student, Rico changed jobs four times since reaching the top of his profession – with each move carrying complicated emotional disturbances for himself and his family. Rico works in the hi-tech electronics industry; it is a world that involves him in continual networking, online short communications, flexible contracts and the like. In discussion with Sennett, Rico confesses to feeling emotionally adrift and vulnerable; he worries that his highly demanding job leads him to neglect his wife and children; he worries about the weak ties that define his few friendships; he worries, above all, about a lack of ethical discipline, fearing the superficial morality that defines his life. Prosperous as he is, Rico is a man whose life is dominated by the imperatives of the money market; the more he tries to adjust to the dynamic pressures of the global market, the more he feels he is losing control of his purpose in life and his sense of self.

When people are inserted into a world of detachment and superficial cooperativeness, of weak ties and interchangeable relationships, and when all this is shaped by the pursuit of risk-taking and self-reinvention, the power of traditional social norms and cultural traditions begins to diminish. This can be potentially liberating: the self finds the potential to define itself anew and create fluid and innovative social relationships. But there is also something deeply unsettling. For a self that is constituted entirely through episodes and fragments has little to hold itself together in emotional terms; and it is this drift of character, of corrosion of the self, that Sennett fixes his attention firmly upon. According to Sennett, as the coherent life narrative breaks down, so does the symbolic texture of the self. In contemporary social conditions durable selfhood is replaced by a kind of supermarket identity – an assemblage of scraps, random desires, chance encounters, the accidental and the fleeting. Moreover, as Sennett notes (1998: 133), this suits the requirements of dynamic global capitalism: 'A pliant self, a collage of fragments unceasing in its becoming, ever open to the new experience – these are just the psychological conditions suited to the short-term work experience, flexible institutions, and constant risk-taking.' According to Sennett, the flexible regime of the new capitalism – with its instant global transfers of money, its hi-tech cultural production, and its radical restruc- turing of the labour market – begets a character structure geared towards the superficial, the fleeting and the fragmented. 'In the flexible, fragmented present,' writes Sennett (1998: 135), 'it may seem possible only to create coherent narratives about what has been, and no longer possible to create predictive narratives about what will be.'

Uncertain lives in the global electronic economy

Globalization has been debated continuously – by neoliberals who want to push it further, and by anti-globalists who underscore the harm it does – and nowhere more intensively than regarding its impact upon local communities. Globalization, so some argue, erodes local communities. Just as the emergence of industrialism in the nineteenth century was judged destructive to family and community, so many critics today lament the erosion of a common culture and communal cooperation as a consequence of the global economy.

The idea that we have moved from a generous world of the caring community to a wholesale corrosion of communal sentiment is, however, open to question. Blinded by nostalgia for a bygone age, such a viewpoint ignores considerable evidence of the flourishing and expansion of global communal loyalties. These include, to name just a few, communities of global protest (Make Poverty History), worldwide communities for the protection of human rights (Amnesty International), and communities for the protection of the environment (Greenpeace).

Given the increasing hold of globalization over our lives, it is perhaps hardly surprising that multiple communal loyalties are on the increase for more and more of us – or, at least, for those of us who live in the expensive cities of the West. But in the same way that globalization blurs national boundaries and can promote a global civic outlook, so it also transforms experience of local, regional and national communities. The increasing mobility of people today, particularly the sharp rise in the number of those relocating for jobs, is a case in point. Such sociological and demographic changes are of major consequence when considering the future of national communities.

To give depth to the debate over community in our own time of globalization, it is vital to adopt a comparative approach. This means looking in particular at how countries around the world are responding to the challenges of globalization. If, for example, practical life today is increasingly affected by global processes, then it is arguable that progressive politics requires a more robust defence of the value of the community sphere, of public goods, rights and obligations, than so far achieved. It is crucial, in particular, that contemporary societies widen their existing definitions of 'vulnerable communities' – of those individuals and families who are potentially open to, as well as the recipients of, policy initiatives. The emergence of a globally interconnected world arguably shifts politics away from nationally based community policy frameworks, in which vulnerable groups are defined in traditional terms of social dysfunction, to more inclusive definitions of government assistance, as a result of the impact of the global electronic economy. Assessment of community needs and potential welfare recipients can no longer be limited to only disadvantaged or marginalized groups.

In this regard, the speed of change unleashed by the global electronic economy – and particularly the impact of institutional change upon our working and private lives – is critical. In 2006, Princeton economist Gene Grossman spelled out, as transforming and universalizing, a new stage of globalization, one which centres on the virtually instant transfer of service jobs to low-wage economies. Grossman's argument takes its cue from the West's outsourcing of manufacturing, which soared during the late 1980s and 1990s; such outsourcing, he argues, has been transformed today into an apparently unstoppable societal dynamic. The outsourcing of industrial production over recent decades, says Grossman, finds its counterpart today in the outsourcing of knowledge-intensive jobs. He calls this 'global electronic offshoring', which he argues is fast changing our ways of living and working – and will continue to do so in dramatic ways over the coming years. Electronic offshoring for Grossman refers to more than the rise of call centres in countries such as India. For any service job can be electronically outsourced if it involves substantial reliance upon information technology and involves little face-to-face interaction. And this is the really dramatic part of Grossman's research: he estimates that somewhere between thirty and forty million service jobs in the US will become open to electronic offshoring in the near future. Thirty to forty million jobs!

Clearly, if Grossman is right, this spells major change not only for the US but more broadly for the global North. Workers throughout the service sectors of the expensive cites of the West, as with manufacturing some decades previously, will be exposed to intense competition from overseas as never before. And not just unskilled or semi-skilled workers are at risk. The highly skilled and highly educated – working in finance, legal, medical and hi-tech sectors – will come under increased competition from overseas workers. This, he suggests, will carry profoundly traumatic consequences for individual identities and local communities, especially as regards the provision of economic and emotional support for the many whose livelihoods are threatened. Where does this leave people in terms of their work? Consigned to the spectre of uselessness? Not necessarily, thankfully. For one thing, retraining and redeployment are now key offshoots of many large-scale organizational retrenchments. Moreover, offshoring to date has only affected a small proportion of jobs in the advanced economies, and so it is not possible to say with any degree of confidence how the global job market will develop in the future. But while this may be reassuring in one sense, it clearly isn't in another. How could anyone now believe, say, in the long-term management of companies or organizations, or for that matter in long-term careers, after reading Grossman? Dilemmas and quandaries are now the plight of contemporary women and men seeking to sketch out a basically safe psychological platform when moving from job to job, contract to contract, network to network. But in our fast-globalizing electronic economy, the more astute accept that short-term jobs, contracts and networks are the new realities. What matters is flexibility – the plastic, reshaped sense of self which these new institutional forms of the global economy at once produce and demand. Thus the typical modern dilemma: How to be flexible enough to survive high levels of personal and cultural drift without being left drained of identity?

Globalization, communication and culture

Thanks to today's vast global flows of information, imagery and identity, the icons of popular culture are legion. McDonald's, Coke, Nokia, Apple, Gucci, Nike: these are just a few of the transnational companies advancing global products and brands in and through which people's identities are remade and transformed in the context of an intensive consumer culture. Sociological studies have devoted much attention to the rise of electronic media globalization in terms of addressing the huge expansion in information diffusion and advertising of consumer goods and other cultural products. In these diverse studies, people's identities and experience of everyday life are understood as marked irrevocably by the emergence of global communication networks and new information technologies. The sheer scale, intensity and speed of mass communication and media technology emerges, in this viewpoint, as an unprecedented feature of global society. In historical terms, it is of course the case that people have, by and large, lived out their daily lives in a web of local cultures – consisting largely of set routines and local interactions structured along national and territorial lines. In an age of so-called global mass culture, however, such cultural fixity well and truly fragments; the more the global spread of communication networks and telecommunications systems occurs, the denser and more complex become patterns of cultural life and layers of identity. Or, as we will see, so say some sociological authors.

In the past few decades, major transformations have occurred within the media industries. The spread of communication infrastructures – radio, television, the Internet, satellite and digital technologies – has made instant communication across the globe a daily reality for many. Such transformations in communication stem from the early 1970s, when the first telecommunications satellites were positioned in geo-synchronous orbits, thus allowing for the emergence of virtually instantaneous electronic communication between individuals, institutions, societies and cultures. These and related new technologies have, in turn, spelt a shift away from national controls over media information and towards a global market in which information cuts through and across geo-political boundaries. Also striking about today's media globalization is that it is largely driven by corporate interests: the producers and distributors of contemporary global media encompass about twenty multinational corporations, from TimeWarner to Rupert Murdoch's News International.

For many critics, the rise of global communication systems has gone hand in hand with the erosion of national culture. The massive cultural flows of electronic media globalization, in this view, fragment the power of national identity and territorial axes of identity more generally. There are various political anxieties at work here. Some critics worry about the threat that unrestricted global media pose to the workings of democracy. Edward Herman and Robert McChesney (1997), for example, point to the dangers of a commercialized media dominated by global corporations in which entertainment triumphs over political debate and civic participation. Other critics, while still concerned with commercialization and the power of transnational corporations, are more concerned with the structural changes associated with media globalization. According to these critics, the global media are little more than the purveyors of a new cultural uniformity. This is, in short, the thesis of *global cultural imperialism* – in which the media function to implant American values and ideologies in less developed countries.

M edia globalization effects, while still hard to sort out, are dominated by commercialization and its impact on the public sphere. For smaller and less economically developed countries, there is a further force of economies of scale and technical and

As we have seen throughout this book, however, we need to be especially
careful when such comprehensive claims are made about the future
direction of society. While many worry about the Westernization or
Americanization of communication networks today, there is considerable
sociological evidence to suggest that the picture remains more complex,
perhaps even puzzling. According to critics of the cultural imperialism
thesis, for example, the globalization of communication does not, in fact,
spell the globalization of culture. Globalization, it is argued, does not have
any single one consequence. Notwithstanding the growing corporate control
of communication networks today, as social theorist John B. Thompson
argues in his book *The Media and Modernity* (1995), media messages are
continually interpreted in novel ways by national audiences. Whether watching American serials like *The Sopranos* or *Six Feet Under* in Asia, listening
to hip-hop in China, or surfing the Net in Lagos, there are a multiplicity
of background assumptions, discourses, norms, values and ideologies
through which people make sense of media messages and products. This,
according to Thompson, would suggest that cultural diversification is hardly
at an end with the advent of globalization. According to another study by
media theorist John Tomlinson (1991), imported media products are always
locally interpreted and transformed in the process of such local readings.
This is not to deny that cultural imperialism poses significant risks to various
local cultures. It is rather to assert that new global communication systems
create 'hybrid cultures'; electronic media globalization, as Stuart Hall has
suggested, can have a 'pluralizing impact' on identities. The emphasis here
is on the word *can*; the task of future social theory is to critically probe and
interrogate the social conditions through which global media can both
enhance and undermine national cultures and national identities.

> The undeniably high profile of the mass media in contemporary cultural practices set against the evidence that people bring other cultural resources to their dealings with it, suggests that we can view the relationship between media and culture as a subtle *interplay of mediations*. Thus we may think of the media as the dominant *representational* aspect of modern culture. But the 'lived experience' of culture may also include the discursive interaction of families and friends and the material-existence of routine life: eating, working, being well or unwell, sexuality, the sense of the passage of time and so on.
>
> John Tomlinson (1991) *Cultural Imperialism: A Critical Introduction*. London: Pinter, p. 61.

Globalization and the new individualism

Globalization, to repeat the argument of this chapter, reshapes not only institutions and organizations but also the very fabric of identity and personal life. In some of my own recent writings with the American sociologist Charles Lemert, notably *The New Individualism: The Emotional Costs of Globalization* (Elliott and Lemert 2006), we have sought to broaden the debate over globalization by examining how individuals react to, and cope with, corporate and networking pressures at the level of self-identity. Our contention, broadly speaking, is that throughout the polished, expensive cities of the West there is an emergent 'new individualism' centred on continual self-actualization and instant self-reinvention. Today this is nowhere more evident than in the pressure consumerism puts on us to 'transform' and 'improve' every aspect of ourselves: not just our homes and gardens but our careers, our food, our clothes, our sex lives, our faces, minds and bodies. This reinvention trend occurs all around us, not only in the rise of plastic surgery and the instant identity makeovers of reality TV but also in compulsive consumerism, speed dating and therapy culture. In a world that places a premium on instant gratification, the desire for immediate results has never been as pervasive or acute. We have become accustomed to emailing others across the planet in seconds, buying flashy consumer goods with the click of a mouse, and drifting in and out of relations with others without long-term commitments. Is it any wonder that we now have different expectations about life's possibilities and the potential for change?

What are the broader social forces sustaining this new individualism? We suggest three key institutional features impinging on people's emotional experiences of globalization: consumerism, neoliberalism and privatization.

In conditions of advanced globalization, our language for expressing individualism is more and more fixed into the syntax of possession, ownership, control and market value. What we are suggesting is that people today increasingly suffer from an emotionally pathologizing version of neo-liberalism. What is pathological is the blinkered fixation on *instant change* – whether of the body, selfhood or society. The desire for instant reinvention of the self, Lemert and I argue, links to much broader institutional transformations of the world order. For the culture of globalization, as Richard Sennett rightly notes, is governed by the logic of acute short-termism. Authors such as Sennett see the flexibility demanded of workers by multinational corporations as demonstrating the reality of globalization, promoting a dominant conception of individuals as dispensable and disposable. But Sennett fails to critically probe, we argue, just how far down the global ethos of short-termism penetrates the emotional landscape of the self. For it is precisely the emergence of an ambient fear of disposability – of not measuring up to the craze for reinvention in personal and intimate life, family and work – that fuels the emergence of 'the new individualism'. This is a form of individualism based on a new cultural imperative for people to be more efficient, faster, leaner, inventive and self-actualizing than they were previously – not sporadically, but day-in day-out. Such an imperative lends to social life a radically experimental quality, with the thrills and spills of the new individualism to the fore. But the emotional costs are also high, and indeed many of the stories we recount of contemporary women and men in *The New Individualism* are those of personal confusion, intense anxiety and disquieting depression. Such emotional tribulations are not simply private problems however, as the new individualism is first and foremost a consequence of our world of intensive globalization. In smashing apart traditional national boundaries, globalization, ironically, offers people a kind of 'absolute freedom' to do whatever they like. The irony is that the world of 'everything goes' has become crippling, as the anxiety of choice floats unhinged from both practical and ethical considerations as to what is worth pursuing. For those enticed and seduced by the new individualism, the danger of self-reinvention is a form of change so rapid and so complete that identity becomes disposable. Instead of finding ourselves, we lose ourselves.

Summary points

1   Globalization refers to the chronic intensification of patterns of interconnectedness (economic, technological, organizational,

administrative, among others) generating transnational or inter-regional flows of activity and networks of interaction.

2 Globalization impacts on all aspects of current social life, from the rise of multinational companies to global warming.

3 Some critics equate globalization with Americanization or Westernization. Others focus on the historical dimensions of global-ization, tracing its conditions to the 'age of discovery'.

4 There are three core social theories of globalization. *Global sceptics* question an overall shift towards world integration. *Radical glob-alists* see globalization as heralding new forms of social life based on free trade and open markets. *Global transformationalists* see less the dawning of an entirely new age than a transformation of previous structures.

5 Today's world of global interconnectedness permeated by supra-national, intergovernmental and transnational forces gives rise to novel possibilities for the spread of cosmopolitanism and global governance.

6 Global networks are also intricately interwoven with the emergence of new political threats and risks, such as hi-tech terrorism. Some critics view transnational terror networks – such as Al-Qaeda – as threatening the fabric of the world as we know it.

7 The routine corporate downsizing, and associated job insecurity, associated with the global electronic economy has profound conse-quences for people's working lives. Globalization, in the view of sociologist Richard Sennett, is producing a 'corrosion of character'.

8 There is much sociological debate over the consequences of global-ization as regards culture and everyday life. Some critics equate globalization with the erosion of national culture. Such new patterns of social uniformity are the result of *global cultural imperialism*. But other critics doubt that globalization produces any single one consequence. There is considerable sociological evidence which demonstrates, on the contrary, that global media are producing 'hybrid cultures' and pluralized social identities.

9 Globalization is said to be tied to the emergence of new forms of individualism. The *new individualism* is fixated on instant change and short-term living.

Further questions

1 To what extent is the world globalized? Is the 'global turn' merely partial to the West, or is it now wall-to-wall across all societies?

2 It is easy to grasp the economic forces of globalization, but harder to understand the globalization of culture and personal life. Discuss.

3 When did globalization arise?

4 How does globalization give rise to new job insecurities?

5 What are the prospects for global cosmopolitan society?

Further reading

Anthony Giddens, *Runaway World: How Globalization is Reshaping Our Lives* (Profile Books, 2002).
David Held *et al.*, *Global Transformations* (Polity Press, 1999).
Robert Holton, *Global Networks* (Palgrave, 2008).

Internet links

The Centre for the Study of Global Governance

http://www.lse.ac.uk/Depts/global/

Economic Policy Institute: Trade and Globalization

http://www.epinet.org/

The Globalist

http://www.theglobalist.com

Globalizaton Index

http://foreignpolicy.com/story/cms.php?story_id=2493

The Globalization Website

http://www.sociology.emory.edu/globalization/

International Forum on Globalization

http://www.ifg.org/

Afterword: Social Theory Today and Towards 2025

From Giorgio Agamben to Manuel DeLanda

In the course of this book we have critically considered a number of key perspectives in contemporary social theory. From the Frankfurt School to globalization theories, we have looked at the profound troubles arising from the whole language and culture of modernity. Social theory, we have seen, is vitally engaged with the repression, oppression and indignity of unequal social relations: it is a deeply political, sometimes melancholic, but profoundly humane critique of the structural forces which underlay the self-destructive pathologies of contemporary societies. Indeed, so serious is the damage done to human life today that much social theory insists it is only by confronting the worst and most painful aspects of current global realities that we may hope to develop plausible alternative social and institutional possibilities. Hence the surprising innovations of recent years – post-feminist, queer, postmodern, risk and liquidity theories – which address anew why modernity leaves so large a number of the world's population unsatisfied, displaced and outcast.

When social theory does the excavating work of digging behind cultural illusions, it engages most directly with the public sphere and the whole issue of the future direction of political society. Yet some critics claim that social theory is merely obscurantist jargon. The criticism, in brief, is that social theory inserts arid abstractions which have little to do with the concrete realities of politics. Still more: the charge is made that social theory is near powerless in changing how we think about politics and social things.

Against the backdrop of such criticism, let us in conclusion briefly consider some recent public interventions by social theorists – both for what they have to tell us about the political nature of social theory and its capacity to impact upon our worlds. In a series of articles over recent years, published in the Opinion columns of such newspapers as *International Herald Tribune* and *The Guardian*, Anthony Giddens has addressed the massive disconnect between the high-consequence risks of globalization on the one hand, and the lifestyle changes necessary to combat these worldwide risks on the other. He has argued, in a provocative and polemical fashion, that the major issues of our time do not reduce to traditional divisions in politics between Left and Right. From climate change to energy security to coping with international crime, today's major political problems transcend nation-state boundaries, as well as traditional national categories of thought used for so many years to frame nation-state politics. The core changes arising from the global electronic economy help to create, says Giddens, a new agenda for politics – at least in terms of policy thinking. The political challenge today – on global economic crises, transnational terrorism, global warming – is for nations to find new ways of working together, cooperating through transnational forums and processes and intergovernmentalism to develop novel models of 'global governance'. This is, in effect, the quantum leap for politics in the early twenty-first century: shifting from nation-state politics to globally cosmopolitan politics.

Giddens' call for a more cosmopolitan approach to politics in our age of globalization is born partly out of his social theory of reflexivity and structuration – discussed in detail in Chapter 5. This, to be sure, is not necessarily easy to spot or substantiate. In the large bulk of his newspaper articles, for example, Giddens does not use the more difficult social-theoretical terminology of 'structuration', 'time-space distantiation' or 'reflexivity'. To the extent that he shies away from such specialist discourse, his political interventions may be likened to, say, a paediatrician or computer scientist commenting in plain language on some aspect of their research competence. There is thus something of a divide between the conceptual analysis informing Giddens' recent political contributions and his media framing of them. But the point is that social theory is at the core of this analysis, at least for anyone who cares to look. Giddens' arguments in favour of 'positive welfare', for instance, derive from his social theory – which holds that globalization ushers into existence an increasingly reflexive citizenry. In the shift to post-traditional or post-industrial society, the old social stratification has gradually been replaced by a new pattern of 'individualization' – where people are much more involved in the self-design of their lifestyles. This necessitates for Giddens a transformation from the traditional welfare state of support and dependency to novel forms of enabling welfare.

It is one thing to write opinion articles, and yet another to actually influence the shape of contemporary politics. But it is just that which Giddens has done, giving the slip in the process to the charge that social theory is removed from concrete politics. For Giddens, as noted in Chapter 5, developed the notion of 'the third way' in political thinking, first, as an adviser to UK Prime Minister Tony Blair (where he also played a role in Blair's dialogues with US President Bill Clinton from 1997 onwards), and second, as a member of the House of Lords in the British Parliament. The level at which Giddens has moved in British political circles clearly represents an extraordinary contribution to civic and public life. But the power of Giddens' social and political theory does not end there, as both his account of 'third way' politics as well as his broader social theory penetrates well beyond the UK and US to encompass Europe, Asia, Latin America and Australia. At work on projects as diverse as the future of the European social model on the one hand, and the obesity epidemic and associated lifestyle issues on the other, Giddens has become the most sought-after social theorist – by political leaders, think-tanks and universities – in the world today.

Compare Giddens' political interventions as a social theorist with those of Manuel Castells. In 2008, Castells appeared as part of the 'Big Thinker' lecture series sponsored by Yahoo! Research. Acknowledging that for too long social theory had sidelined the social implications of communications technology, Castells reappraised the relationship between society and the Internet. Social theory may have been silent on the socially beneficial aspects of new information technologies, but so at the same time had nearly everyone. The media was especially to blame in this connection. 'Media sensationalism', argued Castells (2008), 'is responsible because it always picks up on bad news.' Yet there are many ways in which the Internet extends and reshapes social relations, and Castells is particularly attentive to how such technology might be harnessed to create a more autonomous society. 'The Internet', says Castells, 'does not isolate users, nor does it depress or alienate. The more you use the Internet, the more social you are offline. The Internet adds, rather than subtracts, sociability.' Elsewhere, Castells details statistics on blogs and the Internet thus: of the sixty million blogs worldwide, one is created every second and 55 per cent of new bloggers remain active after two months of Internet use. While only 9 per cent of blogs are directly political in scope, Castells points out 'still, that's a lot of blogging'. In the end, says Castells, the Internet in general increases political interests and activities.

contemporary social theory

However, as it happens, there is no need to rehearse the exceptional contributions of Giddens and Castells as somehow unique in terms of the import of social theory for public political debate. In fact, the bulk of luminary social theorists reviewed in the course of this book have not only contributed to the public sphere and politics, but have found ways of extending and enriching it. The pioneering contributions of Herbert Marcuse, Theodor Adorno, Roland Barthes, Michel Foucault and Jacques Derrida have been of lasting value to debates on both repression and freedom in contemporary politics. Jürgen Habermas, Zygmunt Bauman, Ulrich Beck, Judith Butler, Slavoj Žižek, Fredric Jameson, Homi Bhabha, Julia Kristeva: these too are social theorists who have spent their lives not only studying the social world and its struggles, but as politically engaged public intellectuals. Their contribution has been, among other things, an engagement with fundamental questions about power, domination, repression, identity, sexuality and intimacy in contemporary social processes. And it has been through consideration of these matters – in outlining social theories which are, admittedly, sometimes dense or difficult, but for the most part arrestingly original – that these authors have had a great deal to say about contemporary politics, culture and society.

There remain some key questions which as yet have not been raised. What is the future of social theory? Do recent developments in society, culture and politics give us any indication of where social theory might be headed over, say, the next five to ten years? And will social theory continue to promote the general good of society? Will social theory still engage sizeable publics in 2025? These questions cannot be answered in a simple fashion, partly given the complexity of social theory as an interdisciplinary enterprise and partly because social theory is not really in the business of seeking to predict the future. Yet there is another reason why it is not easy to speculate about the future of social theory. The review of contemporary developments in social theory provided in the course of this book suggests that the prevailing violence, risks and dangers facing the planet are coming closer and closer to smashing the established social structures of modern life. This is perhaps but another way of saying we may be facing the end of the world as we know it – although whether new, more dynamic types of societies and spaces are likely to emerge remains, as some post-structuralists are fond of saying, 'undecidable'. But what surely is self-evident – at the levels of both professional and practical social theory – concerns those radical transformations in social institutions with which intellectuals, political activists and policy-makers, as well as ordinary people, have long traded. I refer to core transformations in the very institutional units of society, from identity and sexuality to the family and work to the nation and politics. These institutional units are both eroding and recombining right before our eyes in these early years of the twenty-first century, and in the remainder of what follows I want to briefly examine some of the more interesting attempts in social theory to develop, if not exactly the answers, at least some interesting-sounding questions about our possible global futures.

Contemporary social theory, I have suggested, began with the German School of Frankfurt critique. In the works of Adorno, Marcuse and Fromm, there was a powerful attempt to understand the pain of those who suffered under Hitler – as well as the wider society living under conditions of 'the administered society' – in both emotional and historical terms. Social theory following the Frankfurt School, right through to the present day, has continued to be shaped by forms of political and ideological turmoil occurring in contemporary societies. In more recent social theory, for example, Zygmunt Bauman has also discussed political themes such as violence, suffering and death, and how they apply to our increasingly global world. For Bauman, the killing of six million Jewish people by the Nazis cannot be explained as a simple reversion from civilized modernity to pre-Enlightenment barbarism. The Holocaust, says Bauman, could only happen because of modernity's twin combination of bureaucracy and technology. Along with gas chambers and other modern technologies facilitating mass murder, the hold of bureaucratic rationality in Hitler's Germany created the social conditions in which moral responsibility evaporated. Similarly the keynote to life lived in today's so-called global cosmopolitan society, at least according to several leading European social theorists, remains that of the *concentration camp*. In the relatively short historical march from Auschwitz to Guantanamo Bay, says the Italian social theorist Giorgio Agamben, a 'state of emergency' has been turned into the norm for constitutional political power in Western democracies. While legal systems may make provisions for interventions of various kinds, there is a wider change of governance across the world – or so Agamben argues – in which the rule of law is routinely displaced by the 'state of exception', understood as the platform through which extra-judicial state violence is inflicted upon citizens.

Agamben understands the political emergence of permanent states of exception largely in terms of Foucault's critique of biopolitics, of which the United States' response under the Bush presidency to the terror attacks of 11 September 2001 is surely a signal example. The political irony of post-9/11 biopower politics, for a critic such as Agamben, is that the state of emergency that was the 'war on terror' was meant to protect the general population from terrorism – whereas it resulted, arguably, in a weakening of the freedoms of democratic society. What Agamben calls 'bare life' is precisely an attempt to think through the violence, degradation and suffering of extra-judicial violence inflicted upon the bodies of individuals today, from camp inmates to terror hostages. Agamben's 'bare life', in the words of

Malcolm Bull, 'provides the perfect metaphor for the naked and humiliated prisoners on Abu Ghraib' – the notorious prison in post-war Iraq, where US soldiers brutalized Iraqi prisoners.

One newly emerging task of social theory, broadly conceived, consists in the dissection of the political conditions under which the planet is shared – probing the structured violence underpinning mass death, diseases and malnutrition, and ever-rising levels of poverty. From this vantage point, over half the world's population may be said to live the hell of 'bare life'. 'Each year,' as David Held summarizes one of the most pressing global issues of our times,

> some 18 million die prematurely from poverty-related causes. This is one third of all human deaths – 50,000 every day, including 29,000 children under the age of five. And, yet, the gap between rich and poor countries continues to rise and there is evidence that the bottom 10% of the world's population has become even poorer since the beginning of the 1990s.

Held's summary of the global challenges to be faced reflects not only the extensive and intensive reach of 'bare life' today, but perhaps also the possibility that such a truly shocking reality might just one day erupt unpredictably on the political scene, transforming the very structured violence which maintains modernity's self-destructiveness. Any such possible eruption is what the leading French philosopher Alain Badiou (2007) calls an 'Event', some exceptional break with the status quo or political consensus. According to Badiou, whose work has influenced Agamben, an Event can erupt on the edges of the very coordinates of social reality, at that point or void where meaning threatens to dissolve into non-meaning. As a result, new truths can be expanded, to the extent that individuals and groups are genuinely committed to the radical implications of such an Event. There is, no doubt, a great deal of French philosophical idealism about this notion, but it is worth noting that Badiou's thinking has inspired various new directions in social theory for confronting some of the most pressing global issues of our times.

If Badiou's work has pursued the philosophical possibilities for the breakup, symbolic ruin and broader transformation of received political meanings, other social theorists have been concerned to map the restructuring of the very coordinates of social reality. While the motive driving society has been interpreted by Marxists and post-Marxists as economic or materialist, and by Freudians and Lacanians as unconscious or affective, there is an emerging consensus that today's social coordinates are being rewritten around the politics of survival itself. In *High Noon: Twenty Global Problems, Twenty Years to Solve Them* (2002), Jean-François Rischard sets out core global challenges ranging from water and energy deficits to global warming, from toxic waste disposal to nuclear proliferation of weapons of mass destruction. But given the complexity of global social processes, it is far from settled or secure whether it is still possible to speak of a 'we' for confronting the variety of political challenges faced today. In *The Sense of The World* (1997), Jean-Luc Nancy reflects on what it means to say we live in 'the world'. Worlds, rather than world, is for Nancy a better way to grasp our 'being-with' others – including all the others separated from us in space and in time that we are unlikely to ever meet, but to whom we have a 'radical responsibility'. What Nancy calls 'naked existence' represents our increasing exposure today to a post-traditional world – one in which the meaning and destination of life is far from fixed or predetermined. The global challenge, according to Nancy, is living within a plurality of worlds without guarantees. The challenge lies in embracing human contingency.

We have seen that a particular version of post-structuralism, sometimes transmuted as postmodernism, was the essential relay by which the whole notion of contingency entered the terrain of radical politics in the late 1980s and throughout the 1990s. In our own time, there has been a further inflation of the value of the 'contingent' in radical social theory. In a number of works bridging complexity theory with Deleuzian philosophy, Manuel DeLanda firmly rejects the kind of determinism of classical physics – which rendered the past as given and treated the future as pre-set – and instead faces head-on the radical implications for society of indeterminacy, multidirectionality and the 'politics of becoming'. In *A New Philosophy of Society* (2006), DeLanda considers the disabling gap between subject and object, between past and future, pointing out that there is in fact no given order in social reality at all. Behind this Nietzschean approach to theorizing social space and time lies DeLanda's attempt to conceptualize history without a determinate beginning or end. Speaking up for the contingent, the indeterminate and ambivalent, DeLanda is out to capture multiple times, plural spaces and divergent social possibilities. Such a heady decentring of causality has a certain undeniable euphoric quality, in the sense that there may be nothing more life-affirming than to say 'we can become whoever we wish to be'. (This may be the point to note that, while born in Mexico, DeLanda now resides in the United States.) But if this can-do philosophy is uplifting at the level of considering possible alternative worlds, it may be less than useful for grasping why my credit card statement arrives at the beginning of every month without fail or why the rent is due at month's end. In other words, this is a social theory that makes more of the world's future possibilities than adequately theorizing much of the social control exerted over cultural affairs that we take for granted.

Whatever we might make of these political limitations, DeLanda is much preoccupied with *creation*, but refers this issue to certain frames of reference derived from biology and 'matter'. What DeLanda calls 'morphogenesis' refers to particular states of 'becoming' (both at the levels of identity and society) which are organized intensively – involving differentiation, profusion, excess. The creativity of society for DeLanda is plastic, the future is radically open-ended, and the shaping of self and society involves a shaping of plural temporalities and spaces and a multiplicity of values. A similar sense of the unpredictable, but none the less ordered or contained, emerges as central to complexity theory dealing with the intricate interrelations between the physical and the social worlds (see e.g. Fritjof Capra's *The Web of Life* (1996)).

The notion of 'creation' suggests, finally, the writings of the late European social theorist Cornelius Castoriadis. While I have not introduced the work of Castoriadis in previous chapters, there is a sense in which much of the argument of this book would not be possible without his contribution. For what has come about with the later development of global capitalism, so Castoriadis argues, is a progressive hollowing-out of the radical imagination of individuals, social relations and the resources of cultural tradition. Such radical imagination, bound up as it is with selfhood and the Freudian unconscious, lies at the core of *human creation* in the strongest sense of the term. It is this creative dimension of both identity and society to which the large bulk of Castoriadis' writings are devoted. What he wishes to capture for social theory is the creation of an imaginary which is radically new, multidimensional and invented, literally, out of thin air. In the broadest sense of the term, he writes of imagination as an unconscious eruption, of creation '*ex nihilo*' – meaning 'out of nothing'. The flip side of such imaginative creativity are the personal and emotional straitjackets resulting from a sociocultural system based on bureaucratic know-how and capitalistic greed – both of which enfeeble the depth and power of human creativity.

In *The Imaginary Institution of Society* (1987), Castoriadis argues that the creativity of the psyche is a site of multiple, fractured and contradictory *representations* of the individual in relation to self, to other people, and to society and history. He argues that the psyche is continually elaborating representations, fantasies, affects; as the flow of representations is produced, so new positionings of self and other are defined, which in turn leads to newer forms of fantasy, identification and cultural process. There is for Castoriadis a delicious indeterminacy at the heart of the Freudian unconscious, such that the regulative hierarchies of self, sexuality, gender and power are constantly rearranged and sometimes transformed, at least partially as a consequence of this ceaseless psychic flux.

At its simplest, Castoriadis' emphasis on the creative nature of the imagination underscores the permutation of fantasies and identifications that selves produce endlessly in relation to society and history. We insert ourselves, through the psychic flux of imagination, at one and the same moment as both creator and created, self and other, identity and difference; we draw on existing social institutions and cultural conventions to produce new images of self and society, which in turn feed back into the cycle of representations. In all this, Castoriadis' central theme is creativity – of the individual self and of the broader society. Underlining creativity, his theoretical position is a far cry from the insipid, commercially constructed notion of the 'ever-new' in popular culture. What distinguishes his position from popular understandings of creativity is his stress on the open-ended and ambivalent nature of psychic representation and cultural production, and it is this stress which necessarily involves reflecting on the more distressing aspects of violence, aggression and destruction in contemporary culture. 'Creation', writes Castoriadis (1991: 3–4), 'does not necessarily – nor even generally – signify "good" creation or the creation of "positive values". Auschwitz and the Gulag are creations just as much as the Parthenon and the *Principia Mathematica*.' It is hard – says Castoriadis – to grasp, and harder to understand, that socio-political paths or fields of imagination stretch all the way from progressive politics to fanaticism and fascism. But the search for alternative futures, and the search for autonomy and justice, are among the creations in Western history that people value highly and judge positively; the practice of critique, of putting things into question, forms a common starting point for a radical challenge to received social and political meanings.

Agamben, Badiou, Nancy, DeLanda, Castoriadis: these are just some of the path-breaking social theorists of recent years. Will their originality and political ambitiousness be discussed and debated in 2025? Possibly. But the point is that no one can say with any degree of confidence what the future holds for social theory. Social theories derive from the serious attempts of women and men to make sense out of the unthinkable social things that harm, constrain, repress or damage life; social theories are of value when they most directly engage, and seek to transform, the political and ideological turmoil out of which they were born, and in the process offer alternative visions of how our personal and social lives could be lived otherwise. In terms of the important writers I have been discussing, it is clear that the themes of human creation, imagination, our 'being-with' others, and the question of autonomy present social theory with fresh challenges. In other words, what social theory requires are multi-perspectival approaches through which it can at once critique the failure of human life to flourish under specific social conditions on the one hand, and defend human needs and desires for alternative forms of life concerned with pleasure, creativity and autonomy on the other. Undeniably, the global challenges we face demand global solutions, and ones that are both future-regarding and geared to the actual needs and desires of others.

Further reading

On the political contribution and impact of social theorists, any regular glance at good-quality broadsheets should reveal a great deal. As discussed in this Afterword, current social theorists contributing on a regular basis to the media include Anthony Giddens, Ulrich Beck, Jürgen Habermas, Manuel Castells, Slavoj Žižek, David Held, Julia Kristeva, and many others.

For Giddens' recent contributions, see his article 'This Time It's Personal', *Guardian*, 2 January 2008. The Castells lecture to Yahoo! Research is available at www.research.yahoo.com/node/2189.

The best place to start reading Agamben is *State of Exception* (Chicago University Press, 2005). See also his *Homo Sacer: Sovereign Power and Bare Life* (Stanford University Press, 1998). For starting Alain Badiou, see his *Being and Event* (Continuum, 2007). For Jean-Luc Nancy, see his collection *Corpus* (Continuum, 2008). For Manuel DeLanda, try *A Thousand Years of Nonlinear History* (Zone Books, 2000). And for Cornelius Castoriadis, read his classic *The Imaginary Institution of Society* (Polity Press, 1987).

References

Adorno, T. (1950) *The Authoritarian Personality*, New York: Harper.

Adorno, T. (1973) *Negative Dialectics*, London: Routledge.

Adorno, T. (1974) [1951] *Minima Moralia: Reflections from Damaged Life*, London: New Left Books.

Adorno, T. (1991) [1951] 'Freudian Theory and the Pattern of Fascist Propaganda' in J. M. Bernstein (ed.) *The Culture Industry: Selected Essays on Mass Culture*, London: Routledge, pp. 132–57.

Adorno, T. (1994) *The Stars Down to Earth: And Other Essays on the Irrational Culture*, London: Routledge.

Adorno, T. (2001) *The Culture Industry*, London: Routledge.

Adorno, T. and M. Horkheimer (2002) [1944] *Dialectic of Enlightenment: Philosophical Fragments*, Stanford, CA: Stanford University Press.

Agamben, G. (1998) *Homo Sacer: Sovereign Power and Bare Life*, Stanford, CA: Stanford University Press.

Agamben, G. (2005) *State of Exception*, Chicago, IL: University of Chicago Press.

Alexander, J. C. (1996) 'Critical Reflections on 'Reflexive Modernization', *Theory, Culture and Society*, 13(4): 133–8.

Alford, C. F. (1985) *Science and the Revenge of Nature: Marcuse and Habermas*, Gainesville, FL: University of Florida Press.

Althusser, L. (1971) 'Ideology and Ideological State Apparatuses', in *Lenin and Philosophy and Other Essays*, London: New Left Books, pp. 121–73.

Anderson, P. (1998) *The Origins of Postmodernity*, London: Verso.

Arato, A. and E. Gebhardt (eds) (1982) *Essential Frankfurt School Reader*, New York: Continuum.

Archer, M. (1982) 'Morphogenesis Versus Structuration: On Combining Structure and Action', *British Journal of Sociology*, 33(4): 455–83.

Archer, M. (1990) 'Human Agency and Social Structure: A Critique of Giddens', in

contemporary social theory

J. Clark, C. Modgil and S. Modgil (eds) *Anthony Giddens: Consensus & Controversy*, London: Falmer Press, pp. 73–84.

Badiou, A. (2007) *Being and Event*, London: Continuum.

Barber, B. (1996) *Jihad vs. McWorld*, New York.

Barthes, R. (1967) [1964] *Elements of Semiology*, London: Jonathan Cape.

Barthes, R. (1972) [1957] *Mythologies*, London: Jonathan Cape.

Barthes, R. (1983) [1967] *The Fashion System*, New York: Hill and Wang.

Baudrillard, J. (1975) [1973] *The Mirror of Production*, St Louis, MO: Telos.

Baudrillard, J. (1981) [1972] *For a Critique of the Political Economy of the Sign*, St Louis, MO: Telos.

Baudrillard, J. (1990a) *Fatal Strategies*, New York: Semiotext(e).

Baudrillard, J. (1990b) *Seduction*, Basingstoke: Macmillan Education.

Baudrillard, J. (1994) [1981] *Simulation and Simulacra*, Ann Arbor, MI: University of Michigan Press.

Baudrillard, J. (1995) *The Gulf War Did Not Take Place*, Sydney: Power Publications.

Baudrillard, J. (1996) [1968] *The System of Objects*, New York: Verso Press.

Baudrillard, J. (1998) *America*, London: Verso.

Baudrillard, J. (1998) [1972] *The Consumer Society: Myths and Structures*, London: Sage.

Baudry, J.-L. (1970) 'The Ideological Effects of the Cinematographic Apparatus', in P. Rosen (ed.) *Narrative, Apparatus, Ideology: A Film Reader*, New York: Columbia University Press, pp. 286–98.

Bauman, Z. (1972) *Between Class and Elite*, Manchester: Manchester University Press.

Bauman, Z. (1973) *Culture as Praxis*, London: Routledge.

Bauman, Z. (1976) *Socialism: The Active Utopia*, London: Allen & Unwin.

Bauman, Z. (1982) *Memories of Class*, London: Routledge.

Bauman, Z. (1987) *Legislators and Interpreters: On Modernity, Post-modernity, and Intellectuals*, Ithaca, NY: Cornell University Press.

Bauman, Z. (1989) *Modernity and the Holocaust*, Cambridge: Polity Press.

Bauman, Z. (1991) *Modernity and Ambivalence*, Ithaca, NY: Cornell University Press.

Bauman, Z. (1993) *Postmodern Ethics*, Oxford: Blackwell.

Bauman, Z. (1995) *Life in Fragments: Essays in Postmodern Morality*, Oxford: Blackwell.

Bauman, Z. (1997) *Postmodernity and Its Discontents*, Cambridge: Polity Press.

Bauman, Z. (2000) *Liquid Modernity*, Cambridge: Polity Press.

Bauman, Z. (2001a) *Community: Seeking Safety in an Insecure World*, Cambridge: Polity Press.

Bauman, Z. (2001b) *The Individualized Society*, Cambridge: Polity Press.

Bauman, Z. (2001c) 'Quality and Inequality', *Guardian*, 29 December.

Bauman, Z. (2002) *Society Under Siege*, Cambridge: Polity Press.

Bauman, Z. (2003) *Liquid Love: On the Frailty of Human Bonds*, Cambridge: Polity Press.

Bauman, Z. (2004a) *Identity: Conversations with Benedetto Vecchi*, Cambridge: Polity Press.

Bauman, Z. (2004b) *Wasted Lives: Modernity and Its Outcasts*, Oxford: Polity Press.

Bauman, Z. (2005) *Liquid Lives*, Cambridge: Polity Press.

Bauman, Z. and P. Beilharz (2001) 'The Journey Never Ends: Zygmunt Bauman talks with Peter Beilharz', in P. Beilharz (ed.) *The Bauman Reader*, Oxford: Blackwell, pp. 18–29.

Bauman, Z. and N. Gane (2004) 'Zygmunt Bauman: Liquid Sociality', in N. Gane (ed.) *The Future of Social Theory*, London: Continuum, pp. 17–46.

Bauman, Z. and B. Vecchi (2004) *Identity: Conversations with Benedetto Vecchi*, Cambridge: Polity Press.

Bauman, Z. *et al.* (2001) 'The Telos Interview', in P. Beilharz (ed.) *The Bauman Reader*, Oxford: Blackwell, pp. 334–44.

Beauvoir, S. de (1988) [1949] *The Second Sex*, London: Picador Classics.

Beck, U. (1991) *Ecological Enlightenment: Essays on the Politics of the Risk Society*, Amherst, NY: Prometheus Books.

Beck, U. (1992) *Risk Society: Towards a New Modernity*, London: Sage.

Beck, U. (1996) 'Risk Society and the Provident State', in S. Lash, B. Szersynski and B. Wynne (eds) *Risk, Environment and Modernity: Towards a New Ecology*, London: Sage, pp. 27–43.

Beck, U. (1997) *The Reinvention of Politics: Rethinking Modernity in the Global Social Order*, Cambridge: Polity Press.

Beck, U. (1998) *Democracy and Its Enemies*, Cambridge: Polity Press.

Beck, U. (1999) *World Risk Society*, Cambridge: Polity Press.

Beck, U. (2005) *Power in the Global Age: A New Global Political Economy*, Cambridge: Polity Press.

Beck, U. (2006) *The Cosmopolitan Vision*, Cambridge: Polity Press.

Beck, U. and E. Beck-Gernsheim (1995) *The Normal Chaos of Love*, Cambridge, MA: Blackwell.

Beck, U., A. Giddens and S. Lash (1994) *Reflexive Modernization: Politics, Tradition and Aesthetics in the Modern Social Order*, Stanford, CA: Stanford University Press.

Benhabib, S. (ed.) (1996) *Democracy and Difference: Contesting the Boundaries of the Political*, Princeton, NJ: Princeton University Press.

Benjamin, J. (1988) *The Bonds of Love: Psychoanalysis, Feminism, and the Problem of Domination*, New York: Pantheon Books.

Benjamin, J. (1995) *Like Subjects, Love Objects: Essays on Recognition and Sexual Difference*, New Haven, CT: Yale University Press.

Benjamin, J. (1998) *The Shadow of the Other: Intersubjectivity and Gender in Psychoanalysis*, New York: Routledge.

Benveniste, E. (1971) *Problems in General Linguistics*, Coral Gables, FL: University of Miami Press.

Bhabha, H. (1994) *The Location of Culture*, London: Routledge.

Bokina, J. and T. J. Lukes (eds) (1994) *Marcuse: From the New Left to the Next Left*, Lawrence, KS: University Press of Kansas.

Bottomore, T. (1984) *The Frankfurt School*, New York: Tavistock.

Bourdieu, P. (1977) [1972] *Outline of a Theory of Practice*, Cambridge: Cambridge University Press.

Bourdieu, P. (1984) *Distinction: A Social Critique of the Judgment of Taste*, London: Routledge & Kegan Paul.

Bourdieu, P. (1988) [1984] *Homo Academicus*, Cambridge: Polity Press.

Bourdieu, P. (1991) *Language and Symbolic Power*, Cambridge: Polity Press.

Bourdieu, P. (1993) *The Field of Cultural Production*, Cambridge: Polity Press.

Bourdieu, P. (1995) *The Rules of Art: Genesis and Structure of the Literary Field*, Stanford, CA: Stanford University Press.

Bourdieu, P. (1996a) *On Television and Journalism*, London: Pluto Press.

Bourdieu, P. (1996b) *The State Nobility: Elite Schools in the Field of Power*, Cambridge: Polity Press.

Bourdieu, P. (2000) *Weight of the World: Social Suffering in Contemporary Society*, Stanford, CA: Stanford University Press.

Bowie, M. (1991) *Lacan*, London: Fontana.

Braaten, J. (1991) *Habermas's Critical Theory of Society*, Albany, NY: State University of New York Press.

Branaman, A. (2000) *Self and Society*, Cambridge, MA: Blackwell.

Branaman, A. and C. Lemert (eds) (1997) *The Goffman Reader*, Cambridge, MA: Blackwell.

Braun, D. (1991) *The Rich Get Richer*, Chicago, IL: Nelson Hall.

Brooks, A. (1997) *Postfeminisms: Feminism, Cultural Theory, and Cultural Forms*, London: Routledge.

Bryant, C. and D. Jary (eds) (1991) *Giddens' Theory of Structuration: A Critical Appreciation*, London: Routledge.

Bryant, C. and D. Jary (eds) (2001) *The Contemporary Giddens*, New York: Palgrave.

Burston, D. (1991) *The Legacy of Erich Fromm*, Cambridge, MA: Harvard University Press.

Butler, J. (1990) *Gender Trouble: Feminism and the Subversion of Identity*, London: Routledge.

Butler, J. (1993) *Bodies that Matter: On the Discursive Limits of Sex*, London: Routledge.

Butler, J. (1997) *The Psychic Life of Power: Theories in Subjection*, Stanford, CA: Stanford University Press.

Calhoun, C. *et al.*, (eds) (1993) *Pierre Bourdieu: Critical Perspectives*, Chicago, IL: University of Chicago Press.

Capra, F. (1996) *The Web of Life: A New Synthesis of Mind and Matter*, London: HarperCollins.

Castells, M. (2000a) *The End of the Millennium, The Information Age: Economy, Society and Culture*, Cambridge, MA: Blackwell.

Castells, M. (2000b) *The Rise of the Network Society, The Information Age: Economy, Society and Culture*, Cambridge, MA: Blackwell.

Castells, M. (ed.) (2004a) *The Network Society: A Cross Cultural Perspective*, London: Edward Elgar.

Castells, M. (2004b) *The Power of Identity, The Information Age: Economy, Society and Culture*, Cambridge, MA: Blackwell.

Castells, M. (2007) 'Communication, Power and Counter-power in the Network Society', *International Journal of Communication*, 1(1): 238–66.

Castells, M. (2008) 'Big Thinker Manuel Castells Discusses Internet and Society', *Yahoo! Research*, http://research.yahoo.com/node/2189, retrieved 13 June.

Castells, M. and M. Ince (2003) *Conversations with Manuel Castells*, Cambridge: Polity Press.

Castoriadis, C. (1987) *The Imaginary Institution of Society*, Cambridge: Polity Press.

Castoriadis, C. (1991) *Philosophy, Politics, Autonomy*, New York: Oxford University Press.

Castoriadis, C. (1997a) 'Done and to be Done', in D. A. Curtis (ed.) *The Castoriadis Reader*, Oxford: Blackwell, pp. 361–417.

Castoriadis, C. (1997b) *World in Fragments: Writings on Politics, Society, Psychoanalysis and the Imagination*, Stanford, CA: Stanford University Press.

Chesneaux, J. (1992) *Brave Modern World: The Prospects for Survival*, London: Thames and Hudson.

Chodorow, N. (1978) *The Reproduction of Mothering*, Berkeley, CA: University of California Press.

Chodorow, N. (1989) *Feminism and Psychoanalytic Theory*, London: Polity Press.

Chodorow, N. (1994) *Femininities, Masculinities, Sexualities: Freud and Beyond*, Lexington, KY: University Press of Kentucky.

Clarke, S. and A. Moran (2003) 'The Uncanny Stranger: Haunting the Australian Settler Imagination', *Free Associations*, 10B: 165–89.

Claussen, D. (2008) *Theodor W. Adorno: One Last Genius*, Cambridge, MA: Belknap Press.

Cohen, G. A. (1978) *Karl Marx's Theory of History: A Defence*, Princeton, NJ: Princeton University Press.

Cohen, I. (1989) *Structuration Theory: Anthony Giddens and the Constitution of Social Life*, London: Macmillian.

Cooley, J. (1902) *Human Nature and the Social Order*, New York: C. Scribner's Sons.

Cornell, D. (1993) *Transformations: Recollective Imagination and Sexual Difference*, New York: Routledge.

Craib, I. (1992) *Anthony Giddens*, London: Routledge.

Critchley, S. (1992) *The Ethics of Deconstruction*, Oxford: Blackwell.

Crompton, R. (1996) 'The Fragmentation of Class Analysis', *British Journal of Sociology*, 47(1): 56–67.

Culler, J. (1975) *Structuralist Poetics*, London: Routledge & Kegan Paul.

Culler, J. (1976) *Saussure*, London: Fontana.

Culler, J. (1983a) *Barthes*, London: Fontana.

Culler, J. (1983b) *On Deconstruction: Theory and Criticism after Structuralism*, London: Routledge and Kegan Paul.

DeLanda, M. (2000) *A Thousand Years of Nonlinear History*, New York: Zone Books.

DeLanda, M. (2006) *A New Philosophy of Society: Assemblage Theory and Social Complexity*, London: Continuum.

Deleuze, Gilles and Felix Guattari (1983) [1977] *Anti-Oedipus: Capitalism and Schizophrenia*, Minneapolis, MN: University of Minnesota Press.

Deleuze, Gilles and Felix Guattari (1987) *A Thousand Plateaus: Capitalism and Schizophrenia*, Minneapolis, MN: University of Minnesota Press.

Derrida, J. (1973) *Speech and Phenomena, and Other Essays on Husserl's Theory of Signs*, Evanston, IL: Northwestern University Press.

Derrida, J. (1976) *Of Grammatology*, Baltimore, MD: Johns Hopkins University Press.

Derrida, J. (1978) *Writing and Difference*, London: Routledge.

Derrida, J. (1981a) [1972] *Positions*, Chicago, IL: University of Chicago Press.

Derrida, J. (1981b) *Dissemination*, London: Athlone Press.

Derrida, J. (1982) *Margins of Philosophy*, Brighton: Harvester Wheatsheaf.

Derrida, J. (1998) *Resistances of Psychoanalysis*, Stanford, CA: Stanford University Press.

Dinnerstein, D. (1976) *The Mermaid and the Minotaur: Sexual Arrangements and Human Malaise*, New York: Harper & Row.

Douglas, M. (1986) *Risk Acceptability According to the Social Sciences*, London: Routledge.

Douglas, M. (1992) *Risk and Blame: Essays in Cultural Theory*, London: Routledge.

Dreyfus, H. and P. Rabinow (1982) *Michel Foucault: Beyond Structuralism and Hermeneutics*, Chicago, IL: University of Chicago Press.

du Gay, P. (2002) *In Praise of Bureacracy*, London: Sage.

du Gay, P. and S. Hall (eds) (1996) *Questions of Cultural Identity*, London: Sage.

Durkheim, E. (1976) [1912] *The Elementary Forms of the Religious Life*, London: Allen & Unwin.

Eagleton, T. (1990) *The Ideology of the Aesthetic*, Cambridge: Blackwell.

Eagleton, T. (1997) *The Illusions of Postmodernism*, Oxford: Blackwell.

Eagleton, T. (2003) *After Theory*, London: Allen Lane.

Eagleton, T. (2008) *Literary Theory: An Introduction*, Minneapolis: University of Minnesota Press.

Elliott, A. (1992) *Social Theory and Psychoanalysis in Transition: Self and Society from Freud to Kristeva*, Oxford: Blackwell.

Elliott, A. (2002) 'Beck's Sociology of Risk: A Critical Assessment', *Sociology*, 36(2), 293–315.

Elliott, A. (2003) *Critical Visions: New Directions in Social Theory*, Oxford: Rowman & Littlefield.

Elliott, A. (2004) *Subject To Ourselves, 2nd Edition*, Boulder, CO: Paradigm.

Elliott, A. (2007a) *Concepts of the Self, 2nd Edition*, Cambridge: Polity Press.

Elliott, A. (2007b) 'The Theory of Liquid Modernity: A Critique of Bauman's Recent Sociology', in A. Elliott (ed.) *The Contemporary Bauman*, London: Routledge, pp. 46–62.

Elliott, A. and C. Lemert (2006) *The New Individualism: The Emotional Costs of Globalization*, London: Routledge.

Ellis, J. M. (1989) *Deconstruction*, Princeton, NJ: Princeton University Press.

Evans, R. (1981) *Dialogue with Erich Fromm*, New York: Praeger.

Ewald, F. (1986) *L'Etat Providence*, Paris: B. Grasset.

Ewald, F. (1993) 'Two Infinities of Risk', in B. Massumi (ed.) *The Politics of Everyday Fear*, Minneapolis: University of Minnesota Press, pp. 221–8.

Felman, S. (1987) *Jacques Lacan and the Adventures of Insight: Psychoanalysis in Contemporary Culture*, Cambridge, MA: Harvard University Press.

Fishkin, J. S. (1991) *Democracy and Deliberation: New Directions for Democratic Reform*, New Haven, CT: Yale University Press.

Forrester, J. (1990) *The Seductions of Psychoanalysis: On Freud, Lacan and Derrida*, Cambridge: Cambridge University Press.

Foucault, M. (1970) [1966] *The Order of Things: An Archaeology of the Human Sciences*, London: Tavistock Publications.

Foucault, M. (1972) [1969] *The Archaeology of Knowledge*, London: Tavistock Publications.

Foucault, M. (1973) [1963] *The Birth of the Clinic: An Archaeology of Medical Perception*, London: Tavistock Publications.

Foucault, M. (1978) *The History of Sexuality*, London: Allen Lane.

Foucault, M. '(1979) *Discipline and Punish: The Birth of the Prison*, New York: Vintage Books.

Foucault, M. (1980) 'Two Lectures' in C. Gordin (ed.) *Power/Knowledge: Selected Interviews and Other Writings, 1972–1977*, New York: Pantheon Books.

Foucault, M. (1982) 'The Social Triumph of the Sexual Will', *Christopher Street*, 64(May): 36–41.

Foucault, M. (1985) *The Use of Pleasure: The History of Sexuality, Vol. II*, New York: Pantheon Books.

Foucault, M. (1986) *The Care of the Self: The History of Sexuality, Vol. III*, New York: Pantheon Books.

Foucault, M. (1988) 'Technologies of the Self', in L. Martin *et al.* (eds) *Technologies of the Self: A Seminar with Michel Foucault*, Amherst: University of Massachusetts Press.

Foucault, M. (1991) 'Governmentality', in G. Burchell, C. Gordon and P. Miller (eds) *The Foucault Effect*, Chicago, IL: University of Chicago Press.

Fowler, B. (1997) *Pierre Bourdieu and Cultural Theory: Critical Investigations*, London: Sage.

Fraser, N. (1987) 'What's Critical about Critical Theory? The Case of Habermas and Gender', in S. Benhabib and D. Cornell (eds) *Feminism as Critique*, Cambridge: Polity Press, pp. 31–56.

Fraser, N. (1989) *Unruly Practices: Power, Discourse and Gender in Contemporary Social Theory*, Minneapolis, MN: University of Minnesota Press.

Freud, S. (1961) [1900] 'The Interpretation of Dreams', in J. Strachey (ed.) *The Standard Edition of the Complete Psychological Works of Sigmund Freud, Vol. 4*, London: Hogarth Press, pp. 1–610.

Freud, S. (1961) [1930] 'Civilization and Its Discontents', in J. Strachey (ed.) *The Standard Edition of the Complete Psychological Works of Sigmund Freud, Vol. XXI*, London: Hogarth Press, pp. 57–145.

Fromm, E. (1941) *Escape from Freedom*, New York: Farrar & Rinehart.

Fromm, E. (1955) *The Sane Society*, New York: Holt, Rinehart & Winston.

Fromm, E. (1957) *The Art of Loving*, London: Allen and Unwin.

Fromm, E. (1973) *The Anatomy of Human Destructiveness*, New York: Holt, Rinehart & Winston.

Fromm, E. (1985) [1932] 'The Method and Function of an Analytical Social Psychology', in A. Arato and E. Gebhardt (eds) *The Essential Frankfurt School Reader*, New York: Continuum, pp. 477–98.

Funk, R. (1982) *Erich Fromm: The Courage to be Human*, New York: Continuum.

Funk, R. (2000) *Erich Fromm: His Life and Ideas*, New York: Continuum.

Fuss, D. (1989) *Essentially Speaking: Feminism, Nature and Difference*, New York: Routledge.

Gamble, S. (ed.) (2001) *The Routledge Companion to Feminism and Postfeminism*, London: Routledge.

Gane, N. (ed.) (2004) *The Future of Social Theory*, London: Continuum.

Garton-Ash, T. (2004) *Free World: America, Europe, and the Surprising Future of the West*, New York: Random House.

Giddens, A. (1971) *Capitalism and Modern Social Theory: An Analysis of the Writings of Marx, Weber and Durkheim*, Cambridge: Cambridge University Press.

Giddens, A. (1979) *Central Problems in Social Theory: Action, Structure, and Contradiction in Social Analysis*, London: Macmillan.

Giddens, A. (1984) *The Constitution of Society. Outline of the Theory of Structuration*, Cambridge: Polity Press.

Giddens, A. (1990) *The Consequences of Modernity*, Stanford, CA: Stanford University Press.

Giddens, A. (1991) *Modernity and Self-identity: Self and Society in the Late Modern Age*, Stanford, CA: Stanford University Press.

Giddens, A. (1992) *The Transformation of Intimacy: Sexuality, Love, and Eroticism in Modern Societies*, Stanford, CA: Stanford University Press.

Giddens, A. (1994) *Beyond Left and Right: The Future of Radical Politics*, Cambridge: Polity Press.

Giddens, A. (1997) *The Third Way: The Renewal of Social Democracy*, Cambridge: Polity Press.

Giddens, A. (1999) *Runaway World: How Globalisation is Reshaping Our Lives*, London: Profile Books.

Giddens, A. (2006) *Europe in the Global Age*, Cambridge: Polity Press.

Giddens, A. (2008) 'This Time It's Personal', *Guardian*, 2 January.

Giddens, A. and C. Pierson (1998) *Conversations with Anthony Giddens*, Stanford, CA: Stanford University Press.

Grenfell, M. (2008) *Pierre Bourdieu: Key Concepts*, London: Acumen Press.

Gross, N. (2005) 'The Detraditionalization of Intimacy Reconsidered', *Sociological Theory*, 23(3): 286–311.

Grosz, E. (1990) *Jacques Lacan: A Feminist Introduction*, London: Routledge.

Guberman, R. and J. Kristeva (1996) *Interviews*, New York: Columbia University Press.

Gutmann, A. and D. Thompson (2004) *Why Deliberative Democracy?*, Princeton, NJ: Princeton University Press.

Habermas, J. (1987) [1981] *The Theory of Communicative Action, Vol. 1*, Boston, MA: Beacon Press.

Habermas, J. (1987) [1981] *The Theory of Communicative Action, Vol. 2*, Boston, MA: Beacon Press.

Habermas, J. (1989) [1962] *The Structural Transformation of the Public Sphere: An Inquiry into a Category of Bourgeois Society*, Cambridge, MA: MIT Press.

Habermas, J. (1995) 'Reconciliation Through the Public Use of Reason: Remarks on John Rawls's Political Liberalism', *Journal of Philosophy*, 92(3): 109–31.

Habermas, J. (1996) *Between Facts and Norms: Contributions to a Discourse Theory of Law and Democracy*, Cambridge: Polity Press.

Habermas, J. (2001a) *Moral Consciousness and Communicative Action*, Cambridge, MA: MIT Press.

Habermas, J. (2001b) *The Postnational Constellation: Political Essays*, Cambridge: Polity Press.

Harker, R. *et al.* (1990) *Introduction to the Work of Pierre Bourdieu*, London: Macmillian.

Hawke, T. (1978) *Structuralism and Semiotics*, London: Routledge & Kegan Paul.

Held, D. (1991) 'Democracy, the Nation-state and the Global system' in D. Held (ed.) *Political Theory Today*, Cambridge: Polity Press, pp. 197–235.

Held, D. (2004) *Global Covenant: The Social Democratic Alternative to the Washington Consensus*, Cambridge: Polity Press.

Held, D. (2008) 'Global Challenges: Accountability and Effectiveness', *Open Democracy*, http://www.opendemocracy.net/article/globalisation/global_challenges_accountability_effectiveness?1, retrieved 29 August 2008.

Held, D. and A. McGrew (2002) *Globalization/Anti-Globalization*, Cambridge: Polity Press.

Held, D. and J. B. Thompson (eds) (1989) *Social Theory of Modern Societies: Anthony Giddens and his Critics*, Cambridge: Cambridge University Press.

Held, D. *et al.* (1999) *Global Transformations: Politics, Economics and Culture*, Cambridge: Polity Press.

Herman, E. and R. McChesney (1997) *The Global Media: The Missionaries of Global Capitalism*, London: Continuum.

Hirst, P. and G. Thompson (1999) *Globalization in Question: The International Economy and the Possibilities of Governance*, Cambridge: Polity Press.

Hobson, M. (1998) *Jacques Derrida: Opening Lines*, London: Routledge.

Hochschild, A. (2003) 'Love and Gold', in A. Hochschild and B. Ehrenreich (eds) *Global Woman: Nannies, Maids and Sex Workers in the New Economy*, New York: Metropolitan Books, pp. 15–30.

Hollway, W. and T. Jefferson (1997) 'The Risk Society in an Age of Anxiety: Situating Fear and Crime', *British Journal of Sociology*, 48(2): 254–66.

Holton, R. J. (2008) *Global Networks*, New York: Palgrave Macmillan.

Homer, S. (2005) *Jacques Lacan*, London: Routledge.

Honneth, A. (1995) *The Struggle for Recognition: The Moral Grammar of Social Conflicts*, Cambridge: Polity Press.

Honneth, A. (2007) *Disrespect: The Normative Foundations of Critical Theory*, Cambridge: Polity Press.

hooks, b. (1984) *Feminist Theory from Margin to Center*, Boston, MA: South End Press.

Howells, C. (1998) *Derrida: Deconstruction from Phenomenology to Ethics*, Cambridge: Polity Press.

Huhn, T. (ed.) (2004) *The Cambridge Companion to Adorno*, Cambridge: Cambridge University Press.

Huntington, S. P. (1996) *The Clash of Civilizations and the Remaking of the World Order*, London: Simon & Schuster.

Irigaray, L. (1985) *This Sex Which Is Not One*, Ithaca, NY: Cornell University Press.

Irigaray, L. (1993) *An Ethics of Sexual Difference*, Ithaca, NY: Cornell University Press.

Irigaray, L. (2000) *To Be Two*, London: Athlone.

Jameson, F. (1981) *The Political Unconscious: Narrative as a Socially Symbolic Act*, London: Metheun.

Jameson, F. (1991) *Postmodernism: Or, The Cultural Logic of Late Capitalism*, Durham, NC: Duke University Press.

Jarvis, S. (1998) *Adorno: A Critical Introduction*, Cambridge: Polity Press.

Jay, M. (1984) *Marxism and Totality: The Adventures of a Concept from Lukacs to Habermas*, Cambridge: Polity Press.

Jay, M. (1996) *The Dialectical Imagination: A History of the Frankfurt School 1923–1950*, Berkeley: University of California Press.

Johnson, C. (1993) *System and Writing in the Philosophy of Jacques Derrida*, Cambridge: Cambridge University Press.

Kaspersen, L. B. (2000) *Anthony Giddens: An Introduction to a Social Theorist*, Oxford: Blackwell.

Kellner, D. (1984) *Herbert Marcuse and the Crisis of Marxism*, Berkeley: University of California Press.

Kellner, D. (1989) *Critical Theory, Marxism and Modernity*, Cambridge: Polity Press.

Kellner, D. (2003) *From 9/11 to Terror War: The Dangers of the Bush Legacy*, New York: Rowman & Littlefield.

Knapp, G. (1989) *The Art of Living: Erich Fromm's Life and Works*, New York: P. Lang.

Kristeva, J. (1980a) 'From One Identity to an Other', in L. Roudiez (ed.) *Desire in Language: A Semiotic Approach to Literature and Art*, New York: Columbia University Press, pp. 124–47.

Kristeva, J. (1980b) 'Motherhood According to Giovanni Bellini', in L. Roudiez (ed.) *Desire in Language: A Semiotic Approach to Literature and Art*, New York: Columbia University Press, pp. 237–70.

Kristeva, J. (1982) *Powers of Horror: An Essay on Abjection*, New York: Columbia University Press.

Kristeva, J. (1984) [1974] *Revolution in Poetic Language*, New York: Columbia University Press.

Kristeva, J. (1986) 'Stabat Mater', in T. Moi (ed.) *The Kristeva Reader*, Oxford: Blackwell, pp. 160–87.

Kristeva, J. (1987) *Tales of Love*, New York: Columbia University Press.

Kristeva, J. (1989) *Black Sun: Depression and Melancholia*, New York: Columbia University Press.

Kristeva, J. (1991) *Strangers to Ourselves*, New York: Columbia University Press.

Lacan, J. (1977) [1949] 'The Mirror Stage as Formative of the Function of the I', in J.-A. Miller (ed.) *Ecrits: A Selection*, London: Tavistock Press, pp. 1–7.

Lacan, J. (1977) [1953] 'The Field and Function of Speech and Language in Psychoanalysis', in J.-A. Miller (ed.) *Ecrits: A Selection*, London: Tavistock Press, pp. 30–113.

Lacan, J. (1977) [1957] 'The Agency of the Letter in the Unconscious or Reason since Freud', in J.-A. Miller (ed.) *Ecrits: A Selection*, London: Tavistock Press, pp. 146–78.

Lacan, J. (1979) *The Four Fundamental Concepts of Psychoanalysis*, Harmondsworth: Penguin.

Lacan, J. (1988) *The Seminar of Jacques Lacan, Vol. 1: Freud's Paper on Technique 1953–54*, Cambridge: Cambridge University Press.

Lacan, J. (1992) *The Ethics of Psychoanalysis 1959–60: The Seminar of Jacques Lacan*, London: Routledge.

Lacan, J. (1998a) *The Seminar of Jacques Lacan, Vol. 2: The Ego in Freud's Theory and in the Technique of Psychoanalysis 1954–5*, Cambridge: Cambridge University Press.

Lacan, J. (1998b) *The Seminar, Book XX: Encore, On Feminine Sexuality, The Limits of Love and Knowledge*, London: Tavistock Press.

Landis, B. and E. S. Tauber (eds) (1971) *In the Name of Life: Essays in Honor of Erich Fromm*, New York: Holt, Rinehart & Winston.

Lane, J. (2000) *Pierre Bourdieu: A Critical Introduction*, London: Pluto Press.

Lash, S. and J. Urry (1994) *Economies of Signs and Space*, London: Sage.

Leach, E. (1970) *Claude Lévi-Strauss*, London: Fontana.

Lemert, C. (1995) *Sociology After the Crisis*, Boulder, CO: Westview Press.

Lemert, C. (2005a) *Postmodernism Is Not What You Think: Why Globalization Threatens Modernity*, Boulder, CO: Paradigm.

Lemert, C. (2005b) *Social Things: An Introduction to the Sociological Life, 3rd Edition*, Lanham, MD: Rowman & Littlefield.

Lemert, C. (2007) *Thinking the Unthinkable: The Riddles of Classical Social Theories*, Boulder, CO: Paradigm

Lemert, C. and G. Gillan (1982) *Michel Foucault: Social Theory and Transgression*, New York: Columbia University Press.

Lévi-Strauss, C. (1969) *The Elementary Structures of Kinship*, Boston, MA: Beacon Press.

Lévi-Strauss, C. (1970) [1964] *The Raw and The Cooked: Introduction to a Science of Mythology*, London: Jonathan Cape.

Lyotard, J.-F. (1984) *The Postmodern Condition: A Report on Knowledge*, Minneapolis, MN: University of Minnesota Press.

Lyotard, J.-F. (1984) [1979] *The Postmodern Condition: A Report on Knowledge*, Minneapolis: University of Minnesota Press.

Lyotard, J.-F. (1993) [1974] *Libidinal Economy*, Bloomington: Indiana University Press.

Macey, D. (1989) *Lacan in Context*, London: Verso.

Mandel, E. (1975) *Late Capitalism*, London: Humanities Press.

Marcuse, H. (1955) [1941] *Reason and Revolution*, London: Routledge.

Marcuse, H. (1956) *Eros and Civilization*, New York: Vintage Books.

Marcuse, H. (1964) *One-Dimensional Man*, Boston, MA: Beacon Press.

Marcuse, H. (1972) *Counterrevolution and Revolt*, Boston, MA: Beacon Press.

Marcuse, H. (1978) *The Aesthetic Dimensions*, Boston, MA: Beacon Press.

McCann, C. R. and S.-K. Kim (eds) (2002) *Feminist Theory Reader: Local and Global Perspectives*, London: Routledge.

McCarthy, T. (1978) *The Critical Theory of Jürgen Habermas*, London: Hutchinson.

McNay, L. (2000) *Gender and Agency*, Cambridge: Polity Press.

McNay, L. (1994) *Foucault: A Critical Introduction*, Cambridge: Polity Press.

McRobbie, A. (2005) *The Uses of Cultural Studies: A Textbook*, London: Sage.

Metz, C. (1982) *Psychoanalysis and Cinema*, London: Macmillian.

Mitchell, J. (1974) *Psychoanalysis and Feminism*, London: Penguin Books.

Mitchell, J. (1984) *Women: The Longest Revolution*, New York: Pantheon Books.

Mitchell, J. (2001) *Mad Men and Medusas*, New York: Basic Books.

Modleski, T. (1991) *Feminism Without Women: Culture and Criticism in a Postfeminist Age*, New York: Routledge.

Mouzelis, N. (1989) 'Restructuring Structuration Theory', *Sociological Review*, 37: 613–35.

Nancy, J.-L. (1997) *The Sense of the World*, Minneapolis, MN: University of Minnesota Press

Nancy, J.-L. (2008) *Corpus*, London: Continuum.

Oakley, A. (1972) *Sex Gender and Society*, Melbourne: Sun Books.

Ohmae, K. (1990) *The Borderless World: Power and Strategy in the Interlinked Economy*, New York: Harper Business.

Ohmae, K. (1995) *The End of the Nation State: The Rise of Regional Economies*, New York: Free Press.

Outhwaite, W. (1994) *Habermas: A Critical Introduction*, Cambridge: Polity Press.

Paolini, A. (1999) *Navigating Modernity: Postcolonialism, Identity, and International Relations*, Boulder, CO: L. Rienner.

Paterson, M. (2006) *Consumption and Everyday Life*, New York: Routledge.

Pittin, R., A. Seenderg and C. Webel (1988) *Marcuse: Critical Theory and the Promise of Utopia*, London: Macmillan.

Poster, M. (1990) *The Mode of Information: Poststructuralism and Social Context*, Chicago, IL: University of Chicago Press.

Ragland-Sullivan, E. (1986) *Jacques Lacan and the Philosophy of Psychoanalysis*, Urbana, IL: University of Illinois Press.

Ray, L. (2007) 'Bauman's Irony', in A. Elliott (ed.) *The Contemporary Bauman*, London: Routledge, pp. 63–80.

Reich, W. (1972) [1933] *Character Analysis*, New York: Farrar, Straus & Giroux.

Ricoeur, P. (1970) *Freud and Philosophy: An Essay on Interpretation*, New Haven, CT: Yale University Press.

Rischard, J. F. (2002) *High Noon: Twenty Global Problems, Twenty Years to Solve Them*, New York: Basic Books.

Rose, N. S. (1996) *Inventing Our Selves: Psychology, Power, and Personhood*, Cambridge: Cambridge University Press.

Rose, N. S. (1999a) *Powers of Freedom*, Cambridge: Cambridge University Press.

Rose, N. S. (1999b) *Governing the Soul: The Shaping of the Private Self, 2nd Edition*, London: Free Association Books.

Roudinesco, E. (1997) *Jacques Lacan*, Oxford: Polity Press.

Rylance, R. (1994) *Roland Barthes*, New York: Harvester Wheatsheaf.

Saussure, F. de. (1974) [1916] *Course in General Linguistics*, London: Fontana.

Sayers, J. (2007) 'Liquid Love: Psychoanalysing Mania', in A. Elliott (ed.) *The Contemporary Bauman*, London: Routledge, pp. 154–68.

Sedgwick, E. K. (1985) *Between Men: English Literature and Male Homosocial Desire*, New York: Columbia University Press.

Sedgwick, E. K. (1990) *The Epistemology of the Closet*, Berkeley: University of California Press.

Sedgwick, E. K. (1993) *Tendencies*, Durham, NC: Duke University Press.

Segal, L. (1997) *Is the Future Female? Troubled Thoughts on Contemporary Feminism*, London: Virago.

Segal, L. (1999) *Why Feminism?*, New York: Columbia University Press.

Sennett, R. (1998) *The Corrosion of Character: The Personal Consequences of Work in the New Capitalism*, New York: Norton.

Sennett, R. (2006) *The Culture of the New Capitalism*, New Haven, CT: Yale University Press.

Smart, B. (1985) *Michel Foucault*, London: Tavistock Publications.

Smart, C. and B. Shipman (2004) 'Visions in Monochrome: Families, Marriage and the Individualization Thesis', *British Journal of Sociology*, 55: 491–509.

Smith, D. (2006) *Globalization: The Hidden Agenda*, Cambridge: Polity Press.

Sturrock, J. (1993) *Structuralism*, London: Fontana.

Swartz, D. (1998) *Culture and Power: The Sociology of Pierre Bourdieu*, Chicago, IL: University of Chicago Press.

Thompson, E. P. (1978) *The Poverty of Theory and Other Essays*, London: Merlin Press.

Thompson, J. B. (1981) *Critical Hermeneutics: A Study in the Thought of Paul Ricoeur and Jürgen Habermas*, Cambridge: Cambridge University Press.

Thompson, J. B. (1984) *Studies in the Theory of Ideology*, Cambridge: Polity Press.

Thompson, J. B. (1989) *Social Theory of Modern Societies: Anthony Giddens and His Critics*, Cambridge: Cambridge University Press.

Thompson, J. B. (1995) *The Media and Modernity: A Social Theory of the Media*, Cambridge: Polity Press.

Thompson, S. (2006) *The Political Theory of Recognition*, Cambridge: Polity Press.

Tomlinson, J. (1991) *Cultural Imperialism: A Critical Introduction*, London: Pinter.

Turner, B. S. (1982) 'The Government of the Body: Medical Regimes and the Rationalization of Diet', *British Journal of Sociology* 33: 254–69.

Turner, B. S. (1984) *The Body and Society: Explorations in Social Theory*, Oxford: Blackwell.

Turner, B. S. (1992) *Regulating Bodies: Essays in Medical Sociology*, London: Routledge.

Turner, B. S. (1994) *Orientalism, Postmodernism and Globalism*, London: Routledge.

Urry, J. (2003) *Global Complexity*, Cambridge: Polity Press.

Urry, J. (2007) *Mobilities*, Cambridge: Polity Press.

Wacquant, L. (2005) *Pierre Bourdieu and Democratic Politics*, Cambridge: Polity Press.

Weber, M. (1968) *Economy and Society; An Outline of Interpretive Sociology*, New York: Bedminister Press.

Weeks, J. (1977) *Coming Out: Homosexual Politics in Britain from the Nineteenth Century to the Present*, London: Quartet Books.

Weeks, J. (1995) *Invented Moralities: Sexual Values in an Age of Uncertainty*, Cambridge: Polity Press.

Westergaard, J. (1995) *Who Gets What?*, Cambridge: Polity Press.

White, H. (1992) *Identity and Control: A Structural Theory of Social Action*, Princeton, NJ: Princeton University Press.

White, S. K. (ed.) (1995) *The Cambridge Companion to Habermas*, Cambridge: Cambridge University Press.

Wiggerhaus, R. (1994) *The Frankfurt School: Its History, Theories, and Political Significance*, Cambridge, MA: MIT Press.

Wilde, L. (1994) *Erich Fromm and the Quest for Solidarity*, London: Palgrave Macmillian.

Winnicott, D. W. (1976) [1960] 'Ego Distortion in Terms of True and False Self', in *The Maturational Process and the Facilitating Environment: Studies in the Theory of Emotional Development*, London: Hogarth and the Institute of Psychoanalysis, pp. 26–33.

Žižek, S. (1989) *The Sublime Object of Ideology*, London: Verso.

Index